P9-AEY-493

❀ THE · WORLD'S ❀ GREAT · CLASSICS

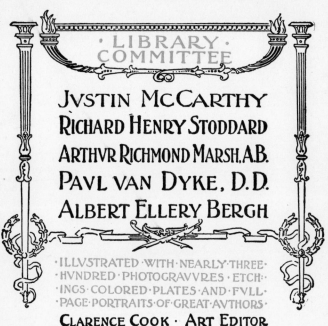

·LIBRARY·
COMMITTEE

JVSTIN McCARTHY
RICHARD HENRY STODDARD
ARTHVR RICHMOND MARSH, A.B.
PAVL VAN DYKE, D.D.
ALBERT ELLERY BERGH

·ILLVSTRATED·WITH·NEARLY·THREE·
·HVNDRED·PHOTOGRAVVRES·ETCH·
·INGS·COLORED·PLATES·AND·FVLL·
·PAGE·PORTRAITS·OF·GREAT·AVTHORS·

CLARENCE COOK · ART EDITOR

·THE·COLONIAL·PRESS·
·NEW·YORK· ❀ ·LONDON·

CHOICE EXAMPLES OF BOOK ILLUMINATION.

Fac-similes from Illuminated Manuscripts and Illustrated Books
of Early Date.

THE THREE DEAD AND THE THREE LIVING MEN.

From a French manuscript Livre d'Heures, written about 1500.

This grim and ghostly conception is taken from a French prayer-book of the
transition period. While the drawing and the idea are distinctly Flemish in character, the border suggests the Italian Renaissance in its richness, its boldness of design, and its freedom. As a design for illustration in a prayer-book it may be said
to be quite in keeping with the theology of the time.

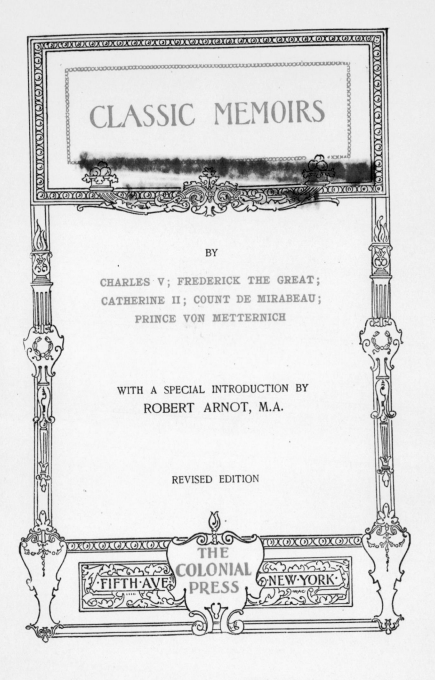

CLASSIC MEMOIRS

BY

CHARLES V; FREDERICK THE GREAT;
CATHERINE II; COUNT DE MIRABEAU;
PRINCE VON METTERNICH

WITH A SPECIAL INTRODUCTION BY
ROBERT ARNOT, M.A.

REVISED EDITION

THE
COLONIAL
PRESS
·FIFTH·AVE·   ·NEW·YORK·

Copyright, 1901,
By THE COLONIAL PRESS.

SPECIAL INTRODUCTION

CONTINENTAL memoir-writers, if we except those of France, seem to exclude the personal element in their written recollections. Leaving out the Semiramis of the North, Catherine II of Russia, we find that the most celebrated of the German, Austrian, and Austro-Spanish writers of memoirs seem to hold that war—the game of kings—and diplomacy—the recreation of statesmen—offer in themselves far more interesting material for record when unmixed with the feelings and opinions of the writer. So it happens that in this volume, with the exception of the recollections penned by that masterful woman, Catherine of Russia, the memoirs gathered present the political and military happenings rather than social records.

Few writers of autobiography have had more fruitful fields to harvest than the conqueror of Barbarossa, Charles V, and the undaunted Frederick the Great. A singular resemblance exists between the memoirs left behind by these two rulers of men, a resemblance which can be best summed up in Montaigne's criticism upon Xenophon and Cæsar, that if the deeds of these two imperial actors had not far surpassed their eloquence, the memoirs probably would never have been written, for the memoirs themselves seem to offer a recommendation, not of their sayings, but of their acts. Charles V undoubtedly stands forth as the most distinguished figure of the sixteenth century. The long-standing injustice done to his memory by the accusations of oppression and ambition has been effaced by the revelations of long inedited documents; and in the light of his autobiography and of the history of his cloister life at Yuste, he is seen to have been superior to the grandeurs he had traversed, and to have been ruled by spiritual, not material influences.

Not even in Carlyle's brilliant pages may the portrait of the great Frederick be better traced than in his own account of those political and military campaigns which reach up to and find temporary cessation at the period of the partition of Poland. One sees him garbed in Spartan simplicity; for crown an old military cocked hat, for robes a snuff-stained blue coat, and yet, despite his garb, a king every inch of him. Not a handsome nor a happy man, but a man of stoical aspect, quite in harmony with the quiet reserve force one feels in the moderation that pervades his writings, which are as clear in statement and comment as his eyes (according to Mirabeau) were vigilant and penetrating.

In the account Catherine II has left to us of her somewhat unpleasant experiences as a grand duchess, wife of the heir-presumptive to the throne of all the Russias, we find many reasons for sympathy with the young German princess, deprived of home influences in early maidenhood, and cast into the most intimate of associations with a brutal, coarse, and partly imbecile prince, surrounded by influences that could hardly be termed civilized. The naïve simplicity of the narrative invites confidence, and we hardly perceive that ruggedness of character and nobility of soul which, despite her private failings, characterized the Empress and Arbitress of the fate of millions, whose reign excited the admiration of her time and still astonishes posterity.

Revolutionists may inspire literature, but they hardly ever produce it. Mirabeau, however, is a distinguished exception. Nature had played pranks with his face and form, and he retaliated by defying law, morals, and authority. Judged by the standard of his own era, he was the saviour of a people in the throes of upheaval, but judged by any other standards he seems little less than a monster. But his capacity was marvellous. His attack on the system of French finance compelled reform, and to get rid of so capable yet dangerous a critic, it is said that the ministry contrived indirectly to compel him to proceed to Berlin, where he found favor with the great Frederick. His ability for intrigue and the obtaining of secret information gave him plenty to do, and it is to this period we owe that series of letters which depict in high relief the closing days of Frederick, and the peculiar atmosphere of scandal and politics which pervaded the court of Berlin.

Metternich is in many respects the most distinguished political figure in Austrian history. Though many times worsted in his diplomatic battles with the unscrupulous Talleyrand, he appears to have retained the confidence of his rulers and the respect of his opponents, and his epistolary accounts of the stirring events and negotiations which covered the Franco-Austrian crisis and culminated in the meeting of the monarchs at Erfurt are invaluable. It was to Metternich without doubt that Napoleon looked for exterior aid in his project of alliance with Marie Louise, and it was Metternich, too, who secretly engineered the final combination that overwhelmed the modern Alexander.

From a purely critical standpoint the memoirs collected in this volume, aside from those of Catherine II, may be said to offer an insight into the secret political annals of the seventeenth, eighteenth, and nineteenth centuries not to be gathered from the writings of historians. They supplement and explain those historical epochs in which the political boundaries of Continental nations were changed and rechanged in a fashion well-nigh kaleidoscopic, and they offer, as it were, a retrospective view of history in mosaic.

Robert Arnot

CONTENTS

ILLUSTRATIONS

AUTOBIOGRAPHICAL LEAVES

BY

Charles V, Emperor of Germany

CHARLES THE FIFTH

1500—1558

Charles the Fifth, Emperor of Germany, was born at Ghent in 1500, and died at the monastery of Yuste, in Estremadura, in 1558. He was the eldest son of Philip, Archduke of Austria, and of Joanna, the daughter of Ferdinand and Isabella of Spain. Philip's parents were the Emperor Maximilian and Maria, daughter and heiress of Charles the Bold, Duke of Burgundy. On the death of his grandfather, Ferdinand, in 1516, Charles took possession of the throne of Spain by the title of Charles I, his mother, Joanna, being of disordered intellect and incapable of reigning. He was not, however, very favorably received by the Spanish nobles, who were doubtful of his right, and jealous of the followers whom he brought from the Low Countries, where he had been educated. All the abilities of his famous minister, Ximenes, were requisite to prevent an open revolt. On the death of Maximilian in 1519, Charles was elected German Emperor from among a number of competitors, chiefly through the influence of the elector Frederic of Saxony. In his earlier years he had been frivolous and dissolute, but he now became mindful of the duties and dignity of his high position. In 1520 he was crowned at Aix-la-Chapelle, and received from the Pope the title of Roman Emperor. He ascended the imperial throne at a time when Germany was in a state of unprecedented agitation concerning the doctrines proclaimed by Luther.

To restore tranquillity, a great Diet was held at Worms in 1521, Luther's declaration of his principles before which forms a well-known and important passage in the history of the Reformation. In 1552 he reduced to subjection the towns of Castile, which had leagued themselves together for the maintenance of their ancient liberties. He was likewise successful in his war against the Turks under Solyman the Great. Charles was involved also in a struggle of long duration with France, in which, after many alternations of fortune, his armies at last drove the French from the greater part of their conquests in Italy; and Francis I of France fell into his hands as a prisoner, after a battle by which the siege of Pavia was raised in 1525.

But the war broke afresh in 1542, and terminated in favor of the Emperor, who also triumphed in the battle of Muhlberg in 1547, over the Protestant princes of Germany, and deprived the elector John Frederic of Saxony of his territories. But he showed so plainly his intention of converting the German Empire into a hereditary possession of his family that new opposition arose, and Charles was compelled to flee before the arms of Duke Maurice of Saxony and the Protestants, and in 1552 to promise them the peaceful exercise of their religion, which was confirmed by the Diet at Augsburg in 1555. Henry II of France also took from Charles some parts of Lorraine. His health failing, Charles now declared, in an assembly of the States of Louvaine, his resolution to seek repose and devote the remainder of his days to God. He resigned the government of his dominions to his son, for whom, however, he vainly sought to secure the imperial throne; and having relinquished to him the crown of Spain, he retired to the monastery of Yuste, in Estremadura, where he spent two years partly in mechanical amusements, partly in religious exercises, which are said to have assumed a character of the most gloomy asceticism, and died in 1558. His autobiography was begun probably at Augsburg in 1550, and completed in his retreat at Yuste between 1556 and 1558.

2

PREFACE OF CHARLES V

THIS history is that which I composed in French, when we were travelling on the Rhine, and which I finished at Augsburg. It is not such as I could wish it, but God knows that I did not do it out of vanity, and, if he has been offended at it, my offence must be attributed rather to ignorance than to malice. Similar things have often provoked his anger; I should not like this to rouse his ire against me! In these circumstances, as in others, reasons will not be wanting to him. May he moderate his anger, and deliver me from the dilemma in which I see myself!

I was on the point of throwing the whole into the fire; but, as I hope, if God gives me life to arrange this history in such guise that he shall not find himself ill served therein, and that it may not run the risk of being lost here, I send it to you that you may have it kept down there, and that it may not be opened until * . . .

I the King.

* Charles V completed his Autobiography at Augsburg. To be nearer Italy he retired to Innsbruck, where he nearly fell a victim to a night attack planned and carried out by his enemies. The abrupt breaking off in these lines, addressed by Charles V to his son Philip, is due to the hurry and disorder attending the sudden compulsory flight from Innsbruck.

AUTOBIOGRAPHICAL LEAVES

After the death of King Philip, there were at intervals various wars in the States of Flanders, which we call the Netherlands. One of those wars was that undertaken by the Emperor Maximilian, in concert with King Henry of England, against Louis, King of France. By the prudence, as well as by the habitual bravery of the Emperor, the French were defeated while endeavoring to relieve Terouane. After the capture of that city, siege was laid to Tournay, which, shortly afterward, also surrendered. The result was, that the Archduke Charles, grandson of the Emperor, proceeded to Tournay, which was then in the hands of King Henry, and to Lille, where he had his first interview with the same King, and where, among other things, his emancipation was discussed and resolved upon.

This took place in the year 1515, during which he was immediately recognized as Lord of the said States of Flanders. Shortly afterward the same archduke sent ambassadors to King Francis of France, who at the same period had inherited that kingdom, on the death of King Louis. These ambassadors negotiated and concluded peace. In the same year his Majesty visited a portion of the States of Flanders, and while making that visit there arrived at the Hague, in Holland, M. de Vendôme, sent by the King of France to ratify that peace. That portion of his States which he had not time to visit this year, was visited by him in the following year, 1516, and he held his first chapter of the Order of the Golden Fleece at Brussels. This was the year of the death of the Catholic King; and, dating from that moment, the archduke assumed the title of King.

At the same period he recovered, not without some resistance, his domains in Friesland: then the King of France, on the occasion of his recent accession, expressed a desire to

4

open other negotiations with his Majesty, which took place at Noyou, at the same time and in the same year. The King of France sent the Seigneur d'Orval to ratify what had been newly agreed upon. His Majesty remained in the Netherlands until September 8, 1517, upon which day he embarked at Flushing for Spain, and he left for the first time, in his absence, Margaret, his aunt, governor of his States.

This same year his Majesty, maintaining the peace concluded in France, and the friendship of the King of England, embarked, as already stated, at Flushing, crossed the ocean, and for the first time saw Spain, where his sojourn was to be prolonged till 1520. Continuing his journey to Tordesillas, he went to kiss the hands of the Queen his mother, and, starting from thence, he proceeded to Mojados, where he met the infant Don Ferdinand, his brother, whom he welcomed with great fraternal love. At this time Cardinal Fray Francis Ximenes, whom the Catholic King had instituted governor of his kingdoms, died. Continuing his journey, his Majesty arrived at Valladolid, where he assembled the Cortes of the kingdoms of Castille; and he was recognized as King conjointly with the Queen his mother.

At this time the King of France intimated to his Majesty a certain intention and wish to go to war with the King of England, to recover, he said, the town of Tournay, which, as has been seen, had been captured. To which his Majesty replied in terms in keeping with the conventions he had concluded with the two kings. This reply, though moderate, just, and reasonable, was interpreted in such guise that the King of France felt insulted, and, shortly afterward, he commenced war. On the other hand, the English monarch did not display the gratitude which such a reply deserved. For soon the two kings came to an agreement, and formed an alliance, taking little into account the conventions which had been concluded between them and the Catholic King. In consequence of this agreement and this alliance, the town of Tournay was restored to the French.

At this time, that is to say in the year 1518, his Majesty and the infant his brother left Valladolid for Saragossa, and during this journey he parted company with the infant at Aranda, who, leaving that town, embarked at Santander, going by sea to Flanders, where he was received by Madam his aunt. His Majesty continued his journey to Saragossa, where, in the same manner, he convoked the Cortes and was recognized as King.

In the year 1519 his Majesty assembled the Cortes at Barcelona, where the same ceremony took place. On his way he learned the death of the Emperor Maximilian, his grandfather; and, while holding the Cortes, the news reached him of his election to the Empire, which Duke Frederick, Count Palatine, was charged to announce to him. From thence he left for Corunna, to embark to receive the imperial crown at Aix-la-Chapelle.

His Majesty embarked at Corunna, leaving as governor Cardinal de Tortosa, to whom he afterward gave as adjuncts the constable and the admiral of Castille, Don Inigo de Velasco, and Don Frederick Henriquez. Having crossed the ocean a second time, he landed for the first time in England, where he had his second interview with the King, and, despite what has been said above, a closer alliance was negotiated and concluded with the said King. From thence he crossed over to his States of Flanders, where he was received by Madam his aunt and by the infant his brother. This was the first return of his Majesty to his States of Flanders: a third interview was the result, at Gravelines and at Calais, between the Emperor and King Henry of England. He then continued his journey to Aix-la-Chapelle, where he was crowned. He again appointed Margaret his aunt governor of Flanders; he also left his brother the infant there, and held his first Diet at Worms. This is the first time that he visited Germany and the Rhine. About this time the heretical doctrines of Luther in Germany and the Communidades in Spain began to manifest themselves.

His Majesty, being at the said Diet, sent for his brother, who from thence went to marry the sister of King Louis of Hungary, according to what had been settled by the Emperor Maximilian.

During the same Diet, Robert de la Mark commenced hostilities. This act had its origin in the reply, mentioned above, which in 1518 the Catholic King Charles had addressed from Valladolid to the King of France. Not only could that King not conceal his mortification and little satisfaction it gave him, but it gradually increased, especially when the Catholic King was elected Emperor.

He was continually making complaints and such unreasonable proposals, and in such exorbitant terms, that the Emperor could neither accept them nor condescend to notice them. From this reason and from other practices, and other communications which the King of France entertained in Italy and in Spain with the Communidades, war commenced in 1521 between his Majesty and the King of France, in which Robert de la Mark lost the greater portion of his domains, which were taken from him by Count Henry of Nassau, then captain-general of the army. These wars lasted till 1525. For this reason the Emperor was obliged to close the Diet at Worms. By so acting, he rather did what he could than what he wished and had resolved to do, and he left to oppose those hostilities.

His Majesty returned by the Rhine, into his States of Flanders for the second time. At this period the Communidades were suppressed in Spain, and the French beaten and driven out of the Kingdom of Navarre, which they had occupied in like manner as they had established themselves at Fontarabia. All these things occurred before the close of the year. At this time the King of France sent an army into Lombardy. It laid siege to Paria, which was defended by the Marquis Frederick of Mantua. An army having been assembled, in virtue of the league entered into by the Emperor with Pope Leo and the Venetians, the French were driven out of the Duchy of Milan. Prosper Colonna was chief of the army of the league; and, in virtue of the same league, the Duchy of Milan was given to Duke Francis Sforza.

At the same time, by the Emperor's orders, the Count of Nassau laid siege to the town of Tournay, which was surrendered by the French to his Majesty, who had occupied it since they received it from the King of England, into whose power it had previously fallen. The army of the King of France again attempted, in 1522, to re-enter the Duchy of Milan, but Prosper Colonna and the army of the league made so valiant a resistance that the French lost the battle of Bicocca. The capture of Genoa followed.

The Emperor, for the third time, leaving the government

of Flanders to his aunt, embarked at Calais, and, for the second time, visited England, where he had his fourth interview with the King. Having remained there some days, he embarked at Southampton, crossed the ocean for the third time, and arrived a second time in Spain, where he again went to kiss the hands of his mother the Queen, and where he remained till 1529. At the very time of his arrival, Pope Adrian, who had been elected on the death of Pope Leo, embarked at Barcelona for Rome. His Majesty continued his journey to Valladolid, where he assembled the Cortes to complete the reconciliation of past differences, excepting a few of the more culpable from the general pardon granted to all those who had offended him.

In the year 1523, during the war with France, the Emperor entertained certain communications and certain correspondence with Duke Charles of Bourbon, who felt himself injured by some acts of injustice done toward him. This is why he entered the service of his imperial Majesty. The Emperor proceeding to Pampeluna with an army to invade France, gave the command of it to Don Inigo de Velasco, constable of Castile, who penetrated into the kingdom, and who on his return recaptured Fontarabia.

This achieved, the Emperor returned in 1524 to the Kingdom of Toledo. He was taken ill with fever, which he got rid of early in the following year, 1525. At this time the King of France laid siege to Paria, which was held by Antonio de Leyra, and, in the battle fought in front of that city, the King was made prisoner by the Duke of Bourbon, captain-general of the Emperor; Charles de Launay, his viceroy at Naples, and Don Francis d'Avalos, Marquis of Pescaria, his principal captains. The King was taken by the viceroy of Naples into Spain to Madrid, where he fell sick, and the Emperor went to pay him a visit. This is the first time they met.

While the Emperor was in the said city of Madrid, peace was negotiated and concluded with the said King, and his marriage with the Queen-widow of Portugal, Eleanor, sister of the Emperor. At the same time the Duke of Bourbon also arrived, who returned soon to Milan, having been invested with that State by his Majesty.

In 1526 the Emperor left Toledo for Seville, where he married. On his journey he received the news of the death of his sister, the Queen of Denmark. In the same city of Seville he was visited by his brother-in-law, the infant Don Louis of Portugal, who accompanied the Empress, his sister. This was the first time his Majesty saw the said infant. At the same time he set at liberty the King of France, receiving in exchange two of his sons as hostages, conformable to the conditions of the conventions made at Madrid. The latter shortly afterward renewed the war, and his imperial Majesty received a message of defiance at Grenada, consequent upon a league concluded between Pope Clement, who had been elected on the demise of Adrian, the Kings of France and of England, and the signoria of Venice. His Majesty sent a reply to that defiance.

In the same city the news reached the Emperor that his brother-in-law, King Louis of Hungary, had been defeated by the Turks and had perished. This is why his Majesty convoked the general Cortes of all his kingdoms of Castile, to concert measures to remedy such a state of things, and to organize the necessary means of defence against the Turks. His Majesty was in this city, in 1527, when his son Philip, Prince of Spain, was born. About the same time, and in the same city, he received the news that the army raised by the Duke of Bourbon had entered Rome, after an assault, in which the said duke was killed, and that Pope Clement was shut up in the fort of St. Angelo. A guard was placed in the fort by the Prince of Orange, who, after the death of the Duke of Bourbon, took command of the army.

The Pope remained in the said fortress until, having come to terms with the army, he was by his Majesty's orders set at liberty.

At the same time, in the city of Burgos, the Emperor received a message of defiance from the Kings of France and of England, under the pretext of the detention of Pope Clement. His Majesty replied that there were no grounds for such an act, as the Pope had already been liberated; and that the fact of the detention of the Pope ought to be reproached less to the Emperor than to those who had compelled him to raise for his defence so many soldiers who did not obey him well.

All this having taken place, his Majesty returned to Madrid, where he convoked the Cortes of the kingdoms of Castile, where his son Philip was recognized prince of the said kingdoms. In the year 1528, his Majesty, on his way to Valladolid, experienced a first attack of gout. He received the news that an army sent by the King of France into Italy, under the pretext of delivering Pope Clement (who, as has already been said, had been liberated,) had advanced to invade and attack the Kingdom of Naples; that it had already conquered a large portion of it, and had laid siege to the capital, into which the army which was before Rome had withdrawn.

In that army were the Prince of Orange, Don Alphonso d'Avalos, the Marquis du Guast, Alarcon, who had occupied the castle of St. Angelo, and Don Hugo de Moncada, who was in the said city of Naples, happening to be there at the time of the death of the viceroy Charles de Launoy; and as each laid claim to the supreme command, they were not on very good terms with each other. Nevertheless they performed their duty so well that, with God's blessing, the said kingdom and capital were defended, and the French army vanquished and routed. During this siege, Don Hugo de Moncada attacked the galleys belonging to the squadron of Prince Doria; but Hugo de Moncada was killed, and most of his galleys captured.

His Majesty, conformably to the resolution he had taken, proceeded to Monzon to hold the Cortes of the three kingdoms of Aragon. This done, he returned to Madrid, where the Empress was residing, who had given birth to the infanta Doña Maria, her first daughter. Soon after envoys arrived from Prince Doria, who, from certain reasons and bad treatment he had received, offered to join his Majesty with his galleys and with those he had captured at Naples. His Majesty willingly accepted the offer, which was most welcome to him, and indispensable for the success of the plans he had in view.

From this city the Emperor proceeded to Toledo; and in this town he charged the Empress to govern in his absence all his Spanish dominions, which he resolved to leave, animated by the desire of counteracting as much as possible the errors in Germany which, owing to the wars he had been engaged in, he had only been able to remedy imperfectly. He also wished, by resisting the attacks incessantly directed against him on the Italian side, at the same time to assume the crowns which he had not yet received, and finally to be in a better position to oppose the Turk, who, it was said, was advancing against Christendom.

From these various motives the Emperor left the city of Toledo for Barcelona, where Prince Doria shortly afterward arrived with his galleys. Here he got his fleet into order so as to embark, as already stated, and have himself crowned in Italy, despite the league already mentioned which had been formed against his Majesty, and which, at the same moment, was beginning to break up: for, while he was still at Barcelona, negotiations were set on foot between Pope Clement and his Majesty. Here the news came that M. de Saint Pol had been defeated in the States of Milan, and that he was the prisoner of Antonio de Leyra, governor of those States. At the same time, his aunt Margaret was negotiating at Cambray a peace with the Queen Regent of France, mother of the King. This done, his Majesty embarked and set sail with his whole fleet, landing for the first time in Italy. While cruising along the French coast, he received the report that peace had been concluded; but he only received the confirmation of it on his arrival at Savona. He consequently sent Seigneur de la Chaulx, one of his household, from Genoa to ratify it. From Genoa he proceeded farther into Italy, where he learned that the Turks had entered Hungary and laid siege to Vienna. This led to the first interview between Pope Clement and the Emperor at Bologna, where his Majesty experienced a second attack of gout.

At Bologna the Emperor was informed that the Empress had given birth to a second son, Ferdinand, whose death was announced to him the following year at Augsburg. To be more free to oppose the Turks and to leave Italy tranquil, he assumed the crowns that belonged to him, in the said city of Bologna.

He concluded peace with the Venetians, and again intrusted the States of Milan to Francesco Sforza. After a long war waged by the Pope and his Majesty against the Florentines, in which the Prince of Orange, who was already viceroy of Naples, fulfilled the functions of captain-general, the house of the Medici was reëstablished in Florence, and Duke Alexander invested with that State. In this expedition the Prince of Orange was killed. He was replaced in his command by Don Ferdinand de Gonzaga, and in the government of Naples by Cardinal Caracciolo, until his Majesty should decree otherwise.

Meantime so valiant a resistance was made by the King his brother, and by those who were with him at Vienna, that the Turk, as well from this reason as from the information he received of the great preparations that were being made to oppose him, thought fit to withdraw. At the same time the Emperor asked his Holiness to convoke and assemble a general council, as most important and necessary to remedy what was taking place in Germany, and the errors which were being propagated throughout Christendom. To this effect his Holiness appointed a legate to attend the Diet at Augsburg, and there to adopt all such resolutions as might seem best suited for such an object.

These matters settled, the Emperor, taking leave of the Pope, left Bologna to proceed to the Diet which he had convoked at Augsburg. Here he was joined by the Pope's legate, to consider the remedies for the said errors, and at the same time to provide for and obviate the evils which were feared on the part of the Turk. The Emperor, passing through Mantua and the territories of Venice, arrived at Trent, and in Germany for the second time. During this voyage he met the King his brother, and they proceeded together to the said Diet of Augsburg, where good measures were concerted against the Turk, which were afterward carried out at Ratisbon. At this time he entered into negotiations with the electors. As the Emperor, because of the great kingdoms and large domains which God had given to him, could not prolong his sojourn in the empire as long as he desired and was suitable, the question of the election of his brother as King of the Romans was brought forward.

On the closing of the Diet they all started together, and for the third time the Emperor visited the Rhine, following it up to Cologne. It was here that, owing to the plague prevailing at Frankfort, the election of the King, his brother, as King of the Romans was concluded on the proposition of his Majesty. From the said city of Cologne the Emperor proceeded to Aix-la-Chapelle to crown the said King. This being done, the

King and the electors commenced treating their private interests, and the Emperor returned a third time into his States of Flanders, to put things into order there, as well on account of his long absence as in consequence of the death of Margaret, his aunt, the news of which reached him on his journey down the Rhine. So as to place everything in the best order, he intrusted the management and direction of affairs to his sister, the Queen of Hungary.

This having been all settled and completed, he made a tour through his States, visiting a portion of his domains. It was with the assistance and in company of the said Queen that he took all the measures that appeared to him most suitable and most necessary. Among other things he held a third chapter of the Order of the Golden Fleece, at Tournay.

At the commencement of this year the Emperor, leaving for the first time the Queen of Hungary, his sister, in the government of the said States of Flanders, started the fourth time for the Rhine, so as to enter Germany a third time, as well as to see whether he could not hit upon some means of putting a stop to the heresies that were spreading there as to oppose the invasion of the Turk, who, as was announced, was preparing to invade Germany with a great army. For this purpose the Emperor convoked an imperial Diet at Ratisbon, to carry into execution what had been agreed upon, as has already been said, at Augsburg. During this journey, while out hunting, he had a fall from his horse, and hurt his leg; erysipelas having ensued, he suffered from it the whole time he was at Ratisbon. He also experienced a third attack of gout. His nephew, the Prince of Denmark, died in the same city.

While his Majesty was thus laid up, the Diet discussed what remedy could be applied to the state of religious matters, and the certain news arrived of the advance of the Turk, with the object mentioned above. For this reason, his Majesty, conjointly with the King of the Romans, his brother, appealed to the States of the empire, who showed themselves full of zeal in the performance of their duty. Religious matters were therefore left aside, as there was no time to discuss them, and they were left in their actual state. Such an army was assembled by the empire, as well as by their majesties the Emperor and the King of the Romans, that the Turk, who wished to besiege

Vienna, where the Emperor and the King of the Romans had anticipated him with their troops, finding that a portion of his troops which had advanced on different points, had been routed by Count Frederick Palatine, the general of the imperial army, resolved to beat a retreat, which resolve he carried out near Neustadt. In fact, the Turk, having crossed the Drave and the Save, returned to Constantinople with great loss and damage to his followers. From this moment his power was no longer so much feared.

In the same summer, by the Emperor's orders, Prince Doria attacked the maritime possessions of the Turk; he captured the town of Coron in the Morea, where he left a garrison; he captured, moreover, many other places, and did great destruction.

The Emperor, seeing that at this moment there was nothing more to be done against the Turk; that the season was too far advanced to reconquer Hungary, and that the plague was devastating the army, resolved to dismiss all his troops, so as to avoid needless expense. This was done without disorder. Only the Italians, whom his Majesty had resolved to leave in Austria, for the defence of that State, excited by some evil-intentioned persons, mutinied without any motive, and returned home. Nevertheless, the Emperor, prosecuting his plans, soon set out to visit Italy a second time; and from thence Spain, which he had a great desire to do, as he had been absent four years from the Empress, his wife. He also desired, on his journey through Italy, to have a second interview with Pope Clement, as well to consider the convocation of the council to remedy the state of religious matters as to concert resistance to the Turk, and also to secure peace and tranquillity in Italy. His Majesty, continuing his journey through Friuli, arrived at Bologna, where he saw his Holiness a second time, without, however, so much result from the interview as his Majesty had expected; and he left for Genoa, where he shortly afterward embarked.

The Emperor for the third time crossed the sea, and, touching Spain for the third time, disembarked at Barcelona, where the Empress, with the Prince of Spain and the infanta Doña Maria, her children, were waiting to receive him. Having remained in that town for some days, the Emperor proceeded to

Monzon, to hold the Cortes of his three kingdoms of Aragon. As soon as the Cortes were over, their majesties started for and arrived at Toledo, in the year 1534. Here another Cortes was held, after which their majesties proceeded to Valladolid, where, in regular course of time, she was delivered of a son. From thence, owing to the plague prevailing there, they proceeded to Palencia, where the Emperor experienced a fourth attack of the gout. In the same year he left that city for Madrid, and spent the winter in the Kingdom of Toledo. At this period was conceived and prepared the expedition to Tunis, which, that very summer, Barbarossa had conquered with a large Turkish army.

His Majesty, leaving for the second time the Empress, who was enceinte, in charge of all his kingdoms of Spain, left Madrid and arrived at Barcelona, to start on the expedition to Tunis. For this object he assembled, in the said city of Barcelona, a great number of vessels-of-war, some sent by the King of Portugal, his brother-in-law, others from Malaga, and from other points of the Spanish coast. Here also arrived the galleys of Prince Doria, his Majesty's lord high admiral. When all these vessels were assembled, as well as the seigneurs, gentlemen and nobles, the gentlemen of the court, and the military and naval officers, the Emperor embarked for the third time at Barcelona, for Tunis. While the Emperor was occupied with these matters, the infant Don Louis of Portugal, his brother-in-law, having learned that the expedition undertaken by his Majesty was directed against the infidels, being a high-minded Christian prince, he joined the expedition at Barcelona, where the Emperor still was, accompanied by many of the leading personages of the Kingdom of Portugal. This is the second time they met. The Emperor received him, and treated him, during the whole duration of the expedition, as a brother ought to treat a brother, and to the best of his means.

All the preparations having been completed, they embarked in the spring; having set sail, they were driven by stress of weather to Majorca, where the Emperor arrived for the first time with his whole fleet, and then to Minorca, where he also arrived for the first time. From thence, steering toward Sardinia, where he also touched for the first time, he there found all his officers, ships, and men, who had made the island a chief point of rendezvous. Here he was joined by six galleys, sent by Pope Paul, who had been elected Pope on the death of Clement.

This junction having taken place, they all sailed from the island of Sardinia, first recommending themselves to God, by whose favor and grace they hoped before daybreak to touch the African coast. In the morning the Emperor, with his galleys, discerned the land, and he awaited the ships that were behindhand at Port Farino. Then, after having made a reconnaissance as to best point for landing, he, for the first time, set foot on African soil, with his whole army, commanded by General Marquis du Guast. After being delayed by some skirmishes, he besieged Goulette for some days with heavy artillery, and finally carried it by storm.

At this time the Emperor received the news that the Empress had given birth to the infanta Doña Juana, her second daughter. A few days afterward, leaving Goulette, and the fleet well provided for, he advanced toward Tunis with his infantry and cavalry and some pieces of artillery. While advancing, Barbarossa made a sortie from Tunis with a large body of Moors on horse and foot, supported by numerous artillery, and attacked the Emperor between some pits and swamps, where he had halted to rest his army.

The Emperor took possession of the ground, and compelled the enemy to withdraw, with the loss of their artillery and of a portion of their troops. His Majesty also suffered some loss on his side. On the same day Barbarossa beat a retreat toward Tunis.

At daybreak next morning, the Emperor drew up his army in order of battle, and advanced against the said city of Tunis, and neither Barbarossa nor his men could prevent him forcing an entrance with his army. After having sacked the town and liberated the Christian slaves, he restored it to King Hassan, and having returned to La Goulette, which he fortified, he embarked with the intention of taking the city of Africa.* He was prevented from doing so by contrary winds. Leaving Calybia, which is also on the coast of Africa, he again made sail, and landed for the first time in Sicily. Having held an assembly

* Mehedia, the ancient Aphrodisium.

there, and having given suitable orders for the welfare of that kingdom, where he left Don Ferdinand de Gonzaga as viceroy, he crossed the Straits of Messina and proceeded to Naples, via Calabria.

This was his third visit to Italy. During this journey he had a fifth attack of the gout, at four different intervals. While at Naples, the Emperor convoked an assembly, in which he discussed the affairs of the kingdom. Here he received news of the death of the Queen of England, of the Prince of Piedmont, who was in Spain, and of Francis Sforza, Duke of Milan.

Meantime Francis, King of France, commenced a third war, with a view to seize the States of the Duke of Savoy. This compelled his imperial Majesty to leave Naples as soon as possible, to take the necessary measures to meet that invasion.

The Emperor visited Rome, where he had his first interview with his Holiness Pope Paul, as much with a view to negotiate peace, for which propositions had been made to him, as to induce him, should it not be concluded, to take the part of the Duke of Savoy, who, beside being a vassal of the empire, was married to his sister-in-law and cousin-german, the infanta Doña Beatrice of Portugal. All these matters were discussed at Rome, and led to various negotiations, but did not end in anything. A correspondence ensued, which the Emperor declined to reply to, as beneath his notice. He therefore resolved to follow up his plans. Having made all possible arrangements, and desirous of finding the most suitable means to restore to the Duke of Savoy the greater portion of his estates, of which he had been forcibly despoiled, he left a portion of his army near Turin and advanced another army through the Netherlands, the command of which he intrusted to the Count of Nassau, so as to alarm and do harm to the enemy. Finally he accompanied the remainder of his troops, the command of which he gave to Antonio de Leyra, and advanced as far as Aix, in Provençe.

This was the first time he entered France with an army. However, as the season was far advanced, and it was necessary to oppose an attack from the enemy, he withdrew with his whole army to Nice. From thence he proceeded to Genoa, where he dismissed and sent home all that portion of his army which was superfluous or useless. He took care to provide for

2

the safety of the frontiers of Piedmont, of Montferrat, and of the State of Milan, of which he appointed the Marquis du Guast governor and captain-general. He then embarked at Genoa, and returned to Barcelona. This was his fourth visit to Spain.

The Emperor proceeded by post to Tordesillas, where the Queen, his mother, and the Empress, his wife, were residing. From thence he went to Valladolid, where he convoked the Cortes. For the sixth time he experienced a severe attack of the gout. He received the news that Duke Alexander de Medici had been treacherously killed, and he conferred the State of Florence upon Duke Cosmo de Medici. At this time the infant Don Louis of Portugal came to Valladolid to visit his Majesty and the Empress. It was the third visit which he paid to their majesties. A few days afterward the Emperor, leaving the Empress enceinte, proceeded to Monzon, where he convoked the ordinary Cortes. At this time the King of France, with troops hastily levied, invaded Flanders, and successively took Hesdin and Saint Pol, which latter town was soon recaptured by assault by an army assembled by the Queen of Hungary, commanded by General Count de Buren. At the same time this army took Montreuil, and defeated Annibal, who was endeavoring to throw provisions into Terouane, then besieged. Nevertheless, the city was relieved, the siege raised, and Montreuil abandoned.

The King of France, finding that the lands of the Duke of Savoy, which he had conquered in Piedmont, were wanting in provisions, and hard pressed by the Imperialists, and that, moreover, he had no means of coming to their support unless he could get rid of the resistance he encountered in Flanders, proposed a general armistice, which the Emperor had some difficulty in accepting, as he was aware of the sad condition of the territory which the King of France occupied in Piedmont. It resulted from these negotiations that the Emperor, having been informed of the sad condition of the said lands, and knowing that his forces were such as to render it impossible for them to receive succor, and from other reasons, concluded a general armistice with the said King, excepting only Piedmont. It happened, however, that the King of France sent so many men and troops into Piedmont that those lands were succored.

The Cortes being closed, the Emperor returned by post to Valladolid, to see the Empress, who had just been brought to bed of her fourth son, the infant Don Juan, who died shortly afterward. Almost at the same time died the infanta Doña Beatrice of Portugal, Duchess of Savoy. The Empress suffered much after her confinement, and since then until the day of her death was in very bad health. While the Emperor was at Monzon, negotiations for peace were opened between his Majesty and the King of France. The result was a conference between their respective ambassadors, which were, on the Emperor's side, Covos, grand commander of Léon, and M. de Granvelle, and on the King's side, the Cardinal de Lorraine and the Constable of France; and as there were some hopes of an interview between their majesties, the Emperor posted back to Barcelona to see what the negotiations had led to. However, Pope Paul, observing that no conclusion had been come to, wished to interfere, offering to proceed in person to Nice, while the Emperor should go to Villafranca, and the King of France to Antibes, to which the Emperor agreed, because he was always inclined toward peace.

Meantime the Emperor visited Perpignan and the frontier of Rousillon; on his return he found his brother-in-law, the infant Don Louis of Portugal. This prince, from his good inclinations and a desire to work in the service of God and to do good, had proceeded to Barcelona in all haste to see if he could be of any service in helping to the conclusion of peace. He was welcomed and entertained by his Majesty in the most hospitable manner. But, considering that the journey to Nice had already been agreed upon, and that his Holiness wished to act as a mediator in this matter, his Majesty thought that it was more advisable the infant should not leave Barcelona. He therefore returned. This was the fourth visit to his Majesty.

As already stated, the Emperor had posted to Barcelona; and there, conformable to his intention of seeing what would ensue from these conferences, he embarked for Nice. While he was yet at Barcelona, negotiations for an armistice had been opened between his Majesty and the King of France, and the Emperor thought there was no inconvenience in doing so, as he was going to Nice to treat for peace. He therefore gave his assent on the point of embarking, and sent his ratification, although he had not yet received that of the King, because he could not have been informed of it in time.

At the same time a report was spread that a Turkish fleet was proceeding eastward, and with the purpose of preventing this journey to Nice. His Majesty having arrived at Pomè-guev, near Marseilles, discerned some lateen sails coming east-ward. The Emperor, aware that a short time previously the King of France had sent some of his galleys in that direction, and fancying that the vessels seen were of that number, made the usual signals to them, so as to enter into conversation, and ascertain what news they had of the Turkish fleet. But the said galleys either did not or would not understand the signals; and as they knew nothing of the armistice, and were enemies, they opened fire upon the galleys of the Emperor, and by hard rowing endeavored to reach the French coast.

His Majesty, perceiving this, ordered his galleys to give chase, and captured four of them in the open sea; but he did not follow those that had gained the land. The Emperor severely reproached the captains of the galleys which he had captured for the fault which they had committed, and informed the governor of the province of this mistake, and of the dis-order which had ensued, making him acquainted, moreover, with the armistice which had been concluded at Barcelona, of which the governor had not received any intimation. Agree-able to this truce, the Emperor restored the four captured galleys, and shortly afterward he received the ratification of the same by the King of France.

The Emperor continued his journey to Nice, where he had a second interview with his Holiness, and, after having kissed his feet, he discussed with him the different negotiations for peace with the King of France, who had also arrived at Saint Laurent. However, the conclusion of a truce was all that was effected, and various motives led to it.

The Emperor being at Villafranca, near Nice, and desirous of seeing the most Christian Queen his sister, as it was a long time since he had seen her, that princess, anxious to conciliate and comply with the wishes of the Emperor her brother and of the King her husband, proceeded to Villafranca with Madame la Dauphine, the actual Queen,* Madame Margaret,† and many other ladies and high personages of France.

* Catherine of Medicis.   † Margaret, daughter of Francis I, afterward Duchess of Savoy.

As she found the time she spent with him extremely short, she returned a second time with a less numerous suite, and passed one night in the same city. The Queen having left, and the armistice having been concluded, the Emperor accompanied his Holiness as far as Genoa, where he experienced his seventh attack of the gout. This was his fifth visit to Italy. At this time the Pope, the Emperor, and the Signoria of Venice concluded an offensive league against the Turk, after which his Majesty embarked at Genoa to return to Spain.

As it had been agreed that an interview should take place between his Majesty and the King of France, his Majesty announced that on his return he should cruise along the French coast and stop at the port of Aigues-Mortes. The King at once, in a small boat, paid the Emperor a visit on board his galley, and the latter, in return for so great an act of courtesy, and to show equal confidence, paid a visit to the King in the town of Aigues-Mortes. He stopped there till the following day, well treated and feasted by the King, who, not satisfied with the courtesy he had already shown to the Emperor, insisted upon accompanying the Emperor in his gig, with his two sons, Monsieur le Dauphin and Monsieur d'Orléans, other princes of the blood, and high personages, to his galley. They all went on board, and great compliments were exchanged on all sides, and various propositions were made, and the result was (as from the said visits and armistice) a great continuation of good-friendship and greater confidence. This was the second time that his imperial Majesty saw the King of France, and the first time that he set foot in that kingdom as a friend.

The Emperor again set sail, and returned for the fifth time to Spain. He landed at Barcelona and left for Valladolid, where he found the Empress much better than when he left her, but still indisposed. To put into execution the league which he had concluded, he for a second time convoked the General Cortes of all his kingdoms of Castille at Toledo, where their majesties were residing, and where the support and assistance were discussed which it was possible and suitable to grant.

In the same year a great dearth prevailed in Sicily. It was here principally that the fleet had to procure its provisions;

and, although the Emperor was quite prepared on his part,
the Pope and the Venetians were of the opinion that it was
not to be thought of to carry out this year the projected enterprise, and the contributions from the Cortes demanded by
his Majesty were ceased to be levied. It, however, happened
that his Holiness and the Signoria of Venice, deeming that it
was not advisable to allow the year to pass by without doing
something, united their fleets and sent them to oppose and
fight the Turk by sea as well as by land. The result of this
expedition was the capture of Castel-Nuovo.*

The sufferings of the Empress continued, and her malady
made daily progress, especially since it was ascertained that
she was again enceinte: the Emperor remained the greater
part of the year 1539 at Toledo. The state of the Empress
grew worse, and having given birth to a fifth son it pleased
God to call her unto himself, and it may be held for certain
that he did so in his great mercy. This death caused great
sorrow to everyone, especially to the Emperor, who ordered
everything to be done that is customary and suitable under
such circumstances.

Since the interview at Aigues-Mortes, negotiations had continued without interruption for the conclusion of a satisfactory
and permanent peace between the Emperor and the King of
France. As it happened that at this period certain innova-
tions commenced to show themselves in Flanders, from which
his Majesty had been absent since the year 1531, he deemed
that his absence might be an obstacle to the remedy which
those evils required, and gave rise to other and still greater
ones. The Emperor had lost his companion; he was animated
by a great desire to do everything that was possible to obtain
a good result and the conclusion of peace; and although he
felt that the prince his son was still much too young to govern
in his absence and to replace the Empress in her functions,
and despite the other inconveniences which were represented
to him and brought to his notice, he hearkened only to the
good and sincere intention he had to do good, and to fulfil
his duties toward his subjects so as to prevent them suffering
greater inconveniences and giving rise to more scandals.

He was also desirous of bringing to a conclusion certain

* Castel-Nuevo, in Dalmatia, at the mouths of Cattaro.

matters which he had left in suspension in Germany. He had formed the design of embarking at Barcelona for Italy; but at the same time the King of France sent him many pressing invitations to visit his kingdom, offering all security and a hearty welcome, while on the contrary he would have been much grieved had his Majesty shown any mistrust or acted otherwise. The Emperor therefore decided on taking his departure from Spain, leaving for the first time the government of his kingdoms to the prince his son, despite his youth.

At the end of this year the Emperor put this resolution into execution, and, on the word and the promise of the King of France (with whom a truce had been concluded at Villafranca, near Nice), he passed through his kingdom, where his Majesty was fêted and well received. This was the third interview between their majesties, the third time that his Majesty set foot in France, and the second time that he entered the kingdom as a friend.

The Emperor visited Flanders for the fourth time. Here he took the most prompt measures possible to put a stop to the disorders which had sprung up there.

He commenced the fortress of Ghent, assembled the estates, and visited the greater portion of the domains. During this visit he experienced at the Hague, in Holland, an eighth attack of gout, and conformably to the intention he entertained, and to the desire which had always animated him to conclude a good peace, he offered to the King of France, immediately he had arrived in the said States, such favorable conditions that he was surprised to find they were not accepted and the desired peace not concluded.

Some time previously Count Charles of Egmont had died, after having for many years ruled the Duchy of Gueldres, which, however, did not belong to him. More than that, he had seized upon every opportunity to develop and increase his power, and at various periods he had attempted to get possession of Friesland, Overyssel, and Gröningen, from which he was always driven back by the imperialists, and which territories were in the peaceful possession of his Majesty.

Not content with this, he made war against the Bishop of Utrecht, who was a prince of the empire, and took the town of Utrecht from him by force. As soon as the Emperor heard of this, to whom the bishop had sued for assistance (an obligation to which he was bound as lord of the fief), and it was all the stronger, as it was necessary to maintain tranquillity in the Netherlands, he concerted measures with the bishop, and came to his assistance in such guise that the said Count Charles of Egmont was driven out of Utrecht by the imperial troops. The Emperor, who proceeded there in person shortly afterward, ordered a new fortress to be constructed there, and for this purpose obtained from the Pope and from the empire all the necessary acts and ratifications.

After the death of Charles of Egmont, Duke William of Clèves seized upon the government of the Duchy of Gueldres. asserting a claim to it. His imperial Majesty, seeing how matters stood, and how he consequently ought to and could act, made him offers, the conditions of which were such that they ought reasonably to have been accepted. But, at the request, and through the intrigues of France (the French were dissatisfied, although without grounds, with the terms of the peace, which were not conformable to their wishes and designs), the duke, who, moreover, was young and followed the counsel of his mother, would not accept them.

The Emperor having thus achieved all that was to be done in the States of Flanders, and having convoked a Diet at Ratisbon, where he wished distinctly to show his claims relative to the Duchy of Gueldres, resolved to leave for the said Diet, as already, while in Spain, he had opened negotiations on the subject with the States of the empire. The King of the Romans came to visit his brother in Flanders, and the deputies of the empire assembled at Worms to deliberate upon this question. The Emperor finding that all was not quite settled in the Netherlands, requested the King his brother to remain there during his absence, and he also charged M. de Granvelle and his other ministers to push on matters while he was attending the said Diet. However, as this assembly at Worms, and the negotiations which took place, did not lead to the result which he had anticipated, everything was reserved for the future Diet of Ratisbon.

The Emperor, leaving for the second time the government of the Netherlands to the care of the Queen of Hungary, proceeded to the Diet at Ratisbon, for the first time passing through the State of Luxembourg. This was the Emperor's fourth visit to Germany. He had convoked this Diet chiefly to establish concord and to effect a remedy in the state of religious affairs. After various debates, the Emperor observed that the princes of the empire had not attended this Diet, and that they were still far from a conclusion, and still more so from the means of execution which ought to be adopted; moreover, the report was current that the Turk intended to invade Austria, and no order had been given to oppose that invasion and to take the necessary measures of defence.

Already, before this news was received, the Emperor, from various reasons which actuated him, had on his return to Spain made great naval preparations for an expedition to Algeria. He therefore left Ratisbon before he was fully informed of the invasion of the Turk, and started for Italy to embark, and commence the said enterprise. This was his Majesty's sixth visit there. Immediately on his arrival, positive news was received that the Turk was making great preparations to invade Hungary. From this reason the Emperor proceeded to Lucca, where he had his third interview with Pope Paul to arrange the means for organizing a defence against the Turk. But finding that this interview and these negotiations led to no result, he proceeded to Spezzia, a port in the Gulf of Genoa, to wait there until his fleet was in perfect readiness.

Already the equipment and preparations for this fleet had occupied more time than was necessary; and although the season was almost passed, nevertheless, as the outlays incurred could not be turned to any other account, and from other reasons which, as already said, actuated the Emperor, considering that weather is in the hands of God, he embarked at the said port of Spezzia for Corsica, which he saw for the first time, and from thence for Algiers, touching at the island of Sardinia, at Majorca, and at Minorca, for the second time. This was the eighth time that he crossed the Mediterranean, and the second time that he landed in Africa. During this journey the weather was seasonable. The Spanish fleet also arrived, and after a few skirmishes, when the troops were already suitably posted to attack the town, and provided with everything that was necessary to open their batteries, so fierce a tempest arose on sea that many vessels perished and the army on land also suffered considerably.

Nevertheless the men mutually assisted each other, and the best order possible was organized, as well to resist the fury of the sea as the attacks of the enemy by land. Finally the annoyances became so great that the Emperor deemed it the wisest plan to relinquish the expedition and put to sea. But this could not be done immediately, as the tempest had not subsided. He was therefore obliged to march twenty miles by land, to cross two large rivers, so as to reach Cape Matafous, where he reëmbarked.

The whole time the army was on land (it remained there twelve days before reëmbarking) it suffered from great want of provisions, because, as already said, the weather was so boisterous that nothing could be got from the ships. After those twelve days the Emperor set sail during a great storm, and was compelled to touch at Bougie. The winds were so contrary, and he was retained so long that he and his troops suffered much from the scarcity of provisions; and the evils would have been still greater had the fine weather not returned. The tempest was so fierce that everyone sought shelter where best he could, and many ships were driven in directions quite contrary to where they wished to go. Nevertheless the troops recovered so well that, without so much loss as might have been expected from such weather, they all returned to the appointed rendezvous. The Emperor dismissed the superfluous men and those least wanted, and the others returned to their garrisons. The Emperor, having embarked at Bougie, arrived with fair weather at Majorca for the third time, from whence Prince Doria returned to Genoa with his galleys, after passing by Barcelona.

The Emperor, with the Spanish galleys, touched for the first time at Irica; for the ninth time he navigated the Mediterranean. He arrived at Carthagena: this was his sixth visit to Spain. He then continued his route as far as Ocaña, where he met his children, the Prince of Spain and the infantas.

In the commencement of the year 1542, the Emperor proceeded to Valladolid, to hold the Cortes of the Kingdom of Castille. Here he experienced a ninth attack of gout, and at the monastery of La Mejorada he suffered from it generally in nearly all his limbs. At this time negotiations were on foot for the marriage of the prince his son with the infanta

Doña Maria of Portugal, and of Prince Juan of Portugal with the infanta Doña Juana, second daughter of his Majesty.

As soon as the Cortes had terminated, the Emperor, although unwell, proceeded as quickly as he could, passing through Navarre, to hold the Cortes of the three kingdoms of Aragon at Monzon, with the intention of returning as soon as possible to Germany to provide some remedy for the affairs of religion, and to recover by all means in his power the Duchy of Gueldres, which belonged to him. The King of France, however, seeing the bad success which had attended the Emperor in his enterprise against Algiers, and fancying that the outlays he had been put to must have drained his finances, commenced by making a small complaint, and the Emperor replied to him by offering all the justifications to which he was bound by the conditions of the truce concluded at Nice.

The King of France nevertheless transmitted to him from all parts the assurance that he had not the slightest intention of going to war with him; but he suddenly attacked the Emperor in the Netherlands, Martin Van Rossem commencing operations in Gueldres, M. d'Orléans in Luxembourg, and M. de Vendôme in the States of Flanders and in Artois. Moreover, he ordered his son the Dauphin to lay siege to Perpignan, and proceeded himself as far as Narbonne to stimulate the enterprise. Nevertheless, by the grace of God, the Emperor, and those who had the management of his affairs, set things so well in order, and organized so able a defence, that this time the said King did nothing of importance.

At this period Pope Paul, not satisfied with having issued a bull, which was a testimony of his good-will, but which had scarcely any other effect, convoked a general council at Trent, and at the same time sent his legates to his Majesty and to the King of France, not only to invite them and to exhort them to peace, but also to restrain them by ecclesiastical censure if they would not obey his behest to conclude a truce.

This happened, as already said, at the period his Majesty was attacked and when the French were repulsed on all sides and compelled to withdraw. His imperial Majesty, seeing with what intentions his Holiness wished to effect a peace between their majesties, and that thereby his imperial Majesty would have been mulcted and dispossessed of all that had been taken from him by a sudden and unexpected invasion, did not think it either equitable or suitable to accept such propositions of peace; but he felt indignant, and obliged to reconquer what belonged to him, and to show his resentment for such an injury. The Emperor, therefore, rejected the said propositions, and would not hearken to them at all. He somewhat dryly dismissed the legate, who had addressed him in a tone without that respect which was due to his Majesty. He, however, still protested that he was, as he always had been, inclined to treat for peace, provided that the adverse party was governed by reason and provided that the peace was sure and suitable to the service of God and to the welfare of Christianity.

The Cortes of Aragon having terminated, the Emperor left for Barcelona. He had sent the prince his son from Monzon to Saragossa, that he should be recognized prince of that kingdom; from thence his Majesty proceeded with him to Barcelona, where he was also recognized. Having passed through Valencia, where the same ceremonial was observed, the Emperor took the direction of Alcala to see his daughters. Here the affiance *per verba de futuro* of his daughter the infanta Doña Juana took place with Prince Don Juan of Portugal, according to what had been agreed upon. This done, the Emperor proceeded to Madrid, which city he left as soon as he could, because he much desired, according to his first intention, to return to Germany.

In fact he had convoked a Diet at Nüremberg, to discuss defensive measures against the Turk, and matters of religion. The King his brother and M. de Granvelle proceeded there, in the name of his Majesty, with many others of his ministers whom he had sent there. The Emperor, having terminated all that he had to do in the kingdoms of Spain, commenced his journey, having left for the second time the prince his son governor of the said kingdoms. He therefore left Madrid, and arrived at Barcelona, which city he would willingly have left earlier, but various obstacles prevented his embarking before May 1st, and in consequence of storms and boisterous weather he was not able to gain the open sea till the nineteenth of that month, when the weather was still unsettled and doubtful. When off Pomègues, near Marseilles, some French galleys sallied out and commenced skirmishing, supported by the land batteries; but they were so ably responded to that they were compelled to retreat, and place themselves under the protection of the artillery on shore. The Emperor, not wishing any delay, continued his journey to Genoa. This was the tenth time he crossed the Mediterranean, and the seventh time he landed in Italy.

While passing in front of Nice the Emperor learned that the galleys of France wished to capture the castle of that town, and, while his Majesty was landing at Genoa, Prince Doria approached with his galleys to watch the movements of those of France. Observing that they came with the intention of executing the project attributed to them, he attacked them so briskly that he captured four of them. At this period his Majesty learned that Barbarossa was expected with a large fleet to support the King of France.

This Barbarossa arrived later, remained at Toulon during the whole time the war against the Emperor lasted, and returned without having performed any act of importance. His Majesty proceeded to Busseto, where he was joined by his Holiness, as much to discuss the affairs of Germany as to see if there were no possible means of concluding a peace. This was the Emperor's fourth interview with Pope Paul, and he experienced a tenth attack of gout. A few days afterward, perceiving how little good resulted from this interview, he continued his journey toward Germany, where he found himself for the fifth time.

As the Diet had not been long sitting, and the Emperor, in a time so replete with troubles, did not see any chance of regulating and discussing the affairs of religion, he continued his journey as far as Spires, where he made all the necessary preparations to enter the campaign with a good army, at the head of which he placed Don Ferdinand de Gonzaga. He was desirous of resenting the injuries and damage perpetrated by the King of France, who had penetrated into the territory of Hainault as far as Binche, and had taken Landrecies, which he was fortifying. He was also compelled to do so by the war waged against him by Duke William of Clèves, who had taken up arms at the instigation of the King of France, and in concert with him. On his way, the Emperor heard of the defeat and rout of the duke's troops at Heinsburg.

Nevertheless his Majesty, on his arrival at Spires, wished, the better to justify himself, to propose to the electors, who had assembled on the banks of the Rhine, to treat with the said Duke of Clèves by means of a pacific arrangement as regarded the Duchy of Gueldres. This proposal did not meet with a good reception, and the only plan left for him was to reassemble his army and advance with it (this was the sixth time he was on the Rhine) as far as Bonn, from whence he took the direction of Duren. Having there made a reconnoissance of the ground, he established his batteries, bombarded the town, and carried it by storm. The Prince of Orange then came up with his army from the Netherlands. The two armies having united, and Duren having been captured, as already stated, with other possessions and lands appertaining to the Duchy of Gueldres, as also to the Duchy of Clèves and of Juliers, his Majesty took the direction of Ruremond, which immediately surrendered, and from thence he advanced in the direction of Venloo. And as Duke Henry of Brunswick arrived as a friend of the said Duke of Clèves, the Emperor demonstrated and exposed to him his error, exhorting him to renounce it.

At this time the mother of the Duke of Clèves died. This latter recognized the bad counsel he had received, and the wisest men of the States of Gueldres also entreated him to withdraw from the danger he was in, and follow better advice; he did so, and came and threw himself at the feet of his Majesty, confessing his fault and asking pardon. He handed over and restored the whole State of Gueldres to the Emperor. But the Emperor, considering that the error of the duke originated rather in his youth than from any evil inclination or wish to do evil, ordered the towns and localities taken from him in other territories to be restored to him. Not content with what he had done, and seeing the duke's repentance, and how well he persevered in his good intentions, he took his marriage into hand; in fact he gave him in marriage his niece, a daughter of the King of the Romans. This marriage increased the obligations of the said duke toward his Majesty, and the love of his Majesty for that prince. At the commencement of the spring, the King of France, to be the first in the field, and to be enabled to oppose superior forces to the Emperor, brought forth two armies destined to wage war in the Netherlands. A portion of one of these armies, in which the King was present in person, occupied Landrecies, and the other portion established itself in the neighborhood while the fortifications were strengthened.

The two sons of the King had meantime marched on Binche, from whence they were driven back with loss, without having accomplished anything. Finally, M. de Orléans joined the other army, which was at Luxembourg. This town, not being in a state of defence, had surrendered, and had been fortified by the French. At the same time happened what has already been related before of the war, that the Duke of Clèves, at the instigation of the same King, had commenced in Brabant. The Emperor, having put an end to that war of Clèves, and having taken possession of Gueldres, as already stated, left, suffering from the gout, Venloo for Diest, where the Estates of the Netherlands were assembled. They granted him a large subsidy, on the footing of the one granted to him the preceding year. This was the fifth visit of his Majesty to the Netherlands. The King of France, apprised of all these facts, withdrew with his troops into his kingdom, after having fortified Landrecies.

This done, the Emperor, leaving under the walls of Landrecies the army which was in the Netherlands, with the gendarmerie which the King of England had sent to him in virtue of conventions which had been concluded, ordered the army which he had with him to march, as also that which had arrived from England, as far as Guise. But as the season was already advanced, and the weather inclement, he soon ordered it back to join that before Landrecies. The Emperor, although suffering much from the gout, left Diest to attend the siege; and knowing that the King of France was assembling new troops to relieve the besieged, he did not wish to be absent from his armies. He therefore established his quarters at Avesnes, although, as already stated, suffering from the gout, and he remained there until the troops sent to the succor of the garrison of Landrecies had withdrawn. This was his tenth attack of the gout.

The King of France, knowing that his troops were in danger and in want of provisions, proceeded with his army to

Château-Cambrésis, from whence he sent a heavy body of cavalry to reconnoitre the ground, so as to attempt to succor the garrison of Landrecies. To prevent this the armies of the Emperor formed a junction, and made such a resistance that this cavalry did not attain its object and had little subject of congratulation. It is true that during this time some French knights, with sacks of gunpowder and a small supply of provisions, of which the besieged stood much in need, succeeded in entering Landrecies at a point where there was no obstacle, which rallied the besieged a little. As the season was advanced and the weather bad, and as, moreover, the chief object of the Emperor, when he ordered his army in France to besiege Landrecies, was to compel the King to give battle, he ordered his army to decamp, and approached France.

On the same day the Emperor, still unwell and carried in a litter, left Avesnes and passed the night at Quesnoy. From thence he rejoined his army, which had already taken up a position opposite that of the King of France. On the following morning his Majesty, leaving his quarters, advanced with all his men within cannon range of the enemy, close to the King's camp, and offered him battle. A few skirmishes and discharges of artillery took place on both sides, and finally a bold charge against the French, who had the worst of it, and they thought it advisable not again to leave their entrenchments. The Emperor, finding they would not come out, advanced with his army close up to the enemy's camp.

The following day was passed in skirmishing: at nightfall the King withdrew with his army and retreated as far as Guise. The Emperor, through the negligence of his scouts, was ignorant of this retreat until the following day; the result was that he could not come up with the King and his army. He advanced as far as a wood or thicket, to a distance of three leagues, but he could not, owing to the disorder of his matchlock-men (who, most of them, were followed or accompanied by more baggage than soldiers ought to have), attempt to cross the wood with his army. A few light cavalry and matchlock-men and a disorderly few traversed the thicket. M. le Dauphin observed it, and having collected his French gendarmes he turned round and charged his pursuers. The latter sought refuge in the thicket, and then returned to the infantry. It may easily be believed that, if the Emperor had had his matchlock-men, with whom he could have passed through the thicket in safety, he might have attained in part the object of his desires; but as nothing else was to be done on this day, and as it was already late, he left the thicket and established his quarters in the very camp and on the very spot which the King of France had left. He arrived there at one hour after midnight.

The Emperor remained some days at Château-Cambrésis, to see if he could not undertake something against his enemy. But the latter resolved to disband his army at once, and sent the troops back to their garrisons. The Emperor, considering also that the festival of All Saints had already passed, determined to do likewise; and consequently he proceeded to Cambray, and from thence to Brussels, where he was taken ill (not from the gout), and was laid up during the rest of the year. At the end of this same year the Princess of Spain, the infanta Doña Maria of Portugal, was, conformably to the engagements which had been made, taken to Castille, and handed over to the Prince of Spain and Salamanca, where their nuptials were solemnized, after having been contracted *per verba de presenti*.

The Emperor, leaving the Queen of Hungary, his sister, for the third time governor of the Netherlands, left Brussels, and for the sixth time went up the Rhine as far as Spires. This was also the sixth time that he entered Germany, where he had convoked a Diet with a view to explain to the electors of the empire the causes which had induced him to undertake the Gueldres expedition and to march against the King of France, causes which have been briefly given above, but which were more developed in the proposition then made. And seeing that at this moment there did not appear any likelihood of the Turk advancing against Christendom, and that it was also impossible to do anything in matters of religion, or to discuss any important affairs, he demanded a subsidy against the King of France, who had seized upon various towns and lands of the empire, and who daily accomplished or negotiated things to its great detriment. This having been well considered and fully appreciated, all granted good aid to his imperial Majesty.

While the Emperor was on his way to Spires, Pope Paul

sent Cardinal Farnese to his Majesty, under color and pretext of making representations to him and of endeavoring to
treat for peace. The Emperor, well aware that these were
empty words and sheer pretext, would not allow himself to be
caught, nor relinquish the plans and pursuit of the enterprise
which he had commenced to recover the territory, of which
he had been despoiled. Thus he soon dismissed the said cardinal, declaring that he was always willing to negotiate for a
sincere, good, and permanent peace. Then, supported and
strengthened by the aid he had received from the empire, he
commenced reassembling his army.

Meantime the Emperor received the news that the army
which he had in Italy had been defeated near Carignano. It
was a bad time and under bad circumstances. Whatever
might come of it, having previously learned that the city of
Luxembourg, although carefully fortified, was short of provisions, and that the King of France was endeavoring to throw
supplies into it, he ordered, in all haste, Don Ferdinand de
Gonzaga, to whom he had intrusted the command of his army,
to prevent any supplies reaching that city. This general, with
a small body of men, performed his mission so well that the
city shortly surrendered.

The Emperor soon reinforced his army in such guise that
his said captain-general captured in a few days many towns
and strongholds on the French frontier, on the Lorraine side,
and laid siege to Saint Dizier. On his part, the Emperor left
Spires and passed through Metz, to join him with the remainder of the army. This was the fourth time that his
Majesty entered France, and the second time as an enemy.
Fire was opened against Saint Dizier, the assault given, and
the town captured in a few days. At this siege the Prince of
Orange was struck by a cannon-ball in the trenches, and died
shortly afterward.

According to what had been agreed upon between his Majesty and the King of England, the said King had come in person with a large army to molest and attack the Kingdom of
France, and his Majesty had also sent to him the forces he had
promised by the said convention, under the orders of M.
de Buren. The said King had stopped at the siege of Boulogne
and of Montreuil; and during the long lapse of time, during

which his Majesty was before Saint Dizier, the King of France had leisure to assemble his whole army, and to garrison the greater portion of the frontiers of his kingdom. The Emperor, taking all this into consideration, observing, moreover, that he had not at his command as sufficient a supply of provisions as he required, and that the season was far advanced, found difficulties for any ulterior enterprise.

However, not to leave the King of England alone against his enemy, he would not retire with his army. Already previously during the siege of Saint Dizier he had captured Vitry, defeated the French light cavalry there, and made other incursions. The Emperor, leaving the town of Saint Dizier and other more important places in a good state of defence, and persevering in the intention already mentioned above, of employing every means to bring the King of France to give battle, resolved to penetrate into the interior of that kingdom as far as he could, always seeking the said King and his army. Consequently, the Emperor, passing by Vitry, established himself in a plain near Châlons. Here some good skirmishes took place, where the French gained nothing, and where they had no reason to be satisfied with the pistols and small matchlocks of the German horsemen.

But as Châlons had a strong garrison, and there was a French army at three short leagues from it on the other side of the Marne; considering, moreover, that the Emperor and his army had no other provisions to depend upon except what they found in the country villages and small towns, it appeared to his Majesty that he ought not to make a longer stay in this locality. And although he had marched during the whole of the day upon which he arrived there, he left with his whole army at ten o'clock in the evening; and so quick was the advance that at daybreak he found himself in view and in face of the spot where the French had taken position with their entrenchments, carefully fortified, especially on the side on which the Emperor had arrived.

The Marne flowed between the two armies. His Majesty might certainly have crossed the Marne, as there was a wooden bridge, which, although broken down, might have been repaired so as to allow the passage of the infantry. There was also one where both cavalry and infantry might cross. But when that was accomplished there would still have been much to be done, to the great disadvantage of the Emperor's troops. For, supposing the bridge and ford crossed—which could only be done in file—it would have been necessary to reform in order, as a fine open plain lay in front, which could be swept by the enemy's artillery. It would have been necessary to advance to the attack under continual fire; and when all this was done, there was still a branch of the Marne, which, though narrow, was deep, and offered some difficult points which could not be overcome without disorder. Then it was necessary to climb a hill or mound to reach the enemy, who counted a good number of Swiss in his ranks.

The Emperor saw that all these difficulties rendered it impossible to put the army in good order of battle; he therefore persisted in the resolution which he had taken to make a long march that day to get ahead of the French army. In fact, it was the Emperor's intention to advance, so as to find the places he passed through undefended, and he hoped that he should force the French to advance so far as to offer him the opportunity he desired. On the same morning Count William of Fürstenberg, not knowing what he was about, crossed the above-mentioned ford, and fell into the hands of the French. On the other hand, Prince de la Roche-sur-Ton, while endeavoring to join the French camp with his company, came across some imperial light-horse, who pursued him, and charged in such guise that he, his lieutenant, and many others were made prisoners, and his men put to flight.

On the same day the Emperor continued to advance, and almost reached Ay, where he was stopped by the bad state of the road and the numerous streams. Moreover, his rear-guard did not arrive till ten in the evening. Thus the army had been marching for twenty-four hours, and on the preceding day it had performed the same march. If it is permitted to form a judgment on what might have happened if the Emperor had that day reached Epernay, which was only a short French league farther on (the thing was impossible), so as to have enabled the army to cross the river on the morrow, over the stone bridge of that city, and by the boats constructed on the same river, he might have, by following the ridge of hill above mentioned, attacked the French camp by the slopes, which had not yet been fortified, and God would have given the victory to whom it pleased him. However, in consequence of the obstacles already mentioned, the Emperor did not reach Epernay till the evening of the following day, and he proposed, in council, what has been related above. But this project could not be carried out, because in consequence of the delay of this day which had been lost, the French had time to fortify all the slopes as they had done on the other side; of which fact the Emperor received speedy information.

In consequence, the Emperor left Epernay, advancing always with great diligence and precaution. But the road offered great obstructions, owing to the numerous streams and rivulets that intersected them. In some localities they were so bad that it was often necessary to make long detours, so that, when it was hoped to get over two or three French leagues during the day, it happened that, owing to the circuitous road taken, not more than one was accomplished. This decided the Emperor to send forward in advance a good number of men without their baggage, that they might capture—and they did capture it—the town of Château-Thierry. The Emperor followed them as fast as he could, always with the intention of advancing farther and continuing his route.

MILITARY AND POLITICAL CAMPAIGNS

BY

Frederick the Great

FREDERICK THE GREAT

1712—1786

Frederick II, King of Prussia, surnamed " The Great," was the son of Frederick William I and the princess Sophia-Dorothea, daughter of George I of Great Britain, and was born in 1712. His early years were spent under the restraints of an irksome military training and a rigid system of education. His impatience under this discipline, his taste for music and French literature, and his devotion to his mother gave rise to discussions between father and son, and resulted in an attempt on the part of Frederick to escape to the court of his uncle, George II of England. Being seized in the act, his conduct was visited with severity, and he was kept in close confinement. According to some reports, the prince's life would have been sacrificed to the fury of his father, had not the kings of Sweden and Poland interceded in his favor. Having humbly sued for pardon, he was liberated, and allowed to retire to Ruppin, which, with the town of Rheinsberg, was bestowed upon him in 1734. Here he continued to reside till the King's death, surrounded by men of learning, and in correspondence with Voltaire, whom he especially admired, and other philosophers; but on his accession to the throne in 1740, he laid aside these peaceful pursuits, and at once gave evidence of his talents as a legislator, and his determination to take an active share in the political and warlike movements of the age.

His first military exploit was to gain a victory at Mollwitz over the Austrians, in 1741, which nearly decided the fate of Silesia, and secured to Prussia the alliance of France and Bohemia. Another victory over the Empress Maria Theresa's troops made him master of Upper and Lower Silesia, and closed the first Silesian war. The second Silesian war, which ended in 1745, from which Frederick retired with augmented territories and the reputation of being one of the first commanders of the age, was followed by a peace of fourteen years, which he devoted to the improvement of the various departments of government, and of the nation generally, to the organization of his army, and the indulgence of his literary tastes. The third Silesian war, or " the Seven Years' War," was begun in 1756 by the invasion of Saxony—a step to which Frederick was driven by the fear that he was to be deprived of Silesia by the allied confederation of France, Austria, Saxony, and Russia. This contest, which was one of the most remarkable of modern times, secured to Frederick a decided influence in the affairs of Europe generally, as the natural result of the preeminent genius which he had shown both under defeat and victory; but although this war crippled the powers of all engaged in it, it left the balance of European politics unchanged. It required all the skill and inventive genius of Frederick to repair the evils which his country had suffered by the war. In 1772 he shared in the partition of Poland, and it is with the military and political campaigns immediately preceding this event that the memoirs here given deal. He left to his nephew and successor a powerful and well-organized kingdom, one-half larger in area than it had been at his own accession, with a full treasury, and an army of 200,000 men. He died at the château of Sans Souci, August 17, 1786. Frederick the Great is said to have " inherited all his father's excellences and none of his defects." His courage, fertility of resource, and indomitable resolution cannot be too highly praised.

MILITARY AND POLITICAL CAMPAIGNS

THE acquisition of the duchy of Berg met with many difficulties in carrying it into execution. To obtain precise ideas, it is necessary to imagine ourselves in the exact state in which the King, at that time, found himself. He scarcely could bring 60,000 men into the field; his only resource for the support of any enterprise, was in the treasure which the late King had left. If he wished to undertake the conquest of the duchy of Berg, it was necessary to employ all his forces; because, it was strongly to be presumed, he must struggle with France, and at the same time take the city of Düsseldorf. The superiority of France was alone sufficient to make him desist, had he not had other impediments, equally considerable and repugnant to his views.

These difficulties arose from similar claims to those of the King, which the house of Saxony made to Juliers and Berg; and from the jealousy with which the house of Hanover beheld that of Brandenburg. If under such circumstances, the King had led his whole forces to the banks of the Rhine, he might well expect that, leaving his hereditary domains void of troops, he would expose them to be invaded by the Saxons and the Hanoverians, who would not have failed to have made a diversion: and should he leave a part of his army in the marche of Brandenburg, to guard his States against the ill-intentions of his neighbors, he would then be everywhere too feeble. France had guaranteed the Palatine succession to the Duke of Salzback; thereby to obtain the neutrality of the old elector during the war she made on the Rhine. It would not have been this guarantee which would have stopped the King; for guarantees are generally only words, which are no sooner given than broken; but it was the interest of France to have

41

feeble neighbors on the banks of the Rhine, and not puissant princes, capable of resistance.

About the same time Count Seckendorff, who had been confined in the prisons of Graetz, obtained his liberty, on condition of remitting into the hands of the Emperor all the orders by which he had been authorized to give the late King of Prussia the most solemn assurances of assistance; which the Emperor had promised him in support of his rights of succession to the duchies of Juliers and Berg.

This introduction shows how little favorable circumstances were to the house of Brandenburg; and what were the reasons which determined the King to abide by the provisional treaty, which his father had concluded with France. But, if these forcible arguments moderated that ardor after fame with which the King was animated, motives not less powerful impelled him to give, at the beginning of his reign, marks of vigor and fortitude, which should render his nation respectable in Europe.

Good citizens sighed to see the little respect in which other powers had held the late King, particularly during the latter part of his reign, and at the contempt thrown on the Prussian name, by the world in general. As these considerations had a great influence on the conduct of the King, we think ourselves obliged to say a few explanatory words on that subject.

The sage and circumspect conduct of the late King had been imputed to his weakness. In the year 1727 there were some differences between him and Hanover, concerning trifles, which ended in reconciliation. Shortly after he had other disputes, equally unimportant, with the Dutch, and which were in like manner accommodated. From these two examples of moderation, his neighbors and those who envied him concluded he might be insulted with impunity; that, instead of real, his was but apparent strength; that his officers were not men of understanding, but fencing-masters; and his brave soldiers mercenaries, who had little affection for the State; and that, with respect to himself, he continually threatened, but never struck.

The world, superficial and frivolous in its judgment, gave credit to such opinions; and these prejudices were soon spread over Europe. The fame to which the late King aspired, a fame more just than that of conquerors, was to render his country happy, to discipline his army; and to administer his finances with the wisest order and economy. War he avoided, that he might not be disturbed in the pursuit of plans so excellent. By these means he travelled silently on toward grandeur, without awakening the envy of monarchs. In the last years of his life the infirmities of his body had entirely ruined his health; and his ambition never would have consented that the command of his troops should have been confided to any other than himself. These various causes, united, rendered his reign happy and pacific.

Had the opinion which was entertained of the King been only a speculative error, truth would in time have undeceived the public; but princes presumed so much to the disadvantage of his character that his allies treated him with as little ceremony as his enemies. As a proof of this, the courts of Vienna and Russia agreed with him to place a prince of Portugal on the throne of Poland. This project was quickly abandoned, and they declared themselves in favor of Augustus II, Elector of Saxony, without deigning to send the least intimation of such a change to the King. The Emperor Charles VI had, on certain conditions, obtained a succor of 10,000 Prussians, whom in 1734 the late King sent to the banks of the Rhine against the French. The Emperor believed himself placed above the necessity of fulfilling such paltry engagements. George II of England called the late King, his brother, the corporal, and said he was King of the highroads and archdustman of the Holy Roman Empire. Every act of this monarch stamped an impression of the most profound contempt. Tre Prussian officers, who, according to the priveleges of electors, enlisted soldiers in the imperial cities, were exposed to a thousand vexations; they were arrested and thrown into dungeons, where they were confined with the vilest rascals. In fine, these excesses became insufferable.

An insignificant bishop of Liège prided himself on the mortifications which he gave the late King. Some subjects of the lordship of Herstall, appertaining to Prussia, had revolted, and the bishop granted them his protection. The late King sent Colonel Kreutz to Liège, with a credential letter to accommodate the matter. And who should think proper to refuse, to allow him to come into his presence? Why, truly my lord bishop who, three successive days, saw the attendant of this envoy in the court of his palace, and as often refused him admission.

This event, and many others, the omission of which brevity occasions, taught the King that a monarch ought to make himself, and particularly his nation, respected; that moderation is a virtue which statesmen ought not too rigorously to practise, because of the corruption of the age; and that, at the commencement of a reign, it was better to give marks of determination than of mildness.

That we here may collect whatever might tend to animate the vivacity of a youthful prince ascending the throne, let us add that Frederick I, when he erected Prussia into a kingdom, had, by that vain grandeur, planted the scion of ambition in the bosom of his posterity; which, soon or late, must fructify. The monarchy he had left to his descendants was, if I may be permitted the expression, a kind of hermaphrodite, which was rather more an electorate than a kingdom. Fame was to be acquired by determining the nature of this being: and this sensation certainly was one of those which strengthened so many motives conspiring to engage the King in grand enterprises. If the acquisition of the duchy of Berg had not even met with almost insurmountable impediments, it was in itself so small that the possession would add little grandeur to the house of Brandenburg.

These reflections occasioned the King to turn his views toward the house of Austria, the succession of which would become matter of litigation at the death of the Emperor, when the throne of the Cæsars should be vacant. That event must be favorable to the distinguished part which the King had to act in Germany, by the various claims of the houses of Saxony and Bavaria to these States; by the number of candidates which might canvass for the imperial crown; and by the projects of the Court of Versailles, which, on such an occasion, must naturally profit by the troubles that the death of Charles VI would naturally excite. This accident did not long keep the world in expectation. The Emperor ended his days at the palace La Favorite, on October 26, 1740. The news arrived at Rheinsburg when the King was ill of a fever.

Infatuated by ancient prejudices, the physicians would not administer the bark; he took it in their despite, for he meditated things much more important than the cure of a fever. He immediately resolved to reclaim the principalities of Silesia, the rights of his house to which were incontestable; and he prepared, at the same time, to support these pretensions, if necessary, by arms. This project accomplished all his political views; it afforded the means of acquiring reputation, of augmenting the power of the State, and of terminating what related to the litigious succession of the Duchy of Berg.

Before, however, he would come to a fixed resolution, he weighed the dangers he had to encounter in undertaking such a war, and the advantages he had to hope.

On one hand stood the powerful house of Austria, which, possessed of advantages so various, could not but procure resources. The daughter of an Emperor was to be attacked, who would find allies in the King of England, the republic of Holland, and the princes of the empire; by whom the Pragmatic sanction had been guaranteed. Biron, Duke of Courland, who then governed Russia, was in the pay of the Court of Vienna, and the young Queen of Hungary might incline Saxony to her interest by the cession of some circles of Bohemia. The sterility of the year 1740 might well inspire a dread of wanting supplies to form magazines and to furnish the troops with provisions. These were great risks. The fortune of war was also to be feared; one lost battle might be decisive. The King had no allies, and only had raw soldiers to oppose to the veterans of Austria grown gray in arms, and by so many campaigns inured to war.

On the other part, a multitude of reflections animated the hopes of the King. The state of the Court of Vienna after the death of the Emperor was deplorable. The finances were in disorder; the army was ruined, and discouraged by ill-success in its wars with the Turks; the ministry disunited, and a youthful, unexperienced princess at the head of the government, who was to defend the succession from all claimants. The result was that the government could not appear formidable. It was, beside, impossible that the King should be destitute of allies. The subsisting rivalry between France and England necessarily meant the aid of one of those powers;

and all the pretenders to the succession of the house of Austria would inevitably unite their interests to those of Prussia. The King might dispose of his voice for the imperial election; he might adjust his pretensions to the Duchy of Berg in the best manner, either with France or Austria. The war which he might undertake in Silesia was the only offensive war that could be favored by the situation of his States, for it would be carried on upon his frontiers, and the Oder would always furnish him with a sure communication.

The death of Anne, Empress of Russia, which soon followed that of the Emperor, finally determined the King in favor of this enterprise. By her decease the crown descended to the young Ivan, Grand Duke of Russia, son of Prince Anthony Ulric of Brunswick, brother-in-law to the King, and of the Princess of Mecklenburg. Probabilities were that, during the minority of the young Emperor, Russia would be more occupied in maintaining tranquillity at home than in support of the Pragmatic sanction, concerning which Germany could not but be subject to troubles. Add to these reasons, an army fit to march, a treasury ready prepared, and, perhaps, the ambition of acquiring renown. Such were the causes of the war which the King declared against Maria Theresa of Austria, Queen of Hungary and Bohemia.

This seemed to be the period of change and revolution. The Princess of Mecklenburg-Brunswick, mother of the Emperor Ivan, was with her son under the tutelage of the Duke of Courland, to whom the Empress Anne, dying, confided the administration of the Empire. This princess supposed herself by birth superior to subjection. As the mother of the Emperor, she imagined she herself was his proper guardian rather than Biron, who was neither a native of Russia nor a relation of Ivan. She artfully excited the ambition of Marshal Munich; Biron was arrested, banished to Siberia, and the Princess of Mecklenburg seized on the government.

This change appeared to be advantageous to Prussia; for its enemy Biron was exiled, and the husband of the regent, Anthony of Brunswick, was brother-in-law to the King. To a good understanding the Princess of Mecklenburg united the caprices and defects of a woman ill-educated. Her husband, weak and destitute of genius, had no merit except the bravery

of instinct. Munich, the engine of their elevation and the true hero of Russia, was the depositary of foreign authority. Under the pretence of this revolution, the King sent Baron Winterfeld on an embassy into Russia, to congratulate the Prince of Brunswick and his consort on the fortunate success of their undertaking. The real motive, the hidden object of this mission, was to gain Munich, who was the father-in-law of Winterfeld, that he might favor the designs which were soon to be put into execution. In executing this Winterfeld had all the happy success that could be hoped.

Whatever precaution might be taken at Berlin, to conceal the meditated expedition, it was impossible to form magazines, prepare artillery, and put the troops in motion so secretly as not to be seen; the world began to suspect something was intended. Damrath, the imperial envoy at Berlin, informed his court that a storm was gathering and that it might probably burst on Silesia. The Council of the Queen replied, from Vienna, " We will not, we cannot, give faith to the intelligence you send." The Marquis of Botta was, however, sent to Berlin, to compliment the King on his accession to the throne, or rather to judge if Damrath had not excited false alarms. The art and penetration of the marquis perceived what was intended, and, on the day that he received his audience after having paid the usual congratulations, he enlarged on the inconveniences of the journey he had made, and dwelt much on the bad roads of Silesia, which had been so destroyed by inundations that they could no longer be travelled. The King did not seem to understand him, and answered that the worst that could happen to those who should travel these roads, would be to bespatter themselves.

Though the King was firmly determined on the part he should take, he thought proper to attempt accommodation with the Court of Vienna, for which purpose Count Gotter was sent thither. He was to declare to the Queen of Hungary that in case she should do justice to the claims of the King of Silesia, he offered his assistance against all her enemies, open or covert, who should wish to dismember the succession of Charles VI, and to give his vote for the imperial election of the Grand Duke of Tuscany. As it was to be supposed these offers would be rejected, Gotter was, in that case, authorized to declare war against the Queen of Hungary.

The diligence of the army was superior to that of the ambassador; it entered Silesia, it will be seen, two days before the arrival of Count Gotter at Vienna. Twenty battalions and thirty-six squadrons were sent toward the frontiers of Silesia, and were to be followed by six battalions, destined to blockade the fortress of Glogan. Feeble as such an army was, it appeared to be sufficient to seize on a defenceless country. It had beside the advantage of amassing magazines for the coming spring, which a large army would have devoured during the winter.

Before the King departed to join his forces, he gave another audience to the Marquis of Botta, in which he repeated the declarations that were to be made at Vienna by Count Gotter. Botta exclaimed, " You are going, Sire, to ruin the house of Austria and overwhelm yourself." " It depends upon the Queen," replied the King, " to accept the offers which are made." This occasioned the marquis to pause; he recollected himself, however, and replied, with an ironical air and tone: " Yours are fine troops, I allow, Sire; ours have not the same appearance, but they have seen the wolf. Think, I conjure you, on what you are going to undertake." The King was vexed and answered warmly, " You think my troops are fine, I will convince you they are good." The marquis made further remonstrances that the execution of this project might be deferred; but the King gave him to understand it was too late, and that the Rubicon was passed.

The attack on Silesia, having become public, was thought so daring as to cause a singular effervescence in the minds of men. The feeble and timorous presaged the destruction of Prussia. Others supposed the prince abandoned everything to chance, and apprehended that he had taken Charles XII for his model. Soldiers hoped for good-fortune and foretold preferment. The grumblers, some of whom are found in all countries, envied the State that increase of which it was susceptible. The Prince of Anhalt was enraged that he had not conceived the plan, and that he had not been the great engine of its execution. He, like another Jonah, prophesied of miseries which fell neither on Nineveh nor Prussia. This prince regarded the imperial army as his cradle; he had obligations to Charles VI, who had bestowed the brevet of prin-

cess on his wife, and he feared the aggrandizement of the King, who would annihilate a neighbor like himself. These subjects of discontent induced him to inspire diffidence and terrors in all minds. He wished to intimidate the King himself, had that been practicable, but everything had been too well planned, and affairs were too far advanced to be able to recede.

To prevent, however, the ill-effect which the opinions of a great general, as was the Prince of Anhalt, might make upon the officers, the King thought proper, before his departure, to assemble those of the garrison of Berlin, and speak to them in the following terms: " I have undertaken a war, gentlemen, in which my only allies are your valor and good-will. My cause is just and my resources are in the hands of fortune. Remember incessantly the fame your ancestors have acquired, on the plains of Warsaw, at Fehrbellin, and during the expedition into Prussia. Your destiny is in your own hands. Distinction and recompense attend the acts of those by whom they shall be merited. But I have no need to incite in you the love of renown, for that is continually before your eyes, and is the sole object worthy your attention. We are to face soldiers, who, under Prince Eugene, obtained the highest reputation. Although this prince no longer is in existence, still conquest will be an increase of honor, when we shall have tried our strength against such brave warriors. Adieu, depart; I will immediately follow to the rendezvous of fame, which now awaits us."

The King departed from Berlin after a grand masked ball, and arrived at Crossen on December 21st. As chance would have it, on that very day a cord, apparently worn out, to which the cathedral bell was suspended, broke; the bell had a fall, and this was interpreted to be a bad omen, for superstitious opinions still influence the national spirit. To eradicate such ill-impressions, the King, on the contrary, interpreted this to be an advantageous token. The fall of the bell, according to him, denoted the abasement of the high; and as the house of Austria was infinitely higher than that of Brandenburg, it very clearly prognosticated the advantages the latter would obtain. Whoever knows the public, knows that such reasons are very sufficient and convincing.

4

The army entered Silesia on December 23d.* The troops
marched by cantonments, as well because there was no enemy
as because the season would not admit of encampment.
Wherever they came, they dispersed a written abstract of the
rights of the house of Brandenburg to Silesia. A manifesto
at the same time was published, the substance of which was
that the Prussians took possession of this province to guard
it against irruption from any third power; which clearly indicated that they would not be expelled with impunity. These
precautions made the people and nobility not regard the entrance of the Prussians into Silesia as the invasion of an enemy,
but as the aid which an officious neighbor would lend his ally.
Religion likewise, that sacred prejudice among the vulgar,
concurred in favor of Prussia. Two-thirds of Silesia are composed of Protestants, who, long oppressed by Austrian fanaticism, looked up to the King as a saviour sent from heaven.

Ascending the Oder, the first fortress that is met with is
Glogau. This place is situated on the left side of the river.
It is of moderate extent and surrounded by a bad rampart,
the smallest part of which was of stone. The moat was ford-
able in many places; the counterscarp was almost destroyed.
As the severity of the season prevented a formal siege, it was
blockaded; neither, indeed, was the heavy artillery come up.
The Court of Vienna had sent precise orders to Wenzel Wallis,
the governor, not to commit the first hostilities. He thought
that a blockade was not a siege, and suffered himself peace-
ably to be cooped up in his ramparts. After the peace of
Belgrade, the greatest part of the Austrian army had remained
in Hungary. On hearing of the irruption of the Prussians,
General Braun (Brown) was sent into Silesia, where he scarcely
could assemble 3,000 men. He attempted to seize on Breslau
both by force and artifice, but without effect.

This city enjoyed privileges similar to those of the imperial
towns. It was a small republic, governed by its magistrates,
and was exempted from receiving a garrison. The love of
liberty and Lutheranism preserved its inhabitants from the
scourge of war. They resisted every solicitation of General
Braun, who, however, might at length have prevailed, had
not the King hastened his march to force him to retreat.

* 1740.

While this passed, Prince Leopold of Anhalt arrived at Glogau with six battalions and five squadrons. He relieved the troops that were at the blockade, and the King immediately departed with the army grenadiers, six battalions and ten squadrons, to gain Breslau without loss of time. After a march of four days he came to the gates of that capital, while Marshal Schwerin, filing along the foot of the mountains, directed his march by Liegnitz, Schweidnitz, and Frankenstein, to drive the enemy from that part of Silesia.

On January 1st the King seized on the suburbs of Breslau without resistance, and sent Colonels Borck and Goltz to summon the city to surrender. Some troops at the same time passed the Oder and cantoned at the Dome. Thus the King was master of both sides of the river, and effectually blockaded this ill-provided city, which soon was obliged to treat. It is further to be observed that, the moats of the city being frozen, the citizens had reason to dread a general assault. The zeal of the Lutheran religion cut short the tediousness of negotiation. A fanatical shoemaker brought over the low people, inspired them with his own enthusiasm, and raised them in such numbers that they obliged the magistrates to sign an act of neutrality with the Prussians, and open the city gates.

No sooner had the King entered the capital than he discharged all persons in office, who were in the service of the Queen of Hungary. This stroke of authority prevented all the private plotting which might have been practised by the old servants of the house of Austria, and all after-cabals against the interests of Prussia.

This affair ended, a detachment of infantry passed the Oder to attack an Austrian garrison of 300 men in Namflau, who, a fortnight afterward, surrendered themselves prisoners of war. One regiment of foot only was left in the suburbs of Breslau, and the King directed his march toward Ohlau, into which Braun had thrown Colonel Fromentini, with 400 men. This town takes its name from a small river which runs under its walls. It was surrounded by a bad rampart, half in ruins, and a dry ditch. The castle, which was somewhat stronger, could not be taken without artillery. While dispositions were made for general assault on this paltry place, the commander capitulated. The garrison deserted at leaving the town, and 120 men only remained, who with their commander were escorted to Neifs. The enemy had a garrison of 1,200 men at Brieg, to blockade which, as well as other places, General Kleist invested it with five battalions and four squadrons.

While the King had taken or blockaded the fortresses on the banks of the Oder, Marshal Schwerin had arrived at Frankenstein, approaching the river Neisse, which separates Upper and Lower Silesia. He fell in with the dragoons of Lichtenstein, whom he drove toward Ittmachau. This episcopal castle has a bridge over the Neisse. Braun to cover and facilitate his retreat, threw in three companies of grenadiers. These Marshal Schwerin blockaded, and on the morrow the King joined him with mortars and some twelve-pounders. As soon as the batteries were capable of playing, Major Mufflin, commander of the garrison, surrendered at discretion. There was now only the town of Neiss to take; but this by its strength was superior to all the others. This place was situated beyond the Neisse, fortified by a good rampart of earth, with a moat of seven feet water in depth, and surrounded by low and marshy lands, which had been overflowed by Rothe, who was the governor. It is overlooked, toward Lower Silesia, by a height which is 800 paces distant. The severity of the season prevented the operations of a formal siege. It therefore only could be taken by assault, bombardment, or blockade. Rothe rendered assault impracticable; he caused the ice of the moat to be broken every morning; he watered the ramparts, which were immediately frozen; and he had furnished the bastions and curtains with quantities of beams and scythes to repel assailants. Bombardment, therefore, was attempted, and 1,200 bombs and 3,000 red-hot balls were thrown in vain. The firmness of the commander obliged the Prussians to abandon the place, and go into winter quarters. Colonel Camas, who had been sent on an expedition against Glatz, rejoined the army; he had failed in his attempt for want of taking his measures well.

While the Prussians were cantoned around Neisse, Marshal Schwerin, at the head of seven battalions and ten squadrons, penetrated into Upper Silesia. He dislodged General Braun from Jaegerndorff, Troppau, and the castle of Graetz. The Austrians retired into Moravia; the Prussians took up their quarters behind the Oppa, and extended as far as Jablunka, on the frontiers of Hungary.

Count Gotter was at Vienna while these military operations were passing, where he negotiated, rather in conformity to custom than with any hope of success. The haughtiness of his language might have intimidated any other court than that of Charles VI. The courtiers of the Queen of Hungary proudly replied that it was not for a prince whose office, in quality of arch-chamberlain of the Empire, it was to present the basin to wash the hands of the Emperor, to prescribe laws to his daughter. Gotter, that he might not be outdone by Austrian ostentation, had the boldness to show the grand duke a letter which the King had written him, in which were these words: " If the grand duke will seek destruction, let him." The fortitude of the duke seemed shaken. Count Kinsky, chancellor of Bohemia, the most haughty man of this supercilious court, took up the conversation, treated every proposition of Count Gotter as injurious to the successors of the Cæsars, reanimated the grand duke, and contributed more than all the other ministers to break off the negotiation.

Europe was amazed at the unexpected invasion of Silesia. Some accused it of being the flourish of levity; others regarded it as the enterprise of frenzy. Robinson, the English ambassador, who resided at Vienna, affirmed that the King of Prussia deserved political excommunication.

At the same time that Count Gotter departed for Vienna, the King sent General Winterfeld into Russia. He there found the Marquis of Botta, who sustained the interests of the Court of Vienna with all the warmth of his character. The good sense of the Pomeranian was on this occasion superior to the sagacity of the Italian. Winterfeld, by the credit of Marshal Munich, concluded a defensive alliance between Russia and Prussia. This was an event as advantageous as could be desired under such critical circumstances.

After the troops had entered into winter quarters, the King left Silesia and came to Berlin to make the requisite preparations for the next campaign. A reinforcement of ten battalions and twenty-five squadrons was sent to the army; and as the intentions of the Saxons and Hanoverians appeared to be equivocal, it was determined to assemble thirty battalions

and forty squadrons near Brandenburg under the command
of the Prince of Anhalt, to observe the conduct of these neighboring powers.   The prince chose Genthin as the most proper
place for his encampment, and where he might equally keep
both Saxons and Hanoverians in check.   Most sovereigns
still remained in a state of uncertainty; they could not foresee
the approaching catastrophe.   The embassy of Count Gotter
to Vienna, at the very time that the Prussian troops made an
irruption into Silesia, was to them enigmatical, and they were
endeavoring to divine whether Prussia was the ally or the
enemy of the Queen of Hungary.

Of all the powers of Europe, France was undoubtedly the
most proper to assist the Prussians in their conquest.   The
French had so many reasons to be the enemies of the Austrians
that their interests must lead them to declare themselves the
friends of the King.   That he might sound the coast, he wrote
to Cardinal de Fleuri, and, though he touched but lightly on
affairs, he said enough to be understood.   The cardinal spoke
plainer in his reply.*   He answered without disguise, " That
the guarantee of the Pragmatic sanction granted by Louis
XV to the Emperor was no tie upon the former, because of
the clause, ' save and except the claims of a third; ' that,
farther, the late Emperor had not fulfilled the principal article
of the treaty, by which he had undertaken to procure to France
the guarantee of the Empire for the treaty of Vienna."

The remainder of the letter contained an angry declamation against the ambition of England, a panegyric on France,
and on the advantages which might result from her alliance,
with a detail of the reasons that might induce the electors to
place the Elector of Bavaria on the imperial throne.   The
King continued his correspondence; he showed the cardinal
the sincere desire he had to ally himself to the most Christian
King, and assured him of every facility which should depend
upon himself, promptly to terminate the negotiation.

Sweden wished to play a part in the rising troubles.   She
was the ally of France, and at the instigation of that power
had sent a body of troops into Finland under the command of General Buddenbrock.   This having inspired Russia
with jealousy, accelerated the alliance the latter made with

* In a letter dated Iffi, January 25, 1741.

Prussia. But that alliance was no sooner formed than it was in danger of being destroyed. The King of Poland had sent the handsome Count Lynar to St. Petersburg. This ambassador pleased the Princess of Mecklenburg, the Regent of Russia; and, as the passions greatly influence the deliberations of the understanding, the regent was presently on good terms with the King of Poland. This amour might have become as fatal to Prussia as that of Paris and the beautiful Helen had been to Troy. Its effects were prevented by a revolution which we shall relate in its place.

The greatest enemies of the King were, as usual, his nearest neighbors. The kings of Poland and England, who relied upon the intrigues which Lynar carried on in Russia, concluded between them an offensive alliance, by which they divided the Prussian provinces. Their imaginations fattened on that prey, and, while they declaimed against the ambition of a youthful prince, they were already enjoying his spoils in the hope that Russia and the princes of the Empire would concur in giving success to their own avidity. The Court of Vienna ought to have seized this moment to have come to an accommodation with the King. Had it then ceded the duchy of Glogau, he would have been satisfied, and would have assisted this court against its other enemies; but it seldom happens that the compliances or refusals of men are well timed. The signal for war was given to Europe. Ministers were everywhere sounding, negotiating, and intriguing to arrange their parties and to form alliances; but the troops of no power were ready; none were provided with magazines; and the King profited by this crisis to execute his grand projects.

The reinforcement for the army in Silesia arrived at Schweidnitz in the month of February. The Austrians on their part also prepared for war. They released Marshal Neuperg from the prisons at Brunn, where he had been detained ever since the peace of Belgrade, to confide to him the command of that army which was to reconquer Silesia. The marshal assembled his troops in the environs of Olmutz, and sent General Lentulus with a detachment to occupy the defiles of the principality of Glatz, by which Lentulus found himself able to cover Bohemia, and join the army of Neuperg in its meditated operations on the Neisse. The Austrian hussars already preluded war; they slipped in between the Prussian posts and endeavored to carry off small parties and intercept convoys. Some trifling skirmishes occurred, which were all as favorable to the infantry as they were unfavorable to the cavalry of the King.

Arriving in Silesia the King proposed to visit all his quarters that he might inform himself concerning a country with which he was unacquainted. For this purpose he left Schweidnitz and came to Frankenstein. General Derschau, who commanded in that part, had advanced two posts further. The one was at Silberberg, the other at Wartha, both in the defiles of the mountains. The King wished to visit them; the enemy got intelligence of this and attempted to take him. By mistake they fell on an escort of dragoons, posted in relay near the village of Baumgarten between Silberberg and Frankenstein. Colonel Ditfort, who commanded that escort, was too ignorant to manœuvre with advantage against light troops; he was beaten and lost forty horsemen. A firing was heard at Wartha. The King, who was there, hastily assembled some troops to fly to the aid of his dragoons, who were at a mile's distance; but he arrived after all was over. It was a thoughtless act of the sovereign to become an adventurer so illaccompanied. Had the King been taken prisoner on this occasion, the war had been ended; the Austrians would have been triumphant without a blow; the Prussian infantry, excellent as it was, would have become useless; and all the great projects of the King would have vanished.

The nearer the opening of the campaign approached, the more serious was the aspect of affairs. The spies were unanimous in their reports that Austrians strengthened themselves in their posts, that new troops were arriving, and that they meditated the surprise of the Prussians in their quarters, either by penetrating through Glatz or Zuckmantel. A hundred dragoons and 300 Austrian hussars threw themselves into Neisse about the same period. This was sufficient indication of the designs of the enemy, and was the reason that the King gave orders to narrow his quarters. He ought immediately to have assembled his troops, but he was inexperienced, and this was, properly, his first campaign.

The season was not sufficiently advanced to convert the blockade of Glogau and that of Brieg into sieges. A project, however, was formed suddenly to seize on Glogau, and Prince Leopold of Anhalt was ordered to put it into execution without loss. On March 9th the town was at once attacked in five different parts, and taken in less than an hour. The very cavalry fired the ramparts, so ruinous were the works. Not a house was pillaged, not a citizen was insulted; the Prussian discipline shone in all its glory. Wallis and his whole garrison were made prisoners of war. A new-raised Prussian regiment was put in possession, the works were instantly begun to be repaired, and Prince Leopold, with the corps he commanded, joined the King at Schweidnitz.

The taking of Glogau was not all. The troops were too much scattered to be able, in case of necessity, to unite. Those quarters, especially, which Marshal Schwerin occupied in Upper Silesia occasioned the most inquietude. The King wished the marshal to collect them and fall back toward the Neisse, where the King would join him with all the forces of Lower Silesia. Schwerin was not of this opinion; he wrote that if he might be reinforced he would engage to maintain his quarters till the spring.

For once the King put more faith in his marshal than in himself. His credulity had nearly become fatal to him; and, as if it were necessary that he should add error to error, he put himself at the head of eight squadrons and nine battalions to repair to Jaegerndorff. He came up with the marshal at Neustadt. "What news of the enemy?" was the first question. "I have none," replied the marshal, "except that the Austrian troops are dispersed along the frontiers f.om Hungary as far as Braunau in Bohemia, and expect the return of my spies every moment." The King arrived at Jaegerndorff on the morrow and his intention was to depart the next day to open the trenches near Neisse, where Marshal Klackstein waited his coming with ten battalions and as many squadrons. The Duke of Holstein, who was then at Frankenstein, was also to join the King, with seven battalions and four squadrons.

At the very moment of the King's departure, and while he was giving his last orders as well to the marshal as to Prince Leopold, seven Austrian dragoons arrived. The information

these deserters gave was that they had quitted the army at
Freudenthal, which is only a mile and a half from Jaegerndorff, that cavalry was there encamped, awaiting the arrival
of the infantry and the artillery to traverse the Prussian quarters and oblige them to raise the blockade of Neisse. Skirmishing at this very instant was heard before the town, and
everybody believed the vanguard of General Neuperg was on
the point of investing Jaegerndorff. There were only five
battalions in this unfortunate place, five three-pounders and
sufficient powder for forty charges. The situation would have
been desperate had Neuperg known how to profit by occasion ;
but the mountain brought forth a mouse. The enemy wished
to know if the Prussians were still in their quarters, and for
this purpose they sent their light troops to skirmish before
each town, in order to bring their reports to the officers.

The design of the enemy being manifest, the King did not
hesitate a moment to assemble the army. The troops of
Lower Silesia had orders to pass the Neisse at Sorge, and
those of Upper Silesia to join the King at Jaegerndorff. On
April 4th the King left Neustadt with all these troops collected, keeping pace with the enemy's army, which marched
by Zuckmantel and Ziegenhals toward Neisse. On the morrow he inclined toward Steinau, a mile distant from Sorge,
where he had constructed bridges over the Neisse. The
blockade of Brieg must be raised and General Kleist received
orders to join the army with his detachment. The Duke of
Holstein had like orders sent to him repeatedly ; those who
were sent with them could not deliver their message, and he
remained in great tranquillity at Frankenstein, seeing the
enemy pass on his right and on his left without in the least
troubling himself. Deserters from the Austrian army arrived
at Steinau, who affirmed that General Lentulus had the same
day joined Marshal Neuperg near Neisse. On receiving this
news the Prussian quarters were contracted immediately round
Steinau, and the King chose a post where he might give the
enemy a proper reception, in case the Prussians were attacked.

To heighten vexation, the quarters at Steinau took fire during the night, and it was only by good fortune that the artillery
and ammunition were saved, dragged through narrow streets,
the houses of which were all in flames. The troops passed

the night under arms on the ground which the King had chosen for his camp. On the morrow* this small corps of thirteen battalions and fifteen squadrons arrived after a fatiguing march at Falckenberg, where information was received that Colonel Stechow, who covered the bridge of Sorge with four battalions, had seen a large body of the enemy fortifying themselves on the other side of the river, and who even kept up a warm fire on the Prussians. Prince Charles marched thither immediately with four battalions, and sent the King word that Lentulus was on the opposite shore of the Neisse with fifty squadrons, and rendered the passage absolutely impracticable because the ground was too confined. The direction of the marching must therefore be changed.

The route of Michelau was taken, where there is another bridge over the Neisse, where General Marwitz already was with the troops assembled from the quarters of Schweidnitz and the blockade of Brieg. The bridge of Sorge was raised without loss of time, and in the evening all these different troops joined the King.

On the morrow the army crossed the Neisse at Michelau, intending to march to Grotkau. A courier who had passed that town brought dispatches to the King, so that he had no suspicions. A very heavy snow fell and interrupted the light so as to prevent the discernment of objects. The march was continued. The hussars of the vanguard entered the village of Leipe, which is on the road, and without knowing it fell in with a regiment of the enemy's hussars who were there cantoned. The Prussians took forty of the enemy, some on foot, others on horseback, and from them intelligence was gained that half an hour before Neuperg had taken Grotkau. A lieutenant named Mitzschefahl had commanded there, with sixty men, and defended himself for the space of three hours against the whole Austrian army. The deserters further deposed that the enemy would march on the morrow to Ohlau to take the heavy artillery which had there been deposited by the King.

On this news the different columns of the army, which were all on the march, were assembled. The King separated them into four divisions and cantoned them in four villages each sufficiently near to the other for the army to be assembled

* April 6th.

at the given rendezvous in less than an hour. The King took
up his quarters in the villages of Pogrel and Alsen, from which
he dispatched various officers to the garrison of Ohlau to inform them of his approach, and to draw to himself two regiments of cuirassiers who had lately arrived in these parts.
None of the officers could get thither, because of the enemy's
parties that infested the country. The next day the snow was
so heavy that objects twenty paces distant could scarcely be
distinguished. Intelligence, however, was received that the
enemy had approached Brieg. Had the bad weather continued, the difficulties of the Prussians must have increased.
Provisions began to be scarce. Ohlau was to be succored, and
in case of misfortune there was no place of retreat; but chance
supplied the want of prudence.

On the morrow, April 10th, the weather appeared clear
and serene, and though the snow was two feet deep there
were no obstacles to oppose any undertaking. The army was
assembled at five in the morning near the mill of Pogrel. It
consisted of twenty-seven battalions, twenty-nine squadrons of
cavalry, and three of hussars. It began its march in five columns: the artilery was in the centre, the two next were columns
of infantry and the two wings of cavalry. The King knew
that the cavalry of the enemy was superior to that of the
Prussians, to obviate which inconvenience he placed two battalions of grenadiers between the squadrons of each wing.
This was the disposition made by Gustavus Adolphus at the
battle of Lutzen, and which, according to all appearances,
will never more be practiced.

In this order the army advanced toward the enemy, following the road which leads to Ohlau. General Rottembourg,
who led the vanguard, passing near the village of Pampitz,
took some twenty prisoners, who confirmed the intelligence
which the peasants of the village of Molwitz had come to give
the King, which was that the enemy's army was cantoned in
Molwitz, Grunigen, and Hüneren.

As soon as the columns came within about 2,000 paces of
Molwitz, the army extended itself in order of battle, though
there was no appearance of the enemy in the field. The
right was to be supported by the village of Herrendorff.
Schulenbourg, who commanded the cavalry of that wing, took

his measures so awkwardly that he did not arrive there. The left was supported by the rivulet of Lauchwitz, the banks of which are marshy and deep. As the cavalry of the right, however, had not left sufficient room for the infantry, three battalions were obliged to be withdrawn from the first line, of which by some lucky chance a flank was formed to cover the right of the two lines of infantry. This disposition was the principal cause of victory. The baggage was stowed near the village of Pampitz about a mile behind the lines, and it was covered by the regiment of La Motte, which just then joined the army.* Rottembourg with the vanguard approached Molwitz, which he saw the Austrians leaving. He ought to have attacked them in this disorder, if he had not received precise orders not to engage; he therefore returned with his corps to the right wing, of which it was a part.

It may appear surprising that an experienced general like Marshal Neuperg should suffer himself to be surprised in any such manner. He, however, was excusable. He had given orders to different officers of hussars to scour the country, especially toward Brieg. Whether it was the result of indolence or negligence, these officers did not do their duty, and the marshal had no intelligence of the approach of the King until he saw his army in order of battle facing his cantonments. Neuperg was obliged to arrange his troops while played upon by Prussian artillery, which was served with promptitude and care. The right wing of his cavalry, under the command of Raemer, arrived the first.

This intelligent and determined officer saw that the right wing of the Prussians was nearer Molwitz than the left, and saw that if he kept his post, Neuperg risked the loss of the battle before the left of his cavalry could come up; therefore, without waiting for orders, he resolved to attack the right of the Prussians. Schulenbourg, to gain the village of Herrendorff, made an ill-conceived quarter-wheel to the right by squadrons. Raemer saw this, and without forming attacked the wing that Schulenbourg commanded, full speed in a column. The thirty squadrons of the Queen's troops led by him immediately overturned the ten Prussian squadrons, each of which presented its left flank. This routed cavalry, passing

* From Oppeln.

by and between the lines of infantry, would have totally broken
them had they not fired upon the fugitives, which fire at the
same time repulsed the enemy.   Raemer was killed; but what
may surprise every military man was that the two battalions
of grenadiers, who had been placed between the squadrons of
the right, singly maintained their ground and joined the right
of the infantry in good order.

The King, who thought he might rally cavalry as he would
stop a pack of hounds, was carried away in their route to the
centre of the army, where he accomplished the rallying of
some squadrons, which he led to the right.   They were obliged
to attack the Austrians in their turn, but these beaten and
hastily collected troops did not long make head.   They dis-
banded and Schulenbourg perished in the charge.   The victorious cavalry then falling on the right flank of the Prussian
infantry, where, as we have said, the three battalions that could
not enter into the first line were placed, made three vigorous
attacks on this infantry.   The Austrian officers fell wounded
among the ranks, the enemy's horsemen were dismounted by
the bayonet, and the bravery of the infantry repelled the
Austrians, who lost many men.

Marshal Neuperg seized this moment.   His infantry was
in motion to attack the right of the Prussians, unsupported
by cavalry.   Seconded by the Austrian horse, he made incredible efforts to break the ranks of the Prussians, but in-
effectually.   This brave infantry resisted attacks like a rock,
and by its fire destroyed many of the enemy.

The left of the Prussians was in less danger.   This wing,
which they had refused the enemy, was supported by the
rivulet of Lauchwitz.   Beyond this marsh the King's cavalry
had charged that of the Queen, and was victorious.   The fire
of the infantry on the right, however, continued for nearly
five hours to be very hot. and soldiers began to want ammunition and robbed the cartridge-boxes of the dead in order to
obtain powder.   The crisis was so great that the oldest officers thought there was no resource, and foresaw the approaching moment when the corps, deprived of ammunition, would be
obliged to yield to the enemy.   So, however, it did not happen,
and this ought to teach young commanders not to despair
too soon, for the infantry not only maintained its ground,

but gained upon the enemy.   Marshal Schwerin, perceiving
this, made a motion with his left, which he brought upon the
right flank of the Austrians.   This motion was the signal of
victory, and of the enemy's defeat.   The rout was total.
Night prevented the Prussians from pursuing their advantages farther than the village of Lauchwitz.

Ten squadrons from Ohlau now arrived, but too late.   The
causeway which they had to pass had been barred by the
Austrian hussars, who long had stopped them there, and who
did not abandon the place until they saw their army routed.
This battle cost the Queen of Hungary 180 officers and 7,000
horse and foot killed.   The enemy lost seven pieces of cannon,
three standards, and 1,200 men taken prisoners.   The Prussians enumerated 2,500 dead, among whom was the Margrave
Frederic, cousin of the King, and 3,000 wounded.   The first
battalion of guards sustained the principal effort of the enemy,
lost half its officers, and of 800 men, had only 180 capable of
serving that remained.

The battle was one of the most memorable of the present
century, because two small armies there decided the fate of
Silesia and because the troops of the King there acquired that
fame of which they never can be deprived either by time or
envy.

The reader must no doubt have remarked in the relation of
the opening of the campaign that it is difficult to say who committed the most faults, the King or Marshal Neuperg.   If the
projects of the Austrian general were superior, execution was
in favor of the Prussians.   The plan of the marshal was
judicious and wise.   By entering Silesia he separated the
King's quarters, penetrated to Neisse, where Lentulus joined
him, and was on the point not only of seizing the royal artillery,
but of carrying the Prussian magazines at Breslau, the only
magazines of which they were possessed.   But the marshal
might have surprised the King at Jaegerndorff, and by this
single stroke have terminated the war; he might from Neisse
have carried the corps of the Duke of Holstein, which was
cantoned only at a distance of a mile.*   Had he been a little
more active he might have prevented the King from passing

* The word mile frequently occurs, and it is presumed it always signifies a German mile,
which contains from four to six, or seven English miles.

the Neisse at Michelau. From Grotkau he ought to have marched day and night to take Ohlau, and cut off the King from Breslau. Instead of seizing these opportunities, by an unpardonable security, he suffered himself to be surprised, and was beaten chiefly in consequence of his own fault.

The King afforded still greater cause for censure. He received timely intelligence of the plan of the enemy, to prevent which he took no sufficient measures. Instead of marching to Jaegerndorff, by which he still more divided his troops, he ought immediately to have assembled his whole army, and to have placed it in close cantonments in the neighborhood of Neisse. He suffered the Duke of Holstein to be cut off, and put himself to the necessity of fighting in a situation from which, had misfortune come, he could not retreat, and in which he risked the loss of his army and being himself taken.

Being come to Molwitz, where the enemy was cantoned, instead of immediately pressing his march to separate the cantonments of the Queen's troops, he lost two hours in methodically forming before the village, where there was no appearance of the enemy. Had he only attacked the village of Molwitz he would have taken the whole Austrian infantry, in much the same manner as twenty-four French battalions were taken at Blindheim; but he possessed, in his whole army, only Marshal Schwerin, who was a man of genius and an experienced general. His troops had all possible good-will, but they were acquainted only with the inferior parts of war, and, having never been in action, they durst only creep, fearful of being decisive. The real salvation of the Prussians was their bravery and their discipline. Molwitz was the school of the King, and of his soldiers; he made profound reflections on all the faults he had committed, and endeavored to correct himself in future.

The Duke of Holstein had an opportunity of striking a great stroke, but occasions on him were lost. Not having received any orders from the King, he had marched, without very well knowing why, from Ottmachau to Strehlen. Here he was on the very day of battle, and heard the firing of the two armies. On the eleventh the flying Austrian armies passed within a mile of his post. He might have destroyed the remainder, but for want of being able to form any resolution, he left an open field to Marshal Neuperg, who assembled the fugitives

on the other side of the Neisse, and the Duke of Holstein very contentedly joined the King's army near Ohlau. After this junction and the arrival of other reinforcements, the whole army consisted of forty-three battalions, fifty-six squadrons of cavalry, and three of hussars.

In order to profit by the victory, it was resolved to undertake the siege of Brieg. Marshal Klackstein was charged with the conduct of this siege, and the army of the King encamped near Molwitz to cover his operations. Eight days after the trenches were opened the governor, Piccolomini, capitulated, before the covered way was carried or any breach had been made in the works. The army remained three weeks encamped near Molwitz, to afford time to fill up the trenches and re-victual Brieg, the ammunition of which had all been expended. The King profited by this inactivity to exercise his cavalry, to teach it to manœuvre, and to change its heaviness to celerity. It was often sent in divisions that the officers might learn to take advantage of the ground and acquire greater confidence in themselves.

At this time Winterfeld, who had negotiated an alliance in Russia, performed so remarkable an action at the head of a detachment that he obtained the reputation of being as good an officer as he was a negotiator. He surprised and beat General Baranay at Rothschlot, and took three hundred prisoners. As the Prussians enjoyed the countenance of the country, they obtained the best intelligence, which in a partisan war procured them various advantages. We shall not, however, relate all similar small actions; for instance, of the manner in which the Austrians ruined, near Leubus, a new-raised regiment of hussars of Baudemar; took about a hundred uhlans near Strehlen, and burnt Zobten; or how the Prussians beat them at Friedwalde and in other rencontres, for it is not our intention to write a history of the hussars, but of the conquest of Silesia.

The battle by which this conquest was almost decided occasioned very different sensations throughout Europe. The Court of Vienna, in expectation of success, was irritated and enraged at its losses. In hope of obtaining revenge it drew troops and a numerous militia from Hungary, with which it reinforced Marshal Neuperg. The kings of England and Po-

5

land began to respect the army commanded by the Prince of Anhalt, which at first they had contemned. The Empire stood amazed, as it were, to learn that Austrian veterans had been defeated by such raw soldiers. France was delighted at the news of this victory; its court flattered itself that by taking part in the war it should in time be able to give the last blow to the house of Austria.

In consequence of this favorable disposition, Marshal de Belleisle, ambassador from France to the Diet of election, which then sat at Frankfort, came to the camp * and proposed a treaty of alliance, on the part of his master, to the King, the principal articles of which related to the election of the Elector of Bavaria, the dismemberment and division of the provinces of the Queen of Hungary, and the guarantee which the French promised for Lower Silesia, on condition that the King would renounce the succession of the duchies of Juliers and Berg, and promise his vote for the Elector of Bavaria. A sketch was made of this treaty, and it was further stipulated that France should send two armies into the Empire, one of which should march to succor the Elector of Bavaria, and the other establish itself in Westphalia, to keep both the Hanoverians and Saxons in awe; and finally that, in preference to all things, Sweden should declare war on Russia, to give the latter employment in the protection of its frontiers.

Advantageous as this treaty appeared, it was not signed. The King would not be too precipitate in affairs of such consequence, and he reserved to himself the liberty of acceding to it as a last resource. Marshal Belleisle indulged his imagination too often. Listening to him, it might have been supposed that all the provinces of the Queen of Hungary were put up to auction. One day, in company with the King, he appeared to be more thoughtful and absent than usual, and the King asked him if he had received any disagreeable news. "None," replied the marshal, "but I am embarrassed to know what we shall do with Moravia." The King proposed it should be given to Saxony, that by this lure the King of Poland might be drawn into the grand alliance. The marshal thought the idea admirable, and afterward put it in execution.

The negotiations of Prussia were not confined to France

* At Molwitz.

alone; they extended to Holland, England, and throughout
Europe. The King having thrown out some propositions in a
letter which he wrote to the King of England, the latter replied that it was true that his engagements required him to
maintain the succession of Charles VI entire, and that it was
with pain that he beheld any interruption of the good intelligence which had subsisted between the Prussians and Austrians; that, however, he would willingly interpose if his mediation could produce a reconciliation between the two courts.
He sent Lord Hyndford as ambassador for England, and the
Sieur Schwichelt as Hanoverian envoy. These two negoti-
ators, though in the service of the same prince, had received
very different instructions. The Hanoverian required that the
neutrality of his master should be purchased by a guarantee of
the bishoprics of Hildesheim, Ofnabruck, and the balliages
that were mortgaged to him in Mecklenburg.

A counter-project was given him, in which the interests of
Prussia were better managed. Hyndford offered the inter-
position of his master, to engage the Queen of Hungary to
cede some principalities in Lower Silesia; but all formal negotiation on these points was eluded until instructions were first
received relative to the disposition of the Court of Vienna.
These ministers were in the King's camp, and it seemed singular that Lord Hyndford gave greater umbrage to Schwichelt
than Marshal Belleisle, and still more singular that the Hanoverian should, as he did, most especially recommend his negotiations to be kept secret from the English ambassador.

These English and Hanoverians, who flattered the King in
his camp, wished only to lull him into security. They did not
act thus in the other courts of Europe. In Russia, the English
minister, Finch, secretly promoted war. The intrigues of
Botta and the charms of the handsome Lynar were the destruction of the brave Munich. The Prince of Brunswick gen-
eral-in-chief in Russia, incited by his grandmother, by the
Empress-dowager, and by those foreign ministers, who were
so many firebrands, would have engaged Russia to declare
immediate war against Prussia. Troops were already assembling in Livonia, of which the King was informed, and this it
was that made him suspect the English, whose duplicity he
discovered. Their intrigues had in like manner extorted a

letter from the grand Pensionary of Holland,* which exhorted
the King to withdraw his troops from Silesia. These various
machinations of the English, and especially what was foreseen
in Russia, finally determined the King to sign the treaty with
France, on the conditions which had been stipulated by the
Marshal Belleisle. The two following articles were added:
That the French should begin their operations before the end
of August; that this treaty should be kept secret till its publication should not be prejudicial to the interests of Prussia.

No time was lost in concluding the alliance; expedition
was necessary, for the ill-will of the Russians began to be apparent. Six thousand Danes and 6,000 Hessians, to whom
England granted subsidies, were added to the Hanoverian
forces, who had been encamped ever since the month of April.
The Saxons were also preparing, and it was in agitation to join
their troops to those of Hanover. Time, therefore, only could
be gained until succors should arrive from France, by amusing
as much as possible Lord Hyndford and the Sieur Schwichelt,
that they might not even suspect the treaty which had been
signed. In this the King and his ministers were so successful
that the negotiations with these ambassadors, which appeared
always on the point of conclusion, continually found some new
impediment which obliged Lord Hyndford to send for more
ample instructions from his court. It was ever near an end,
but never ended.

The camp of the King seemed to become a congress, but the
army was put in motion, and recovered a military air. No sooner
was Brieg revictualled than the army marched to encamp near
Grotkau. Marshal Neuperg was three miles distant from that
place, behind the town of Neisse, and in an impenetrable camp.
The Prussian camp was changed for the convenience of subsistence; the army occupied the heights of Strehlen, from
whence, by approaching Breslau, it might draw provisions,
and dry-fodder the horse, the rest of the campaign. In this
post it was at an equal distance from Berg and Schweidnitz,
and covered all Lower Silesia. Advantage was taken of the
eight weeks which it remained in this position to recruit the
infantry and to remount the cavalry, which was performed with
so much success that the army had not been more complete
than it was since it had taken the field.

* Presented by Ginkel, June 15th.

While the King was thus employed in rendering his army more formidable, Marshal Neuperg was conceiving plans which would have been dangerous had time been left him to put them in execution. We do not suppose it will be here unseasonable to relate in what manner the King discovered these plans. In Breslau there was a considerable number of old ladies, natives of Austria and Bohemia, who long had been settled in Silesia. They had relations at Vienna and Prague, some of whom served in the army of Neuperg. Austrian pride and the fanaticism of the Romish religion augmented their attachment to the Queen of Hungary. They ached with anger at the very name of Prussia; they caballed in secret, intrigued, and held a correspondence with the army of the marshal by the intervention of monks and priests, who became their emissaries, and were informed of all the designs of the enemy. To strengthen their party, these women had appointed what they called their sittings, which were assemblies held almost every evening, where they communicated their intelligence and deliberated on the means that might be employed to expel an army of heretics from Silesia, and to destroy all such miscreants. The King gained intelligence of the chief things that passed in these congregations, and he spared no pains to introduce an insidious sister into their assemblies, who, under the pretence of hatred to the Prussians, could find a welcome and inform him of all their plots.

It was by this channel that intelligence was obtained that Marshal Neuperg proposed by his motions to draw the King from Breslau, to return thither himself by forced marches, and by the aid of the information he obtained to seize the capital. This would be to take from the Prussians all their magazines, and at the same time cut off all their communications with the electorate which they enjoyed on the Oder. It was immediately determined, at all events, to forestall the enemy, and with respect to Breslau to break that neutrality which the magazines themselves had made more than one attempt to infringe. To effect this the syndics and sheriffs most attached to the house of Austria were sent for to the camp of the King. The foreign ministers were at the same time invited thither, that their persons might not be disposed to any disorders which the surprise might occasion. Some battalions were detached, which by

different routes arrived at the suburb.* A passage through the
city was demanded for a regiment. While it entered at one
gate, a cart made a delay at another. Three battalions and
five squadrons profited by this to glide into the city. The infantry occupied the ramparts and squares, and took charge of
the gates; the cavalry cleared the principal streets. In less than
an hour all was quiet.

Neither disorder, pillage, nor murder was committed. The
citizens paid homage. Three battalions continued in garrison,†
and the remainder joined the army. Marshal Neuperg, who did
not suspect he was discovered, had marched toward Frankenstein in the hope that the King would immediately fall upon
Neisse, and that he might then execute his design on Breslau;
but, perceiving that his project had failed, he wished to console himself by carrying the magazine which the Prussians had
at Schweidnitz. In this, likewise, he was disappointed by being
prevented. The vanguard of the King arrived at the time that
his van was at Reichenbach. The Austrians beat their way
back, and retired toward Frankenstein.

The King was joined at Reichenbach by new levies, consisting of ten squadrons of dragoons and thirteen of hussars.
The marshal had chosen his position judiciously: he maintained a communication with the fortress of Neisse by Patsch-
kau, drew substance out of Bohemia by Glatz, and foraged a
country which he could not preserve. His right was supported
at Frankenstein, his left on the hills not far from Silberberg,
and two rivulets covered his front and secured all approaches.
Difficulties did but animate the King; he wished to have the
honor of making the Austrians decamp and of driving them
to Upper Silesia. But before we come to this operation, it will
not be amiss first to cast a glance on what was passing in other
parts of Europe.

The Queen of Hungary then began to see the perils by which
she was menaced. The French passed the Rhine and coasted
the Danube, making long marches. Fear caused her pride to
abate. She despatched Mr. Robinson, the English ambassador
at her court, to make some proposals of accommodation. Robinson, assuming a haughty tone, informed the King that the
Queen wished to forget the past; that she offered him Lim-

---

* August 7th.   † General Marwitz was appointed governor.

bourg, Spanish Guelderland, and two millions of crowns to liquidate his pretensions on Silesia, on condition that he would make peace and his troops should instantly evacuate that duchy.

This ambassador was a kind of enthusiast with respect to the Queen of Hungary, and negotiated with all the emphasis with which he would have harangued the House of Commons. The King, who was sufficiently apt at perceiving ridicule, assumed a similar tone, and replied that, "It was for princes who had no sense of honor basely to sell their rights; that such propositions were more injurious than the contemptuous haughtiness of the Court of Vienna had been," and, with a louder voice, added:

"My army would hold me unworthy of the command, were I to sign a disgraceful treaty and lose the advantages it has given me by acts which valor has rendered immortal. Know, further, that it would be the blackest ingratitude to abandon my new subjects—those numerous Protestants whose wishes have called me hither. Would you have me yield them victims to the tyranny of their persecutors, by whom they would be sacrificed for vengeance? How shall I, in one single day, belie all the sentiments of honor and probity with which I was born? Were I capable of so cowardly, so infamous an act, I should imagine I beheld my ancestors rise from their graves and tell me, 'Thou art no descendant of ours. It is thy duty to combat for the rights which we have transmitted to thee, and these thou hast bartered: the honor which we gave thee as the most precious part of thy inheritance hast thou also bartered. Unworthy to be a prince; a sovereign prince, thou art a vile trader who has preferred gain to glory.' But no; I shall never merit such reproaches; I will bury myself and my army under the ruins of Silesia sooner than permit the honor and renown of the Prussian name to suffer the smallest taint. This, sir, is the answer I have to return."

Robinson stood amazed at this reply, which he little expected, and with which he returned to Vienna. But though the King sent back the fanatic, he continued to flatter Lord Hyndford, and to lull him into perfect security. The time for discovery was not yet come. To keep well with the maritime powers, the propositions of Robinson were communicated to them. The King's refusal was palliated by alleging that, knowing that the barrier treaty tied the hands of the Queen of Hungary, the cessions she had made of Limbourg and Guelderland could not be accepted. In Holland, particularly, great stress was laid on the deference in which the King held the interests of that republic, a deference which he would carry even so far as to refuse Brabant itself were it offered.

It was about this period that the King signed the treaty with Bavaria, and promised his vote at the Diet. These two princes mutually guaranteed to each other Silesia, on the one part, and on the other upper Austria, Tyrol, Brifgau, and Bohemia. The King purchased of this Elector the principality of Glatz for 400,000 crowns, which the Bavarian sold, though he never had it in his possession.

But one of the most advantageous and decisive events which then happened broke forth in the North. Sweden declared war on Russia, and by this diversion destroyed the plans of the kings of England and Poland, and of Prince Anthony Ulric, against Prussia.

Augustus, fallen between his high hopes of dividing between himself and the King of England the States of Prussia, swam with the stream, and unable to do better, leagued with the Elector of Bavaria for the annihilation of the house of Austria. Marshal de Belleisle, who had not known what to do with Moravia and Oberhartmannsberg, erected them into a kingdom and bestowed them on the Saxons; who, in consequence of these alms, signed the treaty on the thirty-first of August.

The Court of Vienna, unable any longer to depend on the intended diversion of the Russians, and pressed on every side, sent back her English negotiator, to the Prussian camp, whither he brought a map of Silesia, on which, with a stroke of a pen, the cession of four principalities was indicated. His reception was cold, and he was given to understand that what might be good at one conjuncture might at another be the reverse. The courts of London and Vienna had placed too much dependence upon the succors of Rusia. According to their calculation, the King must infallibly be humbled, sunken, and reduced on his knees to request peace, and little, indeed, did this fail of happening. Such are the sports of fortune, so common in war, and which so often put the conjectural art of the most able politicians to the rout.

The French and Bavarians were already openly in action. Austria was entered; the troops approached Lintz. By one common and unanimous effort only could they hope to subdue the Queen of Hungary. This was not a time to remain with folded arms. The King, who burned with impatience to act, endeavored to cut off Marshal Neuperg from the fortress of Neisse, and to give him battle on the march. The project was not ill imagined, but it failed in execution. Kalkstein was commanded to march hastily with 10,000 men and pontoons to the village of Woitz, there to throw a bridge over in order that the army, which soon would follow, might find a passage on its arrival. He departed at sunset, marched all night, and on the morrow found himself within cannon-shot of the camp. Whether it was slowness, want of proper disposition, or that the roads were bad and so spoilt by the rains as to stop him, the army outmarched its vanguard and arrived even before Kalkstein at the camp of Toupadel and Siegroth.

This lost day could not be recovered; the King himself marched to Woitz,* and threw his bridges over the Neisse, but the Austrian army appeared drawn up in order of battle at about eight hundred paces from the river. From some prisoners it was learned that Marshal Neuperg had only been there a few hours before the King. The army could not march to this bridge in less than two hours. It might have been passed if the enemy had not prevented the King, but to have crossed the bridge in presence of an army, which certainly must have beaten the troops in detail, and as they took ground to form, would of all imprudent acts have been the most imprudent. This was the cause that it was determined to take post for the day on the heights of Woitz. Soon after the Prussians took the camp of Neudorff, and that they might derive their subsistence from Brieg, they ascertained a communication by occupying the posts of Loewen and Michelau.

The storms which threatened the house of Austria and the dangers which daily became more evident at length made the Queen of Hungary seriously determined to disencumber herself of one of her enemies and break the formidable league by which she must have been overwhelmed. She was sincere in her requisitions for peace. She no longer cavilled for the

* September 4th.

city of Breslau; she only insisted upon preserving Neisse. Lord Hyndford, who then negotiated in her name, pretended that the King in favor of cessions so great must assist the Queen of Hungary with his whole force. To this the King replied that he was sorry he was under the necessity of neglecting his offers, but he could not violate the faith of treaties which he so lately signed with France and Bavaria. So great was the distress at Vienna that the Bavarians were every moment expected there. The roads swarmed with none but fugitive travellers; the court was about to depart. During this general consternation, the Empress-dowager wrote to Prince Ferdinand of Brunswick, who then served in the army, the following letter, which is too singular to pass unnoticed:

VIENNA, September 17, 1741.

MY DEAR NEPHEW:

I break that cruel silence which your conduct in serving against us imposed upon me. This I should not do had I any other means of conjuring the King of Prussia to restore me in himself, a nephew whom I no longer can call dear and worthy of esteem, after the affliction you have mutually brought upon me.

Consolation is in the power of the King. The Queen, my daughter, will grant him all that, which no other person will guarantee, if he will aid to restore her to a state of entire tranquillity and to extinguish the fire which he himself has kindled, and will not assist to increase his own enemies—for nothing more than the death of the Elector Palatine is wanting to acquire him new foes, since the aggrandizement of Bavaria and Saxony will not allow that he should remain in peaceable possession of what the Queen has relinquished to him in Silesia. Persuade the King, therefore, to become our good ally, to assist the Queen with troops to preserve those States the possession of which she is envied by so many enemies. A strict alliance between the two houses would be to their mutual advantage, the situation of their States being such as to aid and sustain their reciprocal rights. I wholly rely upon your representation and upon the high qualities of the King, who, having drawn so many evils upon us, would naturally wish to have himself the honor of snatching us from the precipice and of paying some attention to his individual interest as well as to an afflicted aunt and mother, who yet without rancor is able to sign herself

Your affectionate aunt,
ELIZABETH.

The substance of Prince Ferdinand's reply to the Empress-dowager was that the King could not with honor depart from

the engagements he had entered into with France and Bavaria;
that he sincerely pitied the Empress; that he wished he was
able to change her situation, on which he had compassion;
but that the time of accommodation and of freely acting with
the Court of Vienna was past. A few days later another letter
from the Empress-dowager, written to Prince Louis of Brunswick, who then was in Russia, was intercepted. In this,
though the style was not better, there was more sincerity.
The following is a copy of this letter:

SEPTEMBER 21, 1741.

MY DEAR NEPHEW:
  Our affairs have taken so desperate a turn that our case may be
called that of generally abandoned. We have no longer any one for us.
What may console us in our misfortune is that God may cast more than
one Pharaoh into the Red Sea and confound our false seeming friends, the
most of whom cannot any longer believe in a God. True it is I have not
been lulled by such false appearances, and though the Elector of Bavaria
has drawn the French upon us and drives me hence, I esteem him to be
a worthy Prince; he has not acted with dissimulation and falsehood, but
honestly, and shown himself immediately. I doubt whether I shall any
more date from this place. This is a mournful year. Preserve our alliance, and beware of false and apparent friends.
                    I am your affectionate aunt,
                                          ELIZABETH.

  The style of these letters discovers the anger of the Court
of Vienna at the progress of the Prussians in Silesia, and that
this court breathed only vengeance. But what language is
here? Whoever attacks the house of Austria does not believe in God! To offer peace at a time when there is liberty
to make peace and to refuse proposed conditions after other
treaties have been signed is falsehood and perjury? This is
the language of self-love and pride suppressing truth and
reason. Thus the alliance formed against the Pragmatic
sanction was considered at Vienna as the war of the Titans,
who would have scaled the heavens to dethrone Jupiter.
  The Swedes were not for their part so successful as their
allies. A detachment of 12,000 men had been cut in pieces by
the Russians, near Willmanstrand. This was a considerable
check to a kingdom enfeebled and ruined as it had been ever
since the time of Charles XII. France was mortified and

proposed in other parts to repair that reverse of fortune which her allies had sustained. She intended that Marshal Maillebois with the army that he commanded should penetrate into Hanover and make himself master of that electorate.

The King at this time committed a great error by employing his whole credit to dissuade the French people from this purpose, alleging that such an enterprise would render them odious to all Europe; would make every prince of Germany revolt against them; and that by employing themselves on a thing of little importance, they would neglect the principal object, which was to crush the Queen of Hungary with their whole forces. The French might easily have refuted such feeble reasoning. Had they at that time taken Hanover, the King of England never could have made diversions on the Rhine as he did in Flanders.

Nothing was wanting to render the treaty perfect which the King had entered into with the Elector of Bavaria but the guarantee of the French. This M. de Valori was pressed to procure. His court continued to start difficulties relative to the cession of the principality of Glatz and other portions of Upper Silesia. It happened as he was speaking to the King, that he by chance let fall a letter from his pocket. The King, without taking any notice, put his foot upon it, and dismissed the ambassador with all possible expedition. This letter was from M. Amelot, the Secretary for Foreign Affairs. It indicated that Glatz and Upper Silesia should not be guaranteed to Prussia unless some other greater inconvenience should result from refusal. This discovery being made, M. de Valori was obliged to accede to whatever was proposed.

The designs of the French on Hanover took vent, and presently came to the ear of the King of England, who believed his electorate lost. He wanted time to parry this blow which menaced him so immediately. The measures he had taken with Russia and Saxony having equally failed, he became serious in endeavoring to establish peace between the King of Prussia and the Queen of Hungary. In consequence of this Lord Hyndford repaired to the Austrian camp, where he made such strong remonstrances to the Court of Vienna, and pressed this court with so much energy by showing that in order to save the remainder of its States how necessary it

was seasonably to lose a part, that this court consented to the cession of Silesia as well as the town of Neisse and a slip of Upper Silesia, renouncing at the same time all assistance against its enemies.

The King, who knew the duplicity of the English and Austrians, understood these offers to be snares, and that he might not be amused by fine words which would have kept him idle in his camp, he stole a march on the enemy, passed the Neisse at Michelau, and encamped the next day at Katscher, while a detachment seized on Oppeln, which was made a deposit for provisions. Marshal Neuperg on these motions quitted Neisse and inclined toward Oppersdorff. The King turned by Friedland and encamped at Steinau.

Perhaps these different manœuvres accelerated the negotiation of Lord Hyndford. He came to inform the King that his negotiation had been so successful that Marshal Neuperg was ready to abandon Silesia, provided the King would verbally declare he would undertake nothing against the Queen. The enemy would rest satisfied by a word, by which Prussia would acquire provinces, and the troops winter quarters after having been fatigued by eleven months' operations. The temptation was strong. The King wished to try what would be the result of this conference. Accompanied only by Colonel Glatz, he secretly repaired to Oberschnellendorff, where he found Marshal Neuperg, General Lentulus, and Lord Hyndford.

It was not without reflection that the monarch took this step. Though he had some cause of complaint against France, this was not sufficient to break with her. He knew from experience the propensities of the Court of Vienna; nothing friendly was there to be expected. It was evident that the Queen of Hungary acceded to this convention only to sow distrust among the allies by making it public. It therefore was necessary to exact from the Austrians, as a condition *sine qua non,* that if they divulged the least part of the stipulations agreed upon, the King should be authorized to break off all further treaty.

The King was certain this could not fail to happen. The draught of the stipulations was in the hands of Lord Hyndford, as ambassador from England. It was agreed that Neisse should for form's sake be besieged, but that Prussian troops should not be disturbed in their quarters, which they should take as well in Silesia as in Bohemia, and particularly that unless rigid secrecy was observed everything that had been agreed upon should be to all intents and purposes null.

It must be acknowledged that if there be such a thing as fatality, it was especially manifest in Marshal Neuperg, who seemed destined to conclude the most humiliating treaties for his sovereigns. The marshal soon after led his army toward Moravia. The siege of Neisse was immediately begun. The town held out only twelve days, nor was it entirely evacuated by the Austrian garrison before the Prussian engineers had traced new works which afterward classed it among the strong towns of Europe. The place being taken, the army was divided: one part marched into Bohemia under the command of Prince Leopold of Anhalt; some regiments were employed in the blockade of Glatz and the remainder of the troops of Schwerin took up their quarters in Upper Silesia.

Francis, Grand Duke of Tuscany, who was at Presburg, flattered himself that the King would regard these parleys as treaties of peace, wrote to demand his vote at the imperial election. The answer returned was civil, but conceived in a style so obscure and perplexed that the author himself understood nothing of what he had written. The campaign terminated eleven months after the entrance into Silesia, and the King after receiving the homage of his new subjects at Breslau, returned thence to Berlin. He began to understand the trade of war by the faults he had committed, but the difficulties he had surmounted formed but a part of those which still remained to be overcome before the finishing hand could be put to the grand work which he had undertaken.

LIFE AS A GRAND DUCHESS

BY

Catherine II, Empress of Russia

CATHERINE II, EMPRESS OF RUSSIA

1729—1796

Catherine II, Empress of Russia, was born at Stettin in 1729, and died at St. Petersburg in 1796. Her father, the Prince of Anhalt-Zerbst, was a Prussian field-marshal, and governor of Stettin. She received the name of Sophia Augusta, but the Empress Elizabeth of Russia having selected her for the wife of her nephew and intended successor, Peter, she passed from the Lutheran to the Greek Church, and took the name of Catharina Alexiewna. In 1745 her marriage took place. She soon quarreled with her husband, and each of them lived a separate life. After the death of the Empress Elizabeth, in 1761, Peter III ascended the Russian throne; but the conjugal difference became continually wider. Catherine was banished to a separate abode, and the Emperor seemed to entertain the design of divorcing her, declaring her only son, Paul, illegitimate, and marrying his mistress, Elizabeth Woronzow. The popular dislike to Peter, however, rapidly increased, and at length, he being dethroned by a conspiracy, Catherine was made Empress. A few days afterward Peter was murdered. What participation his wife had in his murder has never been well ascertained.

Catherine now exerted herself to please the people, and among other things made a great show of regard for the outward forms of the Greek Church, although her principles were, in reality, those of the infidelity then prevalent among the French philosophers. The government of the country was carried on with great energy, and her reign was remarkable for the rapid increase of the extent and power of Russia. Not long after her accession to the throne, her influence secured the election of her former favorite, Stanislaus Poniatowski, to the throne of Poland. In her own empire, however, discontentment was seriously manifested, the hopes of the disaffected being centred in the young prince Ivan, who was forthwith murdered in the castle of Schlusselburg. From that time, the internal politics of Russia long consisted in great part of intrigues for the humiliation of one favorite and the exaltation of another. The first partition of Poland in 1772, and the Turkish war, which terminated in the peace of Kainardji in 1774, vastly increased the empire. The Turkish war which terminated in the peace of Jassy in 1792 had similar results, and also the war with Sweden, which terminated in 1790. The second and third partitions of Poland, and the incorporation of Courland with Russia, completed the triumphs of Catherine's reign. She was a woman of great ability, and she invited to her court some of the literati and philosophers of France. She was ever ready to commence great undertakings, but most of them were left unfinished, though much was accomplished in her reign for the improvement of the country and the progress of civilization. Her memoirs show us a woman of generous impulses, tremendous will, and unflagging energy. Her early life was filled with bitterness, but her generous nature, on her accession to power, enabled her to rule without indulging in private prejudice.

LIFE AS A GRAND DUCHESS

THE grand duke, at the time I arrived in Moscow, had in his service three domestics named Czernicheff, all three sons of grenadiers in the bodyguard of the Empress. Their fathers held the rank of lieutenant, which they received as a recompense for having aided in placing the Empress on the throne. The oldest of the Czernicheffs was cousin to the two others, who were brothers. The grand duke was very fond of all three. They were the persons most in his confidence, and were really very useful. All three were tall and well made, especially the oldest. The duke made use of him in all his commissions, and several times in the day he sent him to me. He it was, too, whom the duke made his confidant when he did not care to come to me.

This man was on very intimate and friendly terms with my valet Yevreinoff, and through this channel I often knew things which I should otherwise have been ignorant of. Besides, both of them were attached to me heart and soul, and I often obtained information from them, on a variety of matters, which it would have been difficult to procure otherwise. I do not know in reference to what it was that the oldest of the Czernicheffs said one day to the grand duke, " she is not my intended, but yours." This expression made the grand duke laugh. He related it to me, and from that time it pleased his imperial Highness, when speaking to me, to call me his intended, and Andrew Czernicheff my intended. After our marriage Andrew Czernicheff, to put a stop to this badinage, proposed to his imperial Highness to call me his mother, and I, on my part, called him my son. Now, between the grand duke and myself there was always some reference to this son, for he was excessively attached to the man; and I liked him very much.

My servants were greatly disturbed on this account; some

through jealousy, others from apprehension of the consequences which might result both for them and for us. One day, when there was a masked ball at court, and I had gone to my room to change my dress, my valet Timothy Yevreinoff took me aside, and told me that he and all my servants were terrified at the danger into which he saw me plunging. I asked what he meant. He said, " You speak of nothing and think of nothing but Andrew Czernicheff." " Well," I said, in the innocence of my heart, " what harm is there in that? He is my son. The grand duke likes him as much and more than I do; and he is devoted and faithful to us." " Yes," he replied, " that is all very true; the grand duke can do as he pleases; but you have not the same right. What you call kindness and attachment, because this man is faithful and serves you, your people call love."

The utterance of this word, which had never once occurred to me, was a thunderbolt; first on account of the opinion of my servants, which I called rash; secondly, on account of the condition in which I had placed myself without being aware of it. He told me that he had advised his friend Czernicheff to pretend illness in order to put an end to these remarks. This advice Czernicheff followed, and his feigned illness lasted pretty nearly to the month of April. The grand duke was much concerned about him, and spoke of him continually to me. He had not the slightest suspicion of the real circumstances. At the summer palace Andrew Czernicheff again made his appearance. I could no longer meet him without embarrassment. Meanwhile the Empress had thought proper to make a new arrangement with the servants of the court. They were to serve in turn in all the rooms, and Andrew Czernicheff like the rest. The grand duke often had concerts in the afternoon, and he himself played the violin at them.

During one of these concerts, which usually wearied me, I went to my own room. This opened into the great hall of the summer palace, which was then filled with scaffoldings, as they were painting the ceiling. The Empress was absent; Madame Krause had gone to her daughter's, Madame Sievers; and I did not find a soul in my room. From *ennui*, I opened the door of the hall, and saw at the other end Andrew Czernicheff. I made a sign to him to approach; he came to the door, though with much apprehension. I asked him if the Empress would return soon. He said, " I cannot speak to you; they make too much noise in the hall; let me come into your room." I replied, " That I will not do." He was outside the door and I within, holding the door half open as I spoke to him. An involuntary impulse made me turn my head in the direction opposite to the door at which I stood, and I saw behind me at the other door of my dressing-room the chamberlain, Count Divier, who said to me, " The grand duke wishes to see you, madam."

I closed the door of the hall, and returned with Count Divier to the apartment where the grand duke was giving his concert. I have since learned that Count Divier was a kind of reporter employed as such, like many others about me. The following day, which was Sunday, after mass we learned—that is, the grand duke and I—that the three Czernicheffs had been placed as lieutenants in the regiments stationed near Orenburg; and in the afternoon of this day Madame Tchoglokoff was placed with me.

A few days afterward we received orders to prepare to accompany the Empress to Reval. At the same time, Madame Tchoglokoff told me from her Majesty that, for the future, her imperial Majesty would dispense with my coming to her dressing-room, and that if I had any communication to make to her it must not be made through anyone but Madame Tchoglokoff. In my own mind, I was delighted with this order, which relieved me from the necessity of being kept standing among the Empress' women; besides, I seldom went to her dressing-room, and then but rarely saw her. During the whole time that I had been going there I had not seen her more than three or four times, and, generally speaking, whenever I went, her women quitted the room one after the other. Not to be left there alone, I seldom stayed long either.

In the month of June the Empress set out for Reval, and we accompanied her. The grand duke and I travelled in a carriage for four persons; Prince Augustus and Madame Tchoglokoff made up its complement. Our plan of travelling was neither agreeable nor convenient. The post-houses or stations were occupied by the Empress; we were accommodated in tents or in outhouses. I remember that on one oc-

casion during this journey I dressed near the oven where the
bread had just been baked; and that another time, when I entered the tent where my bed was placed, there was water in it
up to the ankle.   Besides all this, the Empress had no fixed
hour either for setting out or stopping, for meals or repose.
We were all, masters and servants, strangely harassed.

After ten or twelve days' march we reached an estate belonging to Count Steinbock, forty versts from Reval.   From
this place the Empress departed in great state, wishing to
reach Catherinthal in the evening; but somehow it happened
that the journey was prolonged till half-past one in the morning.

During the entire journey from St. Petersburg to Reval
Madame Tchoglokoff was the torment of our carriage.   To
the simplest thing that was said she would reply, " Such a remark would displease her Majesty;" or, "Such a thing
would not be approved of by her Majesty."   It was sometimes
to the most innocent and indifferent matters that she attached
these etiquettes.   As for me, I made up my mind, and during
the whole journey slept continually while in the carriage.

From the day after our arrival at Catherinthal, the court recommenced its ordinary round of occupations; that is to say,
from morning till night, and far into the night, gambling, and
for rather high stakes, was carried on in the ante-chamber of
the Empress, a hall which divided the house and its two stories
into two sections.

Madame Tchoglokoff was a gambler; she induced me to
play at faro like the rest.   All the favorites of the Empress
were ordinarily fixed here when they did not happen to be in
her Majesty's room, or rather tent, for she had erected a very
large and magnificent tent at the side of her apartments, which
were on the ground floor, and very small, as was usually the
case with the structures of Peter I.   He had built this country
residence and planted the garden.

The Prince and Princess Repnine, who were of the party,
and were aware of the arrogant and senseless conduct of
Madame Tchoglokoff during the journey, persuaded me to
speak of it to the Countess Schouvaloff and Madame Ismaïloff,
the ladies most in her Majesty's favor.   These ladies had no
love for Madame Tchoglokoff, and they had already learned

what had happened. The little Countess Schouvaloff, who was indiscretion itself, did not wait for me to speak to her, but happening to be seated by my side at play, she introduced the whole conduct of Madame Tchoglokoff in such a ridiculous light that she soon made her the laughing-stock of everyone. She did more; she related to the Empress all that had passed. It would seem as if Madame Tchoglokoff had received a reproof, for she lowered her tone very considerably with me. Indeed, there was much need of this being done, for I began to feel a great tendency to melancholy. I felt totally isolated. The grand duke, at Reval, took a passing fancy for a Madame Cédéraparre. As usual, he did not fail to confide the matter to me immediately. I had frequent pains in the chest, and at Catherinthal a spitting of blood, for which I was bled.

On the afternoon of that day Madame Tchoglokoff came to my room and found me in tears. With a countenance greatly softened, she asked me what was the matter, and proposed to me, on the part of the Empress, to take a walk in the garden, to dissipate my hypochondria, as she said. That day the grand duke had gone to hunt with the master of the hounds, Count Razoumowsky. She also placed in my hands, as a present from her imperial Majesty, 3,000 roubles, for playing at faro. The ladies had noticed that I was without money, and told the Empress. I begged Madame Tchoglokoff to thank her Majesty for her goodness, and then went with her for a walk in the garden.

Some days after our arrival at Catherinthal, the high chancellor, Count Bestoujeff, arrived, accompanied by the imperial ambassador, the Baron Preyslam, and we learned, by the tenor of his congratulations, that the two imperial courts had just become united by a treaty of alliance. In consequence of this, the Empress went to see her fleet manœuvre; but, except the smoke of the cannons, we saw nothing. The day was excessively hot, and the sea perfectly calm. On returning from this manœuvre, there was a ball in the Empress' tents, which were erected on the terrace. The supper was spread in the open air, around a basin intended for a fountain; but scarcely had her Majesty taken her seat, when there came on a shower which wet the entire company, forcing it to disperse and seek shelter as best it could, in the houses and in the tents. Thus ended this fête.

Some days afterward the Empress departed for Roguervick. The fleet manœuvred there also, and again we saw nothing but smoke. In this journey we all suffered very much in our feet. The soil of the place is rocky, covered with a thick bed of pebbles, of such a nature that if one stood for a short time in the same spot the feet would sink in and the pebbles cover them. We encamped here for several days, and were forced to walk, in passing from tent to tent, and in our tents, upon this ground. For more than four months afterward my feet were sore in consequence. The convicts who worked at the pier wore sabots, and even these seldom lasted beyond eight or ten days.

The imperial ambassador had followed her Majesty to this port. He dined there and supped with her half way between Roguervick and Reval. During this supper an old woman, who had reached the age of 130 years, was led before the Empress. She looked like a walking skeleton. The Empress sent her meat from her own table, as well as money, and we continued our journey.

On our return to Catherinthal, Madame Tchoglokoff had the satisfaction of finding there her husband, who had returned from his mission to Vienna. Many of the court equipages had already taken the road for Riga, whither the Empress intended to go. But on her return from Roguervick she suddenly changed her mind. Many people tormented their brains, in vain, to discover the cause of this change. Several years afterward it came to light. When M. Tchoglokoff was passing through Riga, a Lutheran priest, a madman or a fanatic, placed in his hands a letter and a memorial addressed to the Empress, in which he exhorted her not to undertake this journey, as if she did she would incur the most imminent risk; that there were people posted in ambush by the enemies of the empire for the purpose of killing her, and such like absurdities. These writings being delivered to the Empress left her in no humor for travelling farther. As for the priest, he was found to be mad; but the journey did not take place.

We returned by short stages from Reval to St. Petersburg. I caught on this journey a severe sore throat, which compelled me to keep my bed for several days; after which we went to Peterhoff, and thence made weekly excursions to Oranienbaum.

At the beginning of August the Empress sent word to the grand duke and myself that we ought to go to our duty. We both complied with her wishes, and immediately began to have matins and vespers sung in our apartments, and to go to mass every day. On the Friday, when we were to go to confession, the cause of this order became apparent. Simon Theodorsky, Bishop of Pleskov, questioned us both a great deal, and each separately, respecting what had passed between the Czernicheffs and us. But as nothing whatever had passed, he looked a little foolish when he heard it asserted, with the candor of innocence, that there was not even the shadow of what people had dared to suppose. He was so far thrown off his guard as to say to me, " But how is it that the Empress has been impressed to the contrary?" To which I replied that I really did not know. I suppose our confessor communicated our confession to the Empress' confessor, and that the latter retailed it to her Majesty—a thing which certainly could do us no harm. We communicated on the Saturday, and on the Monday went for a week to Oranienbaum, while the Empress made an excursion to Zarskoe-Selo.

On arriving at Oranienbaum, the grand duke enlisted all his suite. The chamberlains, the gentlemen of the bedchamber, the officers of the court, the adjutants of Prince Repnine, and even his son, the servants, the huntsmen, the gardeners, everyone, in fact, had to shoulder his musket. His imperial Highness exercised them every day, and made them mount guard, the corridor of the house serving as a guard-room, and here they passed the day. For their meals the gentlemen went upstairs, and in the evening they came into the hall to dance in gaiters. As for ladies there were only myself, Madame Tchoglokoff, the Princess Repnine, my three maids of honor, and my lady's-maids; consequently the ball was very meagre and badly managed, the men harassed and in bad humor with these continual military exercises, which did not suit the taste of courtiers. After the ball they were allowed to go home to sleep.

Generally speaking, we were all dreadfully tired of the dull life we led at Oranienbaum, where we were, five or six women, all to ourselves; while the men, on their side, were engaged in unwilling exercises. I had recourse to the books I had brought with me. Since my marriage I read a great deal. The first book I read after my marriage was a novel called " Tiran the Fair " (Tiran le blanc), and for a whole year I read nothing but novels. But I began to tire of these. I stumbled by accident upon the letters of Madame de Sévigné, and was much interested by them. When I had devoured these, the works of Voltaire fell into my hands. After reading them, I selected my books with more care.

We returned to Peterhoff, and after two or three journeys backward and forward between that place and Oranienbaum, with the same amusements, we finally got back to St. Petersburg, and took up our residence in the summer palace. At the close of autumn the Empress passed to the winter palace, where she occupied our apartments of the previous year; while we moved into those occupied by the grand duke before his marriage. These we liked very much, and, indeed, they were very convenient. They were those used by the Empress Anne. Every evening the members of our court assembled in our apartments, and we amused ourselves with all kinds of small games, or we had a concert. Twice a week there was a performance at the great theatre, which at that time was opposite the church of Kasan. In a word, this winter was one of the gayest and best managed I have ever spent. We literally did nothing but laugh and romp the whole day.

About the middle of the winter, the Empress sent us word to follow her to Tichvine, where she was going. It was a journey of devotion; but just as we were about to enter our sledges, we learned that the journey was put off. It was whispered to us that the master of the hounds, Count Razoumowsky, had got a fit of the gout, and that her Majesty did not wish to go without him. About two or three weeks afterward we did start. The journey lasted only five days, when we returned. In passing through Ribatchia Slobodk, and by the house where I knew the Czernicheffs were, I tried to see them through the windows, but I could see nothing. Prince Repnine was not in the party during this journey; we were told that he had the gravel. The husband of Madame Tchoglokoff took his place on the occasion, and this was not the most agreeable arrangement in the world for most of us. He was an arrogant and brutal fool; everybody feared him, and his wife as well; and indeed they were both mischievous and dangerous characters. However, there were means, as will be seen in the sequel, not only of lulling these Arguses to sleep, but even of gaining them over. At that time these means had not been discovered. One of the surest was to play at faro with them; they were both eager players, and very selfish ones. This weak point was the one first perceived; the others came afterward.

During this winter, the Princess Gagarine, maid of honor, died of a burning fever, just as she was to be married to the chamberlain, Prince Galitszine, who subsequently married her younger sister. I regretted her very much, and during her illness I went several times to see her, notwithstanding the representations of Madame Tchoglokoff. The Empress replaced her by her elder sister, since married to Count Matuschkine. She was then at Moscow, and was sent for accordingly.

In the spring, we went to the summer palace, and thence to the country. Prince Repnine, under the pretext of bad health, received permission to retire to his own house, and M. Tchoglokoff continued to discharge his functions in the interim. He first signalized himself by the dismissal from the court of Count Divier, who was placed as brigadier in the army, and gentleman of the bedchamber Villebois, who was sent there as colonel. These changes were made at the instigation of Tchoglokoff, who looked on both with an evil eye, because he saw that we thought well of them. A similar dismissal had taken place in 1745, in the case of Count Zachar Czernicheff, sent away at the request of my mother. Still these removals were always considered at court as disgraces, and they were therefore sensibly felt by the individuals. The grand duke and myself were much annoyed with this latter one. Prince Augustus, too, having obtained all that he had asked for, was told from the Empress that he must now leave. This also was a manœuvre of the Tchoglokoffs, who were bent upon completely isolating us. In this they followed the instructions of Count Bestoujeff, who was suspicious of everybody.

During this summer, having nothing better to do, and everything being very dull at home, I took a passion for riding; the rest of my time I spent in my room, reading everything that came in my way. As for the grand duke, as they had taken from him the people he liked best, he chose other favorites among the servants of the court.

During this interval, my valet Yevreinoff, while dressing my hair one day, told me that by a strange accident he had discovered that Andrew Czernicheff and his brother were at Ribatchia, under arrest, in a pleasure-house, which was the private property of the Empress, who had inherited it from her mother. It was thus that the discovery was made: During the carnival, Yevreinoff went out for a drive, having his wife and sister-in-law with him in the sledge, and the two brothers-in-law behind. The sister's husband was secretary to the Magistrate of St. Petersburg, and had a sister married to an under-secretary of the secret chancery. They went for a walk one day to Ribatchia, and called on the man who had charge of this estate of the Empress.

A dispute rose about the Feast of Easter, as to what day it would fall on. The host said that he would soon end the controversy by asking the prisoners for a book called " Swlatzj," which contained all the feasts, together with a calendar, for several years. In a few minutes he brought it in. The brother-in-law of Yevreinoff took the book, and the first thing he saw, on opening it, was that Andrew Czernicheff had put his name in it, with the date of the day he had received it from the grand duke. After this he looked for the Feast of Easter. The dispute being ended, the book was sent back, and they returned to St. Petersburg, where some days later the brother-in-law of Yevreinoff confided to him the discovery he had made. Yevreinoff entreated me not to mention the matter to the grand duke, as his discretion was not at all to be relied on. I promised him that I would not, and I kept my word.

About the middle of Lent, we went with the Empress to Gostilitza, to celebrate the feast-day of the master of the hounds, Count Razoumowsky. We danced, and were tolerably well amused, and then returned to town.

A few days afterward, the death of my father was announced to me. It greatly afflicted me. For a week I was allowed to weep as much as I pleased, but at the end of that time, Madame Tchoglokoff came to tell me that I had wept enough; that the Empress ordered me to leave off; that my father was not a king. I told her I knew that he was not a king, and she replied that it was not suitable for a grand duchess to mourn for a longer period a father who had not been a king. In fine, it was arranged that I should go out on the following Sunday, and wear mourning for six weeks.

The first day I left my room, I found Count Santi, grand master of ceremonies to the Empress, in her Majesty's antechamber. I addressed a few casual remarks to him, and passed on. Some days later, Madame Tchoglokoff came to tell me that her Majesty had learned from Count Bestoujeff—to whom Santi had given the information in writing—that I had told him (Santi) I thought it very strange that the ambassadors had not offered their condolences to me on the occasion of my father's death; that her Majesty considered my remarks to Count Santi very uncalled for; that I was too proud; that I ought to remember that my father was not a king, and therefore that I could not and must not expect to receive the condolences of the foreign ministers. I was astounded at this speech. I told Madame Tchoglokoff that, if Count Santi had said or written that I had spoken to him a single word having the least allusion to this subject, he was a notorious liar; that nothing of the kind had ever entered my mind; and therefore that I had not uttered a syllable to him or anyone else in reference to it. This was the exact truth, for I had lain it down to myself as an invariable rule never, in any case, to make any pretensions, but to conform in everything to the wishes of the Empress, and fulfil all her commands. It would seem that the ingenuousness with which I replied to Madame Tchoglokoff carried conviction to her mind, for she said she would not fail to tell the Empress that I gave the lie to Count Santi. In fact, she went to her Majesty, and came back to tell me that the Empress was extremely angry with Count Santi for having uttered such a falsehood, and that she had ordered him to be reprimanded.

Some days afterward, the Count sent several persons to me, and among them the chamberlain, Count Nikita Panine, and the Vice-Chancellor Woronzoff, to tell me that Count

Bestoujeff had forced him to tell this falsehood, and that he was very sorry to find himself in disgrace with me in consequence. I told these gentlemen that a liar was a liar, whatever might be his reasons for lying; and that, in order that Count Santi might not again mix me up with his falsehoods, I should never speak to him. Here is what has occurred to me in reference to this matter: Santi was an Italian. He was fond of intermeddling, and attached much importance to his office as grand master of ceremonies. I had always spoken to him as I spoke to everyone else. He thought, perhaps, that compliments of condolence on the part of the diplomatic corps might be admissible; and, judging by his own feelings, he probably considered that this would be a means of obliging me. He went then to Count Bestoujeff, the High Chancellor, and his superior, and told him that I had appeared in public for the first time, and seemed very much affected; the omission of the condolences might have added to my grief.

Count Bestoujeff, always carping and delighted to have an opportunity of humbling me, had all that Santi said or insinuated—and which he had ventured to support with my name—put into writing, and made him sign this protocol. Santi, terribly afraid of his superior, and above all things dreading to lose his place, did not hesitate to sign a falsehood rather than sacrifice his means of existence. The high chancellor sent the note to the Empress. She was annoyed to see my pretensions, and despatched Madame Tchoglokoff to me, as already mentioned. But having heard my reply, founded upon the exact truth, the only result was a slap in the face for his excellency the grand master of the ceremonies.

In the country, the grand duke formed a pack of hounds, and began to train dogs himself. When tired of tormenting these, he set to work scraping on the violin. He did not know a note, but he had a good ear, and made the beauty of music consist in the force and violence with which he drew forth the tones of his instrument. Those who had to listen to him, however, would often have been glad to stop their ears had they dared, for his music grated on them dreadfully. This course of life continued not only in the country, but also in town. On returning to the winter palace, Madame Krause—

who had all along been an Argus—moderated so far as often even to aid in deceiving the Tchoglokoffs, who were hated by everyone. She did more: she procured for the grand duke playthings—puppets, and such like childish toys, of which he was passionately fond. During the day, they were concealed within or under my bed; the grand duke retired immediately after supper, and as soon as we were in bed Madame Krause locked the door, and then the grand duke played with his puppets till one or two o'clock in the morning. Willing or unwilling, I was obliged to share in this interesting amusement; and so was Madame Krause. I often laughed, but more frequently felt annoyed, and even inconvenienced; the whole bed was covered and filled with playthings, some of which were rather heavy.

I do not know whether Madame Tchoglokoff came to hear of these nocturnal amusements, but one night, about twelve o'clock, she knocked at the door of our bedroom. We did not open it immediately as the grand duke, myself, and Madame Krause were scrambling with all our might to gather up and conceal the toys: for this purpose the coverlid of the bed answered very well, as we crammed them all in under it. This done, we opened the door. She complained dreadfully of having been kept waiting, and told us that the Empress would be very angry when she learned that we were not asleep at that hour. She then sulkily departed, without having made any further discovery. As soon as she was gone, the duke resumed his amusements until he became sleepy.

At the commencement of autumn we again returned to the apartments which we had occupied after our marriage, in the winter palace. Here, a very stringent order was issued by the Empress through M. Tchoglokoff, forbidding everyone from entering either my apartments or those of the grand duke, without the express permission of M. and Madame Tchoglokoff. The ladies and gentlemen of our court were directed, under pain of dismissal, to keep in the ante-chamber, and not to pass the threshold, or speak to us—or even to the servants—otherwise than aloud. The grand duke and myself, thus compelled to sit looking at each other, murmured, and secretly interchanged thoughts relative to this species of imprisonment, which neither of us had deserved. To procure for himself more amusement during the winter, the duke had five or six hounds brought from the country, and placed them behind a wooden partition which separated the alcove of my bedroom from a large vestibule behind our apartments. As the alcove was separated only by boards, the odor of the kennel penetrated into it; and in the midst of this disgusting smell we both slept. When I complained to him of the inconvenience, he told me it was impossible to help it. The kennel being a great secret, I put up with this nuisance, rather than betray his imperial Highness.

As there was no kind of amusement at court during this carnival, the grand duke took it into his head to have masquerades in my room. He dressed his servants, mine, and my maids in masks, and made them dance in my bedroom. He himself played the violin, and danced as well. All this continued far into the night. As for me, under different pretexts of headache or lassitude, I lay down on a couch, but always in a masquerade dress, tired to death of the insipidity of these bal-masqués, which amused him infinitely. When Lent came on, four more persons were removed from attendance on him, three of them being pages, whom he liked better than the others. These frequent dismissals affected him; still he took no steps to prevent them, or he took them so clumsily that they only tended to increase the evil.

During this winter, we learned that Prince Repnine, ill as he was, had been appointed to command the troops which were to be sent to Bohemia, in aid of the Empress-Queen Maria Theresa. This was a formal disgrace for Prince Repnine. He went, and never returned, having died of grief in Bohemia. It was the Princess Gagarine, my maid of honor, who gave me the first intimation of this, notwithstanding all the prohibitions against allowing a word to reach us relative to what occurred in the city or the court. This shows how useless are all such prohibitions. There are too many persons interested in infringing them ever to allow of their being strictly enforced. All about us, even to the nearest relatives of the Tchoglokoffs, interested themselves in diminishing the rigor of the kind of political imprisonment to which we were subjected. There was no one, not even excepting Madame Tchoglokoff's own brother, Count Hendrikoff, who did not contrive to give us useful intimations; and many persons even made use of him to convey information to me, which he was always ready to do with the frankness of a good and honest fellow. He ridiculed the stupidities and brutalities of his sister and brother-in-law in such a manner that everyone was at ease with him, and no one ever thought of distrusting him, for he never compromised anyone, nor had any person ever been disappointed in him. He was a man of correct but limited judgment, ill-bred, and very ignorant, but firm, and without any evil.

During this same Lent, one day about noon, I went into the room where our ladies and gentlemen were assembled—the Tchoglokoffs had not yet come—and in speaking first to one and then to another, I approached the door near which the Chamberlain Outzine was standing. In a low voice he turned the conversation to the subject of the dull life we led, and said, notwithstanding all this, people contrived to prejudice us in the mind of the Empress; that a few days before, her imperial Majesty had said at table that I was overwhelmed with debt; that everything I did bore the stamp of folly; that for all that I thought myself very clever—an opinion, however, in which no one else shared, for nobody was deceived in me, my stupidity being patent to all; and wherefore it was less necessary to mind what the grand duke did than what I did. He added, with tears in his eyes, that he was ordered by the Empress to tell me all this, but he begged me not to let it be supposed that he had told me of this order. I replied, that as to my stupidity it ought not to be objected to me as a fault, everyone being just what God had made him; that as to my debts it was not very surprising I should be in debt when, with an allowance of 30,000 roubles, my mother, at parting, left me to pay 6,000 roubles on her account, while the Countess Roumianzoff had led me into innumerable express which she considered as indispensable; that Madame Tchoglokoff alone cost me this year 17,000 roubles, and that he himself knew what infernal play one was constantly obliged to play with them; that he might say all this to those who had sent him; that for the rest, I was very sorry I had been prejudiced in the opinion of her imperial Majesty, to whom I had never failed in respect, obedience, and deference, and that the more closely

my conduct was looked into the more would she be convinced
of this. I promised him the secrecy he asked for, and kept it.
I do not know whether he reported what I told him, but I fancy
he did, though I heard no more of the matter, and did not care
to renew a conversation so little agreeable.

During the last week of Lent I took the measles. I could
not make my appearance at Easter, but received the communion in my room, on the Saturday. During this illness, Madame
Tchoglokoff, though far advanced in pregnancy, scarcely ever
left me, and did all she could to amuse me. I had then a little
Kalmuck girl, of whom I was very fond. She caught the
measles from me. After Easter, we went to the summer palace, and thence, at the end of May—for the Feast of the Ascen-
sion—to the residence of the Count Razoumowsky, at Gostilitza.

The Empress invited there, on the twenty-third of this
month, the ambassador of the imperial court, the Baron
Breitlack, who was about to leave for Vienna. He spent the
evening there, and supped with the Empress. This supper
was served at a very late hour, and we returned to the cottage in which we lodged after sunrise. This cottage was of
wood, placed on a slight elevation, and attached to the slides.
We had been pleased with the situation of this cottage when
we were here in the winter, for the fête of the master of the
hounds; and, in order to gratify us, he had placed us in it on
the present occasion. It had two stories; the upper one consisted of a staircase, a saloon, and three cabinets. In one of
these we slept, the grand duke used another as a dressing-
room, and Madame Krause occupied the third. Below were
lodged the Tchoglokoffs, my maids of honor, and my lady's-
maids. On our return from supper, everyone retired to rest.
About six o'clock in the morning, a sergeant in the guards,
Levacheff, arrived from Oranienbaum, to speak to Tchoglokoff relative to the buildings which were in the course of
erection there.

Finding everyone asleep in the house, he sat down by the
sentinel, and heard certain crackling noises, which excited
his suspicions. The sentinel told him that these cracklings
had been several times renewed since he had been on duty.
Levacheff got up, and ran to the outside of the house. He

saw that large blocks of stone were detaching themselves from the lower portion. He ran and woke Tchoglokoff, telling him that the foundations of the house were giving way, and that he must try and get everyone out of it. Tchoglokoff put on a dressing-gown, and ran upstairs; where, finding the doors —which were of glass—locked, he burst them open. He thus reached our room, and drawing the curtains, desired us to get up as fast as possible and leave the house, as the foundations were giving way. The grand duke leaped out of bed, seized his dressing-gown, and ran off. I told Tchoglokoff that I would follow him, and he left me. While dressing I recollected that Madame Krause slept in the next room, and went to call her. She was so sound asleep that I had much difficulty in awaking her, and then in making her understand that she must leave the house. I helped her to dress. When she was in a condition to go out, we passed into the drawing-room; but we had scarcely done so, when there was a universal crash, accompanied by a noise like that made by a vessel launched from the docks. We both fell on the ground.

At the moment of our fall, Levacheff entered by the staircase door, which was opposite us. He raised me up, and carried me out of the room. I accidentally cast my eyes toward the slides: they had been on a level with the second story; they were so no longer, but some two or three feet below it. Levacheff reached with me as far as the stairs by which he had ascended; they were no longer to be found, they had fallen; but several persons having climbed upon the wreck, Levacheff passed me to the nearest, these to the others, and thus from hand to hand I reached the bottom of the staircase in the hall, and thence was carried into a field. There I found the grand duke in his dressing-gown.

Once out of the house, I directed my attention to what was passing there, and saw several persons coming out of it all bloody, while others were carried out. Among those most severely wounded was the Princess Gagarine, my maid of honor. She had tried to escape like the rest, but in passing through a room adjoining her own, a stove, which fell down, overturned a screen, by which she was thrown upon a bed which was in the room. Several bricks fell upon her head, and wounded her severely, as they did also a girl who was with

7

her. In this same story there was a small kitchen in which several servants slept, three of whom were killed by the fall of the fire-place. This, however, was nothing to be compared with what occurred between the foundations and the ground floor. Sixteen workmen attached to the slides slept there, and all of them were crushed to death by the fall of the house. All this mischief arose from the house having been built in the autumn, and in a hurry. They had given it as a foundation four layers of limestone. In the lower story the architect had placed in the vestibule twelve beams, which served as pillars. He had to go to the Ukraine, and at his departure told the manager of the estate of Gostilitza not to allow anyone to touch those beams till his return. Yet, notwithstanding this prohibition, when the manager learned we were to occupy this cottage, nothing would do but he must immediately remove the beams because they disfigured the vestibule. Then, when the thaw came, everything sank upon the four layers of limestone, which gave way in different directions, and the entire building slid toward a hillock, which arrested its progress.

I escaped with a few slight bruises and a great fright, for which I was bled. This fright was so general and so great among us all, that for more than four months afterward, if a door was only slammed with a little extra force, everyone started. On the day of the accident, when the first terror had passed, the Empress, who occupied another house, sent for us, and as she wished to make light of the danger we had been in, everyone tried to see little in it, and some none at all. My terror displeased her very much, and she was out of humor with me. The master of the hounds wept, and was inconsolable; he talked of blowing out his brains. I presume he was prevented, for he did nothing of the kind, and the next day we returned to St. Petersburg, and some weeks later to the summer palace.

I do not exactly remember, but I fancy it was about this time that the Chevalier Sacromoso arrived in Russia. It was a long time since a Knight of Malta had visited this country, and, generally speaking, few persons came to St. Petersburg in those days; his arrival, therefore, was a sort of event. He was received with marked attention, and was shown everything worthy of note in St. Petersburg and Cronstadt. A naval officer of distinction was appointed to accompany him. This was M. Poliansky, then captain of a man-of-war, since an admiral. He was presented to us. In kissing my hand he slipped into it a very small note, saying at the same time, in a low voice, " It is from your mother." I was almost stupefied with terror at this act. I dreaded its being observed by some one or other, especially by the Tchoglokoffs, who were near by. However, I took the note, and slipped it into my right-hand glove; no one had noticed it.

On returning to my room, I found, in fact, a letter from my mother, rolled up in a slip of paper, on which it was stated that the chevalier expected an answer through an Italian musician who attended the grand duke's concert. My mother, rendered anxious by my involuntary silence, wanted to know the cause of it; she also wished to know in what situation I was. I wrote to her, giving her the information she required. I told her that I had been forbidden to write to anyone, under the pretext that it did not become a grand duchess of Russia to write any letters but such as were composed at the office of foreign affairs, where I was only to attach my signature, and never to dictate what was to be written, because the minister knew better than I did what was proper to be said; that it had almost been made a crime in M. Olzoufieff that I had sent him a few lines, which I begged him to enclose in a letter to my mother. I also gave her information on several other points about which she had inquired. I rolled up my note in the same manner as the one I had received, and watched with impatience and anxiety the moment for getting rid of it.

At the first concert given by the grand duke, I made the tour of the orchestra, and stopped behind the chair of the solo violinist, D'Ologlio, who was the person pointed out to me. When he saw me come behind his chair, he pretended to take his handkerchief from his coat-pocket, and in doing so left his pocket wide open. Without any appearance of action, I slipped my note into it, and no one had the slightest suspicion of what had happened. During his stay in St. Petersburg, Sacromoso delivered to me two or three other notes having reference to the same matter; my answers were returned in the same manner, and no one was ever the wiser.

From the summer palace we went to Peterhoff, which was then being rebuilt. We were lodged in the upper palace, in Peter the First's old house, which was standing at that time. Here, to pass the time, the grand duke took it into his head to play with me every afternoon at two-handed ombre. When I won he got angry, and when I lost he wanted to be paid forthwith. I had no money, so he began to play at games of hazard with me, quite by ourselves. I remember on one occasion his nightcap stood with us for 10,000 roubles; but when at the end of the game he was a loser, he became furious, and would sometimes sulk for many days. This kind of play was not in any way to my taste.

During this stay at Peterhoff we saw from our windows, which looked out upon the garden toward the sea, that M. and Madame Tchoglokoff were continually passing and repassing from the upper palace toward that of Monplaisir on the seashore, where the Empress was then residing. This excited our curiosity, and that of Madame Krause also, to know the object of all these journeys. For this purpose Madame Krause went to her sister's, who was head lady's-maid to the Empress. She returned quite radiant with pleasure, having learned that all these movements were occasioned by its having come to the knowledge of the Empress that M. Tchoglokoff had had an intrigue with one of my maids of honor, Mademoiselle Kocheleff, who was with child in consequence. The Empress had sent for Madame Tchoglokoff and told her that her husband deceived her, while she loved him like a fool; that she had been blind to such a degree as to have this girl, the favorite of her husband, almost living with her; that if she wished to separate from her husband at once it would not be displeasing to her Majesty, who even from the beginning had not regarded her marriage with M. Tchoglokoff with a favorable eye. Her Majesty declared to her point-blank that she did not choose him to continue with us, but would dismiss him and leave her in charge.

Madame Tchoglokoff at first denied the passion of her husband, and maintained that the charge against him was a calumny; but in the meantime her Majesty had sent some one to question the young lady, who at once acknowledged the fact. This rendered Madame Tchoglokoff furious against her husband. She returned home and abused him. He fell upon his knees and begged her pardon, and made use of all his influence over her to soothe her anger. The brood of children which they had also helped to patch up their difference; but their reconciliation was never sincere. Disunited in love, they remained connected by interest. The wife pardoned her husband; she went to the Empress, and told her that she had forgiven everything, and wished to remain with him for the sake of her children. She entreated her Majesty on her knees not to dismiss him ignominiously from court, saying that this would be to disgrace her and complete her misery.

In a word, she behaved so well on this occasion, and with such firmness and generosity, and her grief besides was so real, that she disarmed the anger of the Empress. She did more; she led her husband before her imperial Majesty, told him many home truths, and then threw herself with him at the feet of her Majesty, and entreated her to pardon him for her sake and that of her six children, whose father he was. These different scenes lasted five or six days; and we learned, almost hour by hour, what was going on, because we were less watched during the time, as everyone hoped to see these people dismissed. But the issue did not answer their expectations; no one was dismissed but the young lady, who was sent back to her uncle, the grand marshal of the court, Chepeleff; while the Tchoglokoffs remained, less glorious, however, than they had been. The day of our departure for Oranienbaum was chosen for the dismissal of Mademoiselle Kocheleff; and while we set off in one direction, she went in another.

At Oranienbaum, we resided, this year, in the town, to the right and left of the main building, which was small. The affair of Gostilitza had given such a thorough fright, that orders had been issued to examine the floors and ceilings in all the houses belonging to the court, and to repair those which required attention.

This is the kind of life I led at Oranienbaum: I rose at three o'clock in the morning, and dressed myself alone from head to foot in male attire; an old huntsman whom I had was already waiting for me with the guns; a fisherman's skiff was ready on the seashore: we traversed the garden on foot, with our guns upon our shoulders; entered the boat together with a fisherman and a pointer, and I shot ducks in the reeds which bordered on both sides the canal of Oranienbaum, which extends two versts into the sea. We often doubled this canal, and consequently were occasionally for a considerable time in the open sea in this skiff. The grand duke came an hour or two after us; for he must needs always have a breakfast and God knows what besides, which he dragged after him. If we met we went together, if not each shot and hunted alone. At ten o'clock, and often later, I returned and dressed for dinner. After dinner we rested; and in the evening the grand duke had music, or we rode out on horseback. Having led this sort of life for about a week, I felt myself very much heated and my head confused. I saw that I required repose and dieting; so for four-and-twenty hours I ate nothing, drank only cold water, and for two nights slept as long as I could. After this I recommenced the same course of life, and found myself quite well. I remember reading at that time the " Memoirs of Brantôme," which greatly amused me. Before that I had read the " Life of Henri IV," by Périfix.

Toward autumn we returned to town, and learned that we were to go to Moscow in the course of the winter. Madame Krause came to tell me that it was necessary to increase my stock of linen for this journey. I entered into the details of the matter; Madame Krause pretended to amuse me by having the linen cut up in my room, in order, as she said, to teach me how many chemises might be cut from a single piece of cloth. This instruction or amusement seems to have displeased Madame Tchoglokoff, who had become very ill-tempered since the discovery of her husband's infidelity. I know not what she told the Empress; but, at all events, she came to me one afternoon and said that her Majesty had dispensed with Madame Krause's attendance on me, and that she was going to retire to the residence of her son-in-law, the Chamberlain Sievers; and next day Madame Tchoglokoff brought Madame Vladislava to me to occupy her place.

Madame Vladislava was a tall woman, apparently well formed, and with an intelligent cast of features, which rather prepossessed me at the first look. I consulted my oracle Timothy Yevreinoff relative to this choice. He told me that this woman, whom I had never before seen, was the mother-in-law of the Counsellor Pougovichnikoff, head clerk to Count Bestoujeff; that she was not wanting either in intelligence or sprightliness, but was considered very artful; that I must wait and see how she conducted herself, and especially be careful not to place much confidence in her. She was called Praskovia Nikitichna. She began very well; she was sociable, fond of talking, conversed and narrated with spirit, and had at her fingers' ends all the anecdotes of the time, past and present. She knew four or five generations of all the families, could give at a moment everybody's genealogy, father, mother, grandfathers, grandmothers, together with their ancestors, paternal and maternal, and from no one else have I received so much information relative to all that has occurred in Russia for the last hundred years. The mind and manners of this woman suited me very well; and when I felt dull I made her chat, which she was always ready to do.

I easily discovered that she very often disapproved of the sayings and doings of the Tchoglokoffs; but as she also went very often to her Majesty's apartments, no one knew why, we were obliged to be on our guard with her, to a certain degree, not knowing what interpretation might be put upon the most innocent words and actions.

From the summer palace we passed to the winter palace. Here was presented to us Madame La Tour l'Annois, who had been in attendance on the Empress in her early youth, and had accompanied the Princess Anna Petrovna, eldest daughter of Peter I, when she left Russia with her husband, the Duke of Holstein, during the reign of the Emperor Peter II. After the death of this princess, Madame l'Annois returned to France, and she now came to Russia, either to remain there, or possibly to return after having obtained some favors from her Majesty. Madame l'Annois hoped, on the ground of old acquaintance, to re-enter into the favor and familiarity of the Empress. But she was greatly deceived; everyone conspired to exclude her. From the first few days I foresaw what would happen, and for this reason: One evening, while they were at cards in the Empress' apartment, her Majesty continued moving from room to room without fixing herself anywhere, as was her custom; Madame l'Annois, hoping, no doubt, to pay her court to her, followed her wherever she went. Madame Tchoglokoff seeing this, said to me, " See how that woman follows the Empress everywhere; but that will not continue long, she will very soon drop that habit of running after her." I took this as settled, and, in fact, she was first kept at a distance, and finally sent back to France with presents.

During this winter was celebrated the marriage of Count Lestocq with Mademoiselle Mengden, maid of honor to the Empress. Her Majesty and the whole court assisted at it, and she paid the newly-married couple the honor of visiting them at their own house. One would have said that they enjoyed the highest favor, but in a couple of months afterward fortune turned. One evening, while looking on at those engaged at play in the apartments of the Empress, I saw the count, and advanced to speak to him. " Do not come near me," he said in a low tone, " I am a suspected man." I thought he must be jesting, and asked him what he meant. He replied, " I tell you quite seriously not to come near me, because I am a suspected man, whom people must shun." I saw that he had an altered look, and was extremely red. I fancied he must have been drinking, and turned away. This happened on the Friday. On the Sunday morning, while dressing my hair, Timothy Yevreinoff said to me, " Are you aware that last night Count Lestocq and his wife were arrested, and conducted to the fortress as State criminals? " No one knew why, but it became known that General Stephen Apraline and Alexander Schouvaloff had been named commissioners for this affair.

The departure of the court for Moscow was fixed for the sixteenth of December. The Czernicheffs had been transported to the fortress, and placed in a house belonging to the Empress, called Smolnoy Dooretz. The elder of the three sometimes made his guards drunk, and then walked into town to his friends. One day a Finnish wardrobe-maid, who was in my service, and was engaged to be married to a servant belonging to the court, a relation of Yevreinoff, brought me a letter from Andrew Czernicheff, in which he asked me for several things. This girl had seen him at the house of her intended, where they had spent the evening together. I was at a loss where to conceal this letter when I got it, for I did not like to burn it, as I wanted to remember what he asked for. I had long been forbidden to write even to my mother. I purchased, through this girl, a silver pen and an inkstand. During the day I had the letter in my pocket; when I undressed I slipped it under my garter into my stocking, and before going to bed I removed it, and placed it in my sleeve. At last I answered it; sent him what he asked for through the channel by which his letter had reached me, and then, at a favorable moment, burned this letter which had occasioned so much anxiety.

About the middle of December we set out for Moscow. The grand duke and I occupied a large sledge, and the gentlemen in waiting sat in the front. During the day the grand duke joined M. Tchoglokoff in a town sledge, while I remained in the large one. As we never closed this, I conversed with those who were seated in front. I remember that the chamberlain, Prince Alexander Jourievitch Troubetzkoy, told me, during this time, that Count Lestocq, then a prisoner in the fortress, wanted to starve himself during the first eleven days of his detention, but he was forced to take nourishment: he had been accused of having accepted 1,000 roubles from the King of Prussia to support his interests, and for having had a person named Oetlinger, who might have borne witness against him, poisoned. He was subjected to the torture, and then exiled to Siberia.

In this journey, the Empress passed us at Tver, and as the horses and provisions intended for us were taken by her suite, we remained twenty-four hours at Tver without horses, and without food. We were dreadfully hungry. Toward night Tchoglokoff had prepared for us a roasted sturgeon, which we thought delicious. We set off at night, and reached Moscow two or three days before Christmas. The first thing we heard was, that the chamberlain of our court, Prince Alexander Michael Galitzine, had received, at the moment of our departure from St. Petersburg, an order to repair to Hamburg as minister of Russia, with a salary of 4,000 roubles. This was looked upon as another case of banishment: his sister-in-law, the Princess Gagarine, who was with me, grieved very much, and we all regretted him.

We occupied at Moscow the apartments which I had inhabited with my mother in 1744. To go to the great church of the court, it was necessary to make the circuit of the house in a carriage. On Christmas Day, at the hour for mass, we were on the point of descending to our carriage, and were already on the stairs, during a frost of twenty-nine degrees, when a message came from the Empress to say that she dispensed with our going to church on this occasion, on account of the extreme cold; it did, in fact, pinch our noses.

I was obliged to keep my room during the early portion of our residence in Moscow, on account of the excessive quantity of pimples which had come on my face: I was dreadfully afraid of having to continue with a pimpled face. I called in the physician Boërhave, who gave me sedatives, and all sorts of things to dispel these pimples. At last, when nothing was of avail, he said to me one day, " I am going to give you something which will drive them away." He drew from his pocket a small phial of oil of Falk, and told me to put a drop in a cup of water, and to wash my face with it from time to time, say, for instance, once a week. And really the oil of Falk did clear my face, and by the end of some ten days I was able to appear.

A short time after our arrival in Moscow (1749) Madame Vladislava came to tell me that the Empress had ordered the marriage of my Finnish wardrobe-maid to take place as soon as possible. The only apparent reason for this hastening her marriage was, that I had shown some predilection for her; for she was a merry creature, who from time to time made me laugh by mimicking everyone, Madame Tchoglokoff especially being hit off in a very amusing manner. She was married, then, and no more said about her.

In the middle of the carnival, during which there were no amusements whatever, the Empress was seized with a violent colic, which threatened to be serious. Madame Vladislava and Timothy Yevreinoff each whispered this in my ear, entreating me not to mention to anyone who had told me. Without naming them, I informed the grand duke of it, and he became very much elated. One morning, Yevreinoff came to tell me that the Chancellor Bestoujeff and General Apraxine had passed the previous night in the apartment of M. and Madame Tchoglokoff, which seemed to imply that the Empress was very ill. Tchoglokoff and his wife were more gruff than ever; they came into our apartments, dined there, supped, but never allowed a word to escape them relative to her illness. We did not speak of it either, and consequently did not dare to send and inquire how her Majesty was, because we should have been immediately asked, "How, whence, by whom came you to learn that she was ill?" and anyone named, or even suspected, would infallibly have been dismissed, exiled, or even sent to the secret chancery, that State inquisition, more dreaded than death itself.

At last her Majesty, at the end of ten days, became better, and the wedding of one of her maids of honor took place at court. At table I was seated by the side of the Countess Schouvaloff, the favorite of the Empress. She told me that her Majesty was still so weak from the severe illness she had just had, that she had placed her diamonds on the bride's head (an honor which she paid to all her maids of honor) while seated in bed, her feet only being outside; and that it was for this reason she was not present at the wedding-feast. As the Countess Schouvaloff was the first to speak to me of this illness, I expressed to her the pain which her Majesty's condition gave me, and the interest I took in it. She said her Majesty would be pleased to learn how much I felt for her. Two mornings after this, Madame Tchoglokoff came to my room, and, in the presence of Madame Vladislava, told me that the Empress was very angry with the grand duke and myself on account of the little interest we had taken in her illness, even carrying our indifference to such an extent as not once to send and inquire how she was.

I told Madame Tchoglokoff that I appealed to herself, that neither she nor her husband had spoken a single word to us about the illness of her Majesty, and that knowing nothing of it, we had not been able to testify our interest in it. She replied, "How can you say that you knew nothing of it, when the Countess Schouvaloff has informed her Majesty that you spoke to her at table about it?" I replied, "It is true that I did so, because she told me her Majesty was still weak and could not leave her room, and then I asked her the particulars of this illness." Madame Tchoglokoff went away grumbling, and Madame Vladislava said it was very strange to try and pick a quarrel with people about a matter of which they were ignorant; that since the Tchoglokoffs alone had a right to speak of it, and did not speak, the fault was theirs, not ours, if we failed through ignorance.

Some time afterward, on a court day, the Empress approached me, and I found a favorable moment for telling her that neither Tchoglokoff nor his wife had given us any intimation of her illness, and that therefore it had not been in our power to express to her the interest we had taken in it. She received this very well, and it seemed to me that the credit of these people was diminishing.

The first week of Lent, M. Tchoglokoff wished to go to his duty. He confessed, but the confessor of the Empress forbade him to communicate. The whole court said it was by the order of her Majesty, on account of his adventure with Mademoiselle Kocheleff. During a portion of our stay at Moscow, M. Tchoglokoff appeared to be intimately connected with Count Bestoujeff and his tool General Stephen Apraxine. He was continually with them, and, to hear him speak, one would have supposed him to be the intimate adviser of Count Bestoujeff—a thing that was quite impossible, for Bestoujeff had far too much sense to allow himself to be guided by such an arrogant fool as Tchoglokoff. But, at about half the period of our stay, this intimacy suddenly ceased—I do not exactly know why—and Tchoglokoff became the sworn enemy of those with whom he had been so intimate a short time previously.

Shortly after my arrival in Moscow, I began, for want of other amusement, to read the " History of Germany," by le père Barre, canon of Ste. Geneviève, in nine volumes quarto. Every week I finished one, after which I read the works of Plato. My rooms faced the street; the corresponding ones were occupied by the duke, whose windows opened upon a small yard. When reading in my room, one of my maids usually came in, and remained there standing as long as she wished; she then retired, and another took her place when she thought it suitable. I made Madame Vladislava see that this routine could serve no useful purpose, but was merely an inconvenience; that, besides, I already had much to suffer from the proximity of my apartments to those of the grand duke, by which she, too, was equally discommoded, as she occupied

a small cabinet at the end of my rooms. She consented, therefore, to relieve my maids from this species of etiquette.

This is the kind of annoyance we had to put up with, morning, noon, and night, even to a late hour: The grand duke,
with rare perseverance, trained a pack of dogs, and with heavy
blows of his whip, and cries like those of the huntsman, made
them fly from one end to another of his two rooms, which
were all he had. Such of the dogs as became tired, or got out
of rank, were severely punished, which made them howl still
more. When he got tired of this detestable exercise, so painful to the nerves and destructive to the repose of his neighbors,
he seized his violin, on which he rasped away with extraordinary violence, and very badly, all the time walking up and
down his rooms.

Then he recommenced the education and punishment of his
dogs, which seemed to me very cruel. On one occasion, hearing one of these animals howl piteously and for a long time, I
opened the door of my bedroom where I was seated, and which
adjoined the apartment in which this scene was enacted, and
saw him holding this dog by the collar, suspended in the air,
while a boy who was in his service, a Kalmuck by birth, held
the animal by its tail. It was a poor little King Charles's dog
of English breed, and the duke was beating him with all his
might with the heavy handle of a whip. I interceded for the
poor beast, but this only made him redouble his blows. Unable to bear so cruel a scene, I returned to my room with tears
in my eyes. In general, tears and cries, instead of moving the
duke to pity, put him in a passion. Pity was a feeling that
was painful, and even unsupportable in his mind.

THE AVENGER OF HIS HONOR.

Photogravure from the original painting by Heinrich von Angeli.

A SECRET MISSION

BY

Comte de Mirabeau

HONORÉ GABRIEL RIQUETTI, COMTE DE MIRABEAU

1749—1791

Honoré Gabriel Riquetti, Comte de Mirabeau, was born in 1749 at Bignon, near Nemours, and died in 1791 at Paris. He was descended from the ancient Florentine family of the Arrighetti, who were expelled from their native land in 1268 and settled in Provence. Honoré was endowed with an athletic frame and extraordinary mental abilities, but was of a fiery temper, and disposed to every kind of excess. He became a lieutenant in a cavalry regiment, but continued to prosecute various branches of study with great eagerness, whilst outrunning his companions in a career of vice. An intrigue with the youthful wife of an aged marquis brought him into danger, and he fled with her to Switzerland, and thence to Holland, where he subsisted by his pen. He and his paramour were apprehended at Amsterdam, and he was brought to the dungeon at Vincennes, and there closely imprisoned for four years. During this time he was often in great want, but employed himself in literary labors, writing an "Essai sur les Lettres de Cachet et les Prisons d'Etat," which was published at Hamburg, and a number of tales by which he disgraced his genius, although their sale supplied his necessities. After his liberation from prison, he subsisted chiefly by literary labor, and still led a very profligate life.

When the States-General were convened, Mirabeau sought to be elected as a representative of the nobles of Provence, but was rejected by them on the ground of his want of property, and left them with the threat that, like Marius, he would overthrow the aristocracy. He purchased a draper's shop, offered himself as a candidate to the third estate, and was enthusiastically returned both at Aix and Marseilles. He chose to represent Marseilles, and by his talents and admirable oratorical powers soon acquired great influence in the States-General and National Assembly. The more that anarchy and revolutionary frenzy prevailed, the more decided did he become in his resistance to their progress; but the King and his friends were long unwilling to enter into any relations with one so disreputable, but at last, under the pressure of necessity, it was resolved that Mirabeau should be invited to become minister. No sooner was this known than a combination of the most opposite parties, by a decree of November 7, 1789, forbade the appointment of a deputy as minister.

From this time forth Mirabeau strove in vain in favor of the most indispensable prerogatives of the crown, and in so doing exposed himself to popular indignation. He still continued the struggle, however, with wonderful ability, and sought to reconcile the Court and the Revolution. In December, 1790, he was elected president of the club of the Jacobins, and in February, 1791, of the National Assembly. Both in the club and in the Assembly he displayed great boldness and energy; but soon after his appointment as president of the latter he sank into a state of bodily and mental weakness, consequent upon his great exertions, and died soon after. His "Secret Memoirs of the Court of Berlin" depict the last days of Frederick the Great in a lifelike manner, and every portrait painted by Mirabeau bears the mark of a master's hand.

A SECRET MISSION

THE true reason why the Duke of Weimar is so feasted is because he has undertaken to bring the Queen to consent to the marriage of Mademoiselle Voss. The Queen laughed at the proposal, and said: "Yes, they shall have my consent; but they shall not have it for nothing; on the contrary, it shall cost them dear." And they are now paying her debts, which amount to more than 100,000 crowns; nor do I believe this will satisfy her. While the King of Prussia is absorbed by meditations on this marriage, to me it appears evident that, if the Emperor be capable of a reasonable plan, he is now wooing two wives, Bavaria and Silesia. Yes, Silesia; for I do not think that so many manœuvres on the Danube can be any other than the domino of the masquerade. But this is not the place in which he will make his first attempt. Everything demonstrates (and give me credit for beginning to know this part of Germany) that he will keep on the defensive, on the side of Prussia, which he will suffer to exhaust itself in efforts that he may freely advance on Bavaria; nor is it probable that he will trouble himself concerning the means of recovering Silesia, till he has first made that immense acquisition.

I say that he may freely advance; for, to speak openly, what impediment can we lay in his way? Omitting the million and one reasons of indolence or impotence which I could allege, let it be supposed that we should act—we should take the Low Countries, and he Bavaria; we the Milanese, and he the Republic of Venice. What of all this would save Silesia? And what must soon after become of the Prussian power? It will be saved by the faults of its neighbors. It will fall! This grand fairy palace will come to the earth with a sudden crush, or its government will undergo some revolution.

The King appears very tranquil concerning future contingencies. He is building near New Sans Souci, or rather repairing and furnishing a charming house, which formerly belonged to the lord marshal, and which is destined for Mademoiselle Voss. The Princess of Brunswick has requested to have a house at Potsdam; and the King has bestowed that on her which he inhabited as prince royal, which he is furnishing at his own expense. It is evident that this expiring princess, crippled by David's disease, and consumed by inanity, is to be lady of honor to Mademoiselle Voss.

The debts of the Queen Dowager, the reigning Queen, the prince royal, now become King, and of some other complaisant people, male and female, are paid; and, if we add to these sums the pensions that have been bestowed, the houses that have been furnished, and the officers that have been created, we shall find the amount to be tolerably large. This is the true way to be prodigal without being generous. To this article it may be added that the King has given to Messieurs Blumenthal, Gaudi, and Heinitz, Ministers of State, each a bailliage. This is a new mode of making a present of 1,000 louis. Apropos of the last of these ministers, the King has replied to several persons employed in the Department of the Mines, who had complained of being superseded, that hereafter there shall be no claims of seniority.

He has terminated the affair of the Duke of Mecklenburg with some slight modifications.

He has given a miraculously kind reception to General Count Kalckreuth; who was aide-de-camp to and principal agent of Prince Henry; who quarrelled with him outrageously for the princess; and whom Frederick II kept at a distance that he might not too openly embroil himself with his brother. Kalckreuth is a man of great merit, and an officer of the first class; but the affectation with which he has been distinguished by the King appears to me to be directed against his uncle; perhaps, too, there may be a mingled wish of reconciling himself to the army; but should Count Brühl persist in assuming, not only the rank which has been granted him, but that likewise of seniority, which will supersede all the generals, with Moellendorf at their head, I believe the dissatisfaction will be past remedy. All that is of little consequence while peace shall continue, and perhaps would be the same, were war immediately declared, for a year to come; but, in process of time, that which has been sown shall be reaped. It is a strange kind of calculation which spreads discontent through an excellent army by favors and military distinctions, bestowed on a race of men who have always been such indifferent warriors.

Not that I pretend to affirm there are not brave and intelligent men in the service of Saxony. There are, for example, two at present, very much distinguished—Captain Tielke of the artillery,* whom Frederick wished to gain but could not, though he offered him the rank of lieutenant-colonel and an appointment of 2,000 crowns; and Count Bellegarde, who is said to be one of the most able officers in the world. But these are not the persons whom they have gained for the Prussian service. Hitherto, in all the Saxon promotions, the thing consulted was the noble merit of being devoted to the sect, or that of being recommended by Bishopswerder.

I forgot to mention to you that Comte d'Esterno had, at my intercession, addressed the Comte de Vergennes on the proposition of inviting M. de la Grange into France. It will be highly worthy of M. de Calonne to remove those money difficulties which M. de Brühl will not fail to raise.

General Count Kalckreuth continues to be in favor. It is a subject worthy of observation, that, should this favor be durable, should advantage be taken of the very great abilities of this gentleman, and should he be appointed to some place of importance, the King will then show he is not an enemy to understanding; he is not jealous of the merit of others; nor does he mean to keep all men of known talents at a distance. This will prove the mystics do not enjoy the exclusive privilege of royal favor. But all these deductions, I imagine, are premature; for, although Kalckreuth is the only officer of the army who has hitherto been thus distinguished; although he himself had conceived hopes he should be; although his merit is of the first order; Moellendorf having placed himself at the head of the malcontents, which the King will never pardon; Pritwitz being only a brave and inconsiderate soldier, the ridiculous echo of Moellendorf; Anhalt a madman; Gaudi

* Well known to officers for his military history of the war of 1756, which has been translated from the German into several of the European languages.

almost impotent, because of his size, and lying likewise under the imputation of a defect in personal bravery, which occasioned Frederick II to say of him, " He is a good professor, but when the boys are to repeat the lessons they have learned, he is never to be found." Although his other rivals are too young, and too inexperienced, to give him any uneasiness; in spite of all this, I say, I scarcely can imagine but that the principal cause of the distinction with which the King has treated him was the desire of humbling Prince Henry. At least I am very intimate with Kalckreuth, of whom I made a tolerably sure conquest at the reviews of Magdeburg, and I have reason to believe that I know everything which has passed between him and the King; in all which I do not perceive either anything conclusive, or anything of great promise.

The King supports his capitation-tax. It is said it will be fixed according to the following rates : A lieutenant-general, a minister of state, or the widow of one of these, at about twelve crowns, or forty-eight French livres; a major-general, or a privy councillor, at ten crowns; a chamberlain, or colonel, eight; a gentleman, six; a peasant, who holds lands in good provinces, three; a half-peasant (a peasant who holds lands has thirty acres, a half-peasant ten), a crown twelve groschen. In the poor provinces, a peasant two crowns, a half-peasant one.

Coffee hereafter is only to pay one groschen per pound, and tobacco the same. The general directory has received a memorial on the subject so strongly to the purpose that, although anonymous, it has been officially read, after which it was formally copied to be sent to the tobacco administration, in order to have certain facts verified. The step appeared to be so bold that the formal copy, or protocol, was only signed by four ministers—Messieurs Hertzberg, Arnim, Heinitz, and Schulemberg von Blumberg.

The merchants deputized by the city of Königsberg have written that, if salt is to continue to be monopolized by the Maritime Company, it will be useless for them to come to Berlin; for they can only be the bearers of grievances, without knowing what to propose. It is asserted, in consequence, that the Maritime Company will lose the monopoly of salt. This intelligence, to say the least, is very premature. Salt is an exceedingly important article; and Struensee, who has exerted his whole faculties to secure it to himself, has been so perfectly successful that he sells 5,000 lasts of salt, twenty-eight muids constituting nine lasts. (The muid is 144 bushels.)

I ask once again, if the Maritime Company is to be deprived of its most lucrative monopolies, how can it afford to pay ten per cent. for a capital of 1,200,000 crowns? When an edifice, the summit of which is so lofty and the basis so narrow, is once raised, before any part of it should be demolished, it were very necessary to consult concerning the props by which the remainder is to be supported. The King has declared that he will render trade perfectly free, if any means can be found of not lessening the revenue. Is not this declaration pleasantly benevolent? I think I hear Job on his dunghill, exclaiming, "I consent to be cured of all my ulcers, and to be restored to perfect health, provided you will not give me any physic, and will not subject me to any regimen."

The munificence is somewhat similar to that which shall restore freedom to all the merchandise of France, by obliging it to pay excessively heavy duties, the produce of which shall be applied to the encouragement of such manufactures as shall be supposed capable of rivalling the manufactures of foreign nations. I know not whether the King imagines he has conferred a great benefit on trade; but I know that throughout Europe all contraband commerce is become a mere article of insurance, the premium of which is more or less according to local circumstances; and that therefore a heavy duty (with respect to the revenue) is equivalent to a prohibition.

The King has ordered his subjects to be numbered, that he may not only know their number, but their age and sex. Probably, the changes which are projected to be made in the army are to be the result of this enumeration. But we know how difficult all such numberings are in every country upon earth. Another affair is in agitation, of a much more delicate nature, and which supposes a general plan and great fortitude; which is a land-tax on the estates of the nobles. The project begins to transpire, and the provincial counsellors have received orders to send certain informations, which seem to have this purpose in view. I will believe it is accomplished when I see it.

Single and distinct facts are of less importance to you than
an intimate knowledge of him who governs. All the characters of weakness are united to those I have so often described. Spies already are employed; informers are made
welcome; those who remonstrate meet anger, and the sincere
are repulsed or driven to a distance. Women only preserve
the right of saying what they please. There has lately been
a private concert, at which Madame Hencke, or Rietz, for you
know that this is one and the same person, was present, and
stood behind a screen. Some noise was heard at the door.
A *valet de chambre* half opened it, and there found the
Princess Frederica of Prussia and Mademoiselle Voss. The
first made a sign for him to be silent. The *valet de
chambre* disobeyed. The King instantly rose, and introduced
the two ladies. Some minutes afterward, a noise was again
heard behind the screen. The King appeared to be embarrassed. Mademoiselle Voss asked what it was. Her
royal lover replied, " Nothing but my people." The two ladies,
however, had quitted the Queen's card-table to indulge this
pretty whim. The King was making a joke of the matter, on
the morrow, when one of the ladies of the palace who was
present said to him, " The thing is very true, Sire; but it were
to be wished that it were not." Another lady asked him, the
other day, at table, " But why, Sire, are all the letters opened
at the post-office? It is a very ridiculous and very odious
proceeding."

He was told that the German plays, which he protects very
much, are not good. " Granted," replied he; " but better
these than a French play-house, which would fill Berlin with
hussies, and corrupt the manners of the people." From which,
no doubt, you would conclude that the German actresses are
Lucretias. You must also especially admire the morality of
this protector of morals, who goes to sup in the house of his
former mistress, with three women, and makes a procuress
of his daughter.

He troubles himself as little with foreign politics as if he
were entirely secure from all possible tempests. He speaks
in panegyrics of the Emperor, of the French always with a
sneer, of the English with respect. The fact is, the man appears to be nothing, less than nothing; and I fear lest those

diversions which may be made in his favor are exaggerated. I shall, on this occasion, notice that the Duc de Deux Ponts escapes us; but he unites himself the closer to the Germanic league, which has so high an opinion of itself that it really believes it does not stand in need of our aid. Under the standard of what chief it has acquired this presumption heaven knows!

There is an anecdote which to me is prophetic, but the force of which you will not feel, for want of knowing the country. Prince Ferdinand has received the 50,000 crowns which were due to him, according to the will of the King, on the simple order of Werder, conceived in these words: " His Majesty has given me his verbal command to lay down the 50,000 crowns to your Highness, which will be paid to you or your order, by the treasury at sight.—Welner." An order for 50,000 crowns, to be paid down, signed by any other than the King, is a monstrosity in the political regulations of Prussia.

Erect a bank, and blessings be upon you; for it is the sole resource for finance which would not be horribly burden-some; the only money-machine which, instead of borrowing with dearness and difficulty, will cause you to receive; the only cornerstone on which, under present circumstances, the basis of the power of the Minister of Finance can be supported. Struensee, who is more stiff in the stirrups than ever, since he must necessarily become the professor of the new Ministry, has charged me to inform you that the King will probably purchase shares to the amount of several millions, if you will send him (Struensee) an abstract of the regulations of the bank, according to which he may make his report and proposals.

Apropos of Struensee, with whom I am daily more intimate. He has desired me to inform you that the change of the commandite* for the dealing in piastres will very powerfully lower your exchange; and the following is his reasoning to prove his assertion:

" The remonstrances of the Bank of St. Charles to preserve the remittances of the Court, on commission, at the rate of ten per cent., have been entirely rejected; it has only been able to obtain them on speculation, and on the conditions

* Money-agents.

proposed by the *Gremois;* * that is to say, at an interest of six per cent. for the money advanced.

"The same bank has lately changed the commandite at Paris for the piastre business, and has substituted the house of Le Normand to that of Le Couteulx. As the former does not at present possess so extensive a credit as the latter, many people foresee that the Spanish bank will be under the necessity of keeping a greater supply of ready money with their commandite.

"In the interim, it has found itself extremely distressed. Desirous of settling its accounts with the house of Le Couteulx, and other houses in France, it was in want of the sum of 3,000,000 of French livres. To obtain this, it addressed itself to government, and endeavoring to call in 60,000,000 of reals which were its due. Government having, under various pretences, declined payment, the bank declared itself insolvent, and that it must render the state of its affairs public. This means produced its effect; government came to its aid, and gave it assignments for 20,000,000 of reals, payable annually."

The comedy which Prince Henry had promised the world every Monday had its first representation on yesterday evening. The King came, contrary to the expectation of the prince, and highly amused himself. I was a close observer of royalty, as you may suppose. It is incontrovertibly the cup of Circe which must be presented, in order to seduce him, but filled rather with beer than tokay. One remark sufficiently curious, which I made, was that Prince Henry amused himself for his own personal pleasure, and was not subject to the least absence of mind, neither of politics nor of attention to his guests. All the foreign ministers were present, but I was the only stranger who stayed to supper; and the King, who, when the comedy was over, behaved all the evening with great reserve, except when some burst of laughter was forced from him by the obscene jests of Prince Frederick of Brunswick, contemplated me with an eye more than cold. He is incessantly irritated against me by speeches which are made for me; and the most harmless of my acquaintance are represented as personally offensive to his Majesty. For my own part, I am perfectly the reverse of disconsolate on the sub-

* A company of Spanish merchants so called.

ject. I only notice this that I may describe my present situation, exactly as it is, without any hypocrisy.

It is true that Count Hertzberg has been on the point of losing his place, the occasion of which was what follows: He had announced the promised arrangement to the Duke of Mecklenburg, notwithstanding which, the affair was not expedited. Driven beyond his patience, and impatience in him is always brutal, he one day said to the members of the General Directory, " Gentlemen, you must proceed a little faster ; business is not done thus ; this is a State which can only proceed with activity." An account was given to the King of this vehement apostrophe. The sovereign warmly reprimanded his minister, who offered to resign. Blumenthal, it is said, accommodated the affair.

Apropos of the Duke of Mecklenburg, the King, when he received his thanks for the restitution of his bailliages, said to him, " I have done nothing more than my duty ; read the device of my order " *(Suum cuique *)*. The Poles, when the Prussian arms were erected to denote the limits of the frontiers, after dismemberment by the late King, added *rapuit* to the motto.* I do not imagine Frederick William will ever give occasion to a similar epigram.

A very remarkable incident in the history of the human heart was the following: After various retrenchments had been made upon this duke, especially in the promises that had been given him, one of the courtiers represented to the King that he would not be satisfied. " Well," said his Majesty, " then we must give him a yellow ribbon ; " and, accordingly, yesterday the yellow ribbon was given. The vainglorious duke at this moment found the arrangement of the bailliages perfectly satisfactory, and this was the occasion of his coming to return thanks.

Would you wish to obtain a tolerably just idea of the manner of living, in this noble tennis-court, ‡ called the Court of Berlin? If so, pay some attention to the following traits, and recollect that I could collect a hundred of the same species.

* To every one his own.
† *Suum cuique rapuit.*—He took from every one his own.
‡ *Tripot.*—The just value of the author's word seems to be show-booth. Tennis-courts were formerly hired in France by rope-dancers, tumblers, and showmen ; in which we must not omit the allusion to the debauchery of manners of such people in France.

The Princess Frederica of Prussia is now nineteen, and her apartment is open at eleven every morning.

The dukes of Weimar, Holstein, and Mecklenburg, all ill-bred libertines, go in and out of it two or three times in the course of the forenoon.

The Duke of Mecklenburg was recounting I know not what tale to the King. The Prince of Brunswick, awkwardly enough, trod on the toe of a person present, to make him take notice of something which he thought ridiculous. The duke stopped short in his discourse—" I believe, sir, you are diverting yourself at my expense." He went on with his conversation to the King, and presently stopped again—" I have long, sir, been acquainted with the venom of your tongue; if you have anything to say, speak it to my face, and I shall answer you." More conversation and other interruptions. "When I am gone, sire, the prince will paint me in charming colors; I beg your Majesty will recollect what has just passed."

This same Prince Frederick is, as I have very often told you, the chief of the mystics, against whom he uttered the most horrid things to Baron Knyphausen.

" But how is this, my lord? " replied the baron; " I understood you were the Pope of that Church." " It is false." " I have too good an opinion of your honesty to imagine you can be of a sect which you disavow; I, therefore, give you my promise everywhere to declare you despise the mystics too much to be one of them; and thus you will recover your reputation." The prince beat about the bush, and called off his dogs.

A courtier, a grand marshal of the court, petitions for a place promised to five candidates. I remarked to him, " But how, monsieur, if the place be engaged? " " Oh, engagements are nothing at present," answered he, gravely; " for this month past we have left off keeping our word."

Welner, the real author of the disgrace of Schulemburg, went to see him, pitied him, and said, " You have too much merit not to have many enemies." " I, many enemies, monsieur! " said the ex-minister; " I know of but three—Prince Frederick, because I would not give his huntsman a place; Bishopswerder, because I dismissed one of his dependents;

and you, because—I know not why." Welner began to weep,
and to swear that detraction was everywhere rending his
character. " Tears are unworthy of men," said Schulemburg;
" and I am unable to thank you for yours."

In a word, all is sunken to the diminutive, as all was exalted
to the grand.

It is asserted that the Prussian merchants will be allowed
a free trade in salt and wax. I cannot verify the fact to-day;
Struensee will be too much occupied, it being post day; but
if it be true, the Maritime Company, which at once will be
deprived of salt, wax, coffee, tobacco, and probably of wood,
cannot longer support the burden of eighteen per cent. at
the least ; a profit which no solid trade can afford, and which,
perhaps, Schulemburg himself, with all his lucrative exclusive
privileges, could not have paid, but by perplexing the treasury
accounts, so that the gains of one branch concealed the
deficiencies of another.

As to the silk manufactures, which are proposed to be laid
aside, I do not perceive that any inconvenience whatever will
result from this. An annual bounty of 40,000 rix-dollars
divided among the master weavers of Berlin, added to the
prohibition of foreign silks, will never enable them to maintain a competition. Nay, as I have before explained to you,
the very manufacturers themselves smuggle, and thus supply
more than one-third of the silks that are used in the country;
for it is easy to conceive that purchasers will prefer the best
silks, which have more substance than, and are of superior
workmanship to, those which monopoly would oblige them
to buy. Not that the raw materials cost the manufacturer
of Berlin more than they do the manufacturer of Lyons. They
both procure them from the same countries, and the former
does not pay the six per cent. entrance duty to which the
Lyons manufacturer is subject; besides that, the German
workman will labor with more diligence than the French;
nor is labor much dearer here than at Lyons. The one receives eighty centimes an ell for making, and the other ninety-
five centimes for the same quantity, of equal fineness, which
scarcely amounts to one and a half per cent. on the price of
the silk, estimated at five livres the French ell.

The Berlin manufacturer has likewise, by a multitude of

local calculations of trade, to which I have paid severe attention, an advantage of thirty per cent. over the Lyons trader, at the fair of Frankfort on the Oder. And, whether it proceed from a defect in the government, the poverty of the workmen, or the ignorance of the manufacturer, he still cannot support the competition. Of what use, therefore, are so many ruinous looms, of which there are not less than 1,650, at Berlin, Potsdam, Frankfort, and Koepnic?—the product of which, however, is far from being equivalent to the same number of looms at Lyons. The Berlin weaver will not, at the utmost, do more than two-thirds of the work turned out of hand by the weaver of Lyons. Of these 1,650 looms, we may reckon about 1,200 in which are weaved taffetas, brocades, velvets, etc. The remainder are employed in fabricating gauze, about 980,000 Berlin ells of which are annually produced. (The French ell is equal to an ell three-quarters of Berlin measure.)

The 1,200 silk-looms only produce about 960,000 ells; which in the whole amounts to 1,940,000 ells. The sum total of the looms consume about 114,000 pounds weight of raw silk, at sixteen ounces to the pound. (You know that 76,000 pounds weight of wrought silk will require about 114,000 pounds weight of undressed silk.) There are also 28,000 pair, per annum, of silk stockings fabricated at Berlin; which consume about 5,000 pounds weight of raw silk. It is principally in the stocking manufactory that the silk of the country is employed; which, in reality, is superior in quality to that of the Levant; but they so ill understand the art of spinning it, in the Prussian States, that it is with difficulty worked in the silk-loom. The stocking manufacturers use it to a greater advantage, because, being cheap, and of a strong quality, stockings are made from it preferable to those of Nismes and Lyons, in which cities the rejected silk alone is set apart for stockings. From 8,000 to 12,000 pounds weight of silk is annually obtained in the Prussian States, in which there are mulberry trees enough to supply 30,000 pounds weight. This constitutes no very formidable rivalship with the silk produced in the States of the King of Sardinia.

The commission of inquiry has written to inform Launay

that it has no further demand to make from him; and in consequence he has addressed the King for permission to depart.
The King replied, "I have told you to wait here till the commission shall be closed." There is either cunning or tyranny
on one side or the other.

Mademoiselle Hencke, or Madame Rietz, as you think proper
to call her, has petitioned the King to be pleased to let her
know what she is to expect, and to give her an estate on which
she may retire. The sovereign offered her a country house,
at the distance of some leagues from Potsdam. The lady sent
a positive refusal, and the King, in return, will not hear any
mention made of an estate. It is difficult to say what shall be
the product of this conflict between cupidity and avarice. The
pastoral, in the meantime, proceeds without relaxation. "Inez
de Castro" has several times been performed at the German
theatre, imitated from the English, and not from the French.
In the fourth act, the prince repeats with ardor every oath of
fidelity to a lady of honor. This has been the moment of each
representation which the Queen has chosen to leave the house.
Was it the effect of chance, or was it intentedly marked? This
is a question that cannot be answered, from any consideration
of the turbulent and versatile, but not very feeble, character of
this princess.

When her brother-in-law, the Duke of Weimar, arrived, the
King gave him a very gracious reception; but by degrees, his
countenance changed to icy coldness. Conjectures are that he
has been lukewarm, or has wanted address in his negotiation
with the Queen, on the subject of the marriage, which is far
from being determined on. Two private houses have been
bought at Potsdam, and have been furnished with every degree of magnificence. And to what purpose, if marriage be intended? May not the wife be lodged in the palace? Speaking of arrangements, let me inform you that the King has
sent a M. Paris, his *valet de chambre*, into France, to pay his
personal debts there, and to purchase such things as are wanting to these newly bought houses which are consecrated to
love.

The relations of Mademoiselle Voss, who four months since
pressed her to depart for Silesia, there to marry a gentleman
who asked her hand, are at present the first to declare that the

projected royal marriage would be ridiculous, and even absurd. In fact, its consequences might be very dangerous; for, should disgust succeed enjoyment, a thing which has been seen to happen, Mademoiselle Voss must separate with a pension; instead of which, in her rank of favorite, she might rapidly make her own fortune, that of her family, and procure the advancement of her creatures.

Be this as it may, the time is passed at Potsdam in projecting bowers of love; and, though the sovereign might not perhaps be exactly addressed in the words of La Hire to Charles VII: "I assure you, sire, it is impossible to lose a kingdom with greater gaiety," it may at least be said, "It is impossible to risk a kingdom more tenderly." But, whatever tranquillity may be affected, there are proceedings and projects which, without alarming, for he certainly has valor, occupy the monarch. The journey of the Emperor to Cherson, the very abrupt and very formal declaration of Russia to the city of Dantzic, the intended camp of eighty thousand men in Bohemia, for the amusement of the King of Naples, are at least incidents that may compel attention, if not remark. There are doubts concerning the journey of the Empress into the Crimea, Potemkin being unwilling to make her a witness of the incredible poverty of the people and the army, in this newly acquired garden.

The discouragement of the ministry of Berlin still continues to increase. The King, for these two months, has not acted in concert with any single minister. Hence their torpor and pusillanimity are augmented. Count Hertzberg is progressive in his descent, and Werder begins to decline. The King remains totally unconcerned; and never was the mania of reigning in person and of doing nothing carried to greater excess. Instead of the capitation, a tax on houses is talked of as a substitute. I begin to think that neither of these taxes will take place. There is an inclination to retract without disgrace, if that be possible; and the pretext will be furnished by the advice of the provincial presidents. It is the more extraordinary that this capitation-tax should be so much persisted in, since, under the reign of Frederick William I, a similar attempt was made, and which on the second year was obliged to be renounced.

The Prussian army has made a new acquisition, of the same

kind with those by which it has been enriched for these four
months past. I speak of Prince Eugene of Wirtemberg. He
began his career by an excess of libertinage. He since has distinguished himself in the trade of *Corporal-schlag*,* and by
stretching the severity of discipline to ferocity. He, notwithstanding, has not acquired any great reputation by these
means. He has lived at Paris, and plunged into mesmerism.
He afterward professed to be a somnambulist, and next continued the farce by the practice of midwifery. These different
masquerades accompanied and concealed the real object of his
ambition and his fervor, which is to give credit to the sect of
the mystics, of whom he is one of the most enthusiastic chiefs.
A regiment has lately been granted him, which brings him to
Berlin. His fortune will not permit him to live wholly there;
but his situation will allow him to make journeys to that city,
where he will be useful to the fathers of the new church. Singular, ardent, and active, he delivers himself like an oracle, and
enslaves his hearers by his powerful and ecstatic elocution,
with his eyes sometimes haggard, always inflamed, and his
countenance in excessive emotion. In a word, he is one of those
men whom hypocrites and jugglers make their successful pre-
cursors.

I have just had a very deep and almost sentimental conversation with Prince Henry. He is in a state of utter discouragement, as well on his own behalf as on behalf of his country.
He has confirmed all I have related to you, and all I shall now
relate—torpor in every operation, gloom at court, stupefaction
among ministers, discontent everywhere. Little is projected,
less still is executed. When it is noticed that business is suffered to languish, the King's being in love is very gravely
given as the reason; and it is affirmed that the vigor of administration depends on the compliance of Mademoiselle Voss.
Remarks at the same time are made how ridiculous it is thus
to suspend the affairs of a whole kingdom, etc., etc.

The general directory, which should be a council of state,
is nothing more than an office to expedite common occurrences. If ministers make any proposition no answer is returned; if they remonstrate they meet with disgust. What they
ought to do is so far from what they actually do that the

---

*The flogging-corporal; from *schlagen*, to strike or whip.

debasement of their dignity occasions very disagreeable reflections. Never was a public opinion produced more suddenly
than it has been by Frederick William II, in a country where
the seeds of such opinion did not appear to exist.

Prince Henry can find no remedy for domestic vices, but
he has no apprehensions concerning foreign affairs; because
the King is at present wholly decided in favor of France, and
still more destitute of confidence for the favorers of the English
faction. Pray take notice that this is the version of the prince;
not that I am very incapable of believing it, if we do not throw
up our own chances.

What the public papers have announced respecting the
journey of Prince Henry, is without foundation. Some wish
to go to Spa and France, but no plan is yet determined on; a
vague hope, which he cannot suffer to expire, notwithstanding
the blows he receives, will detain him at Rheinsberg. Year
will succeed to year; the moment of rest will arrive, and habit
will enchain him in his frosty castle, which he has lately enlarged and rendered more commodious. To these different
motives, add a nullity of character, a will unstable as the clouds,
frequent indisposition, and a heated imagination, by which he
is exhausted. That which we desire without success, gives
more torment than that which is executed with difficulty.

A second minister is to be appointed for Silesia; one singly
is a kind of viceroy. It is dangerous, say they, to see with the
eyes of an individual only. *Divide et impera.* Thus far have
they advanced in their politics.

Prince Frederick of Brunswick is ardently active in his intrigues against Prince Henry, and the duke, his brother. What
he wishes is not known; but he wishes, and hence he has acquired a certain importance among the tumultuous crowd,
who cannot perceive that a contemptible prince is still more
contemptible than an ordinary man. He neither can be of
any durable utility, nor in the least degree agreeable or estimable ; but, under certain given circumstances, he may be a very
necessary spy.

A grand list of promotions is spoken of, in which Prince
Henry and the Duke of Brunswick are included as field-
marshals. But the first says he will not be a field-marshal.
He continually opposed that title being bestowed on the duke,

under Frederick II, who refused to confer such a rank on the princes of the blood. This alternative of haughtiness and vanity, even aided by his ridiculous comedy, will not lead him far. He intends to depart in the month of September for Spa; he is afterward to visit our southern provinces, and from thence is to continue his journey to Paris, where he is to pass the winter. Such are his present projects, and the probability is sufficiently great that not anything of all this will happen.

The King has declared that he will not bestow any places on persons who are already in office under the princes. This may perhaps be the cause that Count Nostitz has forsaken Prince Henry. The count is a very strange kind of being.

First sent into Sweden, where he erected himself a chief of some envoys of the second order, finding himself dissatisfied with the severe laws of etiquette, he passed a slovenly life in an office which he exercised without abilities. On his return, he procured himself the appointment of one of the gentlemen who accompanied the prince royal into Russia, but the consent of the prince he had forgotten to ask. He was consequently regarded as an inconvenient inspector, and was but sparingly produced on public occasions. Hence arose ill-humor, complaints, and murmurs. The late king sent him into Spain, where he dissipated the remainder of his fortune. The merchants of Embden, and of Königsberg, requested the Spaniards would lower the duties on I know not what species of merchandise. Count Nostitz solicited, negotiated, and presently wrote word " that the new regulations were wholly to the advantage of the Prusisan subjects."

The King ordered the Court of Spain to be thanked. Fortunately, Count Finckenstein, who had not received the regulations, delayed sending the thanks. The regulations came, and the Prussian merchants were found to be more burdened than formerly. His Majesty was in a rage. Nostitz was suddenly recalled, and arrived at Berlin without the fortune that he had spent, destitute of the respect that he had lost, and deprived of all future hopes. Prince Henry welcomed him to his palace, an asylum open to all malcontents. Here he remained eighteen months, and here displayed himself in the same manner that he had done everywhere else—inconsistent in his imaginations, immoral in mind, ungracious in manners, not capable of writ-

9

ing, not willing to read, as vain as a blockhead, as hot as a turkey-cock, and unfit for any kind of office, because he neither possesses principles, seductive manners, nor knowledge. Such as here depicted, this insipid mortal, the true hero of the Dunciad, is in a few days to be appointed envoy to the Electorate of Hanover. In excuse for so capricious a choice, it is alleged that he will have nothing to do in the place. But wherefore, send a man to a place where he has nothing to do?

Madame Rietz, who of all the mistresses of the sovereign has most effectually resisted the inconstancy of men, and the intrigues of the wardrobe,* has modestly demanded the margraviate of Schwedt from the King, to serve as a place of retreat; and four gentlemen to travel with her son as with the son of a monarch. This audacious request has not displeased the King, who had been offended by the demand made of an estate. He, no doubt, has discovered that he is highly respected, now that he receives propositions so honorable.

His former friends no longer can obtain a minute's audience; the gates to them are gates of brass. But a comedian, whose name is Marron, at present an innkeeper at Verviers, lately came to solicit his protection. He chose the moment when the King was stepping into his carriage. The King said to him, "By and by; by and by." Marron waited; the King returned, sent for him into his apartments, spoke with him a quarter of an hour, received his request, and promised everything for which he petitioned. Never, no, never will subaltern influence decline; footmen will be all-puissant. Welner has publicly obtained the surname of viceroy, or of petty king.

The monarch has written to the general of the gendarmes (Pritwitz), noticing that several of his officers played at games of chance; that these games were forbidden; that he should renew the prohibitions under pain of being sent to the fortress for the first offence, and of being broken for the second. The information and the threat were meant at the general himself, who has lost much money with the Duke of Mecklenburg.

It is affirmed that the Duke of Brunswick will be here from January 8th to 15th. But Archimedes himself demanded a point of support, and I see none of any kind at

* *La garde-robe.* "An ounce of civet, good apothecary."

Berlin. There are numerous wishes, but not one will; and the wishes themselves are incoherent, contradictory, and rash; he does not know, nor will he ever know, how to connect a single link in the chain; he will more especially never know how to lop off the parasitical and avaricious sucker. Agriculture is what is most necessary to be encouraged, particularly as soon as commercial oppression shall be renounced; though this oppression has hitherto been productive of gold, thanks to the situation of the Prussian States. But how may agriculture be encouraged in a country where the half of the peasants are attached to the glebe? For so they are in Pomerania, Prussia, and in other parts.

It would be a grand operation in the royal domains, were they divided into small farms, as has so long since been done by the great landholders in England. It is a subject of much greater importance than regulations of trade; but there are so many interested people to be controverted, and the habit of servitude is so rooted, that strength of understanding, energy, and consistency, not one grain of which I can find here, are necessary to make the attempt. More knowledge likewise is requisite than will here be found, for a long time to come, for it to be supposed that there is no town, no province, which would not most gladly consent to pay the King much more than the neat revenue he at present obtains, if he would suffer the inhabitants to assess themselves; taking care, however, continually to watch over the assessments, that the magistrates and nobles might not oppress the people; or for it to be imagined that the subject would not gain three-fourths of the expenses of collecting, and would be free of all those unworthy restraints which are at present imposed upon them by the fiscal treasury.

It is also necessary to recollect that it is not here as with us, where the body, the mass, of national wealth is so great, because of the excellence of the soil and the climate, the correspondence between the provinces, etc., that we may cut as close as we will, provided we do not erect kilns to burn up the grass; and that in France the expenses of collecting only need be diminished; that no other relief is necessary; nay, that we may still prodigiously increase the load, provided that load be well poised. Here, two or three provinces at the utmost excepted, the basis is so narrow and the soil so little fruitful, so damp, so impoverished, that it is only for tutelary authority to perform the greatest part of all which can reconcile Nature to this her neglected offspring. The division of the domains itself, an operation so productive of every kind of resource, requires very powerful advances; for the farmer's stock and the implements of husbandry are, perhaps, those which, when wanting, the arm can least supply.

Independent of this grand point of view, we must not forget the military power, which must here be respected, for here there are neither Alps nor Apennines, rivers nor seas, for ramparts; here, therefore, with 6,000,000 of inhabitants, government is desirous, and, to a certain point, is obliged, to maintain 200,000 men in arms. In war there are no other means than those of courage or of obedience, and obedience is an innate idea in the serf peasant; for which reason, perhaps, the grand force of the Prussian army consists in the union of the feudal and military systems. Exclusive of that vast consideration, which I shall elsewhere develop, let me add it will not be sufficient here to act like such or such a Russian or Polish lord, and say, " You are enfranchised," for the serfs here will reply, " We are very much obliged to you for your enfranchisement, but we do not choose to be free; " or even to bestow lands gratuitously on them, for they will answer, " What would you have us do with lands?"* Proprietors and property can only be erected by making advances, and advances are expensive; and, as there are so few governments which have the wisdom to sow in order that they may reap, this will not be the first to begin. It is little probable that the morning of wholesome politics should first break upon this country.

At present it is almost publicly known that the Comte

---

* It is a melancholy truth that such is, and indeed such must necessarily be, the spirit of serf peasants; nay, in Russia this error is more rooted than in Prussia. The peasants have no examples of the possibility of existing in a state of independence; they think themselves certain of an asylum against hunger and old age in the domains of their tyrants, and, if enfranchised, would imagine themselves abandoned to an inhospitable world (which indeed, locally speaking, they would be), in which they must be exposed to perish with cold and hunger. Men in a body must be led to act from motives of interest, which, when well understood, are the best of motives. Nothing would be more easy than to convince the peasantry of the largest empire, in a few years, of what their true interest, and the true interests of all parties, is, were not the majority of men, unfortunately, incapable of looking far beyond the trifling wants and the paltry passions of the moment. It is a melancholy consideration that so many ages must yet revolve before truths so simple shall be universally known, even now that the divine art of printing is discovered.

d'Esterno is to depart in the month of April for France. I shall submit it to your delicacy, and to your justice, to pronounce whether I can remain here the overseer of a *chargé d'affaires*. During his absence, functions might be bestowed on me; here I certainly would not remain under an envoy *per interim;* nor would this require more than the simple precaution of sending me secret credentials. But, as no such thing will be done, you will perceive that this is a new and very strong reason for my departure about that time. Those who would make me nothing more than a gazetteer are ill-acquainted with mankind; and still more so those who hope to oblige me to consent tacitly or perforce.

The Count de Masanne, a fervent mystic, is the grand master of the Queen's household. Welner supped with her yesterday, and had the place of honor; that is to say, he sat opposite her. If he cede to wishes of such indecent vanity, he will presently be undone.

Yesterday was a memorable moment for the man of observation. Count Brühl, a Catholic, a foreigner, assuming his rank in the Prussian army, was installed in his place of governor, and the capitation-tax was intimated. This capitation, so openly condemned, supported with so much obstinacy, demonstrated to be vicious in its principle, impossible of execution, and barren in product, at once announces the disgraceful inanity of the General Directory, by which it was loudly opposed, and the sovereign influence of the subaltern by whom its chiefs have been resisted. How can we suppose the King has been deceived respecting the public opinion of an operation so universally condemned? How may he be excused, since his ministers themselves have informed him that he was in danger of, perhaps forever, casting from him, at the very commencement of his reign, the title of well-beloved, of which he was so ambitious? Here we at least behold the ambiguous morning of a cloudy reign.

The Queen is not satisfied with the choice that has been made of Count Brühl, neither is she with the regulations of her household, and therefore she is again contracting debts. She is allowed, for expenses of every kind, only 51,000 crowns per annum. It will be difficult for her to make this sum supply her real wants, her generous propensities, and her numer-

ous caprices. Blind to the amours of the King, she can see
the disorder of his domestic affairs. The day before yesterday there was no wood for the fires of her apartments. Her
house steward entreated the steward of the royal palace to
lend him his assistance. The latter excused himself because
of the smallness of his remaining stock. How, you will ask,
can disorder so indecent happen? Because the quantity consumed was regulated by the late King, on the supposition
that the Queen and her children resided at Potsdam. Since
his death no person has thought of the necessary addition.
Such incidents, trifling as they are in themselves, prove to
what excess carelessness and the defects of inconsistency are
carried.

Count Brühl was waited for in order to furnish the house
of the princes. As he is overwhelmed by debts, and is a Saxon
nobleman ruined, it was requisite the King should cause the
sum of 20,000 crowns to be paid at Dresden, to satisfy the
most impatient of his creditors. Opinions concerning him
are divided.

The only points on which people are unanimous are, that
he is one of the flock of the elect (the mystics), and that he
plays exceedingly well on the violin. Those who have been
acquainted with him fifteen years ago speak in raptures of
his amenity. Those whose knowledge of him is more recent
are silent. Those who are totally unacquainted with him say
he is the most amiable of men. His pupil smiles when he is
praised. It is affirmed that the grand duke has sent him here,
and that it is his intention to take him to himself whenever
he shall have the power.

The prince royal will soon be worthy the trouble of observation; not merely because Frederick II drew his horoscope
in the following terms—" I shall reign again in him," for perhaps he only meant by that to testify his contempt for the
present King; but because all things in him proclaim greatness, but ungraciousness of character; awkwardness, but a
speaking countenance; unpolished, but sincere. He asks the
wherefore of everything, nor will he ever be satisfied with a
reply that is not reasonable. He is severe and tenacious, even
to ferocity, and yet is not incapable of affection and sensibility.
He already knows how to esteem and contemn. His disdain

of his father approaches hatred, which he is not very careful to conceal. His veneration of the late King partakes of idolatry, and this he proclaims. Perhaps the youth is destined to great actions; and, should he become the engine of some memorable revolution, men who can see to a distance will not be surprised.

Launay at length departs; and, as I believe, solely from the fear which the ministry, or rather which Welner, has that the King should, in some weary or embarrassed moment, restore him to his place. His dismission has been granted to him only on condition that he would give up 25,000 crowns of arrears, which are his due. This is a shameful piece of knavery. They have exacted an oath from him that he will not carry off any papers that relate to the State. This is pitiable weakness. For of what validity is such an oath? He may afford you some useful, or rather curious, annotations. In other respects, the man is nothing, less than nothing.. He does not so much as suspect the elements of his own trade. His speech is perplexed, his ideas are confused; in a word, he could only act a great part in a country where he had neither judges nor rivals. But he is not, as he is accused of being, a malicious person. He is a very weak and a very vain man, and nothing more. He has acted the part of an executioner, no doubt; but where is the financier who has not? Where would be the justice of demanding the hangman to be racked because of the tortures he had inflicted in pursuance of the sentence which the judge had pronounced?

He will predict deficiencies in the revenue, and in this he will not be wrong; but he perhaps will not inform you, although it is exceedingly true, that economical principles, which are the guardians of this country, are already very sensibly on the decline. The service is more expensive, the houses of princes more numerous, the stables are better filled, pensions are multiplied, arrangements more costly, salaries of ambassadors almost doubled, the manners more elegant, etc. The greatest part of these expenses was necessary. The real misfortune is that there is no care taken for the proportionate increase of the revenue by slow, but certainly productive, means; and that they seem not to suppose there will be any deficiency, which will at length make an immense error in the

sum total; so that, without war, a long reign may see the end
of the Treasury, should the present measures be pursued. It
is not the prodigality of pomp which excites murmurs. It
is a prodigality in contrast to the personal avarice of the King
which is to be dreaded. It is an insensible, but a continual
wasting. Hitherto the evil is inconsiderable, and, no doubt,
does not strike any person; but I begin to understand the
country in the whole, and I perceive these things more distinctly than I can describe.

It was a custom with the late King, every year, on December 24th, to make presents to his brothers and sisters, the
whole sum of which amounted to about 20,000 crowns. This
custom the nephew has suppressed. A habitude of forty years
had led the uncles to consider these gratuities as a part of
their income; nor did they expect that they should have set
the first examples, or rather have been made the first examples,
of economy. Faithful to his peculiar mode of making presents, the King has gratified the Duke of Courland with a
yellow ribbon. It would be difficult more unworthily to
prostitute his order.

To this sordidness of metal, and this debauchery of moral,
coin, examples of easy prodigality may be opposed. The
house of the Jew Ephraim had paid 200,000 crowns, on account, for the late King, at Constantinople, during the Seven
Years' War. The money was intended to corrupt some Turks,
but the project failed. Frederick II continually delayed the
repayment of the sum. His successor yesterday reimbursed
the heirs of Ephraim.*

A saddler who had thirty years been the creditor of the
late King, who never would pay the debts he had contracted
while prince royal, demanded the sum of 3,000 crowns from
his present Majesty. The King wrote at the bottom of the
petition: "Pay the bill at sight, with interest at six per cent."

The Duke of Holsteinbeck is at length to go to Königsberg, to take command of a battalion of grenadiers. I have
elsewhere depicted this insignificant prince, who will be a boy

---

*It is curious to read, in the "History of the Seven Years' War" (Chap. ix) the ac-
count which this conscientious King gives of the corruption he attempted and the profusion with which he scattered the money of the uncircumcised Jew, but whom he takes
good care never to mention. It was the treasure of the State, and the State, with all its
goods and chattels, flocks and herds, biped and quadruped, serfs and Jews included,
were his—for "was he not every inch a King?"

at sixty, and who will neither do harm to the enemies of the
State nor good to his private friends.

The King has lately bestowed his order on four of his subjects. The one is the keeper of his treasury (M. von Blumenthal), a faithful but a dull minister. The second is the master
of his horse,* M. von Schwerin, a silly buffoon under the late
King, a cipher during his whole life, a perplexed blockhead,
and on whom the first experiment that was made, after the
accession, was to deprive him of his place. The third is his
Majesty's governor, a man of eighty, who has been kept at a
distance for these eighteen years past, and who is destitute
of talents, service, dignity, and esteem for his pupil, which
perhaps is the first mark of good sense he ever betrayed. The
last, who is not yet named, is Count Brühl, who is thus rewarded by titles, after receiving the most effective gratifications before he has exercised any office. What a prostitution
of honors! I say what a prostitution; for the prodigality with
which they are bestowed is itself prostitution.

Among others who have received favors, a mystic priest is
distinguished—a preacher of effrontery, who reposes on the
couch of gratifications, at the expense of 2,000 crowns. To
him add Baron Boden, driven from Hesse-Cassel, a spy of the
police at Paris, known at Berlin to be a thief, a pickpocket, a
forger, capable of everything except that which is honest, and
of whom the King himself said he is a rascal, yet on whom he
has bestowed a chamberlain's key. Pensions innumerable
have been granted to obscure or infamous courtiers. The
Academicians, Welner and Moulines, are appointed directors
of the finances of the Academy.

All these favors announce a prince without judgment, without delicacy, without esteem either for himself or his favors;
reckless of his own fame, or of the opinion of the public; and
as proper to discourage those who possess some capacity as
to embolden such as are natively nothing, or worse than
nothing.

The contempt of the people is the merited salary of so many
good works; and this contempt is daily more pointed; the
stupor by which it was preceded is now no more. The world
was at first astonished to see the King faithful to his comedy,

* Grand écuyer.

faithful to his concert, faithful to his old mistress, faithful to his new one, finding time to examine engravings, furniture, the shops of tradesmen, to play on the violoncello, to inquire into the tricks of the ladies of the palace, and seeking for moments to attend to ministers, who debate in his hearing on the interests of the State. But at present astonishment is incited if some new folly or some habitual sin has not consumed one of his days.

The new uniforms invented by his Majesty have this day made their appearance. This military bauble, prepared for the day on which men have the ridiculous custom of making a show of themselves, confirms the opinion that the sovereign who annexes so much importance to such a circumstance possesses that kind of understanding which induces him to believe that parading is a thing of consequence.

Is his heart better than his understanding? Of this men begin to doubt.

Count Alexander Wartensleben, a former favorite of the present King, who was imprisoned at Spandau for his fidelity to him, being sent for from the farther part of Prussia to Berlin, to command the guards, has lately been placed at the head of a Brandenburg regiment; and by this arrangement he loses a pension of 100 guineas, which was granted him by the King while prince royal. This frank and honest officer is a stranger to the sect in favor; and, after having languished in a kind of forgetfulness, finally receives a treatment which neither can be called disgrace nor reward. This is generally considered as a deplorable proof that the King, to say the least, neither knows how to love nor hate.

Mademoiselle Voss has been persuaded that it would be more generous in her to prevent her lover committing a folly than to profit by such folly; for thus is the marriage publicly called, which would have become a subject of eternal reproach whenever the intoxication of passion should have slumbered. The beauty, therefore, will be made a countess, become rich, and perhaps the sovereign of the will of the Sovereign, but not his spouse. Her influence may be productive of great changes, and in other countries might render Count Schulemburg, the son-in-law of Count Finckenstein, first minister. He has acted very wisely in attaching Struensee to himself,

who teaches him his trade with so much perspicuity that the
Count imagines his trade is learned. He has besides an exercised understanding, and an aptitude to industry, order, consistency, and energy. Aided by his tutor, he will find no
difficulties too great; and he is the man necessary for this
King, whose will is feeble and cowardly. The late King was
equally averse to men of many difficulties, but it was from a
conviction of his own superiority. Great talents, however,
are little necessary to reign over your men of Topinamboo.

The memorial against the capitation-tax, which has been
signed by Messieurs Hertzberg, Heinitz, Arnim, and Schulemburg, concludes with these words: "This operation, which
alarms all classes of your Majesty's subjects, effaces in their
hearts the epithet of well-beloved, and freezes the fortitude of
those whom you have appointed to your council." Struensee,
on his part, has sent in two pages of figures, which demonstrate the miscalculations that will infallibly be discovered
when the tax has been collected. Messieurs Werder, Gaudi,
and probably Welner, persist; and the King, who neither has
the power to resist a plurality of voices, nor that of receding,
dares not yet decide.

On February 15th he is to depart for Potsdam, where he
proposes to continue the remainder of the year; that period
excepted when he journeys into Silesia and Prussia.

The King has to-day advanced the Duke of Brunswick to
the rank of field-marshal. This is indubitably the first honorable choice he has made; and everybody approves his having
singly promoted this prince.

The Dutch envoy has thrown me into a state of great embarrassment, and into astonishment not less great. He has
asked me, in explicit terms, whether I consented that endeavors should be made to procure me credentials to treat
with the Princess of Orange, at Nimeguen. If deception
might be productive of anything, I should have imagined he
only wished to induce me to speak; but the question was accompanied with so many circumstances, all true and sincere,
so many confidential communications of every kind, and a
series of anecdotes so rational and so decisive, that, though
I might find it difficult to account for the whim he had taken,
I could not possibly doubt of the candor of the envoy. After

this first consideration, I hesitated whether I should mention the affair to you, from a fear that the presumption should be imputed to me of endeavoring to rival M. de Renneval; but, besides that my cipher will pass under the inspection of my prudent friend, before it will fall into the hands of the King or his ministers, and that I shall thus be certain he will erase whatever might injure me to no purpose, I have imagined it was not a part of my duty to pass over a proposition of so singular a kind in silence.

I ought to add farther, referring to the ample details which I shall give, after the long conference which I am to have with him to-morrow morning, that, if France has no latent intention, and means only to weaken the Stadtholder, in such a manner as that his influence cannot hereafter be of service to the English, the patriots are by no means so simple in their intentions. I have proofs that, from the year 1784 to the end of 1785, they were in secret correspondence with Baron Reede; and that they ceased precisely at the moment when the baron wrote to them: "Make your proposals; I have a *carte blanche* from the princess, and, on this condition, the King of Prussia will answer for the prince." I have also proofs that M. de Renneval cannot succeed, and that the affair will never be brought to a conclusion, "so long as negotiation shall be continued instead of arbitration." These are his words, and they appear to me remarkable. It is equally evident that the implacable vengeance of the Duc de La Vauguyon arises from his having dared to make love to the princess, and his love having been rejected.

I shall leave those who are able to judge of the veracity of these allegations; but it is my duty to repeat verbally the following phrase of Baron Reede: "M. de Calonne is inimical to us, and his enemy opens his arms to receive us. What is it that M. de Calonne wishes? Is it to be Minister of Foreign Affairs? A successful pacification of the troubles of Holland would render him more service, in such case, than the continuation of those troubles, which may kindle a general conflagration. I demand a categorical answer to the following question: Should it be proved to M. de Calonne that the Stadtholder is in reality come over to the side of France, or, which is the same thing, if he shall be obliged to come over,

will he then be against us? Has he any private interest which we counteract? Is it impossible he should explain himself? The chances certainly are all in his favor against M. de Breteuil, whom we have continually hated and despised. Wherefore will he spoil his own game."

I necessarily answered these questions in terms rather vague. I informed him that M. de Calonne, in what related to foreign affairs, continually pursued the line marked out by M. de Vergennes; that the former, far from coveting the place of the latter, would support him with all his power, if, which could not happen, he had need of his support; that a comptroller-general never could be desirous of anything but peace and political tranquillity; that whether M. de Calonne had or had not particular agents in Holland, was a fact of which I was ignorant (this Baron Reede positively assured me was the case, and probably was the reason of his afterward conceiving the idea of making me their substitute); but that he would suppose me a madman, should I speak to him of such a thing; and therefore if, as seemed very improbable, it were true that the Princess of Orange, on the recommendation of Baron Reede, should be capable of placing any confidence in me, it was necessary she should give this to be understood, through some medium with which I should be unacquainted, as, for example, by the way of Prussia; but it scarcely could be supposed that there would be any wish of substituting a person unknown in that walk to those who were already in the highest repute.

Baron Reede persisted, and further added, not to mention that M. de Renneval could not long remain in his station, the parties would undoubtedly come to a better understanding when the princess could speak with confidence; that confidence was a sensation which she never could feel for this negotiator. In fine, he demanded, under the seal of profound secrecy, a conference with me, which I did not think it would be right to refuse; and his whole conversation perfectly demonstrated two things: the first, that his party supposes M. de Calonne is totally their enemy, and that he is the minister of influence in this political conflict; and the second, that they believed him to be deceived. I am the more persuaded these suppositions are true, because he very strongly insisted, even

should I not receive any orders to repair to Holland, I should pass through Nimeguen, on my return to Paris; that, by the aid of the pledges of confidence which I should receive from him, I might sufficiently penetrate the thoughts of the princess, so as to be able to render M. de Calonne a true report of the situation of affairs, and what might be the basis of a sincere and stable conciliation. It is not, therefore, so much another person, instead of M. de Renneval, that they desire, as another Couette Toury, or some particular confidant of M. de Calonne. I shall conclude with two remarks that are perhaps important.

I. My sentiments and principles concerning liberty are so known that I cannot be regarded as one of the Orange party. There is, therefore, a real desire of accommodation at Nimeguen. And would not the success of this accommodation be of greater consequence to M. de Calonne than the machinations of M. de Breteuil? Wherefore will he not have the merit of the pacification, if it be necessary? And is it not in a certain degree necessary, in the present political state of Europe?

II. The province of Friesland has ever been of the anti-Stadtholder party, and it now begins to be on better terms with the prince. Is it not because there has been the ill-address of attacking the Stadtholder in some part hostile to the provinces, and in which neither the nobility nor the regencies do, or can, wish to see the Constitution absolutely overthrown? Has not the province of Holland drawn others too far into its particular measures?

These two considerations, which I can support by a number of corroborating circumstances, perhaps are worthy the trouble of being weighed. I shall send you, by the next courier, the result of our conference; but, if there are any orders, information or directions, to be given me on the subject, it is necessary not to leave me in suspense; for my situation relative to Reede is embarrassing, since I dare neither to repel nor invite advances, which most assuredly I never shall provoke, and which, by the well-avowed state of the Cabinet of Potsdam, it was even impossible I should provoke, had I been possessed of so much temerity.

Noldé has already written several letters to me from Courland, and mentions an important despatch in cipher, which

is to be sent by the next courier. But the evident result is that it is too late to save Courland; that everything which ought to have been prevented is done, or as good as done; and that the best physicians would but lose their time in prescribing for the incurable. The bearer of the letter, which occasioned the departure of Noldé, is a merchant of Liebau, named Immermann. He has been charged with the negotiation of a loan in Holland and elsewhere, but, as it is said, has met with no success. It is supposed in the country that the Duke has thrown impediments in its way. The Diet of Courland is to sit in January. It is worthy of remark that, for two years past, no delegate has been sent from Courland to Warsaw.

Good information is said to be received that four corps of Russian troops have begun their march, purposely to approach the Crimea at the time that the Empress shall be there; and this not so much to inspire the Turks with fear, as to remove the greatest and most formidable part of the military from the vicinage of St. Petersburg and the northern provinces of Russia; and especially from the grand duke, that there may not be any possibility of dangerous or vexatious events; for the unbounded love of the Russians for their grand duke is apprehended. Yet, if such terrors are felt, wherefore undertake so useless a journey, which will cost from 7,000,000 to 8,000,000 of roubles? So useless, I say, according to your opinions, for, according to mine, the Empress believes she is going to Constantinople, or she does not intend to depart.

The troops are to be divided into four corps, of 40,000 men each. The general of these armies will be Field Marshal Potemkin, who will have the immediate command of a corps of 40,000 men, and the superintendence of the others who are under him, to be led by General Elvut, Michaelssohn, and Soltikow. Prince Potemkin has under his particular and independent orders 60,000 irregular troops in the Crimea. It is whispered he entertains the project of making himself King of the country, and of a good part of the Ukraine.

THE FRANCO-AUSTRIAN CRISIS

BY

Prince von Metternich

CLEMENS WENZEL, PRINCE VON METTERNICH

1773—1859

Clemens Wenzel, Prince von Metternich, the eminent Austrian diplomat and statesman, was born at Coblentz in 1773 and died at Vienna in 1859. His father, Franz Georg Karl, Count von Metternich, was also an Austrian diplomatist, and an associate of Kaunitz. He represented a very ancient and distinguished family, whose original seat was in Julich. Young Metternich was educated at the University of Strasburg, and afterwards studied law at Mainz and traveled in England. In 1795 he married the grand-daughter and heiress of the celebrated minister, Kaunitz, by whom he acquired large estates. His diplomatic career commenced at the congress of Rastadt, which he attended as representative of the Westphalian counts. His rise was very rapid ; he added to the advantages of his birth and connections a more than ordinary share of diplomatic ability, with the most graceful and winning manners. In 1801 he became Austrian ambassador at Dresden ; and on the outbreaking of the third coalition war, he negotiated the treaty of alliance between Austria, Prussia, and Russia. In 1806 he went as ambassador to Paris, and concluded, in 1807, the treaty of Fontainebleau, very favorable to the interests of Austria ; but on the outbreaking of the war between France and Austria, in 1809, he was detained some time ere he could obtain his passport. In course of that year he succeeded Count von Stadion as minister of foreign affairs, concluded the treaty of peace with the French minister, Champagny, and accompanied the Empress Maria Louisa to Paris. He guided the course of Austria amid the difficulties of 1812–13.

Metternich maintained at first a temporizing policy and a scheme of an armed mediation of Austria ; but the obstinacy of Napoleon reduced him to the necessity of adopting at last a decided step, and led him to resolve upon that declaration of war by Austria against France, which took place in August, 1813, and he subsequently conducted with great ability the negotiations which ended in the completion of the quadruple alliance. On the eve of the battle of Leipsic, the Emperor of Austria bestowed upon him the princely dignity. He afterward went to Paris and signed the convention of Fontainebleau with Napoleon, and was sent to England to negotiate concerning a new quadruple alliance, and attended the congress of Vienna, of which he was unanimously elected president. He signed, as Austrian plenipotentiary, the second peace of Paris, November 20, 1815. After this, he continued still to conduct the diplomacy of Austria, and in 1821 was appointed chancellor. His efforts were earnestly directed to the maintenance of peace in Europe, and the preservation of the existing state of things in the Austrian dominions by the strictest measures of police and severe despotism. His memoirs, cast in the form of letters to Count Hudson and other diplomats, give a succinct and vivid picture of the troublous times in which he held the helm of the Austrian ship of state.

THE FRANCO-AUSTRIAN CRISIS

METTERNICH TO STADION, PARIS, APRIL 27, 1808

THE catastrophes which overthrew the throne of Spain are assuredly made to fill the measure of the crafty, destructive, and criminal policy of Napoleon; a policy which he has never ceased to follow since his accession. Let us be thoroughly persuaded of this truth, let us get rid of all illusion, and we shall gain that strength which comes only in great crises. The overthrow of Spain is not, so far as regards principle, more than the reunion of Liguria, the present organization of Holland, the hundred and one destructions that we have seen, and at which all the powers of Europe have looked on with more or less good will, with more or less calmness. The shock of a great throne's fall is terrible; it resounds afar, and yet principle is not more violated than it is by the march of the squadron that tears an unhappy Bourbon from his asylum to shoot him at Vincennes.

The sceptre of Charles IV has not been his for several years. He, the weak and feeble heir to the heritage of his fathers, and his unfortunate successor, are now summoned before a new and monstrous tribunal. A king who dare not abdicate in favor of his legitimate successor, and a son who dare not reign, except by the authority of a French ambassador, in reality reigns no longer. Your Excellency will see from the frightful article that I have marked in the semi-official Journal of April 24th, that this tribunal does exist; Spain then has no longer a sovereign; the arbiter of the Grand Empire has in fact declared himself its master. He has long shown that he is master of all Europe on this side the Inn and the Vistula.

In 1805 and 1806 I cherished the dream of opposing to this colossus a barrier marked out by the Weser, the Thuringian forests, and the western frontiers of the Austrian mon-

archy. Prussia has rejected the plans, which would save
herself and her neighbors; she must necessarily be the victim
of her selfish calculations, and not only Prussia, but all powers
who follow the same course, will be so.

This line, the only one which would cover our right flank,
and relieve us from all anxiety in our rear, and which—since
the peace of Presburg and the loss of Venice (the principal
and most precious of all the acquisitions that Austria can
make), above all since the cession of Dalmatia—only leaves
our left flank to be protected, can no longer be maintained.
Prussia is effaced from the list of powers; Turkey, whose
weakness is even a benefit to us, is an immediate point of
contact with France; we shall save her from total destruction
by our geographical position alone. She cannot be attacked
but by passing through us. To remain constant to old ideas,
to old and impracticable plans, would be destruction; to have
no plan would be ruin.

Austria and Prussia are intact; Turkey vegetates, but it
exists. Spain will no doubt change masters, her fall will
not alter our position; it adds nothing to the power of France.
Napoleon will return to his capital neither more strong nor
less troubled than when he left it. To hope that any time
will be allowed to pass without movement on his part would
be a mere illusion; to follow implicitly all his wishes would
be to carry out his projects for destruction; to oppose him
face to face would be to expose ourselves to be crushed under
his weight; we can then only aim at modifying his plans.
We must enter into them to have the right to do this; we must
have a firm and fixed plan to make this possible. To this all
my political calculations tend, and it seems to me that it is
to this end we ought to direct all our efforts.

We should be very wrong to despise what is going on in
Spain, but I freely confess that the fall of that throne is not a
surprise to me; my despatches testify that I have long believed
in the possibility of this catastrophe. Napoleon only lifts the
veil a little more—it is transparent enough—which covers his
general intentions; he himself thinks he has done nothing
extraordinary or new since his return from the Pyrenees.
Everything which is on this side the line of the confederation
seems to him so entirely under his good pleasure that the

changes he has made in Spain seem to him hardly greater than the nomination of his brother-in-law to the government of Piedmont. But as it is impossible that he should not look beyond the confines of what he calls his Empire, we shall no doubt be exposed to great complications in a short time. We have still the power of looking forward, of determining our wishes and our course; we shall not have the time or the possibility of doing so when direct questions are put to us. I am happy to feel convinced that our august master wisely occupies himself in determining the foundations of his future conduct. May he graciously permit me to touch upon some of the most threatening questions!

There remain three powers which may furnish battlefields to the man who cannot be satisfied without them—Austria, Russia, and Turkey. An alliance, however monstrous it may be, guarantees Russia for the time from a direct attack. Nothing points to any hostile views of Napoleon against Austria; all the measures he has taken for some time aim at the destruction of the Porte. It can only be saved by the firm will and close agreement of the cabinets of Vienna and St. Petersburg, by immediate peace with Russia, and by a successful war of these two imperial courts against France. It will not suffice, for Turkey to avoid the blows which Napoleon is preparing, that we should stand on one side; our inaction would not save her, and it would ruin us.

All the powers—I except England, who, having committed the mistake of signing the peace of Amiens, did not make another by not preparing at once for a new war—have lost by attaching to the treaties they concluded with France the importance of a peace. Peace does not exist with a revolutionary system, and whether Robespierre declares eternal war against the Châteaux, or Napoleon makes it against the powers, the tyranny is the same, and the danger is only more general. To believe that we can continue beyond a certain time quiet spectators of the changes present and to come in Europe, and to found this hope on the promises of France, would be strangely to deceive ourselves. If France invites us to rest, it should only be another motive to prevent us from confounding this offer with a state of calm and quiet, which must be renounced so long as Napoleon lives.

Turkey is threatened; she will fall, because this man has never threatened in vain, and because I see nowhere the necessary means of saving it.   Therefore all the anxieties with which the complications resulting from this overthrow can inspire us, far from paralyzing us, should stimulate our faculties. Shall we refuse to act in concert? they will act without us. Shall we refuse a passage to the French troops through our territory? we must then be ready to fight to stop them, or see them effect the passage against our will.   It remains to discover whether our refusal would not suit Napoleon better than our consent.

Nothing assuredly can be more dangerous than to admit French troops into our territory; the recent example of Spain proves this sufficiently.

Your Excellency knows that I have always held that the salvation of Austria and Russia depends on their perfect agreement on all questions of common interest.   Let us suppose that it is possible to establish this agreement, the order of things should be, that these two powers should use all their efforts to dissuade Napoleon from the destructive projects against the Porte, but that they should end by taking common part in it, in case their efforts should be fruitless.   It will then be a question of diplomatic and, above all, military measures, to guard the two empires against the enterprises which the French may attempt beyond the lines which their troops must traverse.   At that moment the Austrian and Prussian armies which are not destined to act in Turkey (and there would remain great masses) should be regarded as one and the same army, and take military positions strong enough to allow them to close the way behind the French armies. Supposing, on the contrary, that the Cabinet of St. Petersburg continues to follow as imprudently as it does the impulsion it receives from France; that it even exaggerates it, as it has not ceased to do—in that supposition it becomes only more urgent to take an active part in projects impossible even to modify, if we do not enter into them immediately.   If France and Russia agree to the destruction of Turkey, and ask of us a passage for the French troops, shall we refuse it?   I suppose that we might refuse it, and that the interests the two allies would have in our not troubling their plans, or hindering their execution, would prevent them from insisting on this demand; but how should we oppose the return of the French army after having conquered Turkey?

Your Excellency sees that I here maintain the possibility that the French armies might arrive at Constantinople only by way of Albania and Ukrania. I do not know whether this possibility exists, but it hardly seems probable that, even in that case, Napoleon would long make the troops respect the neutrality of Galicia by taking them along the frontier.

I resume this long and doubtless too minute reasoning. It appears to me certain—

I. That it is impossible to regard a state of peace with France as a state of repose.

II. That the return of Napoleon after his expedition to Spain will be the signal for fresh movements.

III. That the Western part of Europe being conquered, and having submitted to changes of dynasty and government which Napoleon has long meditated, he can only direct his activity toward the East.

IV. That everything indicates that the partition of Turkey is the first object to which it tends.

V. That an alliance, offensive and defensive, between Russia and Austria, having for its object a successful war against France, alone can arrest Napoleon in his projects.

VI. That this alliance, considering the moral and physical dispositions of the two empires, not being possible, it is essential to think of an agreement likely to guarantee their mutual existence.

VII. That if we cannot arrive at an agreement with Russia, by persuasion, to stop the destructive plans of Napoleon against the Porte, it would be necessary to take an active part in them; that even if Turkey could be protected from the danger which threatens it, it would be no less necessary to concert measures for opposing the restless activity of that prince.

VIII. That if Napoleon does not renounce this attack, which he could scarcely undertake without us, it would be necessary to take diplomatic and military measures to prevent him from departing from the line of conduct agreed upon.

I should look upon this last enterprise as entirely chimerical, if the conquest of Turkey presented as few difficulties as that of Portugal, and if we were as isolated and as weak as Spain; if we had the *élite* of our army in the Baltic, a sovereign such as Charles IV, and ministers such as the Prince de la Paix. But it is in these important matters that the difference of our position from that of Spain consists. Our dangers are great—they are imminent; the fall of the last throne of the Bourbons does not augment them; it will have been an immense benefit if it arouses generally a feeling of indignation, and with us in particular the conviction that peace with Napoleon is not peace, and that we can only save ourselves by the wisest activity, and by the constant employment of our powerful resources.

METTERNICH TO STADION, PARIS, JUNE 23, 1808

Your Excellency sends me reports from our military commanders which render it necessary to keep a watch on the movements of the French army. The remarks of these officers agree with the rumors heard throughout Europe; an imposing force is placed on one of our frontiers, furnished with everything necessary to enable it to cross it. At Paris and in Germany nothing is heard of but the approaching war with Austria; motives often the most ridiculous are alleged for this war. They are sometimes our pretended armaments; sometimes the petitions which they have made to us for the good of the Church and its visible head; sometimes a guarantee that they have demanded our neutrality in case of a rupture between France and Russia. Others say that the Emperor of the French will not any longer endure our imperial title; that we wish to make war on the Turks and divide the spoil with Russia, or rather that we intend to conclude with the Porte a treaty against France. I make here a short *résumé* of the rumors which are circulated, giving a list of specimens; each day destroys those of the evening before, but only contradicts the motives of the war; the rumor of war continues, and nothing contradicts that rumor.

An immense responsibility would rest on the head of the man who should take upon himself to assert the pacific intentions of Napoleon. Your Excellency knows my way of

thinking entirely. His imperial Majesty has often deigned to appreciate my opinion ; there is certainly in me no partiality for a man whom, I believe, I long ago judged more truly than many of his contemporaries. The great confidence of our august master, and that of your Excellency, authorize me to supply as soon as possible, by a reasoning which I have based upon facts, what is lacking in positive data on the great question. Does Napoleon wish to make war with us at the present time or not ? Every sign answers in the affirmative. Our situation is different from what it was before the end of the last war with Prussia ; we no longer go through the intermediate steps which formerly were necessary to precede the opening of a campaign. Napoleon has no preparations to make ; he has 200,000 men in front of us, on our two flanks, and at our rear. He has not to pass the Rhine with the new troops to fall on us : he can enter Galicia before we know at Vienna that he has made war upon us ; he might invade a great part of the Austrian kingdom, and the event would make no more sensation or noise than five or six years ago the arrival of a French squadron in the Margraviate of Baden would have done. Such is the situation of Europe—such is ours in particular.

We cannot, therefore, any longer stop at possibilities ; we must simply calculate probabilities. Napoleon meditates our destruction ; he meditates it because our existence is incompatible, as to principles, and as to the extent of our territory, with a universal supremacy, to which at this moment three powers are opposed, Russia, Austria, and Spain on the part of the Bourbons. The first two up to the present time are but inert masses : the latter will succumb under the weight of the French power. Will Napoleon make war against Austria before having subdued Spain sufficiently to be able to abandon the King he has just proclaimed to his own forces ? Will he make war on us without being certain of the side Russia would take on this occasion ? It seems to me that these are the two points to which all our calculations should be directed.

The different reports which I have added to my preceding despatch must have proved to your Excellency that the submission of the Peninsula will cost great efforts. It seems

that the almost general rising was not foreseen by Napoleon;
we have never before seen him enter on a campaign without
strong reserves; on this occasion he had none. We do not
flatter ourselves that the devotion of the Spanish nation will
prevent its fall; it will succumb as all isolated efforts must;
but at any rate it will make a vigorous resistance; it seems
susceptible of organization and to necessitate strong measures; besides, the season is advancing.

If Napoleon thinks his presence necessary for the subjuga-
tion of a people in revolt, there is all the more reason we
should do him the justice to believe that he would not trust
the management of an enterprise such as the annihilation of
the Austrian monarchy to any other than himself. The affairs
of Spain will not exempt us, except by some extraordinary
chance, from fighting for our very existence. But I do not believe that Napoleon will try this adventure before having finished with the other, thus exposing himself to the probable mis-
carriage of a plan so long conceived, and with the success of
which the fate of one of his brothers and the sort of prestige
which up to this time has accompanied all his enterprises are
intimately connected. Nothing offers less foundation for the
calculation of probabilities than an insurrection; it may be
prolonged indefinitely, it may cease to-day or to-morrow; but
we are in the middle of the year, and I do not think this is
quite the time he would choose by preference for the opening
of a campaign which, although directed toward the South,
may bring complications in the North.

Your Excellency has observed very judiciously the danger
there would be in agitating officially questions which up to
the present time have not been touched upon. This reflection would have always prevented my doing so, except by
express command, even if the Emperor were in Paris. It
nevertheless appeared to me very important to take a step
which, without committing us, may help to clear up a few
questions. I have after mature deliberation decided on the
following, which, being very frank and loyal, must necessarily confuse the adverse party, a position always favorable
to the cause one pleads.

Reports are circulated which succeed each other with a
rapidity which prove direct machination. Whether Napoleon

spreads them or tolerates them, the inference that we draw from the fact and the results are the same; he knows these reports. I went to the Minister of Police. I said to him that for a long time I had been tempted to speak to him of these things, but that I always despised common reports too much to be able to make up my mind. " The case is changed now," continued I. " I receive news from Vienna which proves to me that these same reports are spread there; my letters from Germany contain the same; and there is such similarity in the accounts, which contain too much nonsense to have been invented in perfect agreement in the four corners of Europe, that I cannot but see them to be the result of machinations. I do not enquire the source—that is nothing; but it is necessary that you come to my help to combat these reports. The pacific intentions of my court are known; personally you know my way of thinking; it is not necessary to prove to you that we do not dream of war—no one even asserts it—but to reassure the Austrian, French, and German public of your intentions with regard to us. These are times when one cannot be silent without becoming an accomplice with those who speak; for some time I have had no complaint to make against your journals, but now give me an opportunity of praising them. Have an article inserted which will prove to all readers that our relations are perfect; contradict distinctly the intentions they attribute to you, and which you allow them to attribute to you. On every occasion here I pronounce myself a minister of peace; furnish me with a good weapon to justify to my court the opinion I have always declared of the sincerity of the Emperor's intentions with regard to us."

" I know all these tales," said Fouché. " I am ignorant of their origin; but my reports to the Emperor have always been to the effect that you would lose no opportunity of contradicting them and declaring them to be completely false. You understand that I cannot approach the political question,. Does the Emperor wish to make war upon you, or not? He does not tell me, and I have no right to ask him; if you wish to know my private opinion, I will tell you that I believe he neither wishes nor would do it. To-morrow I will cause an article to be inserted in a journal in the sense you desire; you

understand that I cannot say all I would wish, but I will tell the truth. I detest rumors of that kind. Does the Emperor spread them? He allows them, there is no doubt, for he can stop them in a moment. Does he wish to occupy the nation, to distract its attention from a point which has not gained its assent? Does he wish to impose upon you? Is he afraid that you will seize this opportunity to declare war against him? Does he believe that you will not recognize the changes he is effecting in Spain, in consequence of your rights over that Crown? I know not, but I am too anxious for peace not to seize with pleasure an occasion for serving that cause. All military men, officers, generals, and marshals, are for war. Since the latter have been dukes, they wish to be archdukes, and so on. I believe that a war with you would be not merely, as any war would be, a misfortune: it would have the particular character of dragging the universe into the waves, for where would this scourge stop? When war had been made on you, Russia would remain, and then China. In short, I detest war, and the rumors of which you complain, for they will end sooner or later in leading to it. No one knows better than I do how this concatenation is brought about: all military men wish for war and collect such rumors; there is no wretched maker of projects who does not bring his ideas to the Emperor; his agents and foreign spies, who are all rogues, make their reports in that sense, to pay their court; and the Emperor ends by believing them. To-morrow you shall have an article as good as it is possible for me to make it."

I had no difficulty in agreeing with the minister's opinions. I observed to him that if the Emperor allowed these rumors, with the intention of holding us in check, he deceived himself altogether. We can be won by confidence, but are only estranged by the contrary. "What do you say, for example," continued I, " of the manœuvring of troops which has placed your Silesian army in the most menacing position on our frontier? Why is each officer of that same army allowed to spread the report that in a short time that frontier will be free? The Emperor Francis is animated by one desire, that of peace and harmony between the two courts; he has never ceased to give proofs of this, and his wish is based on the true interests of his Empire. Napoleon, and all the alarmists who

surround him, cannot suspect him. It would be madness on our part to provoke a war with France; it would be weakness not to repulse an attack with vigor. Consider our policy from this point of view, and you will know the whole secret of our policy." Fouché interrupted me to ask if the news I had just told him of a movement of the French army was in a public newspaper, as in that case he would contradict it. " No," said I, " all the reports from our frontiers bring it, and the result has been a sudden fall in the stocks, which cannot be indifferent to us. We defend the same cause; why should influence be used unfavorable to our credit? " Fouché told me that the following day he would take care to ascribe the fall of stocks to speculation. He spoke very frankly with respect to the publication of a report of the death of the King of England * by the Minister of Foreign Affairs, and used among other energetic phrases the following: " I am glad that M. de Champagny has put his name to such an article rather than I; I never would have done it; there is in the publication of a thing known to be false something unworthy of the master and his servant."

It is impossible that Fouché does not know the real source of the disquieting news which was the subject of our interview. He asked me if I had written to Champagny. I told him no, and that if Champagny were here, I should have preferred to speak to him of a thing which I deplore equally as a friend to peace, as a cosmopolitan, and as Austrian ambassador. " I have no complaints to make," said I to him; " no question has been opened between the two courts, still less a subject of any discussion whatever."

Fouché does not, then, oppose the Emperor's intentions, by slipping in articles of more or less tranquillizing views. I have said above that it did not appear to me that it could be intended by the Emperor to subdue Spain and make war upon us at the same time.

A new point of view, which struck me the more inasmuch as I did not yet know the proclamation of Palafox, was that of our pretensions to the Crown of Spain.†

---

* Apparently a false report of the death of the King of England was circulated at this time : he did not die till 1820.

† In the proclamation of the Spanish General Palafox, May 25, 1808, a reference was made to the Archduke Charles of Austria, nephew of Charles III, as King of Spain.—Ed.

Might it not be possible that this was the principal motive of all the reports, which Napoleon spreads and visibly maintains, to keep us, so to speak, at bay? A direct analogy comes to support this supposition. Your Excellency will remember that, at the time of my negotiation at Fontainebleau, there was a ridiculous vehemence in the demand for my recognition of the new King. The Emperor, who, more than anyone, sacrifices to his prejudices, believed that he could more easily obtain the cession of a province than the recognition of the Kings, his brothers; I am not astonished to find the same fear in him at the present moment.

I hope your Excellency will treat the present report with indulgence. It is useless to tell you of the singular position in which I am placed. Deprived, since the departure of M. de Talleyrand, of all means of contact, or connection, otherwise than by writing (the most sterile of all), with the Government with whom I am charged to overlook and defend our interests, deprived even of all means of control in the official way, I am alone, entirely isolated, crushed with an immense responsibility. I should be an alarmist if I were credulous; I should be a quietist if I despised these same rumors.

I would rather risk falling into snares, such as those which befell M. de Lucchesini, than lead my court into error by not giving the alarm. My reports have for some time rather borne the impress of alarm than that of extreme security. It is not with the latter feeling that, at this moment, I have the conviction that we shall not be attacked by France immediately. When shall we be? I do not know, but it is in the nature and policy of Napoleon that it will be at the very first moment that appears favorable to him. I do not believe that he would prefer the present time. But it may immediately become favorable, and it is with extreme satisfaction that I see efforts made, by our august master, well calculated for the good of his house and his States.

METTERNICH TO STADION, PARIS, JULY 1, 1808

If it is difficult to know exactly what Napoleon's plans are, it is possible to understand them to a certain extent by agreements which are much more the result of a military arrangement than mine; but data furnished by an observer, however little instructed he may be, if he is impartial, are precious to the head of military affairs. They acquire much value when they are based on certain facts.

Your Excellency has for some time heard the formation of camps spoken of, which the French armies are to form in Prussia. The scarcity of food in many provinces, the total ruin of the inhabitants of the towns, serve as a pretext, and were perhaps the real reason of these assemblies. Camps are to be formed near Stargard, Berlin, etc.

Subsequent orders assign them a different direction. The troops of Davoust and De Mortier (comprising the Saxons and the Polonese, about 120,000 strong) have received orders to assemble in the neighborhood of Schweidnitz, in Silesia. It is doubtless this movement which has thrown Bohemia into alarm.

The Marshals Soult and Victor, instead of remaining on the right bank of the Oder, are to form two camps near New and Old Ruppin and Rathenau. (Their divisions may be estimated at nearly 70,000 men.)

An army of nearly 20,000 men is to assemble at Merve, on the Vistula.

The idea is secretly being put forward, that the Prussian Government, to lighten their expenses in a moment of extreme penury, will include in the inventory to the French troops the fortresses in Silesia, which they have not yet occupied.

These measures, which I can answer for as exact, seem to be adjourned. The Court is more able than I am to observe the movements of the French troops in Silesia, but it is the fact that a concentration there seems really necessary in consequence of the want of food in the provinces in which the troops are, who, after this movement, will encamp in the most fertile and best preserved part of the Prussian monarchy.

I hope his imperial Majesty will allow me to submit to him a slight sketch which, bearing simply on the military operations, is perhaps on my part only a foolish dream. But I take the map in hand and calculate by analogy: all Napoleon's campaigns resemble each other!

Is it not easy to see in the army of Silesia the principal body, which would be destined to operate in a short straight line toward the centre of the kingdom? Penetrating Moravia, it isolates Bohemia, divides Galicia; it is sixty leagues to Vienna, and would penetrate Hungary as easily as Galicia.

Might not the camps of Rathenau and Ruppin be regarded as the reserves of the principal army?

The assembled army near Merve is obviously only for observation on the Vistula, and is strong enough to dispute some important passages.

Napoleon's movements are always concentric: he does not act from one point alone. The first control of this plan would be the certain connection of the different armies in country formerly Venetian; this would establish a basis of operations of which the extreme angles would be in Italy and Silesia. Austria and Bohemia would be conquered by the fact of the entry of the enemy into Moravia, or at least would find themselves so much beyond the lines that, their defence being impossible for us, their attack would be useless. The troops of Marmont would penetrate Hungary lower down, and any success on the part of the Italian army would immediately send us back into the centre of the kingdom. The Bavarian and Confederate armies would occupy in this manner without difficulty the provinces within their reach. We ought, then, to calculate our defensive measures as if we had a war to sustain against Prussia and France united. Are they not really united under one chief, with more powerful moral and physical means than those which they had formerly?

This plan is, no doubt, only practicable on the supposition of the most perfect impassibility of Russia.

Her army is composed of twenty-three divisions, of which six are in Moldavia and Wallachia, with from 8,000 to 10,000 Cossacks; four in Finland; four in Courland, Livonia, and on the coasts of the Baltic; three never move from Siberia and the Caucasus.

There remain five divisions in the Polish provinces, to which must be added the greater part of the cavalry of the divisions, which are in Finland. These five divisions, which may amount to about 90,000 men, are then the only ones which, in the first moments of an energetic declaration on the part of Russia, we could count upon; but they would probably commence their operations by retaking Galicia, against which no doubt all the moral and military means would be used at first by the French. Could we indeed count, after the first defeat, on the help of a power which was afraid to decide before the hostilities, and would not that help be so tardy as to destroy the chances a victory might offer. I will sum up.

We have, then, an army of nearly 220,000 men, who can begin a campaign on our back and on our flank, in Silesia and in Prussia. This army has lately divided itself into a first line, a reserve, and a corps for observation on the Vistula.

The orders for this division of the army have not been carried out up to this moment.

There are, then, motives for this adjournment, and these motives are, no doubt, the efforts necessitated by the insurgent Spaniards.

This same army has not to wait for immediate reënforcements; all who can possibly be collected are transported in haste toward the Pyrenees.

The Emperor wished to call the conscription of 1810, but strong representations of the extreme youth of the individuals who would compose it have made him prefer to draw from the reserve of 1802, the only one which has not been employed, a measure which will make a great sensation, because it bears only on men established in homes of their own. I have no data of the number of men it can furnish, but we shall soon see it published.

The produce of the new conscription will no doubt, in the first instance, bear toward the coast of Spain, but as certainly will go to recruit the armies in Prussia the day the insurrection is put down.

We have at this moment to direct our means of defence against an army equal in number to our own, and which is disposed at all vulnerable points, not only of the frontier, but even of the interior of our empire.

Does not this embarrassing position demand measures prompt, because fate has given us a moment of respite; energetic, because after them we can dispose of no more? Should secondary considerations prevent precautions which our welfare imperiously demands?

To provoke a war with France would be madness; it must therefore be avoided, but it can only be avoided by strong measures. Those which his imperial Majesty has arranged—all the last military steps—have assuredly tended to put the army on the most respectable footing; but our army, however strong, good, and well ordered it may be, is it in number sufficient to prevent the final ruin of a monarchy attacked on all her frontiers at one time, and deprived at the opening of a campaign of her most precious resources and most important provinces? It is, therefore, not in ourselves alone that we must seek our safety; it is as necessary for our political intelligence as our military measures.

I look upon the present moment as the last in which it will be possible for us to open up chances of preservation; these chances are frail, because, according to my calculations, they depend only on Russia.

It appears to me urgent, and, I should say, of the last urgency, to explain ourselves very frankly, and, above all, very directly with that power. What can there be of a dangerous nature in the following declaration, which a prudent and penetrating ambassador would make, of the urgency of the case? He would say to Alexander:

"Our position becomes more embarrassing day by day. Two hundred thousand men threaten to penetrate the interior of our kingdom. France herself accredits the rumor; she forces us to measures of precaution, which she tolerates because she does not fear them, but of which she will make a grievance the first day she requires a pretext. We wish nothing from anyone: we only wish for peace; but we can only insure it by uniting with you; you owe your existence to our preservation. Not to wish for peace is not to wish to save your existence. Look at Spain. The day which sees the reigning dynasty descend from that throne is an appeal to all the sovereigns; we would never allow a proposal that you should descend from yours. What will you say the day that proposition is made to the Emperor Francis? It is not in the nature of things that two powers should come to an understanding at the time of a crisis, and even if they did, they would do more harm than could be conceived. We demand from you, therefore, a positive declaration of the course you will take when Napoleon, on his return from Spain, or regarding that conquest as certain, will turn his attention toward the East. There he will encounter Austria, Turkey, and lastly, Russia. Are you in agreement with him about the division of Turkey? We will put ourselves on one side: but he cannot amuse both of us with projects tending only to the removal from the centre of our empires of the strength necessary for our own defence. If he wishes to attack us what part will you play? Do you wish to prevent war? Then, pronounce against it with energy at Paris itself, and the odds are against Napoleon forcing it on us.

" Are you afraid to take this step, which the tone of conversation throughout Europe authorizes you to take, the duty of which is even imposed upon you? At least let us agree about military measures; that in the first moment of hostilities we may regard your army in Poland as the right wing of ours, your armies in Moldavia and Wallachia as reserves. Let us combine a military plan on this principle, the only one which would make the French troops against us infinitely more feeble than ours. Let us, at any rate, base a plan of operation upon it. Tell us, in the contrary case, that you will leave us to our own resources, that you will allow the Galicians to rise without being afraid for your Polish provinces, and that you consider yourselves powerful enough to stand alone, while you are afraid to support us. It is necessary that we should have a prompt and precise reply on all these points, and we only wait for that to regulate our political and military conduct."

In admitting the first proposition we should only be fulfilling our duty, a duty dictated to his imperial Majesty by what he owes to his house and his subjects. We should have lost nothing by admitting the second, and we should, in one way or the other, have put an end to the state of uncertainty about our existence and means of defending ourselves against attack, which is often more painful than annihilation itself. Besides, none of the above reasons which I have put into the mouth of our negotiator in Russia is new to them. The Count de Tolstoy always spoke in that tone, and it is impossible that the evidence of facts should not end by a triumph over the apathetic security of that Government.

I submit this report to his imperial Majesty as a proof of attachment and disinterestedness on the part of one of his servants; who, as to the first, will never change, and who proves the second by daring to give his views on military questions, which are beyond his province, for which he claims the indulgence of the enlightened men to whom they may be communicated.

METTERNICH TO STADION, PARIS, JUNE 23, 1808

I have a confused idea of having one day drawn your Excellency's attention to the editors of the Frankfort and Augsburg Gazettes.

There is a most urgent necessity to exercise some influence over newspapers in general, and particularly over these two, which never cease spreading lies, often of the most ridiculous nature, about us. It is from these that most of the articles are extracted which are found in the French journals. Why should not correct news be communicated to the different newspapers? Why do they not control their correspondents at Vienna, and why should they not refute these lies in the places where they are published?

A great fault which all the governments, and particularly our own, have committed since the commencement of the French Revolution, is that they have regarded as useless, as beneath their dignity and that of the good cause, and indeed even as dangerous, to speak truth to the public, and to speak it incessantly. This fact is never more incontestable than when the French are concerned. They have the game to themselves; they have only occupied an empty place by seizing the desks of the journalists, and no one can reproach them with silence; they have taken up the weapon we have disdained to make use of, and they are now employing it against ourselves.

The use of a thing is confounded everywhere with its abuse; the condition of a pamphleteer with that of a political writer; the man who reasons, with the one who simply relates correct facts! Public opinion is the most powerful of all means; like religion, it penetrates the most hidden recesses, where administrative measures have no influence. To despise public opinion is as dangerous as to despise moral principles; and if the latter will rise up even when they have been almost stifled, it is not so with opinion; it requires peculiar cultivation, a continued and sustained perseverance. Posterity will hardly believe that we have regarded silence as an efficacious weapon to oppose the clamors of our opponents, and that in a century of words!

Who can blame us if we will not allow the public to be supplied with lies about us?

There is not one of the above-mentioned papers which does not say under the heading of Vienna that we are in full negotiation on important points, or which does not publish lies about facts and individuals. The public cannot distinguish if news is true or false. False news has the air of being true if no one can be found to contradict it, and I place the Emperor Napoleon at the head of the credulous public. There is a great difference between what he conceives and what is insinuated to him; it would be found very difficult to change what he wishes, but his credulity may be imposed upon.

I beg your Excellency to pay particular attention to this subject. Nothing is more easy than to avoid the official style in these publications, which have no merit if they bear that impression. I speak to you from a place where, more than anywhere else, I can appreciate the success of the efforts of the government to influence the public. The newspapers are worth to Napoleon an army of 300,000 men, for such a force would not overlook the interior better, or frighten foreign powers more, than half a dozen of his paid pamphleteers.

METTERNICH TO STADION, PARIS, JULY 25, 1808

The courier Beck has brought me the despatches sent by your Excellency.

I send him back at once with the news which, according to all accounts, demands the chief attention of his imperial Majesty.   He will be convinced that we have arrived at the moment when the intentions of Napoleon toward us are becoming manifest.   .   .   .*

The great question of peace and war is being agitated, for how can the remarks which are made on our military armaments be otherwise described?

Does Napoleon believe the moment has come to throw off the mask, and execute plans which he has long delayed?

Does he find the present moment suitable to his interests, and does he merely wish to be enlightened as to the organic measures which, by augmenting our real strength, might at any time be inconvenient to him; and which his suspicious nature may lead him to regard otherwise than in the defensive character they so clearly bear?

If we admit the first supposition, we can hardly avoid war; on the second supposition we might do so, unless we directly provoke it.   Eight or ten days should suffice to discover what is Napoleon's real plan.

The course he has followed for some time resembles his well-known tactics, when he wishes to begin a quarrel.   In preceding despatches I have shown my way of judging of the warlike rumors which for some time he has himself positively encouraged; by these rumors he provokes us to take measures for our safety, then he asks us why we are alarming our neighbors: such is constantly his manner of proceeding.   These same rumors have, during the latter part of the Emperor's stay at Bayonne, acquired great intensity among the hangers-on of the court, even in the imperial family itself.   The Emperor gives no explanation.   I receive these facts from an absolutely authentic source.

From the same data which I have quoted, the conviction is forced upon me that the present moment is not the one Na-

---

* The enclosures with this despatch are a letter of Champagny to Metternich, dated Bayonne, and the answer dated Paris.

poleon would choose for opening up complications with us, and that it will be only if we ourselves wish to make war that it will be made upon us.

If we reflect that Napoleon has but to say the one word— " disarm ! "—to place us in the alternative either of making war or of remaining in a state of weakness which would at once make us the victims of the least of his whims, we cannot deny that he has been moderate in the manner he has chosen to speak to us of our armaments. Is not this the beginning of a discussion of which we now first get a first glimpse? Has he not wished to discover our decision, rather than retard it? In eight days we shall know what we are to believe.

I have maintained the sound principle that, our measures being permanent, they cannot be regarded as offensive. I have compared them to the establishment of the conscription in all the States subject to French influence. If ever they ask us in a more peremptory manner for a reduction, I should find in what has gone before a text for all possible replies. France cannot demand from us the revocation of an organic measure suited to the spirit of the century, and provoked by her own example, without coming to this demand, simple, and explicit: " I wish you to be weak, because I and my allies wish to be strong, and remain so." Such is doubtless his real thought; but it is not in the nature of Napoleon to unveil himself thus. One can disperse an assembled army, but one cannot alter constitutional laws. It is therefore important to separate these two things, and to prove that our military measures come under the head of the last category.

METTERNICH TO STADION, PARIS, AUGUST 2, 1808

I send Count de Mier with the enclosed confidential note, which I received yesterday from M. de Champagny, dated Toulouse, July 27th. Your Excellency will find also the private letter to which I thought I ought to limit my reply.

All argument ceases at the reading of compositions such as those which M. de Champagny addresses to me. Does the Emperor wish to make war upon us?—does he wish to sound our inclination to make war upon him? However improbable this latter supposition may be, is it not nevertheless possible?

But neither one nor the other can alter the part we have to take. . . .

Your Excellency will see that I have confined my letter of to-day to explanations as frank as they are simple—as void of oratorical phrases as they are strong in reasoning and in facts. Nothing is left for Napoleon but the power of leaving it unanswered. That is what he did with the one I sent on July 22d; and this it is that makes me desire to approach him as soon as possible—a desire assuredly quite disinterested!

The present crisis is doubtless the most painful that can occur to the Austrian kingdom. Its fate, its existence will depend on the part the Emperor determines to take. To annul measures purely conservative would be to deliver itself bound, hand and foot, to the man who has never yet rewarded concessions except by fresh demands; directly to provoke war, and consequently to depart from the system which his Majesty has so wisely adopted, would be insanity. The question, therefore, will be to find a middle course, which will combine the safety of the Empire with the care required more for our own preservation than our relations with France, and will enable us to await the only end we may reasonably hope to arrive at—that of retarding as long as possible the explosion with which Napoleon will never cease to threaten us.

I have indicated, in one of the reports last sent, a plan for the union of one or more centres of troops, in a position remote enough to be able to offer the enemy a line of attack involving less risk than scattered bodies, which might be cut off or turned—a manœuvre at which he constantly aims. Would it not be possible to draw a political advantage from a measure which would really be military and conservative, by taking upon me to declare to Napoleon " that, in order to give fresh proof of his Majesty's intention not to act hostilely toward any point whatever occupied by the French armies or by the allies of France, and to silence the odious imputations of calumny, his Majesty had ordered a retrograde movement of his armies?" Is this possible, is it feasible in a military sense? It is not for me to decide, but I believe it my duty to suggest to my court the best means of opposing facts to imputations, the most worthy, and consequently the strongest, measure which can be opposed to the whims of a man who is

never so carried away by passion as not to desire to clothe the most odious enterprises with an appearance of right and reason, but unhappily too violent not to overthrow at the last any obstacle to his ridiculously gigantic views.

M. de Champagny, in his note, speaks of Russia; his assurance that she will never come to our assistance shows the Emperor's uneasiness.

He speaks of future arrangements in Europe; this can only refer to Turkey, for there is no need of our coöperation in those arrangements, which he reckons on establishing in States subject to his influence. Such are the measures which, many persons assert, the States of the Confederation will soon be able to submit to him, to satisfy his views as to a new title with which he will replace that of Protector.

As to the march of troops from the interior of France toward the Rhine, this is for the moment nothing but a vain threat. He can create a new army; we have, during the last twenty years, seen too many astonishing examples of such creations to doubt that with which he now threatens us, but it is a fact that he cannot at this moment send an army to the Rhine which would in any way deserve the name.

The Emperor must make a new conscription. His armies in Spain require considerable reënforcements; he must have a reserve in case he should wish to make war upon us. He has not too many soldiers, even supposing the contrary. Spain can no longer serve as a motive in the eyes of a nation indignant at the policy he has followed in that country. The Corps Législatif will soon reassemble. It will be necessary to find a pretext for the senatus-consulte; they will make use of us to demand that, which the nation will agree to willingly.

METTERNICH TO STADION, PARIS, AUGUST 2, 1808

I had barely finished the preceding despatch when I received the enclosed note from M. de Champagny, dated July 30th.

The despatches being concluded, I send the documents, and your Excellency may sign without retouching them. You will see that the questions have, if not changed, at any rate

taken a turn altogether different since the Emperor saw my letters to M. de Champagny, dated July 22d.

There is nothing to add to Champagny's last note, which is evidently dictated by the Emperor himself. He does not wish for war at this moment, but he will make war upon us before very long. This is the result I extract from a composition containing a crowd of considerations which I cannot enter into, not wishing to delay the courier's departure. It is sufficient for me to declare to your Excellency that if we act adroitly, if we know how to turn to our own profit the weak side Napoleon presents to us, we can, with less charlatanism than he, derive great benefit from the present position of affairs.

We will not allow ourselves to be imposed on by grand words; all he has said of his armies and of their number is false. If 60,000 men can march toward the Rhine, what is the meaning of the embarrassment the affairs of Spain are causing him? The enclosed sketches which I send to your Excellency are exact. But let us sacrifice some forms; let us keep from the excesses which he is committing; let us organize our real strength as far as possible without giving rise to complaints which appear only due to the less essential parts of our military organization; let us take him at his word, let him withdraw his troops; let him proclaim peace; let us in revenge punish the guilty, if any exist, at Trieste; let us yield to a pacific impulsion, if he will prove his intentions by facts—and we shall have attained a grand, an immense object, that of the adjournment of the war.

I cannot send to your Excellency the reply I shall make to M. de Champagny. I shall—not to delay the departure of the courier—be content with telling you that I will write to him to-morrow, and that by founding all I shall say to him on the constant desire of the Emperor to maintain peace, I shall leave the course open to my Court.

All seemed to announce the near arrival of Napoleon. Public opinion was divided as to the place where he would dismount. Many people asserted that he would avoid showing himself to the Parisians, and go to Rambouillet. He completely baffled that calculation, and arrived on the fourteenth, at four o'clock in the afternoon, at St. Cloud. We received the same day, at eleven o'clock P.M., the announcement of a diplomatic audience for the next day, his fête day. If his hasty and unexpected arrival at St. Cloud may have been caused by the reports that the public thought he would not show himself in Paris on August 15th, it may also have been caused by the desire of bringing about a scene unique of its kind and unlike anything that had occurred in diplomatic circles up to this time. He wished to speak to me, but not alone; he wished to do it in the face of Europe, and yesterday was on that account a day of very extraordinary interest.

After Napoleon had received the compliments of all the constituent bodies of the State, the Corps Diplomatique was introduced to the audience at the usual hour. The Nuncio not being there, I placed myself first. The Russian ambassador put himself at my right hand; the Dutch and other ministers continued the circle. The Turkish ambassador was the fifth or sixth in the line. All these details are of importance.

He commenced his round with me, and spoke to me of the heat of the past summer, of the health of my family, etc. He addressed questions equally insignificant to my neighbor; and after having hurried round very quickly, he returned to Count de Tolstoy, and said to him: " Well, you have good news from Finland? " The ambassador having confirmed this fact, " The English expedition," replied the Emperor, " has not been of much use to the King of Sweden; they have sent the troops to Spain who should have helped him. I am sorry that the English have not disembarked there 50,000 men; they may remain there one, two, even three months, they will not remain four."

Then, turning toward me, he said, with an air which did not usually announce the approach of a storm: " Well, and is Austria arming considerably? " " No, sire," I replied; " she

is but carrying out the organic measures which, since the
Peace of Presburg, she had conceived, but delayed. In doing
that, she only follows the example of many of her neighbors,
and maintains the position she ought to hold." Seizing upon
that, he said to me, with ample paraphrase, almost word for
word what is contained in the note of July 30th, which was
written to me evidently under his dictation by M. de Champagny. To repeat to your Excellency the replies which I made
to him, would be really to copy my letters to the Minister of
Foreign Affairs. I will content myself with gathering together
here the facts and phrases, which will clear the ground still
better than that correspondence.

The Emperor made no mention to me of the reserves; he
only spoke of calling out the militia, and especially of the
precipitation with which we had executed our military measures. "Do you want to attack anyone," added he, "or are
you afraid of someone? Has anyone ever seen such haste?
If you had put it at a year, or eighteen months, it would have
been nothing; but to order everything to be ready on July
16th, as if on that day you were to be attacked! You have by
that act given an impulse to the public mind which you will
find it very difficult to set at rest. You see what has passed at
Trieste: my consul has been insulted there. That fact alone
was sufficient to have caused war, if I had wished it. I have
treated Austria with much respect; she has not been deprived
of any of her importance. I could demand fifty millions from
Trieste; I have not done so. If ever I return there, I should
have to burn the city! I do not wish for war; I do not want
anything from you. The Emperor Francis, Count Stadion,
Count Metternich, M. de Champagny do not wish it; no sensible men wish it; and I, who know the course of human affairs,
I tell you that I believe we shall have it in spite of the wishes
of sensible people. An invisible hand is at play; that hand is
the hand of England. M. Adair * is again *en route* for Malta;
he has left Vienna quite satisfied. England has gained fifty
per cent. by your armaments—(what a good objection I could
have made to him!); since she hopes to entice you again, this

---

* Robert Adair, English Ambassador at Vienna from June, 1806, to May, 1809, was, as
Napoleon hints, removed from his post at Vienna in consequence of a secret understanding between Austria and England.—Ed.

has made her more tenacious, more intractable than ever. You force me to arm the Confederation, to tell them to hold themselves in readiness. You prevent me from withdrawing my troops from Prussia, and making them return to France. What I had ordered, fifteen days afterward I was forced by you to counter-order, withdrawing not less than 100,000 men.

"I am frank. You are ruining yourselves, you are ruining me. England can give you money, but not enough; and she gives me none. The States of the Confederation, already very unfortunate, are being ruined; and when all the male population of Europe are under arms, it will be necessary to raise the women! Can this state of things last? It must bring us to war against our will. What do you hope for? Are you in agreement with Russia? I do not believe it; but in that case you will present me a respectable line of defence! (These sentences were addressed as much to M. de Tolstoy as to me; that ambassador preserved the most imperturbable attitude.) But on the contrary supposition, what can you do against France and Russia united? And the first war with Austria will be a war to the death; you must either come to Paris, or I must make a conquest of your kingdom. Your armaments are equally displeasing to St. Petersburg. Do you know how this will end? The Emperor Alexander will tell you that he desires you to stop, and you will do it; and then it will be no longer you on whom I shall depend for the maintenance of tranquillity in Europe, it will be Russia. I shall not submit to you the future arrangements of many questions in which you are interested; I shall treat solely with Russia, and you will only be spectators."

From that I could not doubt that he intended to speak to me of Turkey (the Turkish ambassador being but three steps from me). "See," continued he, "the conduct held by your minister at Constantinople. He does all he can to fan the discord with France. We know all; the Turks tell us everything. You have taken steps about the Servians by which they recognize you as their sovereign. Is it by your armaments that you hope some day to go halves with us in our arrangements? You deceive yourselves. I will never allow myself to be imposed upon by an armed power. I will never treat with one who wishes to impose upon me."

I denied strongly all these supposed facts and ridiculously false assertions. I denied emphatically the negotiations with the Servians. I took up the position that our chief end was that of maintaining the Porte in its integrity; and that far from desiring its fall, we should regard its preservation as a safeguard to our interests; that consequently the imputations made to M. de Sturmer,* concerning which I had already had full explanations with M. de Champagny, were either based on gratuitous suppositions, or, if these accusations were true, on a direct contravention to the most explicit instructions which that minister had received, instructions the less doubtful inasmuch as they were founded on the very principles I was here to establish as our own.

This conversation, in which I replied with extreme frankness and the greatest calmness (replies which, indeed, were only paraphrases of my last letters), lasted an hour and a quarter. The Emperor did not raise his voice a single moment; he never quitted the tone and expressions of the most astonishing moderation. He would certainly have said the same thing in a more energetic fashion if we had been alone, and I should have replied to him in the same manner; here we had the appearance of chatting, and of making a political discursion, including and maintaining the most immediate interests of two great powers, touching on the intentions, the most secret relations past, present, and future, between these powers, and concerning the whole of Europe. A conversation such as this, in which the Emperor agitated the question of the division of Turkey before the representative of that power, is doubtless without example in the records of diplomacy.

It is superfluous to tell your Excellency of the effect which this long conversation produced on all who were present. Nothing else is spoken of in Paris: it was so extraordinary, and based upon antecedents of which those present were so completely ignorant, that the versions given of it and conjectures about it partake more of individual passions and desires.

The Emperor did not spare me some military discussions. He at first exclaimed about the uselessness of a national levy,

---

* Austrian Internuncio at Constantinople; father of the subsequent representative of Austria at the Porte.

then contradicted himself in declaring that measure useful under certain conditions; lastly, he blamed our excessive expenditure; a moment afterward he said he had no objection to the provisioning of our fortresses, declaring it a measure of pure defence. He replied to the objection I made as to his armies on the march, we having opposed no assembly of troops which could in any way bear an offensive character: " No, you have no assembly, but your troops are placed in such a manner as to be able immediately to form real *corps d'armées*. These are things," added he, " on which military men cannot be deceived."

I said to him, *à propos* of illusions, that like Prussia we wished to make the most of our real forces. " Believe me, sire, if you count our soldiers, we also count yours, and we know exactly what your strength is." He replied: " But you have 300,000 regular troops; you could have 400,000 if you liked, and what more would anyone have?" Alluding always to the levying of the militia, having laid down a series of principles as to the political views which Austria ought to entertain—very good principles—and having added, " You think the same," I said to him, smiling: " Not only do I think the same, sire, but I feel as if I were debating our interests with the Minister of Foreign Affairs of Austria, so true is much that your Majesty tells me; and assuredly nothing could less resemble a dispute between two powers than our present discussion." The Emperor smiled in his turn, and said to me: " You see, too, how calm I am." I have since seen how important he considered it that this shade in his conduct and proceedings should not escape me.

THE · WORLD'S
GREAT · CLASSICS

LIBRARY ·
COMMITTEE

JVSTIN McCARTHY

RICHARD HENRY STODDARD

ARTHVR RICHMOND MARSH, A.B.

PAVL VAN DYKE, D.D.

ALBERT ELLERY BERGH

· ILLVSTRATED · WITH · NEARLY · THREE ·
· HVNDRED · PHOTOGRAVVRES · ETCH ·
· INGS · COLORED · PLATES · AND · FVLL ·
· PAGE · PORTRAITS · OF · GREAT · AVTHORS ·

CLARENCE COOK · ART EDITOR

· THE · COLONIAL · PRESS ·
· NEW · YORK · LONDON ·

GOETHE AT WEIMAR.

Photogravure from the original painting by Wilhelm von Kaulbach.

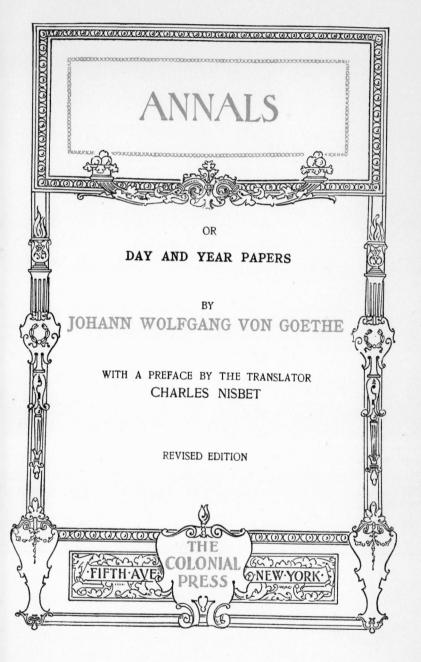

ANNALS

OR

DAY AND YEAR PAPERS

BY

JOHANN WOLFGANG VON GOETHE

WITH A PREFACE BY THE TRANSLATOR
CHARLES NISBET

REVISED EDITION

THE
COLONIAL
PRESS

FIFTH·AVE· ·NEW·YORK·

Copyright, 1901,
By THE COLONIAL PRESS.

TRANSLATOR'S INTRODUCTION

O F the circumstances in which "The Annals" originated and assumed its final shape, Goethe gives the following account, under date 1823, in his "*Biographische Einzelnheiten*":

"Cellini says, 'A man having reached his fortieth year, and convinced that he has accomplished something considerable, and lived an important life, should begin a biography of himself, faithfully writing down the eventful period of his youth, and the subsequent epochs as he advances in life.'

"Cellini is quite right, for undoubtedly the quick, capacious memory requisite for the comprehension of those early times grows gradually dim, and the charm of earthly sense disappears, a charm not to be replaced by the clearness of a cultivated understanding.

"Another important circumstance, however, in the case well deserves consideration. It is necessary not to stand too far aloof from our errors and faults, but, on the contrary, to feel so nearly related to them as to cherish a certain tenderness for them, to recall vividly the situations in which they came to pass, and not to feel ashamed of depicting them to their full extent. In later years all this assumes a different complexion, and at last in reference to such things one falls almost into the attitude of that geometrician who, at the end of a play, called out, 'But what, then, does all this demonstrate?'

"And as activity alone can deliver one from hypochondriac views, whether based on facts or fancies, a man must exert all his powers to transplant himself again into sympathy with the past, to recover that position whence he will look on a defect as a want he can afterward supply, on errors as things to be avoided for the future, on his precipitancy as a rashness

to be curbed, on neglected opportunities as resources he can
yet overtake.

"What, with a view to the purpose above indicated, we
have ourselves essayed and effected, what a junior pupil has
accomplished in the same direction, is, more particularly, as
follows:

"More than once, in the course of my life, I set before me
the thirty neat volumes of Lessing's works, regretted the excellent man especially in that he had lived to see the publication of only the first volume, and rejoiced in the faihtfully devoted brother who, being an active man of letters himself,
could not better express his attachment to the departed than
by unweariedly collecting and unintermittently expediting to
press the works, writings, smaller productions, and whatever
else had been left by the unique man which might serve to preserve his memory in its integrity.

"The man contemplating all this, and sensible of being in
a somewhat similar predicament himself, will not be deemed
presumptuous if he take himself to task and institute a comparison as to how far he has succeeded or failed; what has been
done by and for him, and what in any case it is yet incumbent
on him to do.

"And, accordingly, then, I have to rejoice in a special favor
of the Guiding Spirit. I see twenty volumes of æsthetic works
in regulated order before me, so many others attaching themselves immediately to these, next several to a certain degree
out of harmony with my poetic activity, so that I must fear the
reproach of scattered and disjointed labors. If indeed the man
is to be blamed who, while obeying the native impulse of his
mind, yet at the same time also urged by the demands of the
world, has made endeavors now in this direction, now in that,
and imposed manifold tasks on himself at a time usually allowed for repose.

"There has been, no doubt, this misfortune in such a case,
that important plans were not so much as entered upon, and
many a praiseworthy undertaking was left to perish in its inception. I refrained from executing a great deal in the hope
that with improved culture I should do it better at some
future time; I did not make use of a great deal I had put to-

gether, because I wished to render it more complete; I drew no conclusions out of data I had amassed, from fear of a precipitate judgment.

"Whenever, now, I surveyed, as I often did, the vast mass lying before me, whenever I observed the printed matter, in part arranged, in part not arranged, in part concluded, in part awaiting conclusion, or considered how it was impossible to resume in later years all the threads that had been dropped in earlier times, or even to contrive a re-attachment to pieces the ends of which had disappeared, I felt myself plunged in melancholy confusion, out of which I undertook to deliver myself in a summary manner, at the same time not abjuring special efforts directed toward the same purpose. The main business was a separation of all departments which in earlier or later times had more or less engaged my faculties, and which had been kept in tolerable order by me; a neat, methodic arrangement of all papers, especially such as referred to my literary life; neglecting nothing, depreciating nothing.

"This business is now finished. A young nimble man, expert in the management of libraries and archives, Library-Secretary Kräuter, has this summer so far accomplished the task, that not merely have printed and unprinted writings, collected and dispersed matter been gathered together and disposed in perfect order, but my diaries and all letters, both those sent by and those addressed to me, are locked up in a safe, while a list of those under general and particular headings, including references both alphabetic and numeral, lies completed in my hands. Every sort of labor in relation to the concatenation of my works has thus in the highest degree been lightened to me, while the friends who may be pleased to take on themselves the charge of my literary legacy will find things in the best order to their hands. It now seems appropriate to mention the considerable work in this direction I was induced to undertake, immediately after the completion of the task above referred to.

"So often as I determined, in compliance with the wishes of friends near and distant, to pave the way out of my personal history to some of my poems, to give a satisfactory account of certain events of my life, I found it necessary to return to times which no longer lay clearly displayed before my mind, and I was therefore obliged to subject myself to many preparatory labors, which scarcely promised me the desired result. I nevertheless repeatedly returned to the task, and the fruit of my endeavors is not altogether disappointing.

" The same friendly demand still continues to be addressed to me, while others kindly interested assure me it would be more to their satisfaction if I would, as formerly, present in a consecutive series both my works and the events of my life, and for the future communicate my faithful confessions, not, as I had hitherto sometimes done, in detached pieces. On this point a more particular explanation seems called for.

" As early as 1819, when I purposed to set forth synoptically the contents of my complete writings in order of time, I found myself impelled to deeper and more searching study, and I elaborated a plan of the events of my life, and of the literary works down to the said year proceeding therefrom, a plan laconic, it is true, yet still sufficient for the purpose, separating, next, all that referred to authorship. In this way was drawn up the bare chronological index at the end of the twentieth volume.

" Since the above-mentioned year, I have from time to time in quiet hours proceeded to cast thoughtful glances into my past life, and in the same way as formerly to lay down a plan of the most recent epoch, a work for which more complete diaries seemed desirable. Now, not alone these but many other documents in perfect archive-like order lie arranged in the clearest manner before me, and I find myself stimulated to elaborate that epitome of the whole history of my life so as for the present to satisfy the desire of my friends, and to excite a lively wish for the further development of at least certain portions of it. These conditions, moreover, secure me the advantage that I am at liberty to take in hand any epoch which happens to be the most promising at any particular time, the reader always having one complete thread in his hand which will suffice to conduct him through any gaps.

" To justify such a partial mode of procedure, I need only appeal to every reader who will confess that in a survey of his own life certain events spring up in vital forms to his remembrance, but others both before and after shrink into the shade; that while the former press themselves on his attention, the latter are hardly with any exertion to be fished out of the floods of Lethe.

" First of all, then, it shall be my strenuous endeavor to continue such a task so far as it is begun, to invest the form with flesh and drapery so far as I find it skeleton-like, and to dispose of the whole matter in such a style that people may read the work, not only for instruction, but also for entertainment."

In accordance with the above account we have as the basis of the " Annals " a chronological list of the salient events in Goethe's life down to the end of the year 1819, more particularly of all his literary productions down to the same date, with the circumstances, conditions, and motives in and under which each particular production was conceived, developed, definitely shaped, and happily matured; blighted immediately after its conception; jostled aside shortly after its inception; arrested in its development; resumed after a period, successively resumed after successive periods of abeyance; abortively given to the world; or too long carried and therefore heterogeneously constituted, bearing the impress of epochs distinct from each other and so far incongruous.

This bare chronological chart of Goethe's life and works was drawn up in 1819 and affixed to the twenty-volume edition of his collected writings.

But, as set forth in Goethe's account above quoted, he was induced at the entreaty of friends to set hand again to the chart with a view to elaborating on certain parts of it at least into free-life-like, natural proportions, and in the execution of this task he selected on each occasion that epoch which was then freshest in his memory and in which he felt the most interest, omitting, of course, those selections which had been treated at large in separate publications, such as the Journey to Italy, to Switzerland, etc. The more cultivated, blooming, diversified oases that the reader will thus gladly encounter in the course of a road otherwise rather flat and bare to the outward sense are: Goethe's relations to Schiller; His visit to Göttingen and Prymont; Madame de Staël at Weimar; Herder's death; Dr. Gall and Phrenology; Professor Wolf's visit to Weimar; From Jena to Helmstädt and back; Audience with Napoleon; Rupture between Voss and Stolberg; Hafiz and the West-Eastern Divan.

The " Annals " in this final form was first published in 1830 in the thirty-first and thirty-second volumes of Goethe's collected works.

To the man, however, who looks below the surface, who casts a thoughtful comprehensive glance over the whole, the chief interest of this work will, probably, be, not the personal or sensational attraction, nowhere very strong, of particular passages, but the central position we everywhere here see Goethe holding in relation to the intellectual and artistic culture of Germany. He is here unegoistically, for the most part unconsciously, often with a truly winning naïveté, represented as the origin and fruition of almost all the spiritual interests of his country and his time; as the heart which receives contributions from every effective member of every kind of the national body, and in return sends out the nourishment in improved condition to the remotest parts of the constitution. It may almost literally be said, there is not in Germany a lady distinguished for her beauty of person, her manners, her accomplishments, or her intellectual powers, not a gentleman of distinguished influence or character, not one effective head in any department of science or philosophy, not one poet of any excellence in any respect, not one artist or art-critic of any school, but she, but he, gravitates by a law of nature to Goethe, attaches herself, himself, to the axis of Germany. Almost every distinguished figure in Germany (and so many also outside of it) during the period Germany most abounded in distinguished figures will be found mapped in the " Annals " in distinct relation to the central figure. The Court of Weimar, with all its social graces and accomplishments, Wieland's happy nature, Schiller's aspiration and philosophy, Voss's hexameters, Herder's acumen, Loder's anatomy, Wolf's classics, Batsch's natural science, the Humboldts' wide range of vision, Werner's and Müller's geology, young Mendelssohn's music, but above all and especially the artists and the students of art, Meyer, Bury, Tischbein and a hundred others—they all gyrate round, stream into, are summed up and represented in Goethe.

Practically, too, as Director of the Weimar Theatre and head of the scientific and artistic institutions of Jena, and, indeed, generally, as under Carl August the most influential man of the duchy in all civic enterprises, he approves himself in the highest degree active, zealous, and efficient.

The picture the " Annals " thus presents of Goethe's many- or universal-sidedness, his keen susceptibility and receptivity, his endless versatility, down into his green old age, must astonish every reader, if perhaps many a one is not provoked to exclaim: " If the man runs into so many limbs and arms, can he really have any *body* left at all? If this German Proteus passes so freely and wholly into this, that, and a thousand other persons, is there a decided, central personality culmi- nating above all that, ruling all that? " Goethe, indeed, streams out in full flood into every province and division of nature and human endeavor—is so far commensurate with nature and humanity. He reaches down into the foundations of the world, into the stone-structures of the earth; he attains with his brain to some co-laminability with the sky-skull of the universe, nor are his resplendent eyes wholly dislocated from the sockets of the upper luminaries; the infinity of ani- mal and vegetable forms is not quite sundered from his intel- ligence and personality, but he largely re-attaches them both poetically and scientifically to man; he divines and explores the secret of colors, and diversifies his animal and vegetable structure with endless hues; creatures of the highest develop- ment, men and women, especially, however, engage his study. To comprehend, reproduce, develop, and embellish man and men, to follow man along the course of his brightest achieve- ments in architecture, art, and poetry, to delineate, educate, and edify men, in reference to their present tendencies and so- cial relations—that is the peculiar and chief study of Goethe's whole life.

There is thus no section or function of nature, no operation of man, which is wholly external to Goethe, which is not more or less in communication with Goethe's brain. Here is no vein of nature, but nature; no faculty of man, but man. Ex- tensively (however much or little intensively), Goethe's per- sonality is so far the universe; his intelligence and will reach as far as his outward senses; as far as the chiselled, painted, and written memory of man, he so far animates and modernizes all the past.

The most prominent aspect of him, however, displayed in the " Annals " is, perhaps, the artistic. His whole life long he lives in the most vital sympathy, in the closest intimacy with perennial Greek and Roman art, with the art of all times and all schools, which he not only appreciates with his structural sense of beauty, but discriminates with his understanding as a highly cultivated and accomplished master in this domain; he lives in the most sympathetic relations with all the distinguished artists and art-critics of his time, and especially those of his own country—then among the most eminent in Europe—artists and art-critics who delight to submit their productions and valuations to a sure and friendly judgment, and find their own imaginations and equations ratified beyond further question.

No man ever reproduced more accurately in his own consciousness the aim, the course, the achievement of every great work of art he studied, down to its most hidden detail. Day by day, generally, as the reader of the " Annals " will find, in any case at no distant intervals, he was continually renewing his own integral life, restoring his own body, by resuscitating in himself those perfect figures he contemplated, recreated, appropriated into his inward life and transfused into the substance and style of his literature. It was so far a happiness for him that he was not an artist by profession and had not to spend in long laborious execution over one work, the time he summarily lived through so many works. Goethe *lived* art, daily and hourly elaborating the highest work of art, the work of primal and most imperative obligation on every artist, and so far on every literary man, that of sculpturing and painting his own presence and manners (which so far as they have any *personal* significance are the necessary mould and prototype of every artistic and of every literary work to the extent it is artistic) into the adequate representation of his symmetrical mind. The capital commandment Goethe constantly inculcates both by precept and practice is self-culture, self-union, " Be yourself a whole, a unity, and all your works will be wholes, unities." His frame itself

Goethe kept from being marred or sullied, and even after death Eckermann could not sufficiently admire the unblemished symmetry of the defunct body, the splendor of the complete limbs.

While these "Annals" faithfully record the conditions and circumstances in which each particular poem and work of Goethe originated, so that the student may consult this work as a map assigning at least the exact latitude and longitude of each production, the reader need hardly expect a completely satisfactory account of the integrations of experience, of the transformation of outward circumstances, quite ordinary and prosaic to the dull eye, into vital, ideal poems. Only the man in feeling and thought up to the level of the poem can comprehend that otherwise miraculous transformation. The "Annals," moreover, it must be admitted, is written at by no means a high temperature or a high elevation; and it is impossible for a man at an ordinary to give an adequate account of himself at an extraordinary temperature; impossible for the understanding to communicate the conceptions and achievements of genius.

It would, indeed, appear, too, as though Goethe's habitual life were not very elevated. He is surprised at night by the vision, but after he has fixed it in black on white, and awaked, he returns to genial intercourse with men—not indeed on a low vulgar level—never, never—but still not on a very high and sacred height. After a course, seemingly, of rather worldly life, but which Goethe must have lived, not as a worldling, but on the whole sincerely and heartily, he is caught up in his solitary walking, in his study, into a resplendent world, if not into the seventh heaven; but after the trance he descends to earth with perfect good-will. The comparative absence in the "Annals" of religious feeling will perhaps strike a devout reader. The defect of Goethe's nature comes also strikingly to light on the domestic and political side. But the limits of this notice forbid entering on that interesting question.

One singular merit, however, belongs to the style, as to the substance—that of entire freedom from egoism. The style is never self-conscious, but is every wholly subordinate to the substance. Goethe is a sincere man, much above rhetoric and

eloquence. He speaks simply that which he knows and testifies that which he has seen. Never once does he rouge,
never once does he stick on ornament. " There is no sin but
show and empty words, no virtue but reality." Even gram-
matically, he seldom appears as *" Ich "* in the " Annals "
(though he must often be Englished " I ") ; generally " *man,*"
sometimes " *wir.*"

The translator has, of course, omitted nothing, interpolated
nothing, and in style, also, has striven to render the original
as faithfully as possible, though, unlike the Chinese tailor, not
deeming it incumbent on him to copy every patch or flaw.

CHARLES NISBET.

CONTENTS

ILLUSTRATIONS

ANNALS;

OR,

DAY AND YEAR PAPERS

From 1749 to 1822

1749–1764

TALENT early awakening, diverse impressions labored, in the manner of children, after models to hand in poetry and prose, mostly in the way of imitation, on each occasion according to the model in the ascendant for the time being. Imagination becomes busied with cheerful pictures attaching themselves according to their own sweet fancies to particular persons and immediate situations. By means of occasional poems the mind drew nearer to actual, genuine nature, and so arose a certain conception of human relations, penetrating also into individual varieties, particular cases having to be contemplated and treated. A great deal of scribbling in several languages, favored by early writing to dictation.

1764–1769

Stay in Leipzig. The necessity is felt of a restricted form in order the better to judge one's own productions. The Greek-French, especially in the case of dramas, being the recognized, nay, law-giving form, is adopted. More serious youthful feelings, innocent but painful, press one on the other, and become matter for reflection and expression. On the other hand, many crimes festering beneath the varnished exterior of civil society do not escape the young man's notice. Of works of the first class there remain the "Lover's Caprice" and some songs; of the second, the "Fellow-Culprits," in which, on close inspection, the evidence of diligent study of Molière's world will not be denied, to which source also is due that foreignness of manners which characterizes the piece, and which long excluded it from the stage.

1

1769–1775

Further views into life. Event, passion, pleasure, and pain. The necessity is felt of a freer form, and transition is made to the English side; hence arise " Werther," " Götz von Berlichin-gen," " Egmont." In the case of simpler subjects, there is a return to the more restricted style: " Clavigo," " Stella," " Erwin and Elmire," " Claudine von Villa Bella," the two latter a prose experiment interwoven with songs. To this category also belong the songs to Belinde and Lili, many of which, as also various occasional pieces, epistles, and other social pleas-antries, have been lost.

Meanwhile bolder plunges are made into the depths of human nature; there springs up a passionate antagonism against mis-leading, straitened theories; the laudation of false models is opposed. All this and its corollaries were deeply and truly felt, though often one-sidedly and unfairly expressed. The follow-ing productions: " Faust," the " Puppet-Shows," " Prologue to Bahrdt," are to be judged in this sense; they are clear to everyone. On the other hand, the fragments of the " Wander-ing Jew," and " Hanswurst's (Jack Pudding's) Wedding," were not ripe for publication. The latter piece, however, came off happily enough for the reason that the whole vocabulary of German nicknames was embodied in its characters. A good deal of this ruffian order has disappeared; " Gods, Heroes, and Wieland," however, preserved.

The Reviews in the " Frankfurter Gelehrten Anzeigen " of 1772 and 1773 give a complete picture of the then state of our society and leading personages. An absolute determination to break through all barriers is observable.

The first journey to Switzerland opened to me a manifold view into the world. The visit to Weimar encircled me with beautiful relations, and without any forethought on my part, constrained me into a new, happy course of life.

To 1780

All the above unfinished works had to be suspended on my entrance into the Weimar sphere. Though, by a feeling of presentiment, the poet anticipates the world, yet when it actually storms in on him, he feels himself disturbed and incommoded. The actual world wishes to give the poet what he already has, but in another form, and he is under the necessity of appropri-ating it a second time.

On the occasion of an amateur theatre and festival days, there were poetized and performed " Lila," the " Brothers and

Sisters," " Iphigenia," " Proserpine," the last wantonly and to
the ruin of its effect intercalated into the " Triumph of Sensibility; " the shallow sentimentality which was then in the ascendant provoking many reactions in the direction of hard
realism.   Many little poems, serious, burlesque, and satirical,
on the occasion of festivals great and small, and having the
closest reference to persons and immediate relations, were the
common product of myself and others.   Most of them have
been lost; a part, however, " Hans Sachs " for example, have
been intercalated or otherwise disposed of.   In connection with
this period, too, will be noticed the beginnings of " Wilhelm
Meister," though only in a cotyledonous state.   Its further
development and structure are processes lasting through many
years.

On the other hand, much time and trouble were thrown away
on the purpose of writing the life of " Duke Bernhard."   After
collecting manifold details and drawing up various plans, it
became at last only too evident that the events in the life of
this hero do not compose a picture.   In the lamentable iliad
of the Thirty Years' War he plays a worthy part, but is not to
be detached from the company with which he is associated.
A solution of the difficulty I nevertheless thought I had found.
I would write the life as a first volume imperatively demanding
a second, indications of which in a preparatory manner would
be given in the first; everywhere would appear gaps exciting
regret that a too early death had prevented the architect from
completing his design.   As regards myself, my exertions in
this matter were not altogether lost.   In the same way that my
preparatory studies for writing " Berlichingen " and " Egmont " procured me a deeper insight into the fifteenth and sixteenth centuries, my studies in connection with " Bernhard "
made me conversant better perhaps than I should otherwise
have been, with the confusion of the seventeenth.

Into the end of 1779 falls the second journey to Switzerland.
Attention to external objects, together with the arrangement
and conduct of our social errantry, was not favorable to production.   As memorial of this journey there remains the
" Rambles from Geneva to Gotthard."

Our journey homeward, after we had again reached the
lower levels of Switzerland, suggested to me " Jeri and Bätely."
I at once began the conception, and completely finished the
poem before I re-entered Germany.   The mountain air which
blows through the piece, I am still keenly sensible of every time
its figures disport before me on the stage between linen and
pasteboard rocks.

To 1786

The beginnings of " Wilhelm Meister " had long been kept
in abeyance. The idea originated in a dim presentiment of the
great truth that man is often disposed to attempt a task nature
has denied him the talent to accomplish, disposed to undertake
and diligently labor at a work it is not in him to mature. An
inward feeling admonishes him to desist, but incapable of
clearly appreciating the situation he goes on, in spite of obscure
misgivings, impelled to prosecute his mistaken course in pursuit of a mistaken goal. This description comprises all that is
covered by the terms " mistaken tendency," " dilettanteism,"
etc. If from time to time the situation is half disclosed to him,
there starts up in him a feeling bordering on despair; yet suppressing his painful apprehensions he soon forces himself forward on the road he has so long trodden. In this way very
many squander away the fairest part of their life, sinking at
last into stupefying melancholy. And yet is it possible that all
such false steps may at last conduct to an invaluable good? a
presentiment which in " Wilhelm Meister " ever more and more
unfolds itself into distinct shape and conviction, till at last it
finds clear expression in the words, " You seem to me like Saul,
the Son of Kish, who went out to seek his father's asses and
found a kingdom."

Who, reflectively, reads the little opera " Jest, Cunning, and
Revenge," will discover more in the piece than it can properly
carry. It occupied me a long time. The dimness of my conception of the interlude and at the same time a desire, by dint
of economy and parsimony, to accomplish much within narrow
limits, led me astray. The musical pieces accumulated to such
an extent as to be beyond the compass of three persons to overtake. Then the shameless trick employed to mystify an avaricious pedant has no charm for the true-hearted German,
though it might be enjoyable enough to Italians and Frenchmen. With us no consideration of art can cover the want of
honest-hearted feeling. Another fundamental mistake in the
piece is that three persons caged up, as it were, without the
possibility of a chorus, afford the composer no proper opportunity of displaying his art and delighting his audience.
Nevertheless, my countryman Kayser, staying in Zurich, by his
composition of the opera, procured me much pleasure and gave
me much matter for reflection, besides continuing to me in all
its warmth a happy relationship formed between us in youth
and afterward renewed in Rome.

Here, also, may be mentioned the " Birds " and other festal
plays for Ettersburg, which have been lost. The two acts of

" Elpenor " were written in 1786. At the end of this period the resolution was formed to have a collection of all my works published by Göschen. The editing of the first four volumes was completed Michaelmas, 1786.

1787–1788

The four last volumes were to contain works for the most part only planned and left unfinished. Under Herder's incitement, however, their further prosecution was undertaken. As to the particular execution much will be found in the " Journey to Italy." " Iphigenia " was concluded before the Sicilian trip. While laboring at " Egmont," on my return to Rome, it surprised me to have to read in the newspapers how the scenes in Brussels I had described in that work were almost literally repeated, another evidence of poetical anticipation. During my stay in the land of music, I had thoroughly indoctrinated and manipulated myself into the proper form of the Italian opera and all its advantages. With pleasure, therefore, I undertook a metrical version of " Claudine von Villa Bella," as also of " Erwin and Elmire," handing them over to the composer to run them into his happy musical moulds. Only after my return from Italy in 1788 was " Tasso " concluded, though Göschen's edition was by this time in its entirety in the hands of the public.

1789

Hardly had I settled myself anew into the Weimar existence, and its conditions in respect of business, studies, and literary labors, when the French Revolution ushered itself into the light of day, drawing to itself the attention of the whole world. As early as 1785 the history of the " Necklace " had made an unspeakable impression on me. Out of the bottomless abyss, here disclosed, of city, court, and State immorality, there emerged, spectre-like, before my senses, the most horrible apparitions. These long continuing to haunt my visions so affected my behavior that the friends with whom I was living in the country, at the time the news of the affair arrived, confessed to me long after, when the Revolution had now run a considerable course, that I then appeared to them like one demented. The development of the world-event I followed with great attention, and when in Sicily took pains to procure information respecting it from Cagliostro and his family. At last, in my usual way, in order to get rid of all considerations regarding it, I transformed the whole event, under the title " The Grand Kophta," into an opera, for which, perhaps, the subject was better adapted than for a play. Orchestra Leader Reichardt at once set to work, and composed a good many single pieces, such as the bass air, " Let learned men dispute and fight," etc.; " Go, attend to my suggestions," etc.

This pure opera form, perhaps the most favorable of all dramatic forms, had become so natural and easy to me, that I applied it to many a theme. An opera, " The Dissimilar Housemates," enjoyed a very fair success. The seven persons represented in it, who from family circumstances, choice, accident, and habit, lived together in a castle, or from time to time assembled there, contributed much to the effect, forming, as they did, the most diverse characters, completely opposed to each other as they were, in respect of will and ability, of acting and refraining from acting, and yet incapable of living separately from each other. Its arias, songs, and pieces for several voices I afterwards distributed among my lyric collections, rendering all resumption of the work impossible.

Immediately after my return from Italy, another work afforded me much pleasure. Since Sterne's inimitable " Sentimental Journey " gave the tone to such productions and called forth imitators, descriptions of travel had become almost entirely taken up with the feelings and views of the traveller. The maxim I, on the other hand, had adopted in works of travel was to deny myself as much as possible, leaving the object to imprint itself as purely and integrally as could be on my mind. This principle I followed faithfully when present at the Roman Carnival. A full plan of all the events was presented, while artists politely prepared for me characteristic drawings of the masks. On this basis I founded my representation of the " Roman Carnival," which, being well received, induced ingenious men in their travels to represent also in a pure objective manner the most characteristic features of peoples and their interior relations. I will call to mind only the talented and early deceased Friedrich Schulz and his description of a Polish Reichstag.

1790

My former connection with the University of Jena, which had served to stimulate and favor my scientific studies, I hastened to renew. The augmentation, arrangement, and maintenance of the museums there, under the co-operation of excellent experts, was, furthermore, an employment agreeable as it was instructive for me; and in the observation of nature, and the study of a wide-sweeping science, I felt myself so far compensated for the disadvantages under which I labored in respect of art studies. In writing the "Metamorphosis of Plants," I experienced a veritable lightening of the heart. By having it printed, I hoped to lay down to the instructed a specimen *pro loco*. A botanical garden was prepared.

Painting was at the same time a principal study, and in going back to the elements of this science, I discovered to my great astonishment that Newton's hypothesis was false and untenable. Closer investigation only confirmed my conviction, and so anew I became smitten with a development-mania destined to exercise the greatest influence on my life and labors.

Pleasant domestic-social relations inspire in me spirits and inclination to complete the "Roman Elegies," immediately after which the "Venetian Epigrams" was taken up. A lengthy stay in the wonderful island-town, first while awaiting the return of the Duchess Amalia from Rome, and second in the suite of that princess during her lengthy residence there, a princess who was the life of everything around her, abroad as at home, proved of the greatest advantage to me. A historical survey of the invaluable Venetian school was imprinted on my mind, while, first alone, and then in the company of my Roman friends, Heinrich Meyer and Bury, with the very valuable work, "Della Pittura Veneziana, 1771," for guide, I became completely conversant at once with its art-treasures, which so far as time had spared them, had up to that date been left undisturbed, and with the means by which it was sought to preserve and restore them.

The revered princess, with her whole suite, visited Mantua, feasting on the superabundance of art-treasures there. Meyer returned to his native country, Switzerland, Bury to Rome; the farther journey of the princess afforded pleasure and insight.

Hardly had I returned home when I was summoned to Silesia, where the armed encampment of two great powers favored the Congress of Reichenbach. The quartering in cantonments gave rise to some epigrams, which here and there have been intercalated. In Breslau, on the other hand, where shone a military court and the nobility of one of the first provinces of the kingdom, where uninterruptedly the finest regiments were to be seen marching and manoeuvring, there, however strange it may sound, I was unceasingly engaged in the study of comparative anatomy, living, in the midst of a most tumultuous world, like a hermit shut up in his own thoughts. The study of this branch of natural science had been generated in me in a strange way. In the course of my frequent walks along the dunes of the Lido which divide the Venetian lagoons from the Adriatic Sea, I found a sheep's skull, so happily burst open as not only anew to demonstrate to me the great truth I had formerly recognized, that the skull-bones have all originated in transformed vertebræ, but plainly established the fact of the conversion of inwardly unformed organic masses, through elaboration outward in progressive advancement toward the highest structure and development into the noblest organs of sense; reviving, at the same time, my old faith, already strengthened by experience, that nature has no secret she will not somewhere disclose to the attentive observer.

Now that in the midst of the utmost tumult of life my mind had reverted to osteology, the studies I had years before directed to the subject of the intermaxillary bone must of necessity resuscitate. Loder, whose indefatigable participation and influence I have constantly to celebrate, takes notice of the subject in his anatomical manual of 1788. The little treatise in German and Latin in reference to this matter being, however, still among my papers, I mention briefly only so much: I was fully convinced that a universal type ascending by metamorphosis pervades the whole organic creation, is quite distinctly observable in all its parts in certain middle stages, and cannot be overlooked even when, on the highest stage of humanity, it modestly retires into concealment. On this head were all my labors, including those in Breslau, directed. The problem, however, was so great as not to be solved in a life of scattered activities.

A pleasure trip to the salt-mines of Wieliczka, and an important ride through mountainous and level country by Adersbach, Glatz, etc., increased the sum of my experience and ideas. There are some writings on the subject.

1791

A quiet year spent within the bounds of house and town. A dwelling having the freest situation, and in which a roomy dark chamber was to be fitted up, together with the adjacent gardens, where in the open air experiments of all kinds could be made, induced me to devote myself earnestly to chromatic investigations. I labored especially at the prismatic phenomena, and, endlessly diversifying what was subjective in them, was able to publish the first piece of " Optic Contributions," which the School, with little thanks and empty words, summarily thrust aside.

Not, however, to lose ground too much on the poetical and æsthetic side, I gladly undertook the conduct of the Court Theatre. Occasion was given for a new direction by the retirement of Bellomo's company, which, since 1784, had played in Weimar, and given agreeable entertainment. They had come from Upper Germany, and for the sake of their good singing people had put up with their dialect. The theatres of the whole of Germany being now open to our choice, the places of the retiring actors were the more easily supplied. Breslau and Hanover, Prague and Berlin sent us able members, who in a short time accommodated themselves to each other in their playing and speech, and from the very beginning gave much satisfaction. Of the retiring company, too, some meritorious persons remained, of whom I will mention only the unforgettable Malkolmi. Shortly before the change, died a very estimable player, Neumann, leaving behind him a daughter fourteen years of age, of a most charming natural talent, who entreated me to take charge of the completion of her culture.

As a beginning, only a few plays were given in Weimar. To their great advantage, the company acted throughout the summer in Lauchstädt. There we had to satisfy the demands of a new public, consisting of strangers, the cultivated portion of the neighborhood, the scholarly members of a university close by, and passionately importunate youths. No new pieces were learned, but the old ones thoroughly conned, and in fresh spirits the company returned in October to Weimar. With the utmost care pieces of every kind were now taken in hand, the new company having to learn everything anew.

Very opportune was that bias of mine toward operatic poetry. An indefatigable concert-master, Kranz, and an ever-active theatrical poet, Vulpius, joined in heartily with me. To no end of Italian and French operas we hastened to give a German text, moulding also many a text already in use into better musical adaptation. The scores found acceptance throughout the whole of Germany. The diligence and zeal expended on this matter, however vanished may be the public remembrance of the fact, contributed no small part to the improvement of German opera-texts.

These labors were shared by my friend, Von Einsiedel, who had returned from Italy with a bias as strong as my own in favor of the operas. On this side, therefore, we felt ourselves for many years safe and well provided, and the opera being always the surest and most convenient means of attracting and gratifying a public, we could, with a feeling of security on the operatic side, devote our attention the more undividedly to the reciting plays. Nothing prevented our taking this in hand in a worthy manner and vitalizing it from the very foundation.

Bellomo's repertory was itself important. A manager tries all manner of pieces—what turns out a failure has at least filled out its night; what retains its hold on the public is care-

fully turned to account. Dittersdorf's operas and plays belonging to Iffland's best time we found ready to hand and
utilized. The "Theatrical Adventures," an opera always delightful, with Cimarosa's and Mozart's music, was performed
before the end of the year. Shakespeare's "King John" was,
however, our greatest achievement. Christiana Neumann as
Arthur, a part to which I trained her, had a wonderful effect,
and it was my endeavor to bring up all the others into harmony with her. From the very beginning I made it a practice
to single out the most excellent actor in each piece, and to try
and educate the others up to his mark.

1792

So passed away the winter, and the theatre had already acquired some degree of cohesion. Repetition of former pieces,
valuable and popular, and the trial of all kinds of new, gave
entertainment to as well as exercised the critical faculties of
the public, who now for the first time made the pleasurable
acquaintance of fresh plays, dating from Iffland's most flour-
ishing epoch. Kotzebue's productions were also carefully performed, and as far as possible kept in the repertory. Dittersdorf's operas, easy for the singer and graceful for the public,
were attentively given; Hagemann's and Hagemeister's pieces,
shallow though they be, yet exciting momentary sympathy and
affording momentary entertainment, were not despised. An
important event, however, it was, when, at the beginning of
the year, Mozart's "Don Juan," and, shortly after, Schiller's
"Don Carlos," came to be performed. The accession to our
theatre of young Vohs was of vital advantage. He was highly
favored by nature, and now properly for the first time was
distinguished as an important actor.

The spring infused fresh vigor into my chromatic labors;
I composed the second piece of the "Optic Contributions,"
and published it, accompanied with a table. In the middle of
summer I was again called into the field, this time to more
serious scenes. I hastened by way of Frankfort, Mainz, Trier,
and Luxemburg to Longwy, which on August 28th I found
already taken; thence I followed in the train to Valmy and
back to Trier; then, to avoid the endless confusion of the high-
way, down the Moselle to Coblenz. To the attentive observer,
many experiences connected with nature interlaced the noisy
events of the war. Some parts of Gehler's physical dictionary
I carried about with me. By my continued chromatic labors
I beguiled the *ennui* of many otherwise stagnant days, provoked to work by the fairest experiences in the open world,

such as no dark chamber, no shop-crevice, can afford.   Papers, documents and drawings on the subject accumulated.

During my visit to Mainz, Düsseldorf, and Münster I could notice that my old friends were not minded to recognize me frankly, a fact indicated in Huber's writings, and the psychological explanation of which should not at the present time be difficult.

1793

The cross-grained humor in me to hoot everything sentimental, and half-despairingly to cleave to inevitable reality, found in "Reineke Fuchs" a most congenial subject for treating, half in the way of translation and half of recastment.   The labor I devoted to this "Unholy World-Bible" redounded both at home and abroad to my consolation and joy.   I took it with me to the blockade of Mainz, where I stayed till the end of the siege; nor must I omit observing that my principal motive in undertaking the work was for the sake of practice in hexameters, which then, to be sure, we Germans formed only to the ear.   Voss, who understood the matter, would not, from a feeling of piety, so long as Klopstock lived, tell the good old gentleman to his face that his hexameters were bad—a fault we juniors had to pay the penalty of—we who had lulled ourselves into that rhythm.   Voss disavowed his translation of the "Odyssey," which we reverenced, picked faults in his "Louise," which we took for our model, and so were we at a loss what saint to dedicate ourselves to.

The theory of colors again accompanied me to the Rhine, and in the open air, under a cheerful sky, I gained ever freer views into the manifold conditions under which color appears. The multiplicity involved in this subject, when contrasted with my limited capacity of observing, apprehending, arranging, and combining, seemed to me to prove the necessity of an association.   Such a body with all its limbs I excogitated in my mind, and fixed in black and white, assigning to each member his particular function; in conclusion, pointing out how, by working in co-operation, the object aimed at would soonest be attained.   This essay I submitted to my brother-in-law, Schlosser, whom I met after the surrender of Mainz, following in the train of the victorious army, at Heidelberg.   But how disagreeably surprised was I, when this old expert made merry with my plan, and assured me that in the world at large, but especially in the dear German Fatherland, all disinterested co-operation in a scientific work was out of the question.   I, on the other hand, though no longer a stripling, opposed him like an ingenious believer; whereupon he predicted to me circumstantially a great deal which I at the time laughed to scorn, but which in the sequel I found more than fairly realized.

And so, as far as concerned myself at least, I held ever fast to these studies, as to a plank in a shipwreck, having now for two years immediately and personally experienced the dreadful disruption of all ties. One day in the head-quarters at Hans, and one day in the reconquered Mainz, were symbols of the contemporaneous history of the world such as will still revive in the mind of anyone who endeavors synchronally to call those days to remembrance.

An active productive mind, a truly patriotic man cultivating the literature of his country, will be excused should he feel alarmed at the overthrow of everything established, and discover in himself not the least presentiment of anything better, or even anything different, to take the place of what has been destroyed. Sympathy will not be denied him, even if he feel chagrined that influences of the kind above referred to should extend to Germany, and that crazy, nay, ignoble persons should seize the helm of affairs. In this sense was planned the " Civilian-General," and at the same time " The Alarmed "; next the " Entertainments of the Emigrants "—all productions which for the most part owe their origin, nay, even their execution, to this and the following year.

The " Civilian-General " was performed in Weimar toward the end of the year 1793. A player, Beck, highly expert in the " Schnaps "-parts, had just entered our theatre, and it was properly in reliance on his talent and humor that I wrote the part. He and the actor Malkolmi played their parts most excellently, and the piece was repeated. The prototypes, however, of the images in the play were too dreadful for the reflection of them not of itself to excite anxiety.

The actors Graff and Haide joined our company with a certain amount of preparatory training; the married couple Porth brought us an amiable daughter, who in brisk parts played with genuine gayety, and now under the name of Vohs is still esteemed and beloved by all lovers of the theatre.

1794

Of this year I presumed to hope it would, in compensation for past years wherein I had borne many privations and sufferings, divert my thoughts by manifold activity and quicken me by many congenial experiences—a compensation of which I stood very much in need. For, to have been a personal witness of revolutions of the highest moment and threatening the peace of the world, to have seen with my own eyes the greatest misfortune that can befall citizens, peasants and soldiers, nay, to have borne a part in such disasters, clouded my mind with the utmost sadness.

Yet how was a feeling of relief possible while every day the monstrous tumults within the borders of France alarmed and menaced us! The preceding year we lamented the death of the King and Queen; this year, a like fate overtaking the princess Elizabeth. Robespierre's deeds of horror had terrified the world, and all sense of joy had been so utterly extinguished that no one presumed to rejoice over Robespierre's destruction; least of all while the horrors of war carried on outside the confines of the country by a nation agitated to its innermost centre were still being incessantly pushed forward, shaking the world all around and menacing everything stable with revolution, if not with perdition.

Nevertheless people lived in a dream-like timid security in the North, lulling the feeling of fear by a half-founded hope in Prussia's good relation to the French.

On the occasion of great events, nay, even in the greatest extremity, men cannot refrain from fighting with the weapons of the tongue and the pen. Accordingly, a German pamphlet, "Appeal to all the Nations of Europe," made a great noise. It gave expression to the seething hatred against the French at the moment when the unbridled enemy were powerfully pressing toward our borders. To raise to the highest pitch the conflict of opinions, French revolutionary songs were sent floating about in secret. They reached me also by the hands of persons whom one would not have suspected capable of such conduct.

The dissensions among the Germans in the cause of defending their country and counteracting the designs of the enemy came openly to light in the direction of the political institutions. Prussia, without more distinctly explaining its intentions, demanded maintenance for its troops; a summons to this effect was issued, but nobody would either make contributions or duly arm himself and take other precautions. In Ratisbon a union of the princes against Prussia was spoken of, a union favored by that party which suspected intentions of aggrandizement in the one-sided negotiations for peace. Minister von Hardenberg, on the other hand, endeavored to arouse the estates of the empire in favor of his king, and people vacillated, in the hope of winning over to this side also a half-friend of the French. But whoever brought home to himself the actual situation of affairs would have inwardly to confess that in an element of fear and apprehension people were only trying to beguile themselves with idle hopes.

The Austrians marched hither across the Rhine, the English

into the Netherlands; the enemy spread themselves out over
wider ground, taking possession of richer resources. The news
of fugitives from all quarters swelled; there was no family, no
circle of friends, which had not suffered in its members. From
South and West Germany there were sent me treasure-chests,
spare money, valuables of all kinds, committed to my custody,
gladdening as testimonies of confidence, but saddening as proofs
of a nation's anxiety.

And so, also, on the side of my connection with Frankfort,
solicitudes pressed ever nearer and nearer on me. The fair
burgess possession which since my father's death had become
the fond home of my mother, was now, since the first outbreak
of hostilities, burdensome to her, though she would not trust
herself to confess it. During my visit last year I had opened
up to her the situation, and urged her to deliver herself from
such a burden; but now at this particular time it was unadvisa-
ble to do what, nevertheless, might be deemed a necessity.

A house of burger-like accommodation and respectable appearance, built up anew in our lifetime, a well-furnished cellar,
furniture of all kinds and of good taste in accordance with the
time, collections of books, pictures, copperplates and maps,
antiquities, small works of art and curiosities, really a great
deal that was remarkable, and which my father, from a disposition that way and of good judgment in the matter, had gathered
about him as occasion offered—it all stood there and then together, each part in its particular place fitting comfortably and
usefully into the other, and had in truth only as a whole its
human traditional value. The very thought of its being divided
and scattered, involved the fear of its being dissipated and lost.
It was, too, soon found, after taking counsel with friends and
dealing with brokers, that at the present time any sort of sale,
however disadvantageous, would have to be postponed. Still,
the resolution once taken, the prospect of a life-long tenancy in
a house having a handsome situation, though yet unbuilt, stimulated my good mother's imagination to a cheerful temper, which
helped to tide her over much in the present that was far from
agreeable.

Fluctuating reports of the arrival and invasion of the enemy
diffused a feeling of dreadful insecurity. Merchants transported their goods, several people their movables of value—proceedings which urged on many persons the necessity of thinking
of their personal safety. The inconvenience of emigration
and change of place contended with the fear of bad treatment
at the hands of the enemy. My brother-in-law, Schlosser, was
carried away in the general distraction. Several times I
offered my mother a quiet residence with me, but for herself she

had no fear. She strengthened herself in her Old Testament faith, and finding favorable passages in the Psalms and Prophets, held fast in her attachment to her native city, with which she had grown up, and become almost incorporated. Not one visit would she undertake to me.

Her determination to remain she had already expressed, when Frau von La Roche called at Wieland's, and with this intelligence put him in the greatest perplexity. It was now in our power to render him and ourselves a friendly service. Care and anxiety we had already had our fill of; to stand, over and above, the wail of lamentation seemed beyond the limits of endurance. With her peculiar tact in these matters, my mother, though herself suffering so much, knew how to comfort her friend, and thereby earn for herself our warmest thanks.

Sömmering, with his excellent spouse, held out in Frankfort during the never-ceasing commotions. Jacobi had fled from Pempelfort to Wandsbeck, his people having betaken themselves to other places of safety. Max Jacobi was in my neighborhood, cultivating medicine in Jena.

The theatre, if not an unmixed pleasure to me, served at least to keep me in constant employment; I regarded it as a cheerful school of art, nay, as a symbol of the life of the world and of business, where everything does not proceed smoothly, and so endured in it what was not to be cured.

At the beginning of the year the "Magic Flute" (*Zauberflöte*) was given, and, shortly after, "Richard Lionheart." This, at that time, in the circumstances then prevailing, will mean something considerable. Next came some important Iffland plays, our company getting ever better and better into the way of these representations. The repertory was already respectable; then smaller pieces, even if they did not retain their hold, could always now and again pass as a novelty. The actress Beck, who joined us this year, played to perfection the important parts in Iffland's and Kotzebue's pieces, of indulgent and froward mothers, sisters, aunts, and cateresses. Vohs had married the extremely graceful Porth, fashioned by nature for Gurli, and in this middle region there was little to be desired wanting. The company played some months during the summer in Lauchstädt, thus reaping the advantage of further practising old pieces without tiring the patience of the Weimar public.

And now, turning my attention to Jena and its chairs, I mention the following:

After Reinhold's departure, justly regarded as a great loss for the Academy, with boldness, nay, temerity, Fichte was called as his successor. In his writings Fichte had expressed himself with greatness, but not perhaps with perfect propriety, on the most important subjects connected with morals and the State. He was one of the ablest characters that have ever appeared, and in his motives irreproachable on a high standard; but what moral possibility was there of his keeping even pace with the world which he regarded as a possession of his own creation?

The week-day hours he wanted to devote to public lectures having been otherwise appropriated, he undertook the lectures on Sundays, the introduction of which was attended with difficulties. Hardly had opposition more or less violent connected with this matter been hushed up, not without inconvenience to the higher authorities, when his utterances on God and divine things, on which, of course, it is better to observe a profound silence, provoked disturbances outside, which caused us new troubles. In the Saxon Electorate people were not disposed to put the best meaning on certain passages in Fichte's periodical; and certainly it cost no little pains to interpret by other words in a tolerable sense, or to tone down what had been somewhat strongly expressed, and where the passage could not be made passable to render it at least pardonable.

Professor Gottling, who, after a free-thinking culture acquired in scientific travels, is to be ranked among the very first who adopted the indisputably high conception of the modern French chemistry, came forward with the discovery that phosphor burns also in nitrogen. The repeated experiments this called forth employed us a long time.

Privy-Councillor Voigt, a faithful fellow-laborer in the mineralogical field, likewise returned from Carlsbad, bringing with him very beautiful tungsten, some in large masses, others distinctly crystallized; with which, later on, when such things became rarer, we could gratify many a one whose mind had a turn that way.

Alexander von Humboldt, long expected from Bayreuth, impelled us into the more universal aspects of natural science. His elder brother, likewise present in Jena, interesting himself clearly in all directions of inquiry, shared our aims, investigations, and instruction.

It must not be omitted that Hofrath Loder was at this time lecturing on the science of ligaments—a highly important part of anatomy; for what interlinks muscles and bones, if not the ligaments? Nevertheless, from a strange perversity on the part of the medical youth, this was just the part neglected. We above named, with friend Meyer, made our way in the morning through the deepest snow to an anatomical auditorium almost quite empty, to see this important juncture in the body set forth in the clearest manner, after the most exact preparations.

The excellent ever-active Batsch, who was not above appreciating even the smallest assistance in the way of his pursuits, was this year settled on a small part of the upper Prince's Garden at Jena. The court gardener, however, whose views were all directed toward utility, being placed there in the principal possession, many unpleasant things occurred, to obviate which all that at present could be done was to make plans for the future. This year, too, as if for a good omen, the neighborhood of the garden referred to was rendered more cheerful and congenial. A part of the town wall having fallen in, to avoid the cost of restoration it was determined to fill up the moat at this place, the same operation gradually extending all around.

In view of the great, ever-increasing demands of chromatics, I became more and more sensible of my inadequacy. I therefore intermitted not soliciting friends likeminded with myself. With Schlosser I did not succeed; even in the most favorable times this study would not have engaged his attention. The moral part of man it was which was the subject of his thoughts, and the transition from the inner to the outer world is more difficult than is supposed. Sömmering, on the other hand, shared my studies through all the fatal embroilments. Ingenious was his mode of handling the matter, provocative his very negative, and when I paid good heed to his communications I was ever rewarded with wider views.

Of all the havoc of this year, Nature in her usual way took not the slightest notice. All crops of the field throve splendidly, ripening a month in advance; all fruits matured to perfection; apricots, peaches, melons, chestnuts offered themselves ripe and tempting to the palate: 1794 takes its rank in the series of excellent vintage years.

As to literary matters, the "Reineke Fuchs" was now printed; but the mishaps always cleaving to the transmission of copies did not fail on this occasion also. In this way an accident spoiled for me the fresh sympathy of my Gotha patrons and friends. Duke Ernst had in the most friendly manner lent me various physical instruments; in returning which I packed along with them copies of the burlesque poem, without mentioning the circumstance in my letter—whether from haste or with the intention of surprising my friends I know not; suffice it, the person entrusted by the prince with such business was absent, and the chest was kept long unopened. I, however, waiting in vain for several weeks on some sympathetic response, conjured up all sorts of crazy fancies; till at last, after the chest had been opened, repeated excuses, complaints, regrets, instead of happy recognition, became my sorrowful portion.

From the critical side, moreover, Voss's remarks on the

2

rhythm were not consoling, and instead of having my former good relationship to my friends quickened and improved, I had fain to content myself with not losing ground with them. Yet soon everything again came all right. Prince August continued his literary pleasantries; Duke Ernst showed no break in the well-established confidence he reposed in me, while I directed to the gratification of his art-tastes many an agreeable possession. Voss, too, had reason to be satisfied with me, who for the future showed what respectful heed I had paid to his observations.

The printing of the first volume of " Wilhelm Meister " was begun. The resolution to declare as finished a work in which I had yet so many things to bear in mind was at last taken, and I was glad to wash my hands of the beginning, though the continuation and the conclusion ahead pressed on me with no little anxiety. Necessity, however, is the best counsellor.

In England appeared a translation of " Iphigenia." Unger reprinted the work; but no impression either of the original or of the copy has remained to me.

With the mine at Ilmenau we had now been harassing ourselves for several years. To venture single-handed on so important an undertaking was excusable only to youthful arrogance eager for any kind of activity. With a large established mining-system at hand the scheme might have proved more successful; but with limited means, with foreign though very able functionaries summoned to the place from time to time, though it was clear enough how things should be carried on, the prosecution of the task was neither sufficiently circumspect nor energetic, and the work, especially when a quite unexpected natural structure came to light, was more than once on the point of coming to a standstill.

A meeting of the shareholders having been called, it was not without apprehension and misgiving that I and my colleague, the Privy-Councillor Voigt, a man more expert in business than myself, attended it; but help reached us from a quarter whence we had never expected it. The Time-spirit, of whom so much good and so much ill are spoken, showed himself on this occasion our ally. Some of the deputies found it opportune to build a kind of convent and take on themselves the management of the affair. Instead, therefore, of we commissioners having humbly on our knees to recount a litany of evils, a penance for which we had prepared ourselves, it was at once determined that the representatives themselves should repair to the spot and without prejudice instruct themselves thoroughly as to the facts of the case. We willingly receded into the background; the other party proved themselves above expectation forbearing with the faults they discovered, and confident in the resources they had in prospect. A decision was therefore adopted, such as thoroughly satisfied us; the necessary means being found to carry their plans into execution, the matter was happily concluded.

A remarkable man reduced to poverty by a complication of misfortunes, though not without his own blame, and who under an assumed name stayed at my expense in Ilmenau, was of great service to me. From immediate observation having become, though a hypochondriac, an expert in matters of mining and taxes, he communicated to me much I could not myself have learned to the same degree.

By my journey the year before to the Lower Rhine I had drawn closer my relationship to Fritz Jacobi and the princess Gallitzin. The connection, however, still remained a remarkable one, difficult to describe, and only to be comprehended under the conception of the whole class of cultivated Germans, or rather of Germans now for the first time promoting their mutual cultivation.

On the best part of the nation a light had arisen which promised to lead them out of the desolate, vacant waste of plodding dependent pedantry. Very many people were seized at the same time by the same spirit; they recognized each others' services, respected one another, felt the need of association, sought, loved each other, and yet could no true union be formed. The fact is, the general interest in respect of habits and morals was vague and indefinite; in the whole body as in each individual there was a want of determination toward special activities. The whole invisible circle, therefore, resolved itself into smaller, mostly local, circles, which fashioned and produced much that was praiseworthy; but in reality the important heads isolated themselves ever more and more. We have here, indeed, only another example of the history which, in the revival of inert, stagnant institutions, has often been enacted; and the phasis in question may be regarded as a literary illustration of what we have seen so often repeated in political and ecclesiastical history.

The principal figures worked absolutely according to their own genius, sense, and capacity. To these attached themselves others, who, though conscious of powers of their own, were not disinclined to work socially and in a subordinate way.

Let Klopstock be first mentioned. Intellectually, many turned toward his genius; but his chaste, measured personality, always commanding reverence from those about him, was not calculated to invite approach. Wieland, likewise, was no personal centre for a large circle, though the literary confidence reposed in him was boundless. South Germany, and in particular Vienna, owe to him their culture in poetry and prose. Things sent him, which it was impossible for him not to notice, often brought him to a happy despair.

Herder's influence was later. His attractive character gathered properly no crowd around him, but particular persons shaped themselves by and about him, holding fast to him, and, to their greatest profit, giving themselves entirely to him. Thus were formed little world-systems. Gleim, too, was a centre for many talents. To my share, also, fell many fermenting heads, heads which would almost have degraded to a nickname the honored name of Genius.

The strange thing, however, with all this, was that not only each chieftain, but each of his peers, maintained his independence, endeavoring also to draw others to him and after him into his own ways of thinking; whereby the strangest effects and counter-effects came to light.

While Lavater demanded of everyone that, following his example, he should become transubstantiated with Christ, Jacobi required men to adopt his mode of thinking—a mode individual, recondite, difficult to define. The princess had, in the Catholic conception of things, and within the rites of the Church, found the possibility of living and acting in accordance with her own noble purposes. These two truly loved me, and for the present allowed me my own way, though with a silent, not entirely concealed, hope of winning me entirely over to their sentiments. They, therefore, tolerated many of my wilfulnesses, which from a feeling of impatience, and to assert my liberty in opposition to them, I purposely practised.

On the whole, however, the then state of things was an aristocratic anarchy, somewhat like the conflict in the Middle Ages between powers either in possession of or endeavoring to conquer independence. Like the Middle Ages, too, it preceded a higher culture, as is now apparent when different views have been opened into the situation of that time—a situation indescribable, and for posterity perhaps incomprehensible. On this point Hamann's letters form invaluable archives, to the general comprehension of which a key may be found, but none perhaps will ever be discovered for particular secret compartments in them.

For house-mate I now had my oldest Roman friend, Heinrich Meyer. The remembrance and advancement of our Italian studies remained our daily entertainment. During my last stay in Venice we had come to a thorough mutual understanding, and thereby only the more firmly tightened the bonds of our union. As is, however, usually the case, so in the present instance also, the endeavor to comprehend a subject at a distance from the subject itself, or the anxious effort to attain to clearness of perception in regard to it, only made us sensible of the inadequacy of memory, and incited us to return to the source of artistic forms, to immediate contemplation. And who that has lived in Italy, even though with a less earnest purpose than ours, but ever longs to return thither!

Not that the schism which my scientific studies had produced in my existence was at all healed; for the manner in which I treated experiences in nature seemed to demand all the remaining powers of my soul.

Amid this sharp conflict between my powers, the relationship to Schiller, which all at once developed itself, gave satisfaction to my nature beyond all my wishes and hopes—a relationship which I may rank among the highest that in later years fortune prepared for me. And this happy event I, indeed, owed to my studies in connection with the " Metamorphosis of Plants "; studies whereby a circumstance was brought about which cleared away all the misunderstandings that had long kept me at a distance from him.

After my return from Italy, where I had sought to cultivate myself to greater precision and purity in all branches of art, without any care as to all that meanwhile was going on in Germany, I found poetical works more or less recent in great repute and exercising extended influence, works such as, alas! were extremely repugnant to me; I mention only Heinse's " Ardinghello " and Schiller's " Robbers." The former author was hateful to me because he sought to ennoble and support sensuousness and abstruse modes of thought by the aid of plastic art; the latter because an energetic but immature talent had poured over the country in full torrent just those ethic and theatrical paradoxes from which I was endeavoring to clear myself.

Not that I blamed either of those talented men for what they had undertaken and achieved. Man cannot deny himself the inclination to work in his own way; he makes trials at first unconsciously, crudely, then at each successive stage of culture with ever more consciousness. In this way so much that is excellent and absurd is dispersed over the world, and confusion emerges out of confusion.

The noise, however, excited in the country, the applause universally bestowed on those extravagant abortions by wild students as by the cultivated court lady, fell like a shock on me. All the pains I had taken with myself seemed to me entirely lost. The subjects in which, the ways and means by which, I had cultivated myself, appeared to me all thrust aside and trampled under foot. And what most pained me, all the friends conjoined with me—Heinrich Meyer and Moritz, as also the artists Tischbein and Bury, directing the minds of men in their province in a kindred spirit with my own—these seemed likewise endangered. I was stung to the quick. The study of plastic art, the practice of poetry, I should willingly have renounced *in toto,* had that been possible; for what prospect was there of excelling these productions distinguished by genius and wild form? Conceive my situation! I aspired to appropriate and communicate the purest perceptions, and here was I hemmed in between Ardinghello and Franz Moor!

Moritz, who likewise returned from Italy and stayed some time with me, confirmed himself passionately with me in these views; I avoided Schiller, who was staying in my neighborhood in Weimar. Nor was the appearance of " Don Carlos " calculated to bring me nearer to him; all attempts in this direction on the part of persons standing equally near to him and me I turned aside, and in this fashion we lived some time close to each other.

His essay on " Grace and Dignity " was just as little fitted to reconcile me. The Kantian philosophy, so highly exalting the subject while appearing to set limits to it, he had joyfully adopted; it developed the extraordinary nature had planted in his character, and in the sublime feeling of freedom and self-determination he was ungrateful to the great mother, who certainly did not treat him like a stepmother. Instead of regarding her as self-existent, alive, bringing forth her births, from the lowest to the highest, according to fixed laws, nature was to him the product of certain empiric forms innate in man. Some hard passages, setting my confession of faith in a false light, I could even directly refer to myself, and if they were written without allusion to me, the matter appeared in my eyes all the worse, disclosing, as it would, only the more unmistakably, the immeasurable abyss sundering our modes of thought.

Union was not to be thought of. Even the mild entreaties of a Dalberg, who appreciated Schiller according to his merit, had no effect; the arguments I opposed to any union were indeed difficult to refute. It was not to be denied that two intellectual antipodes were further removed from each other than by one diameter of the earth, and so being, as it were, opposite poles, they could never be brought into one. That, nevertheless, there was some point of affinity between them will appear from the following.

Schiller removed to Jena, where likewise I did not see him. At this time, by incredible pains, Batsch had started a natural research association, having as a basis of study handsome col-

ANNALS **23**

lections and considerable apparatus. Their formal sittings I usually attended, and once I found Schiller there. As we happened to leave at the same time, a conversation struck up between us. He appeared to interest himself in the lecture we had heard, but, with sharp understanding and insight, and to my great pleasure, observed how such a dismembered way of treating nature was not calculated to engage the outsider who would willingly take part in such studies.

To this I replied, that perhaps even to the initiated it was not attractive, and that undoubtedly there was another way of going to work, presenting nature not sundered and detached, but operative and alive, striving with sure determination out of a whole into parts. He desired further light on this subject, but did not conceal his doubts; he could not admit that such a view of nature was, as I maintained, the presentation of experience.

We reached his house, the conversation allured me in; I set forth in a lively manner the metamorphosis of plants, and with many characteristic strokes of the pen caused a symbolic plant to arise before his eyes. He perceived and observed it all with great interest, with a decided power of comprehension; but when I finished he shook his head and said, " That is no observation, that is an idea." I was startled, chagrined in a certain measure; for the line dividing us was by this expression most palpably indicated. An assertion in " Grace and Dignity " recurred to my mind; the old grudge was like to revive in me. I mastered myself, however, and answered, " It can be anything but disagreeable to me to have ideas without knowing it, and even to see them with my eyes."

Schiller, who possessed much more tact and practical prudence than I, and on account also of the " Horen," was disposed to attract rather than repel me, answered like an accomplished Kantian; and my obstinate realism giving rise to a lively debate, a lengthy battle was fought, and then an armistice declared; neither of us could boast himself the victor, each deemed himself invincible. Sentences like the following made me quite unhappy : " How can ever experience commensurate with an idea be given ? For just therein consists the peculiarity of the latter, that experience can never come up to it." If what to him was an idea was to me experience, there must after all be something intermediary, something relational between the two. The first step was, however, taken. Schiller's power of attraction was great, he held fast all who approached him. I took part in his plans, and promised to forward him, for his " Horen," a great deal that was lying hidden by me. His spouse, whom from her childhood I was wont to love and appreciate, contributed her part toward a lasting relationship. Our common friends were all glad, and so, by means of a dispute between object and subject, the most fundamental of all disputes—one, indeed, perhaps never to be wholly composed— we sealed an alliance, which has lasted without interruption, and been, both for ourselves and others, the instrument of much good.

For me, in particular, it was a new spring, in which everything secreted in my nature burst into joyous life, in happy fellowship, all seeds opening, and tender growths shooting up with increased vitality. Our reciprocal letters give the most immediate, the purest, the completest testimony to this fact.

1795

The " Horen " was published; " Epistles, Elegies, Conversations of the Emigrants " contributed by me. We, moreover, considered and held counsel together as to the whole contents of this periodical, the relations of the contributors, and everything else connected with such an undertaking. In this way I got to know contemporaries, and made the acquaintance of authors and productions I should otherwise have never taken the least notice of. Schiller was in general less exclusive than I, and, as editor, was obliged to be indulgent.

With all this I could not refrain from setting off, the beginning of July, to Carlsbad, and staying there over four weeks. In younger years a man gets impatient with the slightest ailments, and Carlsbad had already often proved beneficial to me. To no purpose, however, did I take a lot of work along with me. The crowds of people coming in contact with me in so many different ways distracted me, and prevented all labor; though, to be sure, it also afforded me many a new view of the world and of persons.

Hardly had I returned when news arrived from Ilmenau that a serious crash had put the finishing stroke to the mines there. I hastened thither and saw, not without sad reflections, a work on which so much time, energy, and money had been expended, buried in its own ruins.

Gladdening to me, on the other hand, was the company of my son, five years old, who with his fresh, childlike sense took up for me anew a district on which for twenty years now I had looked and cogitated myself tired, who with new zest apprehended all manner of subjects, relations and activities, and much more decidedly than could have been done by word, expressed by deed, that man dying has yet a living successor, and that man's interest in this earth can never be extinguished.

Thence I was called to Eisenach, where the Court was stay-

ing with several strangers, particularly emigrants. Serious war
tumults warned everyone to be on his guard. The Austrians,
to the number of 60,000 men, had crossed the Main, and events
threatened to become lively in the neighborhood of Frankfort.
A commission which would have brought me near the place of
encampment I contrived to decline. I was too well acquainted
with the havocs of war to seek to visit them.

Here a case occurred to me, on which I have frequently in
life had occasion to reflect. Count Dumanoir—unquestionably
the most highly cultured among all the emigrants, of able character, and clear common-sense, whose judgment I had found
the least prejudiced—met me in a happy humor in the street
in Eisenach, and told me that in the " Frankfort Newspaper "
something was related favorable to the interests of the emigrants. Having a pretty clear conception of the course of the
affairs of the world I was taken aback at this news; it seemed
to me incomprehensible how such a thing should happen. I
hastened to procure the paper, in which on reading and again
reading, I failed to find anything to the effect reported me, till
at last I noticed a passage which might certainly be referred
to the affairs of the emigrants, but in a sense quite the opposite
of that given by the count.

I had already before met with a stronger instance of a similar kind, in which to be sure an emigrant was also concerned.
The French had been slaughtering each other in all ways over
the upper plain of their country; assignats had been changed
into mandats, and these latter had shrunk to the value of nothing. As to all this, people conversed minutely and very regretfully, when a marquis with a degree of composure replied that
no doubt it was a great misfortune; he was only afraid a civil
war would break out and the bankruptcy of the State be inevitable.

Whoever has met with criticisms of this kind in connection
with the immediate relations of life will not be surprised if in
religion, philosophy, and science, where man's isolated, inward
self is called to pronounce sentence, an equal blindness of judgment and opinion should be manifested.

In the same year my friend Meyer returned to Italy; for
though the war was already violently carried on in Lombardy,
the rest of the country was still left untouched; and we lived
in the fond illusion of repeating the years '87 and '88. His
absence robbed me of all conversation on plastic art, and even
my preparations for following him conducted me on other ways.

I was, indeed, quite diverted from art and directed back to
the study of nature, when toward the end of the year the two
brothers Von Humboldt appeared in Jena. At this moment

they both took great interest in the natural sciences, and I
could not but impart to them in conversation my ideas on comparative anatomy, and its methodic treatment. My presentation of the matter being deemed by them congruous and pretty
complete, I was pressingly urged to transfer it to paper; an
advice which I at once followed, dictating to Max Jacobi the
ground-plan of a comparative osteology as it then pictured itself in my mind. I thus both satisfied my friends and gained
for myself a basis from which I could prosecute my further
studies.

Alexander von Humboldt's influence in these matters demands special recital. His presence in Jena furthers comparative anatomy; he and his elder brother induce me to dictate
the general plan, still extant. During his residence in Bayreuth my correspondence with him is very interesting.

In conjunction with him, Professor Wolf, of another side,
yet sympathizing with our general tendencies, entered our circle
at the same time with him.

The circulation of free copies of the first part of " Wilhelm
Meister " employed me for some time. The answers were only
in part gladdening, and on the whole by no means calculated
to further me. Still the letters, both in reference to the time
they reached me and to the present date, are important and
instructive. Duke and Prince of Gotha, Frau von Frankenberg there, von Thümmel, my mother, Sömmering, Schlosser,
Von Humboldt, Von Dalberg in Mannheim, Voss—the most,
if you look closely into it, *se defendendo,* drawing themselves
up in haughty opposition against the secret power of the work.
But, most of all, an ingenious, dear lady friend, by her divina-
tion of many a secret, her search for hidden meanings, and her
intricate decipherings, drove me to despair. What I had desired was that people would take the matter as they found it
and understand things in their palpable sense.

While Unger was busy with the continuation and doing all
he could to accelerate the second volume, an unpleasant relation arose with a leader of the orchestra, Reichardt. Out of
respect to his considerable talent, people had kept on good
terms with him, in spite of his forward and importunate nature.
He was the first who by his musical composition earnestly and
steadily spread abroad my lyric works. It was my way, out
of common kindness, to endure disagreeable people so long as
they did not carry their petulance to a too high pitch; but
when that limit was transgressed to break off, generally with
vehemence, all connection with them. Now Reichardt had with
fury and fanaticism thrown himself on the side of the Revolution. I, on the other hand, who with my own eyes observed

the ghastly, ungovernable consequences of the violent dissolution of all bonds, and who clearly perceived a similar secret agitation in my native country, held fast once for all to established things; for the improvement, vitalization, and direction of which toward a sensible and intelligent organization I had my life long consciously and unconsciously labored; and this my principle, I neither could nor would dissemble.

Reichardt had also begun the happy composition of the songs in " Wilhelm Meister "; his melody to " Know'st thou the land " being still ever admired as excellent. Unger communicated to him the songs of the following volumes, and so on the musical side he continued our friend, but an antagonist on the political. The cleft in the latter respect secretly widened, till at last there was no ignoring it.

In my relation to Jacobi I have next an improvement to report, though the relation still rested on no sure foundation. Love and toleration on one side, and on the other hope of accomplishing my conversion; that will be the briefest statement of the matter. Wandering away from the Rhine he had repaired to Holstein, and at Emkendorf was received in the most friendly manner by the family of Count Reventlow. He painted to me in the most charming colors his satisfaction with the situation there, describing gracefully and circumstantially different family festivals in honor of his birthday and that of the Count, and adding a repeated urgent invitation to me to come.

Such mummeries within a simple family circle were ever repugnant to me, and in the present case the prospect was by no means alluring. Another deterrent element was the feeling that they meditated setting limits to my freedom as a man and a poet by imposing on me certain conventional moralities. So firm was my resolution in this respect that I would not yield even to a pressing claim to accompany thither a son who had studied and taken his degree in the neighborhood, but stubbornly persisted in my refusal.

Jacobi's letters, too, on " Wilhelm Meister " were not inviting. To my friend himself, as also to his distinguished circle, the realism, and that, moreover, of a low class of people, did not seem edifying; the ladies had a great many objections to the morality, and only one person, a man of the world, able and far-seeing, Count Bernstorff, took sides with the much-assailed book. The author felt therefore all the less inclination to hear such lectures personally and allow himself to be cramped up between the horns of a dilemma — a well-meaning, amiable pedantry on one hand and the tea-talk on the other.

From the princess Gallitzin I don't remember to have heard anything on " Wilhelm Meister," but in this year was cleared

up between us a misunderstanding for which Jacobi was to
blame, whether from levity or intention I know not. In any
case it was not to his credit, and had the princess not been of
such a pure nature an unpleasant estrangement would sooner
or later have occurred. She, too, had fled from Münster before
the French. Her high character, strengthened by religion,
supported her, and a tranquil activity everywhere accompanying
her, she remained in benevolent communication with me; and I
was glad in those confused times, in accordance with her recom-
mendations, to establish much that was beneficial.

Wilhelm von Humboldt's sympathy was, however, more
fruitful. His letters show a clear insight into the motives and
achievements, so that genuine furtherance was necessarily imparted by them.

Schiller's appreciation I mention last; it was the most cordial
and the highest. As, however, his letters on the subject are still
extant, I need say no more than that their circulation might
be one of the handsomest gifts to an enlightened public.

The theatre was thrown wholly on me, what I supervised and
directed was executed by Kirms. Vulpius, who was not wanting in talent in this business, joined in with judicious activity.
What in the course of this year was performed is about the following.

The " Magic Flute " continued to exercise its former influence, the operas proving more attractive than all the rest:
" Don Juan," " Doctor and Apothecary," " Cosa Rara," " The
Sun-feast of the Bramins," satisfied the public. Lessing's
works emerged from time to time, but Schröder's, Iffland's, and
Kotzebue's pieces were the regular representations. Hagemann and Grossmann were also somewhat prized. " Abällino "
was ranked almost equal to Schiller's pieces. Our endeavor to
exclude nothing was, however, conspicuously manifested in our
undertaking the performance of a piece by Meyer, " The Storm
of Boxberg," with little success, it must be allowed; still the
public had thereby seen a piece, of so remarkable character, and
had felt if not appreciated its presence.

The fact that our actors had a joyous reception in Lauchstädt, Erfurt, and Rudolstadt, at the hands of the most diverse
public, that they were animated by enthusiasm, and had their
mutual respect raised by the good treatment they received, was
of no little advantage to our stage, and to the maintenance in all
its freshness of an activity which, when the players see always
the same public before them, whose ways and opinions they are
familiar with, is soon apt to slacken.

In passing from these small matters to the immeasurably
higher concern of world-history, I am reminded of the peasant

I saw at the siege of Mainz, within range of the guns, absorbed wholly in the work assigned him behind a gabion trundled forward on wheels. The individual limited to his own part is heedless of the great whole.

There now transpired the Basel peace preliminaries and a gleam of hope lighted on Northern Germany. Prussia made peace, Austria continued the war, and we felt ourselves seized by new apprehension; for the Elector of Saxony refused joining in a special peace. Our officials and diplomatists set off for Dresden, and our most gracious master, himself active above all others, and a centre of activity all round, repaired to Dessau. Meanwhile tumults were heard of among the Swiss country people, especially in the district of the Upper Zurich lake. A process at law arising from these disturbances tended to increase the exasperation. Soon, however, our interest was attracted nearer home. The right bank of the Main again appeared in danger; our neighborhood itself was thought to be threatened; a line of demarcation was spoken of; doubt and apprehension greatly increased.

Clerfayt appears on the scene; we attach ourselves to the Elector of Saxony. Preparations and definite arrangements are called for, and war-taxes having to be imposed, the lucky thought is at last hit on of bringing the intellect also under contribution, though all that was asked in this direction was a *don gratuit*.

In the course of these years my mother had sold her well-furnished wine-cellar; the library, in many departments well supplied; a collection of pictures, including the best works of artists of that time, and what-not all beside; and while she was glad to get rid of what was only a burden, I saw the world my father had earnestly gathered around him disrupted and scattered. This was done at my urgent representation: at that time nobody could advise or help another. The house still remained, but was at last also sold; and the furniture my mother could not take with her was in the end auctioneered away. The prospect of new lively quarters at the Main guard-house was realized, and this change afforded her at the time, new apprehensions having again chased away transient hopes of peace, some distraction for her thoughts.

I have also to remark as a family event, fraught with important consequences, the marriage of my niece, the daughter of Schlosser and my sister, with Nicolovius, resident at Eutin.

Beside the above-mentioned havocs, the attempt to bring pronounced idealists into harmony with the extremely real academic relations, was a source of never-ending vexation. Fichte, who had resolved to lecture on Sundays, and to free

himself from the impediments placed from various quarters in
his way, could not but feel keenly the opposition of his col-
leagues. A knot of students at last gathered in front of his
house and smashed in his windows—a most disagreeable way
of convincing him of the existence of a Not-I.

But not only his character, that of another man also provided
the lower and higher authorities in employment. A young
thoughtful man, by name Weisshuhn, Fichte had called to Jena
to act as his assistant and colleague. He, however, in some
things, which for a philosopher means all things, deviated from
Fichte, and peaceful co-operation was very soon disturbed,
though we did not on that account reject the young man's contributions to the " Horen." A resolute man, but still more incapable than Fichte of adjusting himself to external things, he
had to endure the most disagreeable personal quarrels with
pro-rector and courts; the bitterness intensified at last into accusations of insult, to appease which the proper worldly wisdom
from upper quarters had to be brought into operation.

If now the philosophers from time to time resuscitated for
our entertainment quarrels which scarcely any amount of tact
could compose, we, on the other hand, took every opportunity
to further the interests of those devoted to the study of nature.
The situation of Batsch, a man intellectually aspiring, unrest-
ingly pressing forward, required improvement; he felt the difficulties of his position, knew the means we had at our disposal,
and adjusted himself to small things. It was therefore a pleasure to obtain for him a firmer footing in the prince's garden:
a glass-house, sufficient as a beginning, was set up according to
his direction, opening up a prospect of further favors.

For a portion of the citizens of Jena an important business
was also just at this time concluded. To dry the old arm of
the Saale above the turf-mill (Rasenmühle), which making several windings transformed the fairest meadows of the right
bank into gravel-beds of the left, it had been determined to dig
a trench and divert the stream into a right line. The work
lasted several years, resulting at last in success. The neighboring citizens, for a small outlay, had thereby their lost grounds
restored to them, and the old Saale, together with the gravel-
beds, which had meanwhile become overgrown with useful wil-
lows, handed back to them; a satisfaction surpassing their expectations and causing them to accord a special vote of thanks
to the superintendents of the undertaking.

Not but that there were some grumblers on this occasion.
People interested in the matter, but who, sceptical as to the
success of the enterprise, had refused the little contributions
asked for the work, now came forward claiming a share in the

recovered territory, if not as a right then as a favor. This claim, however, could not be conceded, the master's considerable expenditure on this enterprise requiring some indemnity in the reclaimed soil.

Three works of very different character, but which this year caused a great sensation, require notice at my hands. Dumouriez's "Life" afforded us a deeper insight into the special events, with the general nature of which we were, to our misfortune, sufficiently familiar; many characters were disclosed to us, and the man who had ever commanded much of our sympathy here appeared more distinctly before us and in a favorable light. Intellectual ladies, who, as everybody knows, have always favors they must dispose of somewhere or other, and, as is proper, bestow their friendliest regards on the hero of the day, found zest and edification in this work, which I carefully studied in order thoroughly to master, down to the smallest secret detail, the epoch of Dumouriez's great deeds, of which I had myself been a personal witness. It was also a pleasure to me to find that his presentation entirely harmonized with my own experiences and observations.

The second work pressing on universal attention was Balde's "Poems," which appeared according to Herder's translation, but with concealment of the proper author, and rejoiced in the happiest influence. Richly embodying the time to which they belong and of pronounced German sentiments, they would at any period have been welcome. Warlike confused times, however, alike in all centuries, were imaged back in this poetical mirror, and people felt, as if it were only yesterday, what had distressed and agonized our early ancestors.

The third work drew around it quite a different circle. Lichtenberg's "Hogarth," and the interest in it was, properly, fictitious; for how could the German, in whose simple unsophisticated state such eccentric caricatures of life very seldom occur, have found true pleasure in such things? The tradition, however, of a name highly celebrated by his own nation finding acceptance also on the Continent, the rarity of possessing completely his whimsical representations, the convenience of needing neither a knowledge of art nor any higher sense for the appreciation and admiration of his works, but only a capacity of malice and contempt of mankind, and still more the fact that Hogarth's wit and Lichtenberg's witticisms had paved the way to its acceptance: these were the causes which facilitated its circulation in this country.

Young men who from their childhood, and throughout a course of nearly twenty years, had grown up by my side, were now looking about them in the world, and the news I received

from them could not but give me pleasure, showing me, as it
did, how they were intelligently and actively pursuing their
aims.   Friedrich von Stein was staying in England, where he
found many advantages for his sense in technics.   August von
Herder wrote from Neufchatel, where he thought of preparing
himself for his remaining purposes in life.

A number of emigrants were well received at the court and
in society; but not all of them rested content with these social
advantages.   Many of them, here as elsewhere, desired to earn
their living by some creditable employment.   A worthy man,
already advanced in years, by name Von Wendel, brought to
our attention a Smithy Company in Ilmenau, in which the ducal
exchequer had some shares.   This establishment was certainly
conducted in a peculiar manner.   The masters of the forge
worked only in turn, each by himself with his best ability, and
after short labor handing over the work to his successor.   Such
an establishment is conceivable only in an old-fashioned state
of things, and a man of higher views and accustomed to freer
activity could not succeed in it, though he had the duke's shares
at a moderate rent, which, moreover, would perhaps never have
been demanded.   His love of order and his interest in the whole
concern Von Wendel sought to satisfy by extended plans; now
a number of shares were to be taken, now the whole was to be
acquired, either of which proposals was impracticable, the spare
existence of certain families depending on this business.

Another enterprise he now took in hand; a reverberatory was
built for the smelting of old iron and with a view to establishing
a foundry.   Great things were expected from the heat being
concentrated upward, and, indeed, the fulfilment exceeded expectation; the whole iron apparatus melted into a stream.   Many
other things were tried, but without success.   The good man
at last, sensible of the entirely foreign element into which he
had plunged, and overwhelmed with despair, took an overdose
of opium, which, if not immediately, yet in its consequences
proved fatal.   So great was his unhappiness that neither the
sympathy of the prince nor the well-meaning efforts of the
counsellors charged to undertake the task were able to bring
him round.   Far from his native land, in a still corner of the
Thuringian forest, he, too, fell a sacrifice to the boundless revolution.

Of persons, their fortunes and relations, I remark the following:

Schlosser wanders from home and repairs to Anspach, where
he intends settling, every asylum not being quite desperate.

Herder is painfully sensible of an estrangement which becomes more and more evident, without there being any power

of overcoming it. His disaffection with the Kantian philosophy, and therefore with the University of Jena as well, had always increased, whereas, through my relation to Schiller, I had grown ever more into sympathy with both. Every attempt, therefore, to re-establish the old relation was in vain, the more that Wieland cursed the new doctrine, even in the person of his son-in-law, and as latitudinarian keenly resented a conception of things which threatened to fix Duty and Right by strict Reason, as the phrase went, and make an end of all humorous-poetical free-and-easy notions.

Herder was by nature soft and tender, his tendency great and powerful. Let him work for or against, it was ever with a certain impetuosity and impatience; his was more a dialectic than a constructive mind. He was ever ready with his *heteros logos* against every proposition. Nay, he would inveigh with bitter irony against the expression of a conviction he himself shortly before had taught and communicated as his own opinion.

Saddening, indeed, was a letter I received from Karl von Moser, a man of the highest mark. I had formerly seen him on the pinnacle of ministerial power, when he was called to Carlsbad to draw up the contract between our dear princely married couple. In these times he had put me under many an obligation to him, had even by his force and influence rescued a friend from perdition. For twenty years now his fortunes had been gradually declining, till at length he was reduced to a pitiful existence in his mountain-castle of Zwingenberg. He now wanted, furthermore, to part with a fine collection of pictures he had in more prosperous times tastefully gathered about him; he desired my co-operation in this transaction; and, alas! I could reply to his tender urgent request only by a friendly polite letter. His answer to this, the answer of a man of intellect, hard-bestead and yet resigned, was of such a nature that even now it affects me as it then affected me, it being quite out of my power to help him in his straits.

Anatomy and physiology were this year almost never out of my view. Hofrath Loder demonstrated to a small circle of friends the system of the human brain, in the traditional way, in layers from the top to the interior, with that clearness which distinguishes him. Camper's works were in company with him perused and studied.

Sömmering's attempt to trace more closely the proper seat of the soul gave rise to no little observation, reflection, and examination.

Brandis, in Brunswick, showed himself in the observation of nature a man of talent and stimulating character; like us, he tried the most difficult problems.

Since the time people in Germany began to complain of the abuse of reason, extraordinary cases of crazed brains every now and again came into view. Their exertions revolving in a dark, dismal element, but yet inspiring the hope that by their continued struggles they might at last attain to some degree of sense, we did not refuse such people our sympathy, till in the end they either themselves fell away in despair, or we in despair had to give them up.

A man of this stamp was Von Sonnenberg, calling himself the Cimbrian; physically of fiery nature, not without a certain portion of imagination, which, however, expatiated in purely empty regions. Klopstock's patriotism and Messianism had quite taken possession of the man, filling his head with forms and ideas which drove him into wild enthusiastic extravagances. His grand task was a poem on the Judgment Day, in whose apocalyptic inflated visions, it will readily be conceived, I could find little good taste. I tried to draw him away from all this nonsense, but in vain; no power could induce him to quit his eccentric courses. In this way he went on for a long time in Jena, to the distress of good, sensible associates and well-wishing patrons, till at last, growing ever crazier, he flung himself out of the window and put an end to his ill-starred life.

An event in the civil courts next arrested attention. A young man had inconsiderately reposed trust in a man unworthy of his confidence. The case being tried in the public courts, able men conducted the trial to an issue favorable to the latter. Friends of the former, otherwise sensible people and members of our circle, felt aggrieved at this decision, seeing injustice and harshness where we saw only the inevitable course of law, The most touching protests on the part of those friends did not, of course, in any way affect the verdict, but the difference of views on the case between us and those friends greatly disturbed the harmony of our circle, almost provoking a rupture.

1796

The Weimar theatre had now such a company of actors, and was so well established, as this year to need no new players. To its greatest profit, Iffland played in it fourteen times in March and April. Beside the advantage of his instructive, all-captivating, invaluable example, these representations became the basis of a lasting repertory, and a spur toward higher acquisitions. With this view Schiller, who always held fast by the extant, prepared "Egmont," which was given at the close of the Iffland representations, in much the same form as it is now represented on the German stage.

Altogether, in relation to the German theatre, you find here the most remarkable events in their inception. Schiller, who already in his " Carlos " observed a certain moderation, and by recasting this piece for the theatre, habituated himself to a more restricted form, had conceived the subject of " Wallenstein," and so grasped the boundless material in the history of the Thirty Years' War as to feel himself fairly master of the mass. By reason, however, of this very vastness, the stricter treatment became painful, as I myself could witness, Schiller being disposed to talk over and consider backward and forward with others all his poetical plans and projects. With the constant agitation of matters in which we were interested, with the earnest desire in me to see the theatre attain a robust vitality, I was incited to take " Faust " in hand again; but do what I could I estranged him from the theatre rather than approximated him to it.

The " Horen," meanwhile, continued in its course, my share in it the same; but Schiller's limitless activity seized the idea of a " Muses' Almanac," a poetical magazine, to take the place of companion to the earlier-born periodical, mostly of a prose character. Here, too, the confidence cherished in him by his countrymen was in his favor. The good, aspiring heads ranged themselves on his side. He was, moreover, capitally fitted for an editor of this kind. At one glance he comprehended the intrinsic value of a poem; and if the writer was too diffuse and knew not where to end, Schiller with a stroke of his pen would cancel you out all that was superfluous. I once saw him reduce a poem to a third of its original verses, making it not only available but valuable.

I myself owed much to his encouragement, as the " Horen " and " Almanac " fully testify. " Alexis and Dora," the " Bride of Corinth," " God and Bayadere," were here either executed or planned. The " Xenien," which from innocent, nay, indifferent beginnings, gradually intensified into the utmost sharpness and astringency, kept us going many months, and this very year, when the " Almanac " appeared, created in the German literature the greatest commotion and upheaval. They were damned by the public as the grossest abuse of freedom of the press. Their effect, however, remains incalculable.

A very dear and precious but also heavy burden I dropped from my shoulders toward the end of August. The fair copy of the last book of " Wilhelm Meister " was at last sent to press. For six years it had been my earnest task to mature this early conception, dispose it aright, and gradually hand it over to the printer. It remains, therefore, be it viewed either as a whole or in detail, one of the most incalculable productions. I myself almost want the standard for its valuation.

Scarcely, however, had I gained my freedom by the successive publication of this work, when I imposed a new burden on me; a burden, however, lighter to bear, or rather no burden at all, giving me, as it did, the means of expressing certain ideas, feelings, and conceptions of the time. " Hermann and Dorothea," in its plan and development, kept pace, step for step, with the events of the day. Its execution was begun and ended in September, ready for the hands of friends. With a sense of ease and inward comfort this poem was written, and it communicated a like feeling. The subject and execution had so penetrated me that I could never read the poem without being greatly affected, an influence it still exerts after so many years.

Friend Meyer kept diligently writing valuable papers from Italy. My preparations for following him impelled me to manifold studies, the records of which are still very useful to me. While I was working my way into the art-history of Florence, " Cellini " proved very important, and I formed the resolution, in order to make myself thoroughly at home in that business, to translate his " Autobiography," especially as it appeared to Schiller available for the " Horen."

Nor were the natural sciences neglected. Throughout the summer I found the fairest opportunity of rearing plants under colored glasses, and in total darkness, as also to prosecute the metamorphosis of insects into its details.

Galvanism and chemistry also pressed on my attention. Chromatics was, amid everything else, diligently studied, and to afford me the great advantage of exact presentation, I found a noble company disposed to hear some lectures on the subjects.

As to things abroad, the Saxon Electorate persists in its attachment to the Emperor and empire, and will in this sense cause its contingent to march. Our men also don their ormor; the expenses of this step create much anxiety.

In regard to the great world, the surviving daughter of Louis XVI, Princess Maria Theresa Charlotte, hitherto in the hands of the Republicans, is exchanged for captive French generals, while the Pope pays dear for his armistice.

The Austrians retire across the Lahn, and on the approach of the French keep possession of Frankfort. The town is bombarded, the Judengasse is part burnt, otherwise little is injured, whereupon follows the surrender. My good mother, in her fine new quarters at the chief guard-house, looking up the row, sees before her eyes the threatened and injured parts of the town. Stowing away her goods into the fire-proof cellar, she escapes over the open bridge of the Main to Offenbach. Her letter deserves being appended.

The Elector of Mainz goes to Heiligenstadt; the landgrave's residence continues for some time unknown. The people of Frankfort flee, my mother remains. We live in a kind of soporific timidity. In the Rhine and Main districts constant disturbances and flight. Frau von Coudenhoven tarries in Eisenach, and so what with fugitives, letters, messengers, couriers, the alarm of war rushes once and again as far as to our midst; yet the hope gradually gathers confirmation that for the moment we have nothing to fear, and we think ourselves safe.

The King of Prussia, on some occasion, writes from Pyrmont to the duke, preparing, with diplomatic tact, the accession to neutrality, and facilitating the step. Fear, apprehension, confusion knows no pause. At last the Elector of Saxony proclaims neutrality, at first provisionally, then decidedly. The negotiations, therefore, with Prussia became known to us as well.

Yet we hardly seem quieted by such a step of security when the Austrians again gain the ascendancy. Moreau retires, and all royally minded persons regret the precipitation with which people had let themselves be hurried away; reports increase to the prejudice of the French. Moreau, in his turn, is pursued and watched; it is even reported, shut in. Jourdan, too, retires, and people are in desperation at having saved themselves all too prematurely.

A company of men of high culture meeting at my house every Friday took firmer and firmer footing. I read a book of Voss's " Iliad," acquiring for myself applause, for the poem high interest, for the translator laudatory recognition. Each member communicated, according to his own good pleasure, his employments, works, amateur pursuits, all which was received with frank interest. Dr. Buchholz continued ably and happily to supply us with the latest physico-chemical achievements. No topic was excluded, and the feeling of the company, a feeling which communicated itself even to strangers, of itself precluded everything at all calculated to bore members. Academic instructors attached themselves to us, and of what great benefit this society grew to be, even for the university, is sufficiently indicated by the fact alone that the duke, on hearing, at one of our sittings, a paper read by Dr. Christian Wilhelm Hufeland, at once got him a professorship in Jena, where by his manifold activity he gained for himself an ever-increasing circle of influence. The Society was so managed that my absence caused no break in its meetings, Privy-Councillor Voigt undertaking their conduct in such a case, and for many years we had occasion to bless our common regulated labors.

We had also the pleasure of seeing our excellent Batsch this year in happy activity. The noble, disinterested man, working spontaneously, needed no more than a vigorous plant, large extent of soil, and copious watering: he could draw the richest nourishment out of the atmosphere.

Of this beautiful, silent labor, his writings and reports yet give testimony, and how, contented with his small glass-house, and enjoying the general confidence of contemporary natu-ralists, he saw the respect for his society increase, and the circle of its influence extend; how he communicated his pur-poses to his friends, and with modest confidence spoke of his hopes.

1797

At the close of last year I accompanied my most gracious master on a journey to Leipzig, attending a grand ball there, where Herr Dyk and company, and whoever else had smarted under or been stunned by the " Xenien," eyed us askance as if we were the Evil Principle. In Dessau we enjoyed the re-membrance of former times: the family of Von Loen showed us the open confidence of friends, and we could together call to mind the earliest Frankfort days and hours.

In the first months of this year the theatre received a new. ornament in the accession to it of Caroline Jagemann. " Obe-ron " was given, soon after " Telemach," * and many parts could be filled up with better selection. Outwardly, in the immediate future, the stage continued in its usual course, but inwardly much of importance was in preparation. Schiller, who now had a theatre at hand and under his immediate ob-servation, was bending his mind earnestly to the task of better adapting his plays for the stage, and the vast scope over which " Wallenstein " extended in his mind proving unmanageable in one piece, he determined on breaking it up into several parts. This, in the absence of the company, richly supplied us for the whole summer with matter for instruction and conversation. The " Prologue " was already written, and " Wallenstein's Lager " in visible growth.

I, for my part, too, was in the full swing of activity. " Her-mann and Dorothea " appeared in pocket-book form, and a new epic-romantic poem, immediately thereafter, was con-ceived. The plan was thought out in all its parts, and in an unhappy moment I imparted the argument to my friends. They, however, dissuaded me from the project, and even yet it vexes me to think I let myself be led away by them. The poet alone knows the value of any particular subject, and what

* A German version of " Télémaque."

charm and grace he can elicit from it. I wrote the " New
Pausias " and the " Metamorphosis of Plants " in elegiac form ;
Schiller, with his " Diver," came into competition with me. In
point of fact, we rested neither day nor night. Not till toward
morning did Schiller give himself to sleep. All the passions
were in turmoil : the " Xenien " had thrown all Germany into
agitation, everyone was moved at once to indignation and to
laughter. The wounded tried all their powers of annoyance
on us, and all we opposed to them was the undesisting continuation of our efforts.

The University of Jena was now at its full bloom. The co-
operation there of talented men and favorable circumstances
would deserve the most faithful and brilliant description.
Fichte, in the " Philosophical Journal," gave a new view of
the doctrine of science. Woltmann had become a subject of
interest, justifying the fairest hopes. The Brothers Humboldt
were settled there, and everything connected with nature was
philosophically and scientifically discussed. My " Osteological
Type " of 1795 gave rise to a more rational study and use of
the public collection, as also of my own. I drew up a plan of
the " Metamorphosis of Insects," a subject which for several
years had been my constant attention. Krause's drawings of
the Harz rocks impelled to geological studies. Galvanic experiments were made by Humboldt. Scherer excited the best
hopes in the department of chemistry. I commenced arranging
the color-tables. For Schiller I continued my translation of
" Cellini," and resuming my Biblical studies, with a view to
finding subjects for poetical treatment, I let myself be seduced
into a critical examination of the journey of the children of
Israel through the wilderness. The essay, with affixed map,
was intended to recast into an enterprise, if not sensible, yet
comprehensible, that wonderful forty years' wandering.

An irresistible passion for country and garden life had at
that time taken possession of the people. Schiller purchased a
garden at Jena, and removed thither ; Wieland had settled in
Össmannstädt. Three miles from there, on the right bank of
the Ilm, a small property in Oberrossla was for sale ; I had
some thoughts of buying it.

A visit from Lerse and Hirt gladdened us. The strange
traveller, Lord Bristol, prompted me to an adventurous experience. I make preparations for a journey to Switzerland
to meet my friend Heinrich Meyer returning from Italy. The
building of Weimar Castle forces us to look about for an able
architect and expert workmen. The drawing-school also receives fresh impulse.

Before my departure, out of decided aversion from the pub-

lication of the correspondence of friends, I burn all the letters
sent to me since 1772. Schiller again visits me in Weimar, and
I set out on July 30th. An expert secretary accompanying me,
everything striking and important occurring during the journey was carefully preserved. By due editing, a quite interesting little volume having been compiled from this, only the most
general summary of the journey need here be given.

On the way a minute survey of the districts engaged me, my
attention being directed to geognosy and culture based thereon.
In Frankfort, Sömmering contributes to my instruction by his
conversation, experiments, and drawings. I make the acquaintance of many persons, public and private ; pay attention to the
theatre ; carry on a lively correspondence with Schiller and
other friends, and note the antithesis of the Austrian garrison
and captive Frenchmen : the former, imperturbable seriousness ;
the latter, gay buffoonery. French satyric copperplates.

25th.—Leave Frankfort. Going by way of Heidelberg, Heil-
bronn, Ludwigsburg, I arrive on the 29th at Stuttgart. Merchant Rapp, Dannecker, Scheffauer are visited. Acquaintanceship with Professor Thouret, with skilled workers in ornaments,
stucco-work, quadrants, dating back to the tumultuous time of
Duke Karl. Negotiations with them with a view to engaging
them for the building of Weimar Castle. The " Bachelor and
the Mühlbach " (millstream) dates from the beginning of September, and is at once composed by Zumsteeg ; then the " Young
Men and the Gypsy." September 9th in Tübingen, the guest
of Cotta ; conversed with the most distinguished men there.
Natural museum of Professor Storr inspected ; formerly belonging to Pasquay in Frankfort-on-the-Main, and removed
with the utmost care to Tübingen. Leave there on September 16th. Schaffhausen, Rheinfall, Zürich. 21st, in Stäfa.
Meeting with Meyer. 28th, travel with him by way of Maria
Einsiedeln as far as the Gotthard. October 8th, we returned.
For the third time I visited the little cantons, and the epic
form being just in the ascendant with me, I meditated a " Tell "
in the immediate presence of the classic locality. I needed
such a diversion and distraction for my thoughts, the saddest news having reached me in the midst of the mountains.
Christiana Neumann, by marriage Becker, had departed from
among us. I devoted to her memory the elegy, " Euphrosyne."
Remembrance full of love and honor is all we can give to the
dead.

On the Gotthard I had acquired beautiful minerals ; the highest acquisition, however, was conversation with my friend
Meyer. Italy, in all its fulness of life, he brought back to me
—a land which, alas! war junctures now closed against us.

As consolation, we prepared ourselves for the " Propyläen."
The doctrine of the subjects, and what art assigns as proper
for representation, principally engaged our attention.   The
minute and technical description of art-subjects of ancient and
modern times we reserved as a treasure for the future.   A description of Stäfa having been attempted by me, the journals
revised and copied out fair, we left there on October 21st.
October 26th, leaving Zürich, we arrived on November 6th at
Nürnberg.   In the friendly circle of the district officials we
lived some happy days.   Leave there on November 15th.

In Weimar the arrival of several emigrants of importance
widened our circle, and added to our entertainment there.

To supply omissions, Oberappellationsrath (member of Supreme Court of Appeal), Körner, and his dear and hopeful
family, delighted us the summer of this year with their
presence.   There still remain important events this year un-
mentioned.

Millin's antiquarian activity began to unfold itself.   The
greatest influence, however, was exercised by Wolf's " Prolegomena."

In the theatre I felt acutely the great gap: Christiana Neumann was not there, and yet there was the place where she
had inspired me with so much interest.   She it was who had
accustomed me to the boards, and so now I directed to the
whole the attention I had formerly bestowed exclusively on her.

Her place was filled up with at least a pleasing actress.
Caroline Jagemann, too, meanwhile trained herself ever more
perfectly, and in the drama also acquired unqualified applause.
The theatre had such a good company that all current pieces
could be played with satisfaction and without rivalry.

What, however, redounded to our great and singular advantage was that the most eminent works of Iffland and Kotzebue
had been already appropriated by our theatre, and, on the new
paths they had struck out for themselves, paths hitherto un-
trodden in Germany, had obtained great applause.   Both authors were still in their bloom; the former as actor stood in the
epoch of highest art-culture.

It was also of the greatest advantage to us that we had to
play only before a small public, just sufficiently cultivated, a
public whose taste we could satisfy, while at the same time
maintaining our independence; nay, we dared attempt a great
deal with a view to our own higher culture and that of the
spectators.

Here it was that Schiller proved eminently helpful to us.
He was now minded to have done with the Raw, Extravagant,
Gigantic: his culture already reached the measure of the truly

great and its natural expression. We passed no day in the same
quarter without oral, no week in the neighborhood of each
other without epistolary, intercommunication.

1798

So we labored indefatigably in anticipation of a visit from
Iffland, who in April, by eight of his representations, was to
breathe into us fresh life.   Great was the influence of his presence; for each actor was to measure himself in rivalry with
him.   The immediate effect was that our company proceeded
to Lauchstädt, on this occasion also, in a very respectable state
of efficiency.

They had scarcely left when the old wish revived to have a
better building for the Weimar theatre.   Actors and public
alike thought themselves entitled to a more becoming structure.
The necessity of such a change was indeed recognized by everyone, and it needed but a spirited impulse to determine and speed
the execution of the project.   Architect Thouret was called from
Stuttgart for the further prosecution of the building of the
castle; as a lateral concern he drew up a happy plan for a new
construction of the existing theatre—a plan at once received
with applause, showing, as it did, the greatest skill in accom-
modating itself to the extant edifice.   And so, on this occasion
also, was verified the old remark, that the presence of an architect excites architectural inclinations.   The work was prosecuted
diligently and speedily, so that by October 12th, court and public could be invited to the opening of the new house.   A " Prologue " by Schiller, and " Wallenstein's Lager " gave substance
and dignity to this solemnity.

The whole summer there had been no want of preparatory
labors in anticipation of this event.   The great Wallenstein
Cycle, at first only announced, kept us busy all through that
period, though not exclusively.

My own poetical and literary activity was so extensive that
the " Prophecies of Bakis " engaged me only a little time.
" Achilleïs " I had thoroughly conceived, and one evening communicated the plan in full to Schiller.   He reproached me for
not embodying so ripe a conception in words and verse.   Thus
spurred and exhorted to diligence, I wrote the first book; drawing up also the plan, aided by an extract from the " Iliad."

From such labors, however, I was drawn away by my bias
toward plastic art, a bias which Meyer's return from Italy called
into prominence.   We were principally employed in the further
execution of the first piece of the " Propyläen," which was in
part projected, in part written.   I continued " Cellini's Life "

as a basis for the history of the sixteenth century. " Diderot on Colors " was accompanied with notes more of a humorous than artistic character, and, while Meyer was studiously engaged with the subjects in the main point of all plastic art, I wrote the " Collector," introducing into the free, cheerful world much matter for reflection and consideration.

Natural science, too, engaged much of my thought, observation, and activity. Schelling " On the World-Soul " exercised our highest faculties. In the everlasting metamorphosis of the external world we now saw the world-soul anew embodied. Every living thing around us connected with natural history I studied with great attention. Remarkable foreign animals, in particular a young elephant, contributed to our instruction.

I must not omit here an essay I wrote on " Pathologic Ivory." For several years I had collected pieces of shot and re-healed elephant's tusks—a phenomenon extremely hateful to comb-makers when their saw, often unexpectedly, grates against such a structure—accumulating more than twenty specimens which demonstrated to admiration how an iron ball penetrating the tooth has power, no doubt, to disturb, but not to destroy, its organic life, which here, in a peculiar way, defends and recovers itself. It was a pleasure to me, as an expression of thanks, to incorporate this collection, described and explained, into the cabinet of my friend Loder, to whom I owed so much instruction.

In what order and division the history of the theory of colors was to be set forth was thought out in its different epochs, the various writers being studied, and the doctrine itself carefully pondered and made the subject of conversation with Schiller. He it was who solved the question which long detained me: what the proper grounds are of that strange phenomenon of the confusion of colors in the case of certain people—a phenomenon which led to the conjecture that those persons see some colors, but fail to see others. The conclusion Schiller at last came to was that such people lacked the knowledge of blue. A young man at the head of a guild, and at that time studying in Jena, was in this predicament, and obligingly offered himself for repeated experiments, which at last established the above conclusion.

Further, to represent visually the mental states, we drew up, in common, various symbolic charts. For example, we constructed a temperament-card, in the style of a compass-card, and planned a tabular representation of the advantages and disadvantages to each art of dilettanteism.

A great deal of furtherance in the natural sciences we owed to a visit of Herr van Marum.

Not, however, to lose ground on the side of immediate, common nature, I followed the then prevailing fancy for the country. The possession of the freehold in Rossla necessarily brought me into closer intimacy with the land and soil, country ways, and village relations; imparting to me very many views and sympathies that would otherwise have remained foreign to me. Thus arose, too, for me a neighborly relation with Wieland, who no doubt had gone further in this direction, he having completely abandoned Weimar and taken up his residence in Ossmannstädt. He did not consider, what should have first occurred to him, that for the intercourse of life he had grown completely indispensable to our Duchess Amalia, and she to him. This separation caused a most wonderful despatch hither and thither of messengers on horseback and on foot, and a certain unrest hardly to be assuaged.

An odd visit this summer was paid us in the person of Frau von La Roche, with whom Wieland had never properly agreed, but to whom he was now in direct opposition. No doubt, a good-natured sentimentality which thirty years before, in a time of mutual forbearance, had perhaps been tolerable, was now quite out of fashion and insufferable to a man like Wieland. Her granddaughter, Sophia Brentano, accompanied her, and played a part quite the reverse of that of the grandmother, but equally whimsical.

1799

January 30th, representation of the " Piccolomini "; April 20th, of "Wallenstein." Meanwhile, Schiller was in constant activity. " Mary Stuart " and the " Hostile Brothers " became the subject of conversation. We consider the idea of printing a collection of German dramatic pieces which had maintained their hold on the public, keeping some in their entirety, but altering and abridging others so as to bring them more into conformity with the modern time and taste. The same with foreign pieces, but doing as little violence to their original form as possible. The object aimed at by such work is plain, that of laying the foundation of a substantial repertory for the German theatre, and our zeal to accomplish this testifies to our conviction of the necessity and importance of such an undertaking.

We had by this time become accustomed to work in common, and our mode of co-operation is fully explained in the essay " On the German Theatre." To this year belong the editing of " Macbeth " and the translation of " Mahomet."

The memoirs of Stephanie de Bourbon Conti begot in me

the conception of the "Natural Daughter." Into the plan of this work I desired, with an earnestness worthy of the theme, to fuse many a year's writings and thoughts on the French Revolution and its consequences. In co-operation with Schiller I drew up designs of smaller pieces, some of which, in Schiller's handwriting, still remain.

The "Propyläen" was continued. In September we held the first exhibition of prize pictures. The subject was "Paris and Helena." Hartmann in Stuttgart gained the prize.

If in this way the Weimar lovers of art acquired some measure of confidence from the outside world, Schiller was also thereby incited, in company with me, to the unintermittent observation of nature, art, and manners. Here we became ever more sensible of the necessity of tabular and symbolic treatment. We re-drew together the temperament-card above referred to. We also further elaborated the favorable and prejudicial influences of dilettanteism on all the parts; the papers on which, in both our handwritings, are still extant. In general, such methodic charts, prompted by Schiller's philosophic, systematic mind, and to which, in a symbolic fashion, I adapted myself, formed the most agreeable employment. From time to time we took them up anew, testing them, transposing them. In this way was the plan of the "Theory of Colors" repeatedly labored.

Thus in those branches of science and art which we had marked out as our domain we saw no *termini* before us. Schelling courteously communicated to us the introduction to his "Plan of Natural Philosophy," and talked over with pleasure many physical topics. I composed a general scheme of nature and art.

In August and September I lived in my garden on the Stern, to observe, with the help of a good telescope, a whole lunation, making at last, in this way, a nearer acquaintance with a neighbor of mine so long beloved and admired. All this, however, kept in abeyance a large poem of nature which flitted before my mind.

During my garden-residence, in order to familiarize myself with the most multifarious situations and modes of thought and poetic art, I read Herder's "Fragments," Winckelmann's "Letters and Early Writings," as also Milton's "Paradise Lost." Returned to the town I studied, with the above-mentioned theatrical purposes, the older English pieces, particularly those of Ben Jonson, besides others ascribed to Shakespeare. On good advice I interested myself in the "Sisters of Lesbos," the authoress of which had formerly attracted me as a very beautiful child, and then as a person of high talent. Tieck read to me his "Genoveva," the truly poetic treatment of which gave me great pleasure, and gained the heartiest applause. The presence of Wilhelm August Schlegel was also profitable to me. No moment was passed in idleness, and for many years in the future we looked forward to an intellectual social activity.

1800

This year I spent half in Weimar, half in Jena. January 30th, " Mahomet " was represented, greatly to the advantage of our players. They were thereby forced out of the natural domain they were accustomed to into a more restricted field, the artificial arrangements of which, however, could easily be transformed into natural. It prepared us in every sense for the more difficult and richer pieces shortly to follow. Of operas I will mention only " Tarare."

Subsequently, on October 24th, as on the Duchess Amalia's birthday, " Palæophron and Neoterpe " was given in a more select circle. The representation of the little piece by young lovers of art deserves being called exemplary. Five figures played in masks. The Lady alone was allowed to delight us by the peculiar grace of her own personal features. This representation prepared the way for mask-comedies, which for years to come furnished us with quite a new entertainment.

The composition of different pieces, in common with Schiller, was continued. The " Mother's Secret," by Horace Walpole, was studied and taken in hand, but on closer inspection dropped. The more modern small poems were handed over to Unger; the " Good Women," a social pleasantry, written. At the end of the year, " Tancred " was to be translated for the next January 30th, a day always celebrated. This was done accordingly, notwithstanding an unhealthy feeling of discomfort announcing itself.

In preparing in August this year the second exhibition, we found ourselves favored by contributions from many sides. The subjects, the " Death of Rhesus " and " Hector's Parting from Andromache," had attracted many able artists. The first prize was obtained by Hofmann at Cologne, the second by Nahl at Cassel. The third and last volume of the " Propyläen " was, after increased efforts, published. The way in which envious people opposed this undertaking deserves on fitting occasion to be more fully described, as a consolation to our grandchildren, who, too, will meet with no better treatment.

Natural philosophy pursued its quiet course. A six-foot Herschel telescope was procured for our scientific institutions. I now observed by myself several changes of the moon, and made myself acquainted with the most important light boundaries, thereby obtaining a good idea of the relief of the moon's surface. For the first time, too, the principal division of the " Theory of Colors " into the three great parts, didactic, polemic, and historic, had become quite clear and determinate in my mind.

In Botany, for the sake of a sensible view of Jussieu's system, I arranged in that order the whole of the prints of several botanical octavos, thereby obtaining an insight into the individual form and a survey of the whole such as was not otherwise to be had.

1801

At the beginning of the year I was overtaken with a severe illness, the cause of which was the following: Since the representation of " Mahomet," I had begun and prosecuted a translation of Voltaire's " Tancred." Toward the end of the year, however, it being necessary to set more earnestly to work, I repaired in the middle of December to Jena, where, in the large rooms of the ducal castle, I was at once able to conjure up the spirit of old-fashioned times. The conditions of the place, too, were favorable to my work; but the assiduity with which I labored made me on this, as on many earlier occasions, oblivious of the evil influence of the locality. The building lies in the lowest level of the town, close on the Mill Dam; the stairs and staircase are of gypsum, a very cold and damp stone, which, when a thaw sets in, is apt to contract moisture. Altogether the residence, especially in winter, is of a very doubtful character. But who, busy with any undertaking, thinks of the place where he is working? In short, a violent catarrh laid hold on me, without, however, bending me from my task.

At that time the Brown dogma commanded the allegiance of doctors young and old. A young friend, a devotee of this doctrine, knew by experience that, in the worst cases of chest-affection, Peruvian balsam mixed with opium and myrrh produces an instant arrest of the trouble, and a counteraction to its dangerous course. He advised me to this recipe, and instantly cough, spitting, everything was gone. In happy spirits I returned, in the company of Professor Schelling, to Weimar, when immediately, at the beginning of the year, the catarrh returned with increased violence, and I fell into a state which deprived me of my senses. My friends were in alarm, the doctors in perplexity. The duke, my most gracious master, perceiving the danger, at once interfered, and sent a courier to Jena for Hofrath Stark. Some days passed before I returned to complete consciousness, and when, by the help of nature and the doctors, I again became sensible, I found the

right eye swollen, my sight impeded, and myself otherwise in
a pitiful plight. The prince did not give over his careful at-
tentions, the experienced doctor, a sure hand in practice, did
his best, and so with sleep and perspiration I gradually came
round again.

Inwardly, meanwhile, I had got into such form that on January 19th the *ennui* of the situation demanded some moderate
activity, and I turned to the translation of Theophrast's little
book "On Colors," which had long been in my head. My
nearest friends, Schiller, Herder, Voigt, Einsiedel, and Loder,
were ready to help me over further bad hours. On the 22d a
concert was arranged by me, and on the 24th, when his Highness the Duke set out for Berlin, I was able in blithe spirits to
thank him for the unceasing care about me he had shown to
the end; for on that day my eye again opened, inspiring the
hope of a free and full prospect once more of the world. Next,
with recovering sight, I could with reverence greet the presence of the Most Serene Duchess Amalia and her friendly intellectual circle.

On the 29th I went through the part of Amenaïde with
Mademoiselle Caspers, a rising actress. Friend Schiller conducted the rehearsals, and on the evening of the 30th, after the
representation, he reported to me the success of the affair. I
went, further, through the same part with Mademoiselle Jagemann, whose *naturel* and merit as an actress and singer at that
time deserved an immediate description at the hands of an enthusiastic admirer. Available and agreeable in many parts was
Ehlers as actor and singer, and, especially in the latter capacity,
extremely welcome at a social party. In his quite incomparable rendering of ballads and other such songs in accompaniment to the guitar, he produced the words of the text with the
most exact precision. He was indefatigable in the study of
proper expression, which consists in the singer's bringing out
to one melody the most various meanings of the single verses,
and so filling the place at once of the lyric and epic poet. Perfectly appreciating this property, he was well pleased on my
encouragement several evenings, nay, till late into the night,
to repeat the same song with all its different shades in the most
careful manner. By successful practice he convinced himself
how despicable is all so-called "Durchcomposition" of songs,
by which the general lyric character is quite effaced, and a false
sympathy in details furthered and excited.

By February 7th my productive impatience was astir; I took
up "Faust" again, and executed piecemeal what had long been
sketched and designed in my mind.

When at the end of last year I was working in Jena at

"Tancred," my accomplished friends there loudly reproached me that I was taking myself up so assiduously with French pieces, which Germany in its present temper could not regard with favor, and was producing nothing of my own, though I had given to the world so much in that way. I, therefore, called up before my mind the "Natural Daughter," the complete plan of which had for years been lying among my papers. As opportunity offered I thought out the subject further, but from a superstition, based on experience, that an undertaking to be successful must not be spoken of, I concealed this work even from Schiller, to whom, therefore, I appeared unsympathetic, trustless, and actionless. At the end of December, as I find remarked, the first act of the "Natural Daughter" was completed.

There was no want, however, of deviations, especially in the way of natural science, philosophy, and literature. Ritter visited me often, and though I could not at once get into his way of treating subjects, I yet readily apprehended what he set forth in the way of experiences, and what in accordance with his aspirations he was impelled to cultivate himself to as a whole. Toward Schelling and Schlegel my relation continued active and communicative. Tieck stayed a considerable time in Weimar; his presence was always gracefully furthersome. With Paulus my alliance likewise continued ever the same; all these relationships being maintained in their vitality through the proximity to each other of Weimar and Jena, and still further strengthened by my residence in the latter place.

Natural history did not concern me much. A crooked elephant's tusk was found after a heavy rain-fall in the Gelmeröder defile. It lay higher than all the remains hitherto found of these earlier animals which had been unearthed in the tufa quarries, and found embedded in the stone, a few feet above the Ilm. This specimen, on the other hand, was discovered immediately on the chalk stratum, under the flooded earth, among bowlders, about 200 feet above the Ilm. It was found at a time when, estranged from such subjects, I took little interest in them. The finders took the material for meerschaum, and sent the pieces to Eisenach; only a few fragments reached me, which I left to themselves. Councillor of Mines Werner, however, on a second instructive visit, at once settled the matter, and we were delighted by the solution of a master in his department.

The relations into which my possession of the Rossla freehold brought me demanded much attention for some time, and the days which thus seemed plundered from me were yet turned to useful account in many ways. The first tenant was to be

sued at law, a new tenant to be installed, and the experience
gradually acquired in such foreign affairs could not go for
naught.

By the end of March there was already sufficient feeling of
recreation in a country residence. Business was given over
to agriculturists and lawyers, and in the meantime it was a
pleasure to expatiate in the open air. *Ergo bibamus,* too, being
a fit conclusion to all premises, many a customary and extem-
porized feast was celebrated. There was no want of visitors,
and the costs of a well-furnished table increased the deficit the
old tenant had left behind him.

The new one was passionately fond of tree-nurseries, and a
pleasant slip of valley of the most fruitful soil gave scope for
the gratification of his tastes in this direction. The bushy side
of the declivity, graced with a bubbling spring, called forth,
on the other hand, my old park-fancies for winding paths and
social spaces. In short, all that was wanting was the element
of profit to make this little possession highly desirable. The
neighborhood, too, of an important little town and smaller com-
munities, made social by sensible functionaries and able farmers, gave a particular charm to the residence. The roadway
toward Eckartsberg, now determined on, and marked off immediately behind the house-garden, always suggested thoughts
and plans of a pleasure-house, with the enlivening sight of
animate market vehicles rumbling past. Thus, on the soil
one should have looked to for profit, there were only comfortable preparations made for increased expenses and ruinous
distractions.

One pious, life-important solemnity, however, occurred these
days in the interior of the house. The confirmation of my son,
solemnized by Herder in his noble way, did not pass without
an affecting remembrance of past relationships, nor without
hope of future friendly connections.

Amid these and other events a good deal of time had passed
away. Physicians, as well as friends, solicited me to go to a
watering-place, and, in conformity with the convalescent system then prevailing, I decided on Pyrmont, all the more that
I had now long yearned after a stay in Göttingen.

On June 5th I departed for Weimar, and the very first stages
of the road yielded me the highest refreshment. I could again
look abroad sympathetically on the world, and though unmixed
by any æsthetic feeling, the journey inspired an inward sense
of comfort. I liked to view the succession of landscapes, to
mark the changes in the nature of the country, to think of the
character of the towns, their remote origin, restoration, police,
habits, and perversities. The human form, and its highly re-

markable varieties, also attracted my attention. I again belonged to the world.

Arrived at Göttingen, and entering the " Crown," I observed, while twilight was thickening over the place, some commotion in the street. Students were coming and going, disappeared in side lanes, and reappeared in lively groups. At last, all at once, there resounded a hearty cheering, but in a moment all again was still. I heard that such testimonies of applause were formally repudiated, and it gave me all the greater pleasure that they had ventured spontaneously to greet me in passing. Immediately thereafter I received a note, signed Schumacher from Holstein, intimating in a becomingly confiding way a purpose he and a company of young men had cherished to visit me in Weimar at Michaelmas, and expressing the hope to have their wishes gratified on the spot. I spoke to them with interest and pleasure. Such a friendly reception would have been grateful to a sound man, and was doubly so to a convalescent.

Hofrath Blumenbach received me in his usual way. Always surrounded by the most recent and remarkable things, his presence is at any time instructive. In his house I saw the first aerolite, a product of nature we had only a short time previously come to a sensible belief in. A young Kestner and Von Arnim, formerly known, and of kindred tastes, called on me and accompanied me to the riding-school, where I saluted the celebrated riding-master Ayrer among his pupils. There is always something imposing in a well-equipped riding-school. The horse holds a high rank among animals, yet his considerable far-reaching intelligence is in a wonderful way restricted by his cramped expression. A creature of such respectable, nay, great qualities, capable of utterance only by walking, running, and racing, is a strange subject for contemplation. One almost comes to the conviction that he was created only to be an organ of man, in order through association with higher sense and aims to accomplish almost impossible feats of strength and grace.

The reason why a riding-school has such a beneficial influence on the intelligent man is that here, perhaps alone in the world, is seen with the eye and comprehended with the mind the judicious restriction of action, the expulsion of all arbitrariness, nay, of accident itself. Man and animal here so mingle into one that it cannot be said which properly educates the other. Such considerations attained their climax when the two pairs of so-called white-born horses appeared, which Prince Sanguszko purchased in Hanover for a large sum.

Passing to the stillest and least obvious form of activity, I now had a survey of the library, in which one feels as in the presence of a great capital noiselessly yielding incalculable interest.

Hofrath Heine showed me Tischbein's heads of the Homeric heroes, executed on a large scale. I recognized the hand of my old friend, and rejoiced in his continued efforts, through study of the ancients, to attain an insight into the method by which the plastic artist is to compete with the poet. How much progress has been made since, twenty years ago, the excellent Lessing, with a presentiment of the truth, found it necessary to warn people against the errors of Count Caylus, and in opposition to Klotz and Riegel, defend his conviction that mythologico-epic subjects are to be treated not according to Homer, but as Homer himself did, in a sensuous-artistic way!

New and renewed acquaintanceships were gratefully formed. Under conduct of Blumenbach I again viewed the museums, and in the geological department found hitherto unknown extra-European specimens. And as any place attracts a stranger hither and thither, calling into exercise every moment the capacity in man of rapidly changing his interest with the subject, I justly prized Professor Osiander's pains to show me the important institution of the new and strangely built Lying-in House, as also its mode of operation.

The enticements with which Blumenbach attracts youth and instructs them in an entertaining way captivated, too, my son of eleven years old. The boy, hearing that Hainberg was as if composed of many-shaped petrifactions, urged me to pay a visit to this height, where the usual forms lay exposed to view, while the rarer yielded themselves only to a longer and diligent search.

And so, on June 12th, I left this uniquely important place, in the grateful hope of again spending a longer period there by way of completing my recovery.

The way to Pyrmont offered me new subjects for contemplation. They valley of the Leine, with its mild character, appeared friendly and cosey. The town of Eimbeck, with its high-aspiring roofs, slated with sandstone, made a curious impression. Passing through it and its immediate neighborhood, I thought I could perceive that twenty or thirty years previously it must have had an excellent mayor. This conclusion I drew from the fact of there being important plantations there of about that age.

In Pyrmont I took handsome lodgings in the house of the treasurer of the spa, the house having a quiet situation at the end of the town. No better luck could have befallen me than that the Griesbachs had taken rooms in the same house, arriving shortly after me. Quiet neighbors, tried friends, people of culture and liberal dispositions, they furnished me with the most excellent entertainment. Pastor Schütz, from Bückburg, most welcome to this family as a brother and brother-in-law, and to me as a likeness of his brothers and sisters, my old acquaintances, took likewise warm interest in all that was worthy and elevated. Hofrath Richter, from Göttingen, in the company of Prince Languszko, who was laboring under an eye-ailment, ever displayed most amiable properties: dryly cheerful, rallying and being rallied, now ironical and paradoxical, now grave and open.

With such persons from the very beginning I felt myself at home. I could think of no spa-period I had passed in better company. Our acquaintanceship of years' standing begot a mutual tolerant confidence. Here, too, I made the acquaintance of Frau von Weinheim, the former wife of General von Bauer, Madame Scholin and Raleff, the relative of Madame Sandor in Berlin. Graceful and amiable friends, they added much to the pleasure of our circle.

Unfortunately, stormy, rainy weather hindered frequent walks in the open air. I devoted myself at home to the translation of " Theophrast," and to further labor on the ever-enlarging " Theory of Colors."

The remarkable vapor-cavity in the neighborhood of the place, where nitrogen gas mixed with water is powerfully beneficial to the human body, but by itself an invisible, deadly air, gave rise to a number of entertaining experiments. After a diligent examination of the place, and of the level of that stratum of air, I could more boldly institute striking and enlivening experiments. The soap-bubbles dancing merrily on the invisible element, the sudden extinction of a flickering wisp of straw, the instantaneous relighting, and such like appearances gave stunning gratification to such persons as knew nothing at all of the phenomenon, and excited admiration in those who had not yet seen it produced on a large scale and in the open air. This secret agent being taken home by me in Pyrmont bottles and the miracle repeated of the wax taper becoming extinguished in each apparently empty glass, the company was completely satisfied as to the experiments, and the incredulous spa-master so convinced in the matter that he readily packed up for me some empty alongside of some water-filled bottles. These I took with me to Weimar, where it was shown that their contents had lost none of their efficacy.

We often walked to Lügde along the path leading thither between enclosed meadow spaces. In the hamlet which had been several times burnt down our attention was arrested by a desperate inscription on a house :

> " God grant this house His grace !
> Twice I've run out apace ;
> For twice it has been burnt to the ground.
> If a third time I'm running out found,
> God bless my flight and what's to follow,
> For ne'er again I'll raise its fellow. "

The Franciscan cloister was visited and some milk there offered us tasted. A primitive church outside the place gave us the first innocent conception of such a house of God in early times with nave and cross passages under one roof, with perfectly smooth, unadorned front-gable. It was ascribed to the times of Charlemagne ; in any case it is to be accounted primitive, whether in respect to the actual time of its erection or as answering to the primitive wants of that district.

I, and especially my son, enjoyed a most agreeable surprise through an offer of Rector Werner to guide us to the so-called crystal mountain behind Lügde, where, under clear sunshine, the fields are seen shimmering with thousands and thousands of small mountain crystals. These have their origin in the little holes of a marl stone, and are in every way remarkable, as a more recent product, in which a minimum of the silica contained in the limestone, probably escaping in the form of vapor, passes pure and clear as water into crystals.

We further visited a hardware factory behind the Königsberg established and carried on by Quakers, and were also induced to attend several times their religious services held close by Pyrmont. The rhetoric which there flowed forth after a long pause of expectation and which was to be regarded as improvised would hardly be taken by any person the first time, let alone after repeated hearings, for inspired. It is sad that a pure worship once pinned down to a particular place and losing its true relation to the present through the lapse of time can never quite escape a touch of hypocrisy.

The Queen of France, the Consort of Louis XVIII, under the name of the Countess Lille, appeared also at the Spa, in a small but reserved circle.

I have yet important men to name ; Councillor of Consistory Horstig and Hofrath Marquart, the latter a friend and follower of Zimmermann.

The continuance of bad weather drove society frequently to the theatre. I paid more attention to the actors than the pieces. Among my papers I find a list of all their names and the parts they played ; but the place reserved for the criticism is not filled

up.   Iffland and Kotzebue, here, too, did their best, and Eulalia,
if one understood little of the parts she played, produced by her
soft, sentimental-toned delivery the greatest effect; my lady-
neighbors dissolved into tears.

What, however, winds through and apprehensively agitates
all Pyrmont society, like an evil serpent, is the passion for gambling and the interest in it affecting everyone even against his
will.   Enter the salons to escape wind and weather, or in favorable hours walk up and down the alleys, everywhere among the
ranks of men you hear the same monster hissing.   Now you
witness a wife anxiously beseeching a husband to gamble no
more, now you meet a young man in despair over his losses
neglecting his lady-love, forgetting his bride.   Then, again, all
at once resounds a cry of unbounded admiration, " The bank
is closed for the day ! "   This time it happened indeed in *Rouge
et Noir.*   The prudent winner immediately got into a post-
chaise to secure his unexpectedly acquired treasure in the hands
of near friends and relatives.   He returned, as appeared, with
a moderately filled purse, and continued to live quietly, as if
nothing had happened.

It is, however, impossible to reside in this district without
being reminded of those early histories of which the Roman
writers hand down to us such honorable records.   Here is still
to be seen the circumvallation of a mountain, that series of hills
and valleys was probably the scene of certain marches and battles.   The name of that mountain, of that place, is full of suggestions.   Traditional customs themselves point back to the
earliest times of rude celebrations.   Let one resist the influence
never so much, let one be never so averse from speculations leading from uncertain to still more uncertain ground ; one is here
caught in a magic circle, is constrained to identfy the past with
the present, to localize the most general space to a spot close by.
At last one enjoys the greatest comfort in fancying for a moment that he has rendered the vaguest of traditions a subject of
immediate observation.

By conversations of this kind, together with reading of many
papers, books, and tracts, all more or less pertaining to the
history of Pyrmont and its neighborhood, the thought of a
certain definite picture became alive in me, for which, in my customary way, I at once sketched out a plan.

In the year 1582, all at once streams of travellers began to
pour in a lively manner from all parts of the world toward Pyrmont, a well at that time known, indeed, but not yet highly celebrated—a marvel that nobody could explain.   Incited by the
news of this event, a brave German knight in his best years
commands his squire to make all equipment, and on the journey

keep an exact diary; for the squire having as a boy been destined for a monk was expert enough with the pen. The diary accordingly begins from the moment of the command, with the preparations for departure and the care of the knight's household in his absence; whereby we obtain a clear view of the situation.

They put themselves on the road and find innumerable wayfarers streaming hither from all sides. The knight and his squire are ready with their aid and take the direction and conduct of the crowd. This gives occasion for a description of the state of those times. At last the knight arrives in Pyrmont at the head of a large caravan. Here, as already on the way, all attention is given to local aspects. Of primitive times there was, indeed, yet much remaining to remind one of Hermann and his associates. The church at Lügde here proves of the greatest service. The tumult and throng are brought prominently into view. Of the endless diseases the repulsive are in few words dismissed; the mental, however, as being wonderful and not disgusting, are treated at large, the persons so affected being also described. Ties of affection and manifold relations develop themselves, and the Unsearchable, the Holy, forms a desirable contrast to the sensationally splendid. Kindred spirits draw together, characters seek their like, and so in the midst of the world-commotion there arises a City of God, round whose invisible walls the rabble lashes and rages according to its fashion. For here, too, gathered vulgarity of every kind: charlatans who found special entrance; gamblers, sharpers, who threatened everyone, except the united circle of the good; gypsies, who, by their strange behavior and their knowledge of the future, inspired confidence and reverence; not to forget the multitude of hucksters whose linen, cloths, and hides were at once taken possession of by the knight and thereby a place of residence, though a thronged one, provided for the orderly people.

The dealers finding such speedy and advantageous market for their wares, some of them made haste to return with similar goods; others speculated how to set up with them for themselves and others shelter and protection against wind and weather. In short, a far extended store was soon formed, whereby, under steady sale, the ever-new arrivals found satisfaction for the primary necessities of lodging.

The knight had surrounded the quarter of the noble company with palisades and so secured it against every physical attack. There was no want of spiteful, secretly opposing, violently defiant adversaries, who, however, were incapable of inflicting any injury. The virtuous circle already counted within it several knights, old and young, who at once institute watch and police; nor did it lack for earnest clerical men who practise right and justice.

All this was represented in the style of that time as the subject of immediate observation, and daily written down by the squire with such short natural reflections as would occur to a good opening mind.

Then, however, appeared, causing a sensation, three worthy men, dressed in long-folded, glittering white robes, and whose ages formed an ascending series, a youth, a middle-aged man, and an old man, and stepped unexpectedly into the midst of the well-minded company. Themselves full of mystery, they revealed the mystery of their meeting, opening clear vistas into the future greatness of Pyrmont.

This thought occupied me the whole time of my stay in Pyrmont, as also on my return journey. A great deal of study, however, being requisite to give body to this work and render it instructive, as also to weave the fragmentary material into a whole worthy of the respectful perusal, not only of the spa-residents, but also of all Germans, particularly Low Germans, the conception was in danger of remaining a mere plan or fancy, especially as I had destined my stay in Göttingen to the study of the history of the theory of colors.

The last days of my stay in Pyrmont, during very broken weather, were not spent in the most agreeable manner, and I began to fear my visit there would not prove beneficial to my health. After a disease attended by such high inflammation, to subject me again, according to the Brown method, to a bath of so decidedly exciting properties, was perhaps an indication of no great judiciousness on the part of the doctors. To such a degree of excitability had I attained that by night I could not sleep for the violent pulsation of my blood, while by day the most indifferent event would throw me out of my equilibrium.

The duke, my most gracious master, arrived in Pyrmont on the ninth of July. From him I learned what had been recently going on in Weimar and what was in inception there; but my nervous condition prevented my enjoying a presence so much desired. The continual rainy weather, too, precluded all social pleasure in the open air. I left the place on the seventeenth of July, little edified by the results of my stay.

By the motion and dissipation of the journey, as also by the disuse of the exciting mineral water, I reached Göttingen in happy spirits. I there took pleasant lodgings on the first floor of the house of Krämer, the instrument-maker, in the Alley. The special purpose I had in view in a lengthy stay there was conclusively to fill up the many gaps still sensible in the historic part of the theory of colors. I brought with me a list of all the books and writings I had hitherto been unable to procure. This list I handed to Professor Reuss, from whom, as also from all others in office, I received the greatest assistance. Not only was I supplied with all I asked for, but much yet unknown to me was offered to my attention. I was allowed to spend a large part of the day in the library, many works were sent to my house, and so I passed the time with the greatest profit. Pütter's " History of the Learned of Göttingen " I studied on the spot itself with greatest attention and warmest interest, also carefully perusing the catalogues from the foundation of the university, and thereby acquiring a very fair idea of the history of the sciences of modern times. I next studied all the physical compendiums and the successive editions, concentrating my attention particularly on the chapters on light and colors.

The remaining hours passed very cheerfully. I should have to mention the whole of living Göttingen if I were to cite in particular the friendly parties, the dinners and suppers, the walks and excursions that were apportioned me. I name only one pleasant excursion with Professor Bouterwek to upper-bailiff Westfeld's at Weende, and another set on foot by Hofrath Meiners, in which quite a bright day, first at the paper-mill, then in Pöppelshaufen, next on the Plesse, where a sumptuous refection was provided, was spent in the company of Professor Fiorillo, the evening being closed by confidential talk on the Mariaspring.

The indefatigable efficient instruction of Hofrath Blumenbach, which imparted to me so much new knowledge and insight, aroused the passion of my son for the fossils of Hainberg. Very many walks were taken thither, the numerous specimens there collected, the rarer ones searched for. On this occasion it was curious to observe the difference between two characters and tendencies. While my son with the passion of a collector amassed every species of stone, Eduard, the son of Blumenbach, a born soldier, stuck exclusively by the belemnites, gathering them in order to surround a heap of sand which he regarded as a fort with palisades.

Very often I visited Professor Hoffmann, making a nearer acquaintance with the cryptogams, a province hitherto always inaccessible to me. At his place I saw with admiration the production of colossal ferns which disclosed to ordinary view by day what otherwise is visible only by the microscope. A violent flood of rain inundated the lower garden and some streets of Göttingen lay under water. An odd embarrassment was occasioned by this event. We were to be conveyed in sedan-

chairs to a splendid banquet provided by Hofrath Martens. I
got through all right, but my friend who had my son seated
along with him proving too heavy for the carriers, they dropped
them, as though it had been on the dry pavement, to the no
small admiration of the dressed sitters who felt the water
streaming into them.

Professor Seyffer, too, politely and minutely showed me the
instruments of the observatory. Several important strangers,
such as one is accustomed to find as unattached visitors at fre-
quented universities, I made the acquaintance of, and every day
saw my conquests increase above all expectation. Nor must
I omit mention of Professor Sartorius, who, on all and every
occasion of need, such as one is liable to in foreign places, was
ever ready, both with word and deed, and by his uninterrupted
sociability composed all the events of my stay in Göttingen into
a useful and gladdening whole.

He, too, in company with Professor Hugo, had the kindness
to request of me a lecture explaining the proper object of my
theory of colors. This challenge I could not but half earnestly,
half jestingly accept, for the sake of thereby obtaining a better
comprehension of my materials and facility in their use. Yet,
for want of a thorough mastery of the subject, the experiment
did not turn out either to my own or my friend's satisfaction.

So passed the time as pleasantly as profitably, though I was
at last made sensible how dangerous it is to approach a great
mass of learning; for while for the sake of a few dissertations
bearing on my business, I piled whole volumes of academic writings before me, I found everywhere so many lateral solicitations
that, with my keen susceptibility and previous knowledge in
many departments, I was distracted hither and thither, and my
collections ran the risk of assuming a piebald appearance. I
soon again, however, constrained myself into limits and was
able at the right time to draw to a conclusion.

While, therefore, I spent a series of days with rare profit
and pleasure, I suffered on the other hand by night many disturbances highly disagreeable at the time, though appearing
ridiculous afterward.

My beautiful and talented friend, Mademoiselle Jagemann,
had shortly before my arrival enraptured the public to a high
degree. Husbands thought of her accomplishments with more
enthusiasm than their wives cared about, while excitable youth
was perfectly carried away. Her superiority in gifts, both of
nature and art, occasioned me a serious annoyance. The
daughter of my landlord, Mademoiselle Krämer, had naturally
a very fine voice, which she had happily cultivated, but she
lacked talent for the shake, of the grace of which in its highest

perfection she was now made sensible in a foreign artist.   She
now, therefore, appeared to neglect everything else, and to give
all her strength to the acquisition of this new ornament in song.
How she practised during the day I know not, but at night, just
when we were thinking of bed, her zeal reached its climax.
Till midnight she went on repeating certain cadenzal passages,
whose conclusion should have been adorned with a shake, but
was mostly spoiled, or at least rendered without significance.

Another impulse to despair came from a very different quarter.   A pack of dogs gathered round the corner house, where
they kept barking in intolerable fashion.   To disperse them you
seized the first missile you could lay hands on, and so flew many
of the Hainberg ammonites my son had patiently collected, but
generally to no purpose.   For no sooner did we think them
scared away than the barking revived in full force, till at last
we discovered that a big house-dog at the window over our
heads was always recalling them with his voice.

But this was not enough.   The monstrous sound of a horn
startled me out of deep sleep, as though it were blowing into
me between my bed-curtains.   A night watchman performed
his functions under my window and, to my double and treble
misery, all his companions in office at all corners of the streets
leading to the Alley replied to his call, demonstrating in dreadful tones the solicitude with which they watched over the security of our rest.   My morbid irritability now revived, and
there was no other course open than to enter into negotiations
with the police, who had the particular politeness to bring to
silence first one and then another of these horns for the sake of
the odd stranger, about to play the part of the uncle in " Hum-
phrey Clinker," whose irritability was by a pair of bugle-horns
exasperated into positive madness.

Instructed, happy and thankful I quitted Göttingen on the
fourteenth of August and visited the basalt bridge of Dransfeld,
whose problematic appearance was then attracting the attention
of natural philosophers.   I climbed the high Hahn, on whose
top, by the fairest weather, I enjoyed an extended view and obtained a better conception of the landscape as far as the Harz.
I next repaired to Hanoverian Minden, whose remarkable situation on a tongue of earth, formed by the junction of the Werra
and Fulda, offered a joyous picture.   Thence to Cassel, where
I met my friends with Professor Meyer.   Under conduct of the
brave Nahl, whose presence made us think of our former Roman
residence, we took a view of Wilhelmshöhe on the day when
the fountain glorified the manifold park-and-garden landscape.
We paid careful attention to the costly collection of the picture
gallery and the castle, took a walk through the museum, and

visited the theatre. Gladdening was our meeting with a sympathetic friend, Major von Truchsess, who, in former years, by his upright manliness, had deserved enrolment in the rank of Götz von Berlichingens.

The twenty-first of August we went by way of Hoheneichen to Kreuzburg; the following day, after visiting the salt-pits, we reached Eisenach, saluting the Wartburg and the Mädelstein alive with so many remembrances of the past twenty years. The pleasure-grounds of the merchant Röse had meanwhile grown to a subject of new, unexpected interest.

I next reached Gotha, where Prince August received me hospitably, according to old friendly relations, in his pleasant summer-house, and the whole time of my stay kept a select table, where the duke and the dear Von Frankenberg consorts never failed.

Herr von Grimm, who, fleeing from the great revolutionary disorders, escaped from Paris shortly before Louis XVI, and more happily than he, had found a sure asylum with the court which had shown its friendship for him in olden times. Tried man of the world and pleasant guest though he was, he could not yet suppress an inward bitterness at the heavy loss he had sustained. Let the following account serve as an example of how all property at that time melted into nothing. On his flight, Grimm had left behind in the hands of his man of business some 100,000 francs in assignats. These were reduced by mandats to less value, and every man of sagacity, apprehending the reduction to zero of the latter papers as well, endeavored to change them into some species or other of indestructible goods, storing up eagerly such things as rice, wax candles, and whatever of that kind was offered for sale. Grimm's man of business, feeling the responsibility, hesitated how to act, till at last in despair, and with the thought of saving something, he expended the whole sum on a stock of Brussels cuffs and frills. Grimm readily showed them to the company, humorously boasting the advantage of having costly state-ornaments such as no one else could show.

The remembrance of former gatherings at Gotha in the '80's, when the interest turned on poetical projects and on æsthetic literary communications, formed, of course, a striking contrast to the present moment, when one hope after another had vanished, and when people scarcely felt secure under the shelter of high patrons and friends, just as in the case of a deluge people are filled with dread, though perched on mountain-tops. Still there was no want of cheerful entertainments. They were minded with gracious attention to celebrate my birthday at a select banquet. In the usual courses themselves a difference

was observable. At the dessert, however, the whole livery of
the prince entered in stately procession, the house-steward at
the head. The latter bore a large cake, flaming with parti-
colored wax candles, which, amounting in number to some
half-a-hundred, threatened to melt and consume each other,
whereas, at children's festivals of this kind, space enough is
left for succeeding life-tapers.

This may also serve as an example with what becoming
naïveté we had now for so many years rejoiced in our mutual
affection, in which pleasantry and respectful attention, good
humor and politeness, contended in common, by the exercise
of mind and heart, to adorn the whole course of life.

In the best spirits I returned on August 30th to Weimar,
and, amid the new engagements pressing on me, forgot any
weakness that might have lingered about me as a consequence
of my illness and the venturous cure to which I had subjected
myself. The competition pieces sent in for the ensuing third
exhibition claimed my attention. This exhibition was carefully
arranged, visited by friends, neighbors, and strangers, and gave
occasion to manifold entertainment and to a more intimate acquaintance with living artists. At its close, Nahl, trained in
the Roman antique school to beautiful form ,and the purest
execution, received half of the prize for " Achilles on Skyros,"
while Hoffmann, from Cologne, bred in the color-loving and
life-loving Netherland school, received the other half for
" Achilles in Battle with the Rivers." The two drawings received the further honor of being reserved for the ornamenta-
tion of the rooms of the castle.

And here is the proper place to mention a capital thought
which the provident prince gave for the consideration and execution of the Weimar lovers of art.

The rooms of the castle, which were being renovated, were
to be furnished not only with becoming princely splendor, but
were also to be devoted as a monument of the talents of
contemporary artists. Most purely and completely was this
thought carried out in the corner room occupied by the most
serene duchess, where several competitive and other pieces of
contemporary German artists, mostly in sepia, were placed under glass and in frames on a simple background. In the other
rooms, too, pictures by Hoffmann from Cologne, and Nahl
from Cassel, by Heinrich Meyer from Stäfa, and Hummel
from Naples, statues and bas-reliefs by Tieck, inlaid work and
reliefs by Catel, were disposed in tasteful harmonious order.
That the first plan was not, however, more thoroughly carried
into execution is a fault of the usual course of the world, in
which a praiseworthy intention is marred in its fulfilment more

by the discord of those taking part in it than by external impediments.

My bust executed with great care by Tieck, I may here mention in the way of parenthesis.

As to the course of the building of the castle in the main, one could regard this business with the greater composure inasmuch as a couple of men like Gentz and Rabe began to work at it with full and clear views. Their trustworthy merit precluded all doubts even under conditions which otherwise would have excited a certain anxiety, for in fact the state of matters was unusual. The walls of our old castle were left standing; some recent contrivances resolved on without sufficient circumspection appeared as an impediment in the way of more mature plans, and the old as well as the new were an obstruction to higher and freer undertakings. With all these cross purposes the castle building sometimes looked like a mountain, out of which, in Indian fashion, the architecture was to be hewn. And therefore on this occasion the business was committed to a couple of men who appeared on the scene as talented architects with new views, and from whom were not to be expected alterations requiring alteration, but conclusive steady progress.

I now return to theatrical affairs. On October 24th, the anniversary of the first mask play, " Palæophron and Neoterpe," " The Brothers," elaborated in the style of Terence by Einsiedel, was given, introducing a new series of theatrical peculiarities which found acceptance for some time, brought multiplicity into the representations, and served by way of practice in certain accomplishments.

Schiller worked at Lessing's " Nathan." I was not idle in reference to this work. On November 28th it was performed for the first time, not without perceptible influence on the German stage.

Schiller had this year begun and ended the " Maid of Orleans." Many doubts arose in regard to its representation, doubts which robbed us of the pleasure of seeing so important a work at once on the boards. To the activity of Iffland, and the rich resources at his disposal, it was reserved by a brilliant performance of this masterpiece to acquire for himself an enduring name in theatrical annals.

No small influence on our representations of this year was exercised by Madame Unzelmann, who appeared on our boards in principal parts at the end of September. A great deal of inconvenience, nay, of positively prejudicial influence, attends the appearance of guests at theatres. We as far as possible declined their services, unless they offered occasion of stimulus and improvement to our stock company, an advantage possible only in the case of excellent artists. Madame Unzelmann gave eight successive important representations, in which the whole company appeared in important parts, and both on their own account and in relation also to the new guest were summoned to the exercise of their utmost powers. This proved an incalculable incitement. Nothing is more pitiful than the mechanical dragging performance into which a member, nay, the whole body, of an institution will contentedly sink; but in the case of the theatre such execution is extremely offensive, instantaneous effect being here demanded, and no distant cumulative success having to be expected. An actor who neglects himself is to me the most despicable creature in the world; mostly he is incorrigible. A new public and new rivals are therefore indispensable spurs. The former puts a check on his faults, the latter challenge him to due exertion. May then the insuppressible system of guest-playing in the German theatre produce the best effects throughout the country generally!

Stollberg's public transition to the Catholic faith rent asunder the fairest ties formerly formed. I lost nothing by this event, for my closer relation to him had long ago deliquesced into general good wishes. I early felt a true affection for him as for a worthy, amiable, loving man, but I had soon to observe that he would never stand on his own feet, and I therefore regarded him in the light of one who seeks his salvation and composure outside the domain of my endeavors. Nor did this event in any way surprise me. I long held him for a Catholic, for such he was in his views, course, and surroundings. I could therefore witness without disturbance the tumult which was bound at last to arise out of a late manifestation of secretly false relations.

1802

Actors and spectators had now both attained a high degree of cultivation. Successful above all expectation were the representations of "Ion" (January 4th), "Turandot" (January 30th), "Iphigenia" (May 15th), "Alarcos" (May 29th). They were most carefully and excellently given, though the last failed to acquire any favor. By these representations we testified our earnest purpose to submit everything worthy of attention to a free unprejudiced judgment. This time, however, we had to contend with a narrow, exclusive party spirit.

The great dissension which came to light in German literature operated, especially on account of the proximity of Jena, on our theatrical circle. I ranked myself with Schiller on one side. We confessed ourselves of the party of the new struggling philosophy, and a system of æsthetics derivable from it, without paying much attention to persons who, by the way, played a particularly wanton and insolent game.

Now the brothers Schlegel had most deeply offended the opposite party, and therefore, on the eve of the representation of " Ion," the author of which was no secret, an attempt at opposition unreservedly raised its head. Between the acts people whispered all manner of censure, for which, to be sure, the somewhat dubious passage of the mother afforded wished-for occasion. An article attacking the author, as also the direction, was projected for the *Mode-Journal,* but earnestly and emphatically refused; for it was not yet a principle that in the same State, in the same town, any member might destroy what others had shortly before taken pains to establish.

Once for all we were determined on keeping our stage clean from the personalities of the day, while the other party was bent on degrading it into an arena for detraction. There was, therefore, no little sensation when I struck out of the " Small-town Bodies " (*Kleinstädter*) everything directed against the persons who, in the main, were in harmony with me, though I could not approve their every procedure nor recognize all their productions for praiseworthy. The opposite party bestirred itself powerfully, asserting that when the author was present it was proper to take counsel with him. Such a course was observed in the case of Schiller, and another had a right to equal courtesy. Such a strange inference could not, however, find acceptance with me. Schiller brought to the stage only matter of noble stimulus, of high tendency; they, on the other hand, matter of detraction, caricaturing and frustrating the problematic good; and it is the trick of such fellows, mis-appreciating every true pure relationship, to smuggle their base-ness into the easy indulgence of social conventions. In short, the passages referred to were kept out, and I took the trouble of filling up the gaps thereby occasioned with general pleas-antry, which succeeded in exciting the laughter of the audience.

These, however, were but trifles compared with the decided schism which disclosed itself in Weimar society on the occa-sion of a festival to be celebrated on March 5th. Things had necessarily to come to such a head sooner or later: why par-ticularly that day was chosen I do not remember. Enough, a great display of representations referring to him and his works was to be given in honor of Schiller in the large town-hall, newly decorated by the community. The intention was plain, that of raising a sensation, entertaining society, flattering friends, setting up opposition to the theatre, establishing a pri-vate to the prejudice of the public stage, cajoling Schiller's

favor, winning me over by means of him, or, if that attempt
should fail, detaching him from me.

Schiller had no liking for the business. The part assigned
to him was compromising, intolerable to a man of his style,
as to every right-thinking man—to stand there in his own person before a large assemblage, a target for their grimacing
reverences. He had a mind to announce himself unwell, but
more affable than I, and by conjugal and family ties more involved in society, he was almost compelled to drink the bitter
cup. We assumed the affair would come off, and many an
evening enjoyed good fun in anticipation of it, though he would
fain have been ill to escape the trial.

As far as we could hear, many figures in Schiller's pieces
were to be presented. A " Maid of Orleans " was settled.
Helmet and banner carried complacently through the streets
by carvers and gilders to a certain house had provoked a great
noise, prematurely letting the cat out of the bag. The finest
part, however, was reserved for the leader of the chorus himself. A walled-in form was to be represented, the noble master
in leathern apron to stand beside it. After mysterious salutation spoken, after the melting of the glowing mass, from the
demolished form Schiller's bust was at last to emerge. We
made merry over this secret which gradually oozed out, and
without disturbance saw the business going forward.

Our good-nature was, however, rather over-rated when we
were ourselves challenged to contribute to the performance.
The only bust of Schiller, in the Weimar library, a former
cordial gift of Dannecker, was requested for the above object,
and refused, on the perfectly natural ground that a gypsum
bust never came back from a festival uninjured. Other refusals from other quarters happening at the same time exasperated the allies to the highest pitch. They did not see that,
with the exercise of a little diplomacy, all difficulties might be
overcome; and nothing equalled their astonishment, benight-
edness, and resentment when the carpenters, going with props,
laths, and boards to erect the dramatic structure, found the
hall locked, and had it explained to them that, having been
quite recently fitted up and decorated, it could not be granted
for such a tumultuous purpose, where it was impossible to
guarantee security against injury.

The first *finale* of the " Interrupted Sacrificial Festival "
does not excite such horror as was provoked first in the upper
classes and then down through all grades of the population by
this disturbance, nay, extinction of the praiseworthy enterprise.
So many various hindrances in the way of the project happening to combine in such an artful manner that no other agency

than that of one single Evil Principle could account for it, I was the person on whom the fellest fury was directed, though in truth I did not grudge anyone this satisfaction. People should, however, have reflected that a man like Kotzebue, who by all manner of provocations stirs up ill-will on many sides, will occasionally concentrate swifter and more hostile influences against himself than a regular conspiracy would ever instigate.

If now an important upper stratum of society was on the side of our opponent, the middle-class estranged itself from him, exposing all the faults of his first youthful immature productions. In such violent commotion did the minds of men fluctuate on this and that side.

Our supreme authorities, from their lofty stations, looking abroad with free capacious views, had taken no notice of these petty brabbles. Accident, however, which, as Schiller says, is often *naïve*, was to cap the whole affair. The secretive mayor, as a meritorious practical man, had just at that moment been decreed the title of councillor. The Weimar people, who have never been wanting in pungent ideas to fasten the theatre to actual life, therefore gave him the name of Prince Piccolomini, a distinction that for a long time stuck to him in jovial society.

It will easily be conceived that such a commotion prejudicially affected our social as well as our theatrical circle. How it next touched me personally may here be mentioned.

In the course of the past winter a noble company of persons, quite without any speculative purposes, joined themselves to us, taking pleasure in our intercourse and achievements. On the occasion of picnics, which from time to time were got up by this select union, and held in my house, under my management, there originated several songs, which afterward spread into universal circulation. The familiar " There seizes me, I know not how," was written for the twenty-second of February, when the most Serene Hereditary Prince, leaving for Paris, called on us for the last time, a circumstance alluded to in the third verse of the song. In the same way we had before saluted the New Year, and in the song celebrating the founding of our institution, " Why walkest thou, my pretty neighbor? " the members of the company could easily under transparent masks recognize each other. Other songs, particularly pertinent from their *naïveté*, were contributed by me to this union, in which affection without passion, emulation without envy, taste without pretension, politeness without affectation, and, over and above, naturalness without rudeness, played reciprocally into each other.

Now, in spite of many unfortunate well-considered attempts

in this direction on his part, we had not admitted the opponent, as he never, moreover, entered my house. He was therefore impelled to gather a circle of his own about him, an achievement not difficult for him. By the pleasing, modestly importunate manner which he possessed as a man of the world he knew how to rally people around him. Persons of our circle, too, were attracted over to him. Where sociality finds entertainment, there it makes its home. All looked forward with pleasure to taking an active part in the festival of March 5th, and for a time proportionately denounced me as the supposed extinguisher of such a day of joy and honor. Our little group accordingly broke up, nor did any social songs of the above kind again succeed with me.

Everything, however, that I had purposed with Schiller and other allied active friends pursued its unchecked course; for it was our habitual principle in life to turn our backs on losses, and keep our eye directed on the gains ahead. And in the present instance this procedure was all the easier for us that we felt assured as to the sentiments of our supreme authorities, who, with their higher views, looked down on court and town adventures as indifferent and momentary, though sometimes entertaining.

A theatre, renewing its blood from time to time by the accession of new youthful members, is bound to make vital progress, and on this object our endeavors were constantly bent.

On February 17th, Mademoiselle Maas stepped on to our stage for the first time. Her pretty figure, her gracefully natural manner, her fine-toned voice, in short, her whole happy individuality at once captivated the public. After three trial essays as "Maiden of Marienburg," as Rosine in "Lawyer and Peasant," as Lotty in the "German House-father," she was engaged, and very soon we could depend upon her in the assignment of important parts. On November 29th we again made a hopeful acquisition. Out of respect for Madame Unzelmann, out of affection to her as a most charming actress, I took her son, twelve years of age, on chance to Weimar. I happened to test him in quite a peculiar way. He might have prepared himself for the recitation of various pieces, but I gave him an Oriental book of tales lying at hand, out of which he read on the spot a merry story with so much natural humor, with so much significant expression in the case of change of persons and situations, that I could feel no hesitation about him. He appeared with approbation in the part of Görge in the "Two Billets," and, especially in rôles of natural humor, showed himself everything that could be desired.

While art thus flourished in full youthful bloom on our

boards, a death occurred which I deem it my duty to record.

Corona Schröter died, and as I did not feel myself in a state
to devote to her a monument such as she so well deserved, it
was a grateful relief for me to have so many years before inscribed her memory in such a characteristic style as I could
not now have surpassed. It was also on the occasion of a
death, that of Mieding, the theatre decorator, that in earnest
cheerfulness I remembered my fair friend. Most vividly do I
recall the elegy, copied out fair on black-edged paper, which
I sent to the " Tiefurt Journal." Not that there was any dark
presentiment in such a circumstance in relation to Corona.
Her beautiful figure, her gay spirits, continued long years after
to charm and animate people. She might well have stayed some
time longer within the circle of a world from which she made
a too early exit.

In connection with theatrical affairs it has yet to be mentioned that this year we good-naturedly offered a prize for a
play of intrigue. We gradually received a dozen pieces, mostly,
however, of such a crazy, desperate character that we could
not sufficiently admire the strange false tendencies secretly
active in the dear Fatherland, and which our challenge had
called into the light of day. We reserved our criticism, for in
truth we had none to give, and at the authors' requests returned
them their productions.

It has also to be remarked that in this year Calderon, whom
by name we had known our life long, began to enter our horizon, and by the very first model-pieces of his which we made
the acquaintance of set us in astonishment.

Through all these above-mentioned labors and cares there
wound many an unpleasant employment, in consequence of the
duties in connection with the Jena museums I had for many
years undertaken and performed.

The death of Hofrath Büttner, which happened in the middle of the winter, imposed on me a troublesome task little profitable to the mind. The peculiarities of this strange man may be
comprised in a few words: unbounded desire for scientific
possessions, narrow-minded punctiliousness, no power whatever of comprehensive systematic vision. To the increase of
his considerable library he devoted the pension yearly granted
him in connection with the mother library. Several rooms in
the side building of the castle were allowed him for a lodging,
and these were all packed as full as they could hold. At all
auctions he bade for books, and when the old steward of the
castle, his commissioner, once told him that he had already
two copies of an important book, he answered that one cannot
have enough copies of a good work.

After his death were found on the floor of a large room the whole acquisitions of auctions lying in heaps beside each other, as they had successively arrived from fairs. The wall-shelves were filled with them; on the floor itself it was impossible to set one foot before the other. The frail chairs all groaned under the loads of rough books, the new arrivals being always heaped in layers over the old.

In another room, towered up round the walls, were smoothed and folded books, awaiting a pattern binding. And so in extreme old age this resolute man still appeared eager in prosecuting the activity of his youth, though his energies at last dwindled into mere feeble aspirations. Imagine other rooms, too, filled to excess with useful and useless physical-chemical apparatus, and you will be able to appreciate the embarrassment in which I felt myself when this part of the legacy separated from that of his heirs was taken over, and had to be cleared out of the premises long destined to other purposes. On this business I lost a great deal of time, much of the stock was injured, and many years did not suffice to clear the confusion. You soon discover how necessary in such a case is your prompt personal direction. For when the question is not to achieve the best, but avoid the worst, you are embarrassed with no end of doubts only to be conquered by resolution and action. Unfortunately I was called away to other pressing business, though I accounted myself so far happy in being able to commit the task of disposing the collected mass to fellow-laborers able and willing to work in the proper style.

Several times already, in the course of our theatrical notices, reference has been made to the advantages accruing to our company from their summer stay at Lauchstädt. At this point, however, a more special description of the matter must be given. The stage there was erected by Bellomo as economically as possible. A couple of high wooden gables in an open square, from which on both sides the roof reached down close to the ground, composed this temple of the Muses. The interior space was divided lengthwise by two partitions, the middle room being devoted to the theatre and spectators, the side rooms to the wardrobes. Now, however, with the new growth and expansion of our establishment, both plays and players, but especially the Halle and Leipzig public, demanded suitable accommodation.

The building of the Weimar castle, at first carried on in a dilatory but afterward in a spirited manner, and lasting for several years, attracted talented architects and, as always was and will be the case, building begets a desire for building. As years before, the presence of Herr Thouret caused a worthy

Weimar theatre to arise, so on this occasion the presence of Herren Gentz and Rabe provoked the demand on them to erect a Lauchstädt edifice.

The doubts connected with such an undertaking had frequently been discussed. What with considerable distance, the alien site and soil, and the quite peculiar considerations of those engaged there, the obstacles appeared almost insurmountable. The place of the old theatre was not suited to a larger building, the handsome site alone fit for such an erection was a subject of dispute between different jurisdictions, and one could not but entertain misgivings about raising an edifice on ground to which one had no sure legal claim. Nevertheless, driven by the force of circumstances, by restless activity, by passionate love of art, and by inexhaustible productivity, we ultimately succeeded in overcoming all opposition. A plan was sketched, a model of the stage prepared, and by February full unanimity was arrived at in regard to the whole project. The hut-form which would comprehend the whole under one roof was specially rejected. A moderate vestibule was to be erected for the ticket office and stairs; behind, the higher room for spectators; and at the back the highest for the stage.

Much, nay, everything depends on the situation of a building. This point, therefore, was weighed and considered with the greatest care, so that on the completion of the building there was nothing to regret in that respect. The work went on with might and main. In March the wood granted for our edifice lay frozen at Saalfeld; on June 26th we were sitting comfortably in our new theatre, witnessing our first play. The whole undertaking in all its details, the favorable and unfavorable features in its character, our unslackening three months' energies on the task, the trouble, care, vexation we experienced in connection with it, the personal sacrifices we had all along to make—all this would comprise a little romance, and would furnish a very fair symbol of greater enterprises.

The opening, introduction, and inauguration of such establishments are always a matter of moment. On such an occasion the attention is stimulated and curiosity strained, and the time is well fitted to draw people's minds to the relation between the stage and the public. The opportunity, therefore, was not let slip. In a prelude there was represented in symbolical and allegorical fashion all that in recent times had occurred in the German theatre in general, but especially on the Weimar stage. The farce, the domestic drama, the opera, the tragedy, the *naïve* play, as also the mask, all successively appeared, each in its peculiar character, played and explained themselves, or were explained, the figure of Mercury serving to knit the whole together, to interpret and apply everything. The transformation of a wretched rustic tavern into a theatrical palace, most of the characters being at the same time translated into a higher sphere, furthered cheerful reflection.

On June 6th I repaired to Jena, and wrote the prelude in about eight days. The last hand was put to it in Lauchstädt, and up to the very end the revisions were committed to memory and practised. It exercised a charming influence, and for many years many a friend who visited us on that occasion remembered the high joys of art he had then experienced.

My Lauchstädt residence imposed on me the duty of visiting Halle as well, friends there having in a neighborly way, for the sake of the theatre as also of personal relationships, honored us with frequent visits. I mention, in particular, Professor Wolf, a day in whose company is a whole year's solid instruction; Chancellor Niemeyer, who contributed such an active part to our endeavors as to undertake the revision of "Andria," which gave happy occasion for the increase and multiplicity of our masks.

With equal friendship the whole culture of the surrounding country was disposed to assist me and the institution I had so much at heart. The neighborhood of Giebichenstein enticed me to pay visits to the hospitable Reichardt. He, his worthy spouse, their graceful, beautiful daughters, forming a harmonious whole, and situated in the midst of a romantic landscape, composed a highly attractive circle, where men of merit from far and near found it a pleasure to spend a longer or a shorter time, knitting ties which lasted through life.

Nor must I omit mentioning the pleasure I felt in hearing the melodies which Reichardt was the first to compose for my songs rendered with so much feeling by the fine voice of his eldest daughter.

But the catalogue of important experiences connected with my stay in Halle is not yet exhausted. My visit to the botanical garden under the conduct of Sprengel, the careful inspection, with a view to my own purposes, of Meckel's cabinet, the collector of which I unfortunately found no longer in life: these things were of no little profit to me; for both from the subjects themselves, and from the conversations held on them, I took away matter serving to the promotion and completion of my studies.

Like advantage, such as may always be found at a university residence, I obtained at Jena, in the month of August. With Loder, the anatomical problems formerly mentioned were continued, with Himly a great deal was discussed in reference to subjective seeing and color phenomena. So deeply were we

plunged in the subject that often late into the night we kept
wandering about over hill and dale. Voss had removed to
Jena, and seemed desirous of settling there. His great circumspect learning, his splendid poetical figurations, the friendliness of his household existence attracted me, and I had no
greater interest than in convincing myself of his rhythmic principles. And so was formed a highly agreeable and fruitful
relationship between us.

Begirt by museums and by everything which had early impelled me to and furthered me in the natural sciences, I seized
every opportunity of adding to my knowledge in this respect.
The wolf's milk caterpillar being this year an unusually copious
production, I studied the growth of this creature to its full
maturity and its transition to a chrysalis. By this means I
became disabused of many trivial ideas and conceptions.

Comparative osteology, too, a special and constant subject
of my thoughts, occupied a large part of my busy hours.

The death of the meritorious Batsch was deeply felt as a
loss to science, to the university, and to the Natural Research
Society. Unfortunately the museum collected by him was,
through a strange combination of circumstances, taken to pieces
and scattered. A part belonged to the Natural Research Society; this went to the directors, or rather to a higher authority,
who at a considerable cost paid the society's debts and assigned
the extant members a new gratuitous place of meeting. The
other part, as the property of the deceased, went indisputably
to his heirs. Properly, with a greater effort, the whole, which
did not bear division, should have been taken over and kept
intact, but the reasons for not doing so were also weighty.

If something was hereby lost, a new expected gain was in
the back end of the year acquired. The considerable mineral
cabinet of Prince Gallitzin, which, as president of the society,
he had decreed it, was to be transferred to Jena, and there set
up in the order he wished. The museum, formerly well provided, was by this increase raised to new splendor. The other
scientific institutions under my management were preserved in
as fair a state as finances would permit.

The university was then animated by earnest students whose
hopes and aspirations infused equal enthusiasm into the minds
of their professors. Of important strangers staying some time
in Jena may be named Von Podmanitzky, who, instructed on
many sides, was disposed to take an active part in our aims
and labors.

Along with all these scientific exertions the sociality of Jena
suffered no abatement in its cheerful character. New rising
members added to the grace of life, and gave me ample com-

pensation for the defect in this respect I had for some time experienced in Weimar.

With what gladness should I have spent the remaining part of the beautiful harvest season in a place where I was surrounded with everything pleasant and instructive. The exhibition, however, which had to be prepared for the near future forced me back to Weimar, occupying my attention on through September. For no little time and trouble were required to frame and hang up the different arrivals, setting each in the place where it would show to most advantage and best secure the respectful notice of visitors; and all this work, as well as the careful return of the pictures, was divided between me and my friend Meyer.

The subject of this, the fourth exhibition, was " Perseus and Andromeda." Our intention by this piece was to draw attention to the splendor of the human structure in youthful bodies, for where is the summit of art to be found if not in the full blossom of the creature formed after God's image?

To Ludwig Hummeln, born at Naples and living in Cassel, the prize was adjudicated. With delicate sense of art, with fine feeling had he handled the subject. In the middle of the picture stood Andromeda upright by the rock. Her left hand, now liberated, drawing some folds of the cloak over her person, betoken modesty and sense of shame; resting himself, sat Perseus on the head of the monster at her side; and opposite a genius running to give succor, loosed the bonds of the right hand. His agitated youthful figure heightened the beauty and strength of the worthy pair.

In the province of landscape-painting the prize fell to Rohden from Cassel. The Jena " General Literature-Gazette " of 1803 giving a sketch of the historical picture preserved the memory of this work of art, and, by its minute description and criticism of the different pieces, affords a survey of the production of this fourth exhibition.

While thus in every way we endeavored to call forth and promote all that had long been recognized as alone proper and conducive to plastic art, we heard in our drawing-rooms that a new little book on art had appeared, making a great sensation, a book which maintained that the only foundation for art was piety. By this news we were little affected, for how should a syllogism like the following find acceptance: " Some monks were artists, therefore all artists should be monks." Still it might have prompted some misgivings in us to see how valued friends, interesting themselves in our exhibition and approving our efforts, yet appeared to take pleasure in such suggestions— flattering and fostering human weaknesses, as they were well

observed to be—and to expect from them a new happy departure
in this province.

The exhibition, which was much visited in October, afforded
opportunity for intercourse with lovers of art at home and
abroad; nor, for the time of the year, was there any want of
prized arrivals from a distance. Hofrath Blumenbach indulged
his Weimar and Jena friends with some days of his company;
and on this occasion, as always, his presence imparted the most
cheerful instruction. And as no benefit ever comes alone, the
good understanding in the interior of our Weimar society gradually came round again.

A considerable correspondence caused me to direct immediate
glances into the life and activities outside our borders as well.
Friedrich Schlegel, who, in his travels through our region, was
well satisfied with the pains taken about his " Alarcos," gave
me ample news as to the state of Paris. Hofrath Sartorius,
also, whose visit had refreshed a long-abiding relationship,
and who was now engaged in the study of the history of the
Hanse Towns, sent me from his remote quarter communications
regarding this important undertaking. Hofrath Rochlitz, who
watched the progress of our theatre with increasing interest,
directed letters to me, still preserved, to this effect.

Many other things testifying to happy relationships with
different persons I find noted down. Three young men, Klap-
roth, Bode, and Hain, stayed in Weimar, and with our permission made use of Büttner's polyglot remains.

If, this year, I was kept in unceasing activity with the business which fell to my hands, now in Weimar, now in Jena, and
now in Lauchstädt, the possession of the little freehold of Rössla
gave occasion also for many journeys hither and thither. No
doubt it had by this time become quite evident that to derive
material advantage from so small a property, it was necessary
for the proprietor to cultivate and look after it himself, as his
own farmer and manager, drawing his immediate sustenance
out of it, in which case it would afford a quite decent existence.
Very different, however, is the state of things in the case of a
spoiled citizen of the world. Still, rural life in a pleasant valley, by a little stream bordered with woods and bushes, in the
neighborhood of fruitful heights, not far from a populous and
well-to-do little town, possessed a charm which detained me
there for days, and even inspired cheerful moods for small
poetical productions. Women and children are here in their
element, and the intolerable gossip in towns shows itself in such
a place in at least its simplest form. Even disaffection and
ill-will appear purer, springing as they do out of the immediate
wants of mankind.

Pleasant in the highest degree was the neighborhood of Oss-mannstädt, higher up in the same valley, but on the left side of the water. Wieland, too, began to entertain doubts as to a state of nature. He once set forth very humorously how much con-trivance was needed to wring but a little pleasure out of nature. He represented learnedly and merrily all the outs and ins con-nected with the production of herbage for fodder. The clover, which had been produced by careful cultivation, he collected with much pains by means of a maid whom it took no little ex-pense to support, and then had it consumed by the cow, only in order at last to obtain something white for his coffee.

In those theatre and festival disturbances, Wieland had de-meaned himself very properly. Straightforward and honest he was, though, as will happen with anyone in a momentary passion, under the influence of prejudice whispered into him, and with antipathies not wholly to be blamed, he was sometimes betrayed into a petulant, unfair expression. We often visit-ed him after dinner, getting home in good time across the meadows.

In my Weimar household existence there occurred an im-portant change. Friend Meyer, who, since 1792, with the ex-ception of a few years' absence, had shared my house and table, gladdening me with his knowledge, instruction, and counsel, quitted my domicile in consequence of a conjugal relation he had entered into. Nevertheless the need of uninterrupted com-munication with one another soon overcame the little distance which parted us. Our mutual influence continued in its full force, suffering neither check nor pause.

Amid all the tumults of this year I did not leave off nourish-ing in secret my pet " Eugénie." The whole, in all its length and breadth having become quite familiar to me, I worked away at any moment at any particular part, a circumstance which will explain its unusual completeness. I concentrated my strength successively on each separate point, which thus came emphati-cally into visuality.

" Cellini " belonged more to a wild, disrupted world. It, too, however, I managed, though not without exertion, to push forward, the work at bottom proving to be of more import than I at first imagined.

Reineke Fuchs might now, also, at any moment of wanton vivacity, come to the front. He was sure of good reception and hearty cheer for a certain time.

CHOICE EXAMPLES OF PALEOGRAPHY.

Fac-similes from Rare and Curious Manuscripts of the Middle Ages.

PAGE OF MINNESINGER POETRY.

From a German manuscript, written about 1310.

The name of Minnesinger was first given to the band of Suabian poets who flourished between 1130 and 1350, and from them descended upon the German lyrical poets in general. The Minnesingers were the German correspondents of the French *trouvères*, and both were of important service in the development of their respective literatures. We owe the manuscript from which the fac-simile is taken to the generosity of the Chevalier Manessen, of Maneck, who, about 1310, had the lyrical productions of four hundred German poets collected and transcribed. As will be noticed, the verses are not separated; the first paragraph, first column, which has six lines, gives seven verses. The writing is in the style termed Modern Gothic, and is characterized by legibility rather than elegance.

Klageliche not · clage ich von
kernume de ſi mir gebot ·
de ich mine ſinne · da bewa
re da man mich f v̊ derben
wil · hey minen ſpil · durch dich lide ich
ſendes kumbers al zevil

Wengel roſen var · wol geſteller küin
ogen luter klar · ũ ſinneklichũ kin
ne hat ſi dü mir krenker leben vñ hp
her ſelig wip · durch din beſten tugende
mir min leit v̊trip ·

Sꝛſſe troſterin · troſte mine ſinne ·
durr die mine din · in der mine ich
brinne · vñ der mine füre lide ich ſende
not · hei münde rot · wilt dv mich nibt
troſte ſich ſo bin ich tot ·

Ich wil vngenig raten · de ſi balde
frowen ſich · da wir e den riſen praten · da
iſt nv gar wiſteklich · da entſpringet
blv̊me vñ kle · kalde riſen vñ ſne · ſunt
zergange aber als e

Ich wil miner ſrowen mv̊ten · de ſi mir
genedic ſi · der vil reinen der vil gv̊ten
wer ich gerne nahe bi lieſſe ch̾ mich
ir vngefüger nit · det mir alſo nahe
ir · frö den ſi mich röbet zaller zit ·

Werdet truwer wibe müne machet fꝛo
wid̾ichen mvt · des bin ich wol werde
üne · de nie wüne wart ſo gv̊t · als ich
mich v̊ſinne kan · ſon enwirdet niemā
mähr · tro der minen nie begin̄

Ones libes ögen weide · daſt dü hebū
ﬅiuwe min · ſol ich iemer kome w
leide · de mvſ an ir hulde ſin · de ſi ſpreche
ich bin dir holt · de wer mir ein richer
ſolt · vñ neme es für des keiſers golt ·

Urende dü iﬅ erwacher · dü eꝛ
wuſſe tag · ſo lange in oﬅ lant
die hat vns vf erhaꝯ · d̾ hür
ﬅe friderich · des manig wol er
lacher · der ſin iﬅ werdt rich · er kan die ſie
chen laben · mit milregebend̾ hant · gelebt
ich noch ten tag · d̾ mich vro ſelde erkā
de als ſi erneſwanne pﬂag · min habe iﬅ
wirdt kleine · mir iﬅ v̊ ſchulde ande ſo mā
allẽ ithalbe gat · vñ mich blüſet eine
de lenger mir dü zit ·

Jung mā ich wil dich leꝛe · wie rumb ich ſel
te ſi des din lib wirde hat · wilt dv behalte
das · ſold ſo dv diene gor vñ · alle erbwen
ere · la ſwache ſpot · wis an zorne lag · in
ne wiſe rat wis löſer were vñ · ſwaz dv
ſeheﬅ die breﬅe da ſolt dv wiſe bi nem vñ
ia behalte · do ſolt in eꝛ gleﬅe · wir ſchande
hade den hür · ſo maht mir vreude alꝛ vñ
wirt din ende gv̊t ·

Ich ſach lieblich lachſe ein rees müntelin d̾
wre ſo wol gevar · da ich mun ize wart wiſe ·
ir hehd̾ ôgẽ blig · mag mir wol truke ſwa
che · mich v̊ reiſꝛ ir minen ﬅrik · ſie iﬅ lieb
lich zaller ſüte · vñ alles valſchel · bar · ich
wil ir diener ſin ſwenig ich ſie an ſchone
ſiﬅ miner ſelde ſehin · ſo enzvnder mich
ir müne · ſi wiſe ſ meie töwe · erblöﬅ wüſ
ſer ﬂacht · d̾ ich wꝛlide büne ſi hat ſo wi
ne f zvbt ·

1803

For the new year we gave " Palæophron and Neoterpe " in the public theatre. By the representation of the " Brothers " of Terence, the public had already become accustomed to masks, and the first properly classical piece could not fail of its good effect. The earlier conclusion addressed to the duchess Amalia which we had given to the piece was turned into a more general application, and the good reception of this representation put us in the best humor for serious undertakings.

The performance of the " Bride of Messina " (nineteenth of March) involved much previous labor, the most careful reading and theatrical rehearsals being necessary. The first part of the " Natural Daughter " shortly following (second of April), and then the " Maid of Orleans " demanded all our time. Never, perhaps, had we labored so spiritedly, so judiciously, and to such general satisfaction.

Of our determination to reject and steer clear of everything in the way of malevolence, negation, and detraction, let the following serve as a proof. At the opening of the year a little comedy under the title of " The Phrenologist " was sent me through the hands of a valued friend, a comedy holding up to ridicule and contempt the respectable endeavors of a man like Gall. I returned the production, with a sincere and general explanation, which as applying to all things of that kind, may here be quoted.

" In herewith returning you the smart little piece as unsuitable for our stage, I deem it my duty, in accordance with our old friendly relations, to specify more particularly the reasons for this decision of ours. It is a rule with us to keep our theatre as much as possible clear of everything which in the eyes of the people might tend to degrade scientific inquiry ; partly on principle, partly because, the university being close by, it would look unfriendly in us here to slight and ridicule studies which many a man there is earnestly pursuing.

" Many a scientific investigation aiming at the discovery of some secret or other of nature is, no doubt, apt, partly from the charlatanism of the investigators, to offer a ridiculous aspect ; nor is the comic poet to be blamed if, in passing, he allows himself a side thrust at such things. We, too, are by no means pedantic in this respect. At the same time we have carefully avoided everything of any compass having reference to philosophical or literary matters, to the new theory of medicine, etc. For this reason, then, we should not like to hold up to laughter Gall's curious doctrine, which may, no more than Lavater's, be without some foundation in fact, especially that by so doing

we would have to fear displeasing many of our respected
hearers.—Weimar, January 24, 1803."

With a repertory before satisfactory, but now newly enriched,
we came amply furnished to Lauchstädt. The new house, the
important pieces, the most careful performance, excited general
interest. Terence's "Andria," elaborated by Herr Niemeyer,
was, equally with the "Brothers," represented with an approach to the antique. Spectators came as far as from Leipzig.
They, as well as those from Halle, became ever more acquainted
with our earnest endeavors, a circumstance which redounded
to our great profit. This time I stayed there no longer than
necessary, in order to arrange with Hofrath Kirms, my fellow-
commissioner, some requirements connected with building and
certain desirable points in connection with our surroundings.

In Halle, Giebichenstein, Merseburg, Naumburg, I renewed
many a prized connection. Professor Wolf, Privy-Councillor
Schmalz, Jacob, Reil, Lafontaine, Niemeyer, received me with
their usual friendliness. I surveyed Von Leysser's mineral
cabinet and mounted the Petersburg to get fresh specimens of
porphyry. Before my departure I had the pleasure of observing how, as a whole, our theatre gave signs of vital integrity,
and how in details there was nothing to be taken exception to,
a happy state for which hearty thanks were no doubt due to the
director, Genast. I made my return by way of Merseburg, to
consolidate the good relationship formed with the authorities
there, and then to prosecute further my affairs in Weimar and
Jena.

Though now for a time I had striven to keep the theatre and
its concerns pretty well at arm's length, I was in spirit more
than ever drawn toward it. Two young men of the names of
Wolff and Grüner, from Augsburg, the former hitherto connected with the mercantile, the latter with the military, life,
waited on me, impelled by the decided bent of their natures for
the stage. After short trial, I soon found that they would each
of them prove a particular ornament to our theatre, and that
a couple of young bloods with such mettle in them would rapidly
train themselves in an establishment already so well appointed.
I determined on keeping them, and happening to have leisure
of time as well as of mind, I began a set of lessons with them,
developing the histrionic art to myself as well as to them, from
its primary elements, and with the progress of both pupils attaining a greater clearness on a subject to which I had hitherto
devoted myself instinctively. The grammar of this branch of
human culture I was thus led to construct I afterward used in
my instruction of several young actors. Some writings connected with this subject still remain.

After the two above mentioned, a third young man, Grimmer by name, applied to us with a similar purpose. His appearance and manner also gave the best promise, and he was particularly welcome to Schiller, whose head was now full of " Tell," with its many characters, and who was therefore anxious about a fit presentation of all the parts. We therefore engaged him likewise and soon found him serviceable in his place.

The first part of " Eugénie " was written, played, and printed. The plan of the whole, scene after scene, lay clearly before me, nor had the attraction this piece for several years exercised on me in any way abated. The second part was to be laid in the country-seat, the residence of Eugénie, the third in the capital, where, in the midst of the greatest confusion, the recovered sonnet would have produced no effectual cure, it is true, but yet a momentary scene of beauty. But I must not proceed further in this matter, or I should have to set forth the whole in all its details.

I had to rejoice in the friendliest appreciation from many sides, the most grateful testimonies of which I have collected, and may perhaps find occasion to communicate to the public. The feeling, the conception, the conclusion drawn regarding the piece was all I could wish, but I had committed the great, unpardonable mistake of coming forth with the first part before I had concluded the whole. I call the mistake unpardonable, committed as it was against my old tried superstition. Superstition, but still very capable of rational justification.

A very deep sense lies in the fiction that to dig up and take possession of a treasure it is necessary to set about the business in silence, to drop not a word on the matter, however encompassed on all sides it may be with dread and delight. Just as significant is the fable that in adventuring after a precious talisman in far distant mountain-wilds a man must go on without stopping, nor dare to look about him, even should he hear close behind him on his precipitous path voices of fearful dread or delicious enchantment.

The thing, however, was done, and the fondly prized succeeding scenes visited me only occasionally, like unsteady spirits which return yearning and sighing after deliverance.

As some years before, so now again, the situation of Jena occasioned us no little concern. Since the French Revolution a restlessness had seized the minds of men, so that they hankered after a change in their position, either intrinsically or at least topographically. This description applies in particular to the professors of academic institutions, and many of these being at this time newly erected and particularly privileged, there was no want of attraction and invitation to places where better sal-

ary, higher status, and greater influence in a wider circle were
offered.

These big-world events must be kept in mind in order to a
general comprehension of the events at this time occurring in
the little circle of the Jena Academy.

Christian Wilhelm Hufeland, in the faculty of medicine so
circumspect and endowed with such various talents as regards
both treatment and exposition, was called to Berlin, and bore
there the title of privy-councillor, which in a great kingdom
had now grown to be a mere title of honor, while in smaller
States it still carried with it its original active distinction, and
without which it could not easily be conferred. Such promotions, however, did not remain without influence on those left
behind.

Fichte, in his " Philosophic Journal," had ventured on utterances respecting God and divine things which seemed to contradict the traditional expressions used in reference to such
mysteries. He was called to account. His defence did not
mend matters. He went passionately to work, never imagining
how much disposed in his favor were the authorities on this side,
and what a good interpretation they contrived to put on his
thoughts and words. Notice to this effect could not, of course,
be given him in so many words, and just as little the ways and
means by which it was sought to help him out of his scrape in
the mildest manner. Conversation back and forward on the
subject, guess and assertion, confirmation and determination,
all these fluctuated through each other in manifold uncertain
speeches in the university. A ministerial censure was spoken
of—Fichte might prepare himself for nothing less than a kind of
reprimand. Thereupon, losing all self-control, Fichte deemed
himself justified in addressing a violent letter to the ministry,
in which, assuming the certainty of such a measure, he vehemently and defiantly declared that he would never brook the
indignity, but would rather at once, there and then, withdraw
himself from the academy, in which event he would retire not
alone, but in company with several distinguished teachers like-
minded with himself.

This, of course, at once interposed an effectual barrier in the
way of all the good intentions cherished toward him. There
was no escape, no remedy left; the mildest measure possible
was to accept his resignation. Now, for the first time, when
the matter could no longer be helped, did he become aware of
the expedient devised in his favor, and had to repent, as we also
regretted, his precipitancy. At the same time no one came
forward avowing a common resolution to leave the academy
with him. Things remained for the moment as they had been.

A secret discontent, nevertheless, festered in all minds, causing them to look abroad. At last, Hufeland the jurist left for Ingolstadt, Paulus and Schelling for Würzburg.

On the back of all this we heard in August that the highly prized " Literature-Gazette " was to be transferred from Jena to Halle. The plan was shrewdly enough laid. Things were to be carried on as usual to the end of the year, and the new year entered on as though nothing further was meditated. At Easter, however, a move should be made, apparently as if the place of printing alone were to be changed, and by tactics of this kind, with all decorum and convenience, this important establishment was to be forever smuggled out of Jena.

The matter, it is not too much to say, was of the greatest moment. This insidious procedure threatened the university for the moment with complete dissolution. On this side we were in real embarrassment; for although we had the right to question those concerned in the undertaking, whether there was any foundation for the general rumor, we were yet disinclined in such an ugly business to appear either premature or harsh. At first, therefore, we hesitated how to act, while delay grew every day more dangerous. The first half of August was gone, and everything depended on the counter-measures adopted in the six weeks till Michaelmas.

All at once comes help from an unexpected quarter. Kotzebue, who, since last year's scenes, was a declared enemy to all Weimar designs, cannot celebrate his triumph in secret, but arrogantly flourishes in the " Freimüthige " how the days of the Academy of Jena, which had already sustained a heavy loss in able professors, were now numbered. The " General Literature-Gazette," in consequence of the great favors accorded to the editor, was to be removed from there and set up in Halle.

On our side there was now an end of all scruples; we were completely justified in asking the heads of the enterprise whether that was their intention. It being impossible for them to deny it, their purpose of carrying on the establishment in Jena till Easter was at once frustrated, and they were informed that dating from the new year the " General Literature-Gazette " would be conducted in Jena without their assistance.

This declaration was bold enough, for we could scarce see ahead of us. Our resolution was, however, justified by success. The minutes of those days have been carefully preserved, and posterity will perhaps take pleasure in marking the course of an event of the highest importance for us at least.

The establishment of the " Literature-Gazette " being now secured in all its integrity, we had to look about for men to fill the vacant chairs. Out of several anatomists proposed,

6

Ackermann was elected. He laid the foundation of a permanent anatomical museum in connection with the university, a work which had been long in contemplation. Schelver was also called to the head of the botanical faculty. From the character of the man, at once delicate and profound, the best hopes for natural science were entertained.

The Mineralogical Society, founded by Lenz, awakened the greatest confidence. All interested in this branch of study were desirous of becoming members of the society, and great rivalry was displayed in coming forward with important contributions to the Cabinet. Conspicuous among the contributors was Prince Gallitzin, who, in acknowledgment of the presidentship conferred on him, presented the society with his considerable cabinet. By this and other gifts the establishment grew to such importance that the duke, toward the end of the year, confirmed the statutes of the society, thereby giving it a marked rank among the public institutions.

After the loss of so many important men, we had to congratulate ourselves on the acquisition of new fellow-laborers. Fernow came from Rome to stay for the future in Germany. We attached him firmly to us. Duchess Amalia gave him the librarianship of her own collection of books, a post vacant since the death of Jagemann. In view of his thorough knowledge of the Italian literature, the select library of this department, and his agreeable social qualities, he proved a highly valuable acquisition. He brought, moreover, a considerable treasure with him, the drawings left behind by his friend Carstens, by whose side throughout his career as artist, and down to his early death, Fernow had stood faithfully with counsel and deed, with judgment and assistance.

Dr. Riemer, who had gone with Herr von Humboldt to Italy, and had there for some time worked along with him in his family circle, had left that country in Fernow's company, and was likewise highly welcome to us. He attached himself to my family, lodged in my house, and bestowed his care on the education of my son.

With Zelter, too, a nearer relationship was formed. His fortnight's stay redounded to our mutual profit, both in an artistic and moral sense. He found himself in the strangest dilemma between, on one hand, a craft inherited, and practised from youth up until he had acquired a mastery of it, a craft which, economically, secured him a comfortable existence in the middle class of life, and, on the other, an art-impulse innate, powerful, irresistible, an art-impulse which unlocked the whole wealth of the tone-world out of his individuality. Practising the former, impelled by the latter, possessing facility in the former, aspiring after facility in the latter, he stood, not like Hercules at the meeting of two ways, the one of which he must elect, the other avoid, but attracted on this side and that by two equally prized muses, the one of which he had made his own, while he wished also to appropriate the other. His upright, able, earnest burgess-like nature made him just as anxious about moral culture, this being so intimately allied to, nay, incorporated with, æsthetic culture, so that to their mutual perfection the one cannot be conceived without the other.

A double mutual activity must needs therefore prevail, the Weimar lovers of art being themselves almost in the same predicament. What nature did not intend for them was imposed on them, and what nature intended for them seemed to remain ever out of their reach.

The buildings attached to the library and extending toward the castle were pulled down for the sake of a freer prospect. Instead of them, a new place became necessary, for which Herren Gentz and Rabe politely undertook to furnish the drawings. The area formerly occupied by a stately staircase and the large business and waiting-room was used for this purpose. In the second floor, moreover, room was not only found for several book-cases, but also some places for antiquities, works of art, and such like. No less was the cabinet of coins, comprising a full collection of Saxon medallions, thalers, and smaller coins, also medals, including Roman and Greek specimens, carefully disposed.

Having in my life eschewed above everything else empty words and phrases, covering no real thought or feeling, as an offence not to be endured in others, and impossible in myself, I suffered veritable pain in translating "Cellini," a work which everywhere demands, in order to its due appreciation, immediate contemplation. I regretted from my heart that I had not made a better use of my first through trip and my second stay at Florence, and had not acquired a deeper insight into the art of modern times. Friend Meyer, who, in the years 1796 and 1797, had himself there amassed the most comprehensive knowledge, helped me to the utmost, yet I ever longed after personal inspection, no more permitted me.

The idea, therefore, occurred to me whether Cellini* coins, which he makes so much use of, might not be procurable, or whether anything else might be had which would help to transplant me into those times.

Fortunately I heard of a Nürnberg auction, where copper coins of the fifteenth and sixteenth, nay, of the seventeenth and eighteenth century, were offered for sale, and I succeeded in

* Coins of the time of Cellini.

obtaining the whole lot.   Not only the original series of popes,
from Martin V to Clement XI, that is to the first quarter of
the eighteenth century, became my property, but also within that
period cardinals and priests, philosophers, learned men, artists,
and remarkable women, in distinct, uninjured specimens, part
cast, part stamped.   Strange and vexing, however, among so
many hundreds, no Cellini!   Even as it was, nevertheless, they
served to incite one to study the historical line, to make investigation after " Bonanni," " Mazzucchelli," and others, laying
the basis for altogether new instruction.

The older shooting-house in front of the Frauenthor had now
long been encroached upon all round by the park grounds.   The
space it occupied was already inclosed by gardens and walks.
The practice at the target, but especially bird shooting, had thus
gradually become inconvenient and dangerous.   In exchange,
the town council, with great profit, took a large space of ground,
spreading out pleasantly in front of the Kegelthor.   The far-
extending acres were to be converted into gardens and garden-
grounds, while a new shooting-house should be erected on a
proper site.

The site of a building, when the architect has free scope allowed him in this respect, is ever a point of the utmost moment
with him.   A country edifice and its environs should mutually
adorn each other.   The most careful consultations on th' head
were, therefore, held between the Berlin architects and the Weimar lovers of art, as also between the town council and the
shooters' society.

In the case of a new pleasure-house with its environs, destined
for the reception of a large multitude, the main requirement is
shade, a convenience not so easily procurable.   A pleasant bit
of wood was, therefore, the necessary point on which to lean a
wing of the building.   The site of the body of the building was
next determined by a primitive four-fold linden avenue extending above that thicket.   The wing, and therefore the whole
building, had to be planned rectangularly.

A moderate plan, sufficient at any rate for bare necessities,
became gradually enlarged.   The shooters' society, the public
bent on dancing and enjoyment, all put in claims, all demanded
a suitable and convenient place of accommodation.   Then the
erection of a restaurant close by, but yet detached from the
building, was also found to be a complicated concern.   And so
our original plan was still further extended.   The irregular nature of the ground itself, furthermore, tempted one to give the
freest development to the requirements and conveniences of the
object we had in view. At the end, accordingly, it was found that
æsthetic and other considerations had carried us a long way be-

yond the limits of strict necessity. Still a building is one of
those things which, beside satisfying inward requirements,
should gratify the eye, and when it is finished, there is no more
question how much thought, exertion, time, and money have
been spent on it. Its total effect is the paramount consideration
subordinating every other.

Toward the end of the year I had the pleasure of seeing my
connection with the earth-clods of Rossla finally terminated.
If the former tenant was a man disposed to enjoy life, easy-
minded and careless in his business, his successor, hitherto the
inhabitant of a country town, was distinguished by a certain
petty punctiliousness of his own, of which his procedure in reference to the well already mentioned may serve as a symbol.
The good man in his notions of gardening conceiving a fountain
to be the highest achievement, conducted the water flowing
in moderate measure from the well in narrow tin pipes to the
lowest spot, whence it sprang up a few feet high, but instead
of forming a water-mirror, only created a swamp. The idyllic
aspect of the walk by the well was thus through this silly fancy
of his quite spoiled, while other views, too, of the place no longer
afforded me the pleasure I had formerly found in them.

With all this the frugal man had come to a clear understanding that to one who took the management in his own hands the
property was quite a fair investment, and to the degree in which
the possession lost favor in my eyes it grew in favor in his.
The upshot was that I resigned the estate to him, suffering no
loss except that of the time I had spent on it, and, to be sure,
the outlays I had made on rural festivities, the pleasure of
which, however, must count for something. If, moreover, a
clear view into this mode of life could not be computed at so
much money, I had yet gained a great deal by it, besides the
happiness of socially enjoying many a cheerful day in the free,
open country.

Madame de Staël arrived in Weimar the beginning of December while I was yet busy with the programme in Jena.
Schiller's letter to me of the twenty-first of December respecting her at once served to present to me a clear picture of the
mutual relations which her presence created:

"Madame de Staël will appear to you entirely as you have
already à priori construed her in your mind. She is all of a
piece; not one foreign, false, pathologic trait in her. Despite,
therefore, of the immense distance sundering you from her
nature and way of thinking, you feel perfectly at your ease with
her; you are disposed to listen to everything she says, to say
everything to her. The French culture presents her purely and
integrally in a highly interesting light. In all we understand

by philosophy, that is, in all ultimate and supreme judgments you are, and in spite of all argument remain, in controversy with her.   Her *naturel* and feeling, however, are better than her metaphysics, and her beautiful understanding elevates itself to an intellectual faculty.   There is nothing she will not explain, penetrate into, take the measure of; there is nothing obscure, nothing inaccessible within her clear horizon.   What she cannot illumine with the torch of her understanding has for her no existence.   She has, therefore, a perfect horror of the ideal philosophy which, in her opinion, leads to mysticism and superstition, and that is the nitrogen which would be the death of her. For that which we call poetry, there is in her no sense; of works of this kind she can appropriate only the passionate, oratorical, and general.   Not that anything false will impose upon her: she will only be unable always to recognize the true.   From these few words you will perceive how the clearness, decision, and intellectual vivacity of her nature cannot work otherwise than beneficially.   The only annoyance is the quite uncommon nimbleness of her tongue; to keep up with it, you must be all ear. But seeing that with my poor expertness in French I get quite tolerably along with her, you with your greater practice will find communication with her a very easy affair."

It being impossible for me to remove from Jena till my business was done, many more descriptions and accounts reached me as to how Madame de Staël was demeaning herself, and what reception she was getting, so that I could pretty well prescribe for myself the part I should have to play.   Things, however, were all disposed quite otherwise, as will appear in next year's notices, to which we are about to pass over.

But how inconvenient such an important visit must be at this particular time will be appreciated by him who duly weighs the gravity of the business which then detained me in Jena.   To meet the world-famous " General Literature-Gazette " with the dismissal of its staff, and while it was endeavoring to transplant itself to another place to constrain it to grow in the same old spot, was a bold enterprise.   Nor is one always sufficiently sensible how a bold undertaking requires equal boldness in its execution, uncommon tasks not being achievable by common means.   More than one sensible, shrewd man gave me to understand how astonished he was at our committing ourselves to such an impossible feat.   The feat, however, was rendered possible by the fact that a man of such merit as Herr Hofrath Eichstädt took the resolution of continuing the business to which he had hitherto contributed so important a part.

The Weimar lovers of art now deemed it their duty to put the whole weight of their influence on the scale in our favor.

Prize themes for plastic artists, reviews of the papers sent in, bestowal of the prize, other kindred matters, the drawing up of a new prize theme; this complexity of affairs which had hitherto belonged to the " Propyläen " was now to go to the good of the " General Literature-Gazette." The programme for this employed me in my present isolation, while I remained in constant communication with my friend and fellow-laborer Heinrich Meyer.

Who carefully surveys the first year's course of the new, or " Jena General-Literature-Gazette," will freely confess that it was no small task. The prize problem of 1803 was variously solved, and the prize adjudicated to Professor Wagner, from Würzburg, the various merits of the competitors having been previously estimated and account given of the volunteered pieces. An attempt had then been made to restore Polygnot's picture in the Lesche at Delphi, the task being prosecuted as far as possible in the spirit of this original father of art.

The Weimar lovers of art during the five years they had now carried on this institution had ample occasion to observe how a too strictly defined theme is apt to hamper the artist, and that he should be allowed a certain license of choice, in order to work in accordance with his own sense and ability. The theme appointed for this year, therefore, was : " The Human Race in a Struggle with the Element of Water," a subject which we hoped would give occasion for great variety of treatment.

Out of the programme above referred to we may here cite a passage as conclusion to this subject and as giving occasion for the relation of a graceful incident :

" Among the treasures of the Cassel gallery the ' Charitas ' of Leonardo da Vinci is in the highest degree deserving the attention of artists and lovers of art. Herr Riepenhausen had sent to the exhibition the beautiful head of this figure excellently copied in water-colors. The sweet sadness of the mouth, the yearning expression of the eyes, the meek, entreating inclination of the head, the subdued color-tone itself of the original picture were here repeated with entire purity and effectiveness. Most of those who visited the exhibition contemplated this head with much pleasure. Nay, a lover of art must have been mightily attracted to it, for there on the glass just above the mouth were the unmistakable traces of a heart-giving kiss imprinted by sweet lips."

How much love was expressed in this fac-simile of a kiss will first appear when the circumstances are related in which the kiss was given. Our exhibition this year fell later than usual, but the interest manifested in it by the public induced us to protract it beyond the ordinary time. The rooms grew gradually colder, but were not heated till close on the time of opening. A small charge, to be devoted to the benefit of the institution, was made for one admission, especially in the case of strangers. For the natives a subscription ticket was arranged giving admission at pleasure even beyond the fixed time. While we, then, aware of the pretty evidence of appreciation of an excellent work of art, were, in secret glee, on the watch after the perpetrator, the following was conclusively established. The kiss was that of a young person. This might have been taken for granted, but the features fixed on the glass confirmed the supposition. Then it occurred alone; no one would have ventured on such a thing in the presence of many people. The event happened early, while the rooms were yet unheated. The fond lover suffused the cold glass with his warm breath, imprinted the kiss into his own vapor, which, growing cold, became consolidated. Only a few were acquainted with this affair, but it was easily conjectured who had early made his way into the unheated rooms, and things all pointed in the same direction. Suspicion rising to certainty rested on a young man whose truly kissable lips we had afterward more than one opportunity of greeting in a friendly way.

So far as we know the picture was taken to Dorpat.

A great, though, alas! an anticipated loss befell us the end of the year. Herder, after long languishment, quitted us. For three years now I had been withdrawn from his companionship. For with his disease increased his cantankerous, contradictory humor, overclouding his invaluable, unique, loving, and lovable nature. You could not visit him without rejoicing in his mildness; you could not leave him without being mortified.

How easy to vex anyone by reminding him in cheerful, frank moments by a sharp, hitting, clever word of his own defects, the defects of his spouse, his children, his situation, his dwelling! This was his fault in early days; a fault, however, in which he continued to indulge himself and which at last estranged every man from him. Faults of youth are tolerable; to be regarded as transitional, as the acid in unripe fruit. In mature age, however, they inspire one with despair.

Curiously enough, shortly before his death I was to experience a *résumé* of our many years' joys and sorrows, of our agreement, as also of our painful misrelationship.

After the representation of " Eugenie," Herder, as I heard from others, had expressed himself in the most favorable terms regarding the work, and unquestionably he was the man to discriminate to the bottom, intention from performance. Several friends repeated his own expressions. Pregnant, pointed, in

the highest degree grateful they were to me.   I might even hope
for a mutual *rapprochement,* a happy event which would have
made the piece doubly dear to me.

To this an immediate outlook was opened.   At the time I was
in Jena he was there, too, on business.   We lived in the castle,
under one roof, and exchanged visits of courtesy.   One evening
he came to me, and with calmness and sincerity began to say
the most favorable things about the piece in question.   While as
critic he displayed intimate acquaintance with the structure of
the work, as friend he showed sympathetic interest in it, and,
as in a mirror a picture often appears more charming than on
immediate inspection, so now, for the first time, it seemed to me
I rightly understood my own production and intelligently enjoyed it.   This most inward, beautiful joy was not, however,
to be long indulged me!   He capped his fair speeches with an
expression which, though merrily uttered, pierced me to the
very quick, annihilating all he had said, at least for the moment.
The man of insight will comprehend the possibility of the oc-
currence, but will, at the same time, sympathize with me in the
dreadful shock which staggered me.   I looked at him, answered
nothing, and the many years of our co-existence consummated
in this explosion filled me with the utmost horror.   So we
parted, and I never saw him again.

1804.

The winter had set in with all its force.   The roads lay buried
under snow; the Schnecke, a steep height in front of Jena, denied
all passage.   Madame de Staël sent ever more pressing intimation of her presence; my business was ended, and for many
reasons I determined on returning to Weimar.   This time
again, however, I felt the evil effects of staying in winter in the
castle.   The dearly-bought experience of 1801 had failed to
teach me the lesson of prudence.   I returned with a severe
catarrh, which, though not dangerous, confined me for some
days to bed, and then for weeks to my room.   In this way a
part of the stay of this singular woman became historical to me,
hearing, as I did, from my friends a report of all that passed in
society.   The intercourse between us had to be carried on first
by notes, next in *tête-à-tête* conversations, afterward in a very
small circle, perhaps the most favorable way in which I could
become acquainted with her, and, as far as possible, she with me.

Her presence, both intellectually and bodily, had something
charming about it, nor did she seem to take it amiss when, in
the latter respect also, people showed themselves not insensible
toward her.   How often might she have transfused into one

feeling, sociality, good-will, affection, and passion! Once she said, " I never trusted a man who had not once been in love with me." It is a pertinent remark, for when once a man as happens in love, has opened his heart and committed himself, he is forever committed, and it is impossible for him to harm or leave unprotected a creature formerly loved.

With decided impetus she pursued her purpose of learning the conditions under which we lived, interpreting them according to her own conceptions. She made all inquiries respecting each of us individually, and as a woman of the world sought to obtain a clear view of our social relations, and with her feminine powers of mind to penetrate into our more general modes of thought and all that is understood by philosophy. Though now I had no reason whatever to disguise myself in her presence, but was disposed to meet her with entire frankness, in spite of the fact that people never understand but always misunderstand me, let me commit myself never so unreservedly to them, there was, nevertheless, one circumstance which admonished me to exercise discretion for the moment. I had just received a French book, newly published, containing the correspondence of two ladies with Rousseau. In this work it appeared how nicely they had mystified the inaccessible, retiring man. Engaging his interest by some trifling affairs, they contrived to entice him into a correspondence which, after they had carried on the joke long enough, they collected and published.

I expressed to Madame de Staël my disapproval of such conduct. She, however, took the matter lightly ; seemed rather to admire it, and gave me, in no dubious terms, to understand that she was meditating the same game with us. That was quite enough to put me on my guard, in a certain measure to seal my lips.

The great talents of this high-minded and high-souled authoress are evident to everyone, and the results of her travels through Germany are a sufficient testimony of the good use she made of her time.

Her aims were various. She wanted to know Weimar in its moral, social, and literary aspects, and obtain exact information on all those points. Then it was her wish to make herself known, having as much at heart the diffusion of her own views as the fathoming of our mode of thought. Nor was that all. She aimed at producing an impression on the senses, the feelings, the mind: she would incite people to a certain brisk activity, with the lack of which she reproached us.

Having no idea of what is meant by duty, no idea of the quiet, composed attitude obligatory on him who sets himself seriously to the performance of duty, she would have people concern themselves with everything, be ever accomplishing something for the moment, just as in company a man should be continually speaking and agitating matters.

The Weimar people are certainly capable of enthusiasm, perhaps of a false enthusiasm, but French flash was not their forte, least of all at a time when French ascendancy threatened the whole world, and men of quiet penetration anticipated the inevitable mischief which in the next year was to bring us to the verge of ruin.

In reading and declamation, also, Madame de Staël was bent on gathering laurels. A reading of " Phædra," which I could not attend, had the success to be expected. It again became clear that the German might well forever have renounced this restricted form, this measured and bombastic pathos. The nice, natural kernel hidden under all this he will rather dispense with than take the trouble of picking it out of so much enveloping material repugnant to nature.

Philosophizing in company means carrying on a lively conversation on insoluble problems. This was her peculiar pleasure and passion. Of course, she pursued this exercise in speeches and rejoinders into a domain where properly God and the individual soul are alone permitted to hold communion. In this business, too, as woman and Frenchwoman, she would stick positively by her main positions, without giving exact heed to what the other said. ·

All this provoked the evil genius in me so that I treated everything that came up in a contradictory, dialectic, problematic spirit, and by obstinate antitheses often drove her to despair. In this predicament she first appeared in a truly amiable light, while her nimbleness in thought and reply displayed itself most brilliantly.

I had, on several occasions, *tête-à-tête* conversations with her, in which, too, as usual, she did not fail to dun me. On the most important events she allowed you not a moment's time for reflection, but in discussing momentous affairs, in dealing with the gravest questions, passionately demanded of you to be as swift in your movements as though you were catching a shuttlecock.

An anecdote may here be in point. Madame de Staël came to me one evening before the court time and at once, by way of salutation, exclaimed with vehemence : " I have important news to tell you. Moreau has been arrested, along with some others, and accused of treason against the tyrant ! " Like everyone, I had for a long time been interested in this noble man, following his ways and actions. In silence I recalled the past, in

order, in my way, to try the present by it, and make inferences
as to the future, or at least conjectures in that direction.   The
lady changed the conversation, diverting it as usual on to various indifferent topics, while I, still groping in my mind on the
old subject, was not at once ready with replies to her remarks.
She, therefore, anew began the reproaches I had often before
heard.   I was again this evening, as usual, *maussade*, and no
cheerful conversation was to be got out of me.   This made me
really angry.   I assured her she was incapable of any real
sympathy; she stormed in on you, stunned you with a severe
blow, and then at once called on you to join in a frolic, to skip
with her from one subject to another.   These expressions of
mine were quite to her mind.   *Passim* she wanted to elicit, no
matter what.   To reconcile me she went carefully through the
particulars of the unfortunate event she had referred to, displaying great insight into the situation of affairs as also into
characters.

Another anecdote will likewise show how lively and easy a
game it was to live with her if you would only take things in
her way.   On the occasion of a numerously attended supper at
the duchess Amalia's, I sat at a distance from her, and this time
also was quiet and thoughtful.   My neighbors reproached me
with it, and there was a slight ripple at our end, the cause of
which at last reached the ears of the upper guests.   Madame
de Staël hearing the complaint about my silence, expressed
herself on the matter as ordinarily, adding, " In general I do
not like Goethe when he has not drunk a bottle of champagne."
To this I said, half aloud, so as to be heard only by those sitting
next me: " Then on more than one occasion we must have
been fuddling together."   A moderate laugh broke out.   She
demanded to know the cause.   No one was able and disposed
to frenchify my words in their proper sense, till at last Benjamin
Constant, who sat next me, on her continued importunity,
volunteered, in order to put an end to the matter, to satisfy her
by a euphemistic phrase.

No matter, however, what may be thought and said of such
things, the great and important influence she exercised on the
course of affairs cannot be denied.   That work of hers on Germany, which sprang from such social meetings, is to be regarded
as a powerful machine cleaving the first considerable gap into
that Chinese wall of antiquated prejudices which divided us
from France, bringing us into spiritual communication with the
country beyond the Rhine and finally beyond the Channel, and
so enabling us to exercise vital influence on the more distant
West.   Let us therefore bless those annoyances and conflicts
of national peculiarities which at the time seemed by no means
to our profit.

With Benjamin Constant, too, I enjoyed pleasant, instructive hours. Whoever properly appreciates this excellent man's performances in subsequent times, and the zeal with which he pushed forward undeviatingly on the course he had marked out for himself as the course of duty, will be able to form some idea of the worthy, though as yet undeveloped, tendencies which at that time dominated such a man. In private confidential conversations he communicated to me his principles and convictions; principles and convictions philosophically directed toward moral, political, practical ends. He desired reciprocal communications at my hands, and if my mode of regarding and treating nature and art was not always clear to him the way in which he labored honestly to appropriate it, bring it into harmony with his own conceptions, and translate it into his own language, was of the greatest service to myself, bringing out, as it did, prominently before me all that was as yet undeveloped, obscure, incommunicable, unpractical in my style of treatment.

The evening he would spend sometimes at my hearth with Madame de Staël. Later on would drop in Johannes von Müller, and, the duke, my most gracious master, being also inclined to take part in these select evening circles, there could be no want of highly interesting conversation. No doubt the important and fatal events of the moment were pressing irresistibly into the common occurrences of the day; but to divert our attention from these things the medallion collection of the second half of the fifteenth century formed by me, and just at that time zealously augmented, proved of happy service, turning away our minds from considerations of seriously political or universally philosophical import into particular, historico-human observations. Here Johannes Müller was in his element, having completely at his finger-ends the history of each man imaged in the metal, and relating many a cheerful biographical incident.

Nor in the following weeks of the first quarter of the year was there any want of symathetic strangers. Professor Wolf, the powerful philologist, seemed to find ever more pleasure in our circle, and on this occasion had come from Halle for a short time to visit me. Rehberg, the meritorious painter, whom the warlike junctures had driven from Italy, showed us praiseworthy works with which he intended going to England. We also heard from him a circumstantial report of the havocs to which the beautiful land and especially Rome was exposed. Fernow's presence was in the highest degree refreshing and instructive, he having brought with him much that was stimulating in respect to art and the Italian languages. Voss's stay in Jena was no less influential. His good relationship to Hofrath Eichstädt caused him to take an active part on behalf of the "Literature-Gazette," though he could not quite hide his intention of leaving Jena.

For the rest, how difficult it was to keep one's patience with our excellent foreign guests, let the following serve as an example. Madame de Staël had as good as forced us to a performance of the "Natural Daughter." What could she, however, with the little mimic movement of the piece, get out of the copious speeches wholly unintelligible to her? She told me I had not done well in treating this subject. The book which furnished the material was not prized and the original of the heroine who figures in it was not respected in good society. As I was good-humored enough to decline jokingly the appeal to these tribunals, she replied that this was just the fault of us German authors, not to take heed of the public. She further pressingly demanded a performance of the "Mädchen von Andros." What reception this mask-piece affecting antiquity might have received at her hands, I do not remember.

Toward the end of June I repaired to Jena, and at once, the same evening, owing to a lively St. John's fire, met with a merry enough reception. There is no question but these pleasure illuminations on the mountain seen from the neighborhood of the town as also when driving up and down the valley, affect us with a pleasant surprise.

According to the nature and bulk of the materials employed, and the greater or less degree of swiftness with which they are brandished about, they flame up tongue-wise now in the form of obelisks, now of pyramids; appear to die out in a glow and all at once blaze into new effulgence. A reciprocal play of fire is thus seen disporting up and down the valley in the most varied manner.

Amid all these spectacles there was one in particular imposing and significant, though lasting only for a short time. On the pinnacle of the Hausberg, which seen in front towers up skittle-wise, there flamed aloft symmetrically a considerable fire, though of a mobile and restless character. In a short time it was seen pouring in two diverging streams down the sides of the skittle. These two flaming rows connected in the middle by a fiery cross-line displayed the figure of a colossal blazing A from whose apex a splendid flame, like a crown, shot forth and pointed to the name of our revered dowager duchess. This phenomenon called forth universal applause. Foreign guests in astonishment inquired how such a significant festive fire-picture could be produced.

They very soon learned that it was the work of a class from

whom such a gay and ingenious device was least to be expected.

The university town of Jena, whose lowest and poorest class is particularly prolific—a common feature in large cities—swarms with boys of different ages, not unfitly likened to the *lazaroni*. Without exactly begging, they commend themselves by their importunate services to the beneficence of the inhabitants, and in particular of the students. With the increased attendance at the academy, this tag-rag class of people had grown specially numerous; they crowded the market-place and the corners of streets, ready for any errand. They carried messages hither and thither, ordered horses and carriages, bore the albums up and down, and solicited inscription; doing all services of that kind for small recompense, though counting a good deal to them and their families. They had the name of Moors, probably because from their exposure to the sun they had acquired an obviously dark complexion.

These had now for a long time claimed the right to kindle and feed the fire on the pinnacle of the Hausberg, and to enable them to do this they made use of the following means. As assiduous in their attendance on the female servants as on the students, they knew how to ingratiate themselves into the good-will of the former by many a service, in return for which the besom-stumps were carefully laid by throughout the year and delivered over to them against this festival. To collect all these they distributed themselves through the different quarters of the town, and on the evening of St. John's Day assembled in troops on the pinnacle of the Hausberg. There they set fire to the stumps, waving them about in many various motions, which this time went to the construction of a large A. At the end they stood still, each one holding the flame as long as possible.

This lively spectacle, watched and admired by friends assembled at a cheerful supper, was calculated to arouse some enthusiasm. Glasses were clinked in honor of the revered duchess, and as the police had for some time been making ever more serious preparations to put an end to those pleasure illuminations, we could not help regretting the loss for the future of such joyous scenes, or expressing a wish for the continuance of the custom in the merry toast:

> " St. John's feast give no man the mumps,
>   Each year its bonfire burn;
>   For brooms are ever being swept to stumps
>   And youngsters e'er being born."

A deeper pleasure was afforded us in examining the scientific establishments there, the collection of the mineralogical

society having been particularly enhanced both in its treasures
and arrangement. The vitreous tubes, which at the time had
first come prominently into notice, served, like all important
novelties, to impart fresh interest to this department of study.
To bring geognostic experiences and geologic thoughts into a
consecutive visual series, a model was thought of, which at first
sight should represent a graceful landscape, the undulations of
which were, on taking the whole to pieces, to be explained by
the various sorts of stone indicated inside. A plan in miniature
was sketched, at first not without success, but afterward on
account of the pressure of other interests set aside, and by reason of disputes regarding the mode of representing such problematic things committed to oblivion.

The library left by Hofrath Büttner, the binding of the books
and their arrangement still gave me a great deal to do.

Gladdening to me in the highest degree, in the midst of all
these labors, was the visit of my most gracious master, who
came over with Privy-Councillor Von Voigt, a statesman zealously co-operating with me in these matters. What a rich
reward it was to labor for such a prince, who was ever opening
out new fields to enterprise and activity, confidently committing
the cultivation of them to his servants, who every now and
again looked in on you and at once with perfect accuracy determined how far you had been acting in accordance with his intentions, while sometimes by your unusual activity you would
surprise him with the results you had achieved!

During his present visit, the resolution came to a head to set
up an anatomical museum, which, in case of there being no
professor of anatomy in connection with the university, should
remain attached to the scientific institution. This was all the
more necessary that, through the removal of the important
Loder Cabinet, a great gap was felt in this department. Professor Ackermann, called from Heidelberg, set himself devot-
edly to labor and collect from all quarters toward this purpose,
and under his management the undertaking very soon succeeded, at first in a didactic, which of course is entirely different
from a scientific, sense. The latter at once directs attention and
endeavors toward the new, the rare, nay, the curious, and has
of course no right of action till after the satisfaction of the didactic sense.

The more I advanced in my chromatic studies, the more
important and precious appeared to me the history of the natural
sciences in general. Whoever carefully surveys the course of a
higher knowledge, the course of a higher generalization, will
have occasion to remark how experience and knowledge may
progress and enlarge, but how thought and true insight will yet

by no means advance with equal pace, and this for the perfectly plain reason that knowledge is endless and accessible to every man who will take the trouble attentively to look about him, whereas deliberation, thought, the conjunction of ideas is confined within a certain circle of human capabilities. Knowledge of the world-phenomena around us, from the fixed star to the smallest living point, may, accordingly, grow ever clearer and completer, while true insight into the nature of these things is possible only to the highest intellectual faculty. This will explain the fact that not individuals alone, but whole centuries revolve in a fixed circle from error to truth, from truth to error.

In this year I had arrived at the memorable time when the Royal Society, as it was afterward called, met first in Oxford, then in London. Kept back by various hinderances, next interrupted in its labors by the great fire in London, but always becoming more consolidated, it was at last formally constituted and established.

The history of this society, by Thomas Spratt, I read with great approval and considerable edification. Notwithstanding all the objections that may have been urged against this man, who is no doubt somewhat flighty, by more exacting people, a man of talent he always remains, and gives us right true glances into the situation.

The protocols of this society, published by Birch, are, on the other hand, beyond all dispute quite invaluable. The beginnings of so great an institution furnish us with enough materials for thought. To this work I devoted every quiet hour at my command, and what of it I appropriated I have briefly incorporated into my " History of the Theory of Colors."

Here, however, I must not omit to mention that I obtained these works from the Göttingen library, through the favor of the noble Heyne, whose indulgent kindness I enjoyed uninterruptedly for many years, even though he often could not wholly conceal a little annoyance at the late return of many important works. No doubt my desultory mode of life and study was mostly to blame for the fact that I could only at first make a hasty onset on able productions, and then, called off by external importunities, was obliged to lay them aside in the hope of a more favorable moment, which probably did not arrive for a long time.

Winckelmann's earlier letters to Hofrath Berendis had already long been in my hands, and I had prepared myself for their publication. In order to gather together what in various ways might serve toward the delineation of this extraordinary man, I drew my valued friends Wolf in Halle, Meyer in Weimar, and Fernow in Jena, into co-operation with me in this bus-

7

iness, and in this way was gradually formed the octavo volume as it was then placed in the hands of the public.

A French manuscript, " Diderot's Nephew," was handed me by Schiller, with the expression of a wish that I would translate it. At all times I was quite specially taken, not with Diderot's sentiments and way of thinking, but with his mode of representing things, and I found the packet of the greatest stimulating excellence. A work more insolent and more restrained, more talented and more audacious, more immoral-moral, had scarcely ever before met my eyes, and I therefore very readily undertook its translation. For the sake of making it the more intelligible to myself and others, I recalled out of the treasures of literature things having affinity with the work in question and with which I had formerly been familiar, and so under the form of notes in alphabetic arrangement grew an appendix which I at last got published by Göschen. The German translation was to come out first, and the original to be printed shortly after. With this plan in my head, I neglected to get a copy of the original, a neglect which occasioned quite curious occurrences, as will later on fall to be narrated.

With every month the new " General Literature-Gazette " pressed forward with increased vitality, not indeed without having varied opposition to encounter, but without suffering any real check. To relate in a connected whole all that it had to fight its way through, for and against, would make up no unacceptable publication, and the course of such an important literary undertaking would at all events be instructive. In the present case, however, we can only have recourse to a simile in order to express ourselves. The error of the opposite party was that they did not consider how, though a hostile battery on a favorable military position may be removed and transplanted to another important point on their own side, that in no way hinders the enemy from bringing up his guns to the vacated spot and thereby gaining equal advantage for himself with his adversary. In the conduct of the business I took a continuous active part. Of the reviews I wrote I will here specify only that on Voss's poems.

In the year 1797, with my friend Meyer returning from Italy, I had made a most enjoyable trip to the little cantons, whither now for the third time I felt drawn bythe spell of an incredible longing. The Vierwaldstädter lake, the Schwyz Haken, Fluelen and Altorf, now viewed with free open eye on my way hither and thither, compelled my imagination to people with persons those localities of immense configuration, and who offered themselves more readily to me than Tell and his brave compatriots? Here on the spot itself I meditated an epic poem, to which I gave myself with all the greater devotion that I wanted to undertake a larger work in hexameters, in that beautiful verse to which our language was gradually moulding itself, in order by practice and through counsel with friends to attain more and more perfection in that measure.

Of my plans I will only mention briefly that the " Tell " I had in my mind was a kind of " Demos," whom, therefore, I figured as a gigantically powerful burden-bearer, engaged his life long in carrying hides and other wares hither and thither across the mountains, troubling himself no further about lordship and subjection, but laboriously driving his trade, and as able as resolute to defend himself from the most immediate personal evils. As such he was known to his countrymen, who were richer and of higher social status, and for the rest was looked upon as inoffensive, even by the foreign oppressors. This position assigned to him facilitated to me an exposition unfolding itself in action, an exposition which would have set forth clearly the exact situation of the time.

My governor of the province was one of those easy selfish tyrants who press forward to the accomplishment of their purposes heartlessly and ruthlessly, but otherwise are well pleased to enjoy their comfort, and so far are disposed to live and let live, perpetrating on occasion, at the dictate of their own caprices, this and that deed, which may either be indifferent in its consequences, or may, too, operate for weal and woe. From these sketches it will be seen that the plan of my poem on both sides was so far practicable, admitting of a definite series of actions so suitable to the epic poem. The old Swiss and their faithful representatives, outraged in their possessions, honor, persons, and reputation, should feel their impassioned moral nature agitated into inward fermentation, tumult, and final outbreak, while the two principal figures outlined above should stand in contrast to and operate immediately on one another.

These thoughts and images, however much they employed my mind, gradually coalescing as they did into a mature whole, did not succeed in obtaining definite objective embodiment at my hands. The German prosody, so far as it imitated the old syllable-measure, instead of becoming regulated, grew ever more problematic. The acknowledged masters of such arts and artifices were themselves divided into almost hostile camps. In these circumstances, what was before dubious grew more dubious. In my case, however, when I had any purpose in my mind, it was impossible for me to craze my head with the means by which the purpose was to be attained. The means must be already at hand if I was not at once to abandon the undertaking altogether.

With all this inward creation and outward negation we had entered into the new century. I had often talked over the affair with Schiller, had often enough entertained him with my lively description of those walls of rock and the anguished lot of the people, so that at last this theme could not but shape and mould itself in his mind according to his own structure. He, too, made me acquainted with his views, nor did I wish to have any part whatever in a material which had now for me lost the charm of novelty and of immediate observation, but formally and with pleasure I resigned in his favor all my rights and claims to the property, as I had formerly done in the case of the " Cranes of Ibykus " and many another theme. It will, moreover, clearly appear, when the above representation is compared with Schiller's drama, that the latter is wholly the author's production, and that he owes nothing to me except the incitement to the task and a more vivid view of the situation than the simple legend could have afforded him.

The elaboration of this subject was, as usual, a matter of constant conversation between us. The parts were at last distributed among the actors in accordance with his views, the rehearsals carefully superintended by us both. In costume and decoration, too, we wished to proceed only in moderation, though with an eye to what was fitting and characteristic. On this occasion, as always, we acted but in conformity with the state of our economic resources, and with our conviction that only moderate stress is to be laid on externals, but so much the greater weight to be attached to essence and substance. If externals are made the preponderating element, while in the end they fail to satisfy all the demands of sense, they crush that higher structure which in point of fact is the only justification of the drama. On March 17th came the performance, and by this first, as also by the following representations, and no less by the happiness which this piece all along created, we were completely rewarded for all the care and trouble we had spent on it.

In conformity with the arrangement come to with Schiller to form gradually a repertory for our theatre, I tried my hand at " Götz von Berlichingen," without being able to accomplish the purpose in view. The piece always continued too long. Divided into two parts it became inconvenient, and the flowing historical course of the play entirely hindered a stationary interest in the scenes such as is demanded by the theatre. Meanwhile the work was begun and ended not without loss of time and other disturbances.

In these times, too, I had a visit from Count Zenobio, who came to receive back the fifty carolins which some years before he had deposited in my hands to be given as a prize for the best solution of a question proposed by him. I no longer remember the exact terms of the question, but in strange wording it ran something to this effect: What has been the strict course all along of the culture of men and of human society? It might have been said that the answer to this question was already contained in Herder's "Ideas," and other such writings of his. In the vigor of his earlier years, Herder, to gain this prize, might well have once more constrained his powerful pen to a precise *résumé* of this theme.

The good, well-meaning stranger, who was willing to contribute something on behalf of the enlightment of men, had conceived of the University of Jena as though it were an academy of the sciences. The papers sent in were to be perused and appraised by it. How oddly such a demand corresponded with our position is soon comprehended. Nevertheless I talked over the matter at large with Schiller and then with Griesbach. Both found the theme much too comprehensive and in a certain measure also undefined. In whose name should it be given out, who was to be the judge, and what authority might be expected to examine the competing papers, which could not be other than of large compass even in the case of the best writer? The conflict, moreover, between the Anatolians and Œkumenians was at that time more lively than now. The conviction was beginning to take hold on men that the human race everywhere could have originated under certain conditions of nature, and that each race so arising must have invented its language according to organic laws. Now the theme in question demanded investigation into these beginnings. To adopt either side of the question was to exclude the essay from general approbation, and to vacillate between the two sides was a ticklish business. In fine, after much agitation of the affair, I let both prize and question drop, and perhaps in the meantime our Mæcenas had come upon other ideas and discovered a better use for his money. At all events, it was a relief to me to have his carolins and the whole affair out of my hands and responsibility.

1805

This year was also entered on with the best intentions and hopes, and in particular "Demetrius" was the subject of frequent and minute discussion. Both of us being, however, again and again disturbed in our chief tasks by bodily ailments, Schiller continued the translation of "Phædra," I of "Rameau," efforts which demanding no productivity of our own served to tune and stimulate our talent through communication with foreign and finished works.

My work incited, nay, compelled, me to take the French
literature again in hand, and in order to the understanding of
the eccentric, audacious little book to infuse fresh distinct life
into names which for us Germans at least had lost all meaning.   Musical studies, too, in former times so agreeable to me,
but now long kept in abeyance, I also resuscitated.   In this way
many an hour which otherwise would have been wasted in pain
and languor was turned to good account.   By a happy accident
there came to us at this time a Frenchman of the name of Texier,
whose gay and clever talent for reading French comedies with
change of voice, according to the representations of the French
actors, was the admiration of the Court for several evenings.
To me in particular, who highly valued Molière, devoting a
certain portion of time each year to his works, and thereby ever
anew testing and renewing a reverence I truly felt for him—
to me it was both enjoyable and profitable to hear his living
voice in the person of a countryman of his, who, equally with
me penetrated with a sense of Molière's great talent, by his
representations contended with me in extolling the French
comedian.

Schiller, urged by January 30th, worked diligently at
" Phædra," which was actually performed on the appointed
day, and here at the time, as subsequently in other quarters,
afforded able actors the opportunity of distinguishing themselves and still more highly raising their talent.

In the meantime, owing to two dreadful fire accidents which
happened in succession, within a few nights of each other, and
by both of which I was personally endangered, I was thrown
back into the bad state of health from which I was endeavoring
to recover.   Schiller felt himself in an equally bad plight.   Our
personal meetings were interrupted; we exchanged flying messages.   Some of his letters written in February and March yet
testify to his sufferings, to his activity, his resignation, and his
ever more and more vanishing hopes.   The beginning of May I
ventured out, I found him on the point of going to the theatre,
I did not wish to keep him from it, a sense of discomfort deterred
me from accompanying him, and so we parted in front of the
door of his house, never to see each other again.   In the state
in which I was, bodily and mentally, a state which taxed all my
strength to prevent my sinking under it, no one ventured to
bring to me in my loneliness the news of his decease.   He had
departed on the 9th, and now all my troubles assailed me doubly
and threefold.

As soon as I had so far manned myself, I looked about in
quest of some decided serious work; my first thought was to
complete " Demetrius."   From the time when the purpose was

formed down to the end we had frequently talked over the plan.
Schiller liked well in the midst of his labors to hold argument
with himself and others, for and against, as to how any particular work was to be done; he was just as unwearied in listening to other people's opinions as in scrutinizing his own from
this and that point of view. I thus accompanied him side by
side through all his works from " Wallenstein " onward, for
the most part in a peaceful and friendly way, though sometimes
when at last the play was about ripe for performance I disputed
vehemently with him on some points, till in the end the one or
other of us gave way. In the play of " Demetrius," too, his
ardent and aspiring spirit had conceived the plot in much too
wide compass. I witnessed how he was bent on constructing
the exposition in a prelude, now like " Wallenstein," and now
like the " Maid of Orleans," how he gradually narrowed his
field, compressed the salient points, and began to work this and
that part into conformity with such circumscription. One
event attaining predominance in his mind over another, I was
ever at his side with counsel and co-operation. The piece
became as vital in me as in him. At present, therefore, it was
my passionate desire to continue our intercourse with each other
to the undoing of death, to sustain alive his thoughts, views, and
intentions, down to the smallest particular, and in the elaboration of our own and foreign works to raise for the last time our
wonted co-operation to its highest climax. In this way his loss
would be cancelled; he would still live with me. I hoped to
unite our mutual friends. The German theatre, for which we
had labored in common, he creating and moulding, I instruct-
ing, practising, and executing, should, till the arrival of a like
fresh spirit, not be wholly orphaned on account of his departure.

In short, all the enthusiasm which despair stirs up in us on the
occasion of a great loss had taken possession of me. My hands
were free from all other work; in a few months I should have
finished the piece. To see it at once played in all theatres
would have been a magnificent funeral solemnity, a solemnity
he himself had prepared for himself and his friends. I was
well, I was consoled. Unfortunately, however, many hinderances came in the way of the execution of this design, hinderances which some carefulness and prudence might perhaps
have overcome, but which my passionate, inconsiderate antagonism only aggravated. Obstinate and precipitate, I gave up
the idea, and even now I dare not think of the situation into
which I felt myself plunged. Now, properly, for the first time
was Schiller torn from my side, now for the first time was his
fellowship denied me. My artistic imagination was forbidden
from busying itself with the catafalque I intended raising for

him, a catafalque which should outlast his burial longer than in the case of the one at Messina. Now it was that my imagination turned to follow the corpse to the grave which had desolately closed in on him. Now for the first time I began to feel his dissolution. Intolerable pain seized hold of me, and my bodily sufferings secluding me from all company I sank into the saddest loneliness. My diary records nothing of that time, its blank leaves indicate my blank state, and what scraps of news may elsewhere be found only testify how I followed current business without further interest, and instead of directing it let myself be directed by it. In later times how often had I to smile quietly to myself when sympathetic friends missed Schiller's monument in Weimar. The thought was always present with me how I could have raised the most joyous monument in honor of himself and our co-operation.

The translation of "Rameau's Nephew" had been sent by Schiller to Leipsic. Some manuscript sheets of the "Theory of Colors" I received back after his death. The objections he had entertained to the passages marked by him I could explain in his sense, so that his friendship still exerted itself from the kingdom of the dead, while mine was banished among the living.

My solitary activity I now directed to another subject. Winckelmann's letters, which had come into my hands, caused me to think of this distinguished long-missed man, and to compress into convenient limits all that for many years I had been revolving in my head and heart respecting him. Many friends had been already asked to contribute to this work. Schiller himself had promised to take part in it.

I may well deem it the providence of a friendly disposed genius that an especially prized and revered man, with whom I had formerly stood only in general relations of occasional correspondence and intercourse, now felt himself impelled to draw closer the bonds of intimacy between us. Professor Wolf, of Halle, manifested his interest in Winckelmann and my efforts toward his commemoration by sending me an essay which was highly welcome to me, though he himself declared it to be unsatisfactory. As early as March this year he had announced a visit he intended paying us, and all Weimar friends gladdened at the prospect of having him again in their circle, which, alas! he found diminished by one noble member—found plunged in deep sadness of heart—when on May 30th he arrived in our midst, accompanied by his daughter, who in all the charms of opening youth rivalled the spring itself. I could not but hospitably receive the respected man, spending hours highly delightful and instructive with him. In confidential relations, each of us speaking freely on the subject in which he was most interested, the marked difference between our two characters soon became apparent. The diversity in the present case was of an altogether different character from that unlikeness which, instead of separating, most inwardly united me and Schiller. My realistic could very well consociate with Schiller's ideal tendency. Both tendencies detached failing of their goal, they at last entered into a vital alliance with each other.

Wolf, on the other hand, had devoted his whole life to the literary traditions of antiquity, carefully examining and comparing them as far as possible in manuscripts and editions. His penetrating understanding had so mastered the peculiarities of the different authors according to the time and place in which they flourished, and so sharpened itself in this province, that in the difference of language and style of writings he at once detected the difference in their spirit and sense, tracing their peculiarities from the simple letter and syllable up to rhythmic and prosaic euphony, from the simple structure to manifold complexity of sentences.

Was it any wonder, then, that so great a talent disporting itself with so much certainty in this element, possessing an almost magic skill in recognizing virtues and faults in this sphere, able to assign to every particular writing its particular time and place, and so in the highest degree realizing the past— was it any wonder, that such a man should supremely value these masterful accomplishments and deem the results springing from them to be alone estimable? In short, from his conversations it appeared that he prized that alone as historical, alone truly credible, which was or could be proved to have come down to us in writings from olden times.

The Weimar friends, on the other hand, had come by another road to a corresponding set of convictions. With their passionate attachment to plastic art, they necessarily very soon became aware that in this department also the historical is the only basis of a true judgment, as of practical emulation. They had, therefore, accustomed themselves always to consider ancient as well as modern art historically, carefully surveying its course of development, and imagined that from their point of view, likewise, they had mastered many a characteristic feature by which time and place, master and pupil, originality and imitation, predecessor and successor, could be duly discriminated.

When now in liveliest conversation both modes of realizing the past were discussed, the Weimar lovers of art might well deem themselves at an advantage in comparison with the excellent man, seeing they did full justice to his studies and talents, sharpened their taste on his taste, endeavored with their intellectual faculty to attain to a comprehension of his intellectual habit, and in this way edified and enriched themselves. He, on the other hand, denied the admissibility of their procedure, and there was no means of convincing him of his partiality. It is difficult, nay, impossible, to excite in a man who has not heartily devoted himself to any particular study and thereby gradually attained to some familiarity with the subject and the power of drawing comparisons between it and his own more special branch of culture—it is difficult or even impossible to excite in such a man so much as a presentiment of the matter to be appreciated, the last appeal having ever in such a case to be addressed to faith and confidence. When, now, we very readily granted that some speeches of Cicero, for which we had the greatest respect, inasmuch as they had been helpful to us in building up our little Latin, were to be regarded as patchwork interpolated at a later period and not as especial models of eloquence, he, on the other hand, would by no means allow that the sculpture handed down to us could also trustworthily be disposed of according to a certain series in the order of time.

Though, again, we frankly conceded that with respect to sculpture much might remain problematic, as even the man most deeply versed in writings was for his part also unable, at all times, to satisfy himself or others in regard to some point in his department, it was not for us for one moment to presume to ask of Wolf a reciprocal concession on his side, to ask him to admit that our documents had a like validity with his, that the sagacity we had attained by practice might be of equal value with his! The very obstinacy of this conflict, however, yielded us the considerable advantage that all arguments pro and con were exhaustively discussed, and that each bent on enlightening the other could not fail of himself attaining greater clearness and facility in his special province.

Seeing, however, that the greatest good-will, affection, friendship, need of each other, pervaded these discussions, that both sides during the course of the argument saw each before it an infinity of knowledge, of things to be known, there reigned throughout the whole time of a lengthy coexistence quite an excited gayety of spirits, quite a passionate cheerfulness which tolerated no stagnation, which found within the same circle ever fresh material for entertainment.

The conversation turning on the older history of art, there was, necessarily, often mentioned the name of Phidias, who belongs as much to the world as to art history, for what were the world without art? It thus happened as a matter of course that reference was made to the two colossal heads of the

Dioscuri lying in Rudolstadt. Our incredulous friend made
this the occasion for a trip thither, as a proof of his good-will
to take sides with us, but, as was to be anticipated, without any
special success. Unfortunately, at that time the two gigantic
heads, for which hitherto no suitable site could be found, were
left standing on the bare earth, and all proper contemplation of
their features being denied, only the fondest connoisseur would
have been able to recognize their excellence. Being well
received by the Court there, Wolf enjoyed himself in the beautiful country round about, and after a visit to Schwarzburg
returned in the company of Friend Meyer, in happy spirits, but
as much an unbeliever as ever.

The Weimar lovers of art during the stay of this highly
prized man much extended their knowledge, and at the same
time greatly cleared and vitalized their former intellectual conquests, while his abundant vivacity in the highest degree animated their whole circle. With a pressing invitation to us to
give him a speedy return visit, he went back to Halle in the best
humor.

I had, therefore, the happiest inducement to repair again to
Lauchstädt, although the theatre did not properly require my
presence there. Our repertory contained so much both good
and excellent not yet witnessed there that we could adorn many
of our bills with the attractive words " For the first time." For
the sake of lovers of the theatre, let me here present the constel-
lation with which we then sought to shine in that sphere. As
mostly new, or at least very popular, there appeared of tragic and heroic plays: " Othello," " Regulus," " Wallenstein,"
" Nathan the Wise," " Götz von Berlichingen," " Maid of
Orleans," " Johanna von Montfauçon." Of comic and sentimental pieces: " Lorenz Stark," " Jealousy put to the Blush,"
" Fellow-Culprits," " Hussites," and " Page Tricks." Of
operas: " Saalnixe " (Salon-sprites), " Cosa Rara," " Fanchon," " The Interrupted Sacrifice," " Diggers after Hidden
Treasures," " Soliman the Second," and then, at the close, the
" Song of the Bell," as a prized and worthy commemoration of
the revered Schiller, many obstacles opposing a special and
formal celebration to his memory.

During my short stay at Lauchstädt, I had principally to
arrange things connected with buildings, etc., as also to come
to some definite understanding with the officials there on certain
points. This settled, I repaired to Halle, where in the house of
my friend I met with the most hospitable reception. The conversation lately interrupted was resumed in a lively manner, and
extended on all sides. As I here found the man unintermittently at work, in the midst of his daily, defined, and sometimes

compulsory labors, there were a thousand occasions which
started subjects for intellectual conversation, on which, oblivious of time, we would be engaged for the day and half the
night.

If now I had to admire in him the incarnation of immense
knowledge, I was also inquisitive to learn with what method and
what skill he instructed the youth on each particular subject.
Thanks to the assistance of his daughter, on more than one
occasion I was enabled to listen to his lectures behind a tapes-
tried door.   Everything I could have expected of him was fulfilled—a free discourse springing out of fulness of knowledge,
based on the most thorough comprehension and delivered with
talent and taste.

That under such relations and in such circumstances I gained
much benefit is obvious to the dullest, but how influential on
the rest of my life these few months were only the man of understanding will rightly appreciate.

In another department I had the happiness to be indoctrinated into a far-reaching branch of science.   In the first days of
August, Dr. Gall opened his course of lectures, and I joined
myself to the many hearers who thronged his auditorium.   His
peculiar doctrine, which now began to transpire widely, could
not but after some preliminary investigation find response in
me.   I was already accustomed to contemplate the brain under
the light of comparative anatomy, a light which revealed to
the eye itself that the different senses are but off-shoots branch-
ing from the spinal column, and at first simple and detached are
to be readily recognized in this relation, though gradually their
traces (in this connection) become less perceptible, till at length
the swollen mass wholly conceals distinction and origin.   This
organic operation repeating itself in all animal systems from
below upward, and ascending from the palpable to the imper-
ceptible, the leading conception of Gall's doctrine was by no
means foreign to me: and even should he, as you observed, mis-
guided by his sharp-sightedness, venture into too elaborate
detail, all you had to do by way of correction was to convert
an apparently paradoxical partial application into a more comprehensive general statement.   The dispositions to murder,
robbery, and stealth, as also philoprogenitiveness, friendship,
and philanthropy, might, for example, be comprehended under
more general rubrics, and in this way certain tendencies very
well be associated with the preponderance of certain organs.

Still, whoever bases his instruction on the general is not
likely to attract a large number of desirable pupils.   It is the
particular which charms people, and properly, too, for life is
directed to the particular, and very many men can get along

in a single line without having to strain after more than just so much understanding as will assist the five senses.

At the beginning of his lecture he touched on the metamorphosis of plants, so that Friend Loder, sitting beside me, looked at me with some surprise. In truth, however, the only surprise was that, though the lecturer must have been sensible of the analogy, he did not recur to it, notwithstanding that this idea might well have been made a ruling one throughout the whole length and breadth of the argument.

Beside these public, principally craniologic, lectures, he in private opened up the construction of the brain itself before our eyes, to the enhancement of my interest. For the brain, as the basis of the head, is the key of the whole. It determines, is not determined by, the skull. The inner diploe of the skull is held fast by the brain, and constrained within its due organic limits. On the other hand, in the case of sufficient supply of bone-mass, the outer lamina seeks to expand to a monstrous size, and inwardly to construct so many chambers and compartments.

Gall's instruction may well be regarded as the crown of comparative anatomy. For though he did not deduce his doctrine from that source, and proceeded more from without inward, being, too, apparently bent rather on immediate instruction than deduction, all his facts were in close connection with the spinal column, and the hearer was left perfectly at liberty to classify them in that connection. Gall's interpretation of the brain was in every way an advance on the old traditional exposition, whereby so many stories or cuttings of the brain from the top inward were dubbed with so many names, and the thing left alone. The very basis of the brain, the centres of the nerves, were only so many topographical distinctions, and that was all I could get out of it, so that shortly before a sight of Vicq d'Azyr's fine diagrams fairly drove me to despair.

Dr. Gall was also added to the company which had received me in such a friendly way. We therefore saw each other every day, almost every hour, and the conversation always revolved within the sphere of his wonderful observations. He made jokes about all of us, and asserted that in accordance with the structure of my brow I could not ope my mouth but out there flew a trope, and was every moment catching me in the deed. My whole organization, he maintained in all earnest, denoted the born popular orator. This gave rise to all manner of jests, and I had fain to resign myself to being ranked in the same class with Chrysostom.

All this intellectual activity, joined to social good living, might perhaps not have exactly suited my bodily state. At all

events, I was all unexpectedly overtaken with the paroxysm of
a customary disease, which, proceeding from the loins, painfully announced itself from time to time by morbid symptoms.
On this occasion, however, it procured me the advantage of a
nearer acquaintance with Councillor of Mines Reil, who, treating me medically, became also known to me as a thoughtful,
well-disposed, observant man. What interest he took in my
condition is testified by an opinion of my case in his own handwriting, dated September 17th of this year, a document I have
respectfully preserved among my papers.

Nor was I destined by my illness to lose Dr. Gall's further
course of instruction. He had the politeness to bring the
apparatus used in each lecture to my room, and my sickly state
not hindering me from higher speculations and observations,
he communicated his views to me at great length.

Dr. Gall left for Göttingen. We, however, were attracted by
the prospect of a singular adventure. Hofrath Beireis, in
Helmstädt, an eccentric, problematic man, already for many
years notorious in many respects, had been so often named to
me; his neighborhood, remarkable possessions, strange behavior, and the secret brooding over all, so often described
to me, that I could not but reproach myself with the fact that I
had not seen with my own eyes, and in personal intercourse
endeavored to fathom, in a certain measure at least, this most
singular personality, which seemed to point to an earlier transi-
tory epoch. Professor Wolf being in the same predicament in
this respect with myself, we determined, knowing the man was
at home, on undertaking a journey to the mysterious griffin who
presided over extraordinary and scarcely conceivable treasures.
My humorous fellow-traveller readily allowed my son, fifteen
years old, to take part in this expedition, an addition which contributed greatly to our social entertainment. The able, learned
man constantly plying the boy with railleries, the lad in turn
availed himself of the right of self-defence, nay, on occasion
would assume the offensive. The boundaries prescribed to such
warfare were, moreover, apt to be transgressed, and the two
would turn on each other with nudges and boisterous frolics, not
altogether convenient in a carriage. We drew up at Bernburg,
where our worthy friend could not forbear indulging his tastes
for certain purchases and barters, a circumstance which the
young scapegrace, on the watch over all the actions of our
fellow-traveller, did not fail to turn to the best account in the
way of rough pleasantry.

The excellent but self-willed man had a decided antipathy
to all toll-gatherers, and even when they exercised their rights
with all gentleness and forbearance, nay, all the more on that

account, would express his intolerance of them, bringing us
sometimes to the verge of disagreeable scenes.

The like aversions and peculiarities preventing us in Magdeburg from visiting some meritorious men, I occupied myself
principally with the antiquities of the cathedral, in particular
the monuments to the dead. I speak here of but three bronze
ones erected to the memory of three archbishops of Magdeburg:
Adelbert II, after 1403, stiff and stark, but carefully done, and
to a certain extent natural, below life-size; Friedrich, after 1464,
above life-size, natural and artistic; Ernst, with the year 1499,
an invaluable monument by Peter Vischer, with which few are
to be compared. In the contemplation of these monuments I
experienced no end of delight. For him who studies the development of art—its decline, its deviations, its return to a right
course, the dominance of a leading epoch, the influence of individuals—and cultivates his eye and sense in that way, there is no
conversation so instructive and entertaining as the silent one
evoked by a series of such monuments. I wrote down my
observations, for the sake both of practice in literary delineation
and of remembrance, and am glad to find the leaves still among
my extant papers. Yet in these hours I should like nothing
better than that an exact copy were taken of these monuments,
especially of the splendid Vischer one. (Such a copy was, later
on, laudably communicated to me.)

Town, fortification, and, as seen from the ramparts, the surrounding country were viewed with attention and interest; in
particular, the eye rested long on the large group of trees which,
at not too great a distance, rose venerably to adorn the plain.
They overshadowed the cloister of Bergen, a place which called
up many remembrances. There it was where Wieland, nursing
keen, youthful, tender feelings, had laid the foundation of higher
literary culture. There, too, with pious intentions, labored Abt
Steinmetz, perhaps one-sidedly, yet honestly and vigorously.
And much does the world in its impious one-sidedness need such
springs of light and warmth, if in its erring egotism it is not to
perish of cold and thirst!

In the course of repeated visits to the cathedral, we observed
a lively Frenchman in clerical dress, conducted by the sacristan,
hold very loud conversation with his companion, while we
natives pursued our purposes in silence. We learned it was the
Abbé Gregoire, and though I was very desirous to go and introduce myself to him, my friend, averse to the Gaul, would not
consent, and we contented ourselves, while engaged at some
distance from him, with observing his behavior and overhearing
his opinions, which he expressed aloud.

We resumed our journey, and in passing from one water-

shed to another—my chief interest being geognostic—I noticed
how the sandstone heights now pointed in the direction, not
of the Elbe, but of the Weser. Helmstädt itself has quite a
pleasant situation. There where flows a small stream of water
the sand is belted down by gardens and other agreeable plantations. The traveller who enters this district without the idea
of a lively German university will be agreeably surprised at
finding in such a quarter an old establishment of learning of
limited proportions, where on the basis of an earlier cloister-
existence academic chairs of a more modern type have been
planted, where good livings offer a comfortable settlement,
where old roomy buildings afford sufficient scope for a respectable household, considerable libraries and cabinets, and where
a quiet activity can devote itself all the more assiduously to
literary labors—a small number of students not demanding that
urgent and uninterrupted course of lectures which only deafens
us at thronged universities.

The staff of professors was in every respect considerable.
I need only here name Henke, Pott, Lichtenstein, Crell, Bruns,
and Bredow ; everyone will at once appreciate the circle in which
we travellers found ourselves. Solid learning, free communication, cheerfulness of intercourse, maintained by ever-new
accessions of youth, brisk enjoyment in the prosecution of earnest and judicious tasks, the co-operation, moreover, of the
ladies—the elder wives keeping open table, the younger bright-
ening everything with their graces, the daughters displaying
the greatest amiability—all this played so much the one into the
other that you fancied it was all the manifold totality of one
large family. The large rooms themselves of the old-fashioned
houses invited numerously attended banquets and thronged
festivities.

At one of these gatherings the difference between myself and
my friend came again to light. At the end of a rich supper
two beautifully plaited garlands were brought forth to crown
us. The beautiful girl who set mine on my head I thanked
with a kiss which was heartily returned, and in the vanity of
my heart I was glad to read in her eyes that my presence so
adorned was not displeasing to her. My wilful fellow-traveller,
however, sitting opposite to me, struggled against his vivacious
patroness, and, though under the tugging and flinching which
ensued, the garland was not quite disfigured, the dear thing
could not but feel in a certain measure ashamed not to have got
the gift out of her hands.

With so much that was charming we might have been in danger of forgetting the proper purpose of our visit had not Beireis
himself animated every gathering with his presence. Not tall,

f a good and mobile figure, he looked a man in reference
o whom the legends of his fighting accomplishments might
ass tolerably. An incredibly high and arched forehead, out
f all relation to the fine, compressed lower parts of the face,
ndicated peculiar intellectual powers, and in so advanced years
e could boast of a particularly brisk and unaffected activity.

In company, especially at table, he displayed his gallantry in
n original style, representing quite freely how he had once been
he admirer of the mother and was now the wooer of the daugh-
er. This oft-repeated fable was allowed to pass undisputed,
or, though nobody made any pretensions to his hand, a share
n his legacy was not deemed so despicable.

Announced as we were, he offered us every hospitality. We
leclined quarters in his house, but were thankfully pleased to
pend a large part of the day among his remarkable collections.

A great deal of his former possessions, the name and reputa-
ion of which were still fresh, we found in the most lamentable
tate. The Vaucansonian automatons were utterly paralyzed.
n an old garden-house sat the flute-player in very unimposing
lothes, but his playing days were past, and Beireis showed the
riginal barrel-organ whose first simple pieces had not satisfied
im. On the other hand he let us see a second barrel-organ,
n which he had kept organ-builders for years in his house at
abor, but which, as they went away too soon, was left unfin-
shed; and so the flute-player at the very beginning became
nute. A duck without feathers stood like a skeleton, still de-
oured the oats briskly enough, but had lost its powers of diges-
ion. With all this, however, Beireis was by no means put out,
ut spoke of these obsolete, half-wasted things with much com-
lacency, with an air of much consequence, as if he thought
hat mechanism had since produced nothing new of greater
mportance.

In a large hall devoted to natural history the remark was re-
eated that everything self-preserving was kept in good order
n its place. He showed us a very small magnet-stone that
arried a great weight, a real phrenite from the Cape of the
reatest beauty, and other excellent specimens of minerals.

In the middle of the hall, however, was a closely packed series
f stuffed birds, all eaten to pieces by moths, feathers and vermin
ying heaped up on the stands. Pointing this out, he assured us
t was a stratagem of war he had hit upon. All the moths in the
ouse were by this means drawn to this quarter, and the rest of
he rooms kept clear of the pest. The seven wonders of Helm-
tädt were next, in due order, displayed to our eyes, the Lieber-
ühn preparations, as also the Hahn calculating machine. Of
he former some really wonderful examples were shown, and

8

by the latter complicate problems of different rules worked out.
The magic oracle, however, was dumb.   Beireis had taken oath
never again to wind up the obedient clock, which at his command, though he stood at a distance from it, now stopped and
now went on.   An officer for relating such marvels having been
given the lie was killed in a duel, and since then he had firmly
resolved never again to expose his admirers to such danger nor
be the occasion for unbelievers perpetrating such rash outrages.

After what has been related above, a few additional remarks
may not be out of place.   Beireis, born in the year 1730, felt
himself as a man of parts capable of a wide, comprehensive
knowledge and qualified to attain proficiency in many branches.
Following the impulses of the time, he cultivated himself as
polyhistor, next devoted his energies to medicine, but, having
the happiest all-retentive memory, he presumed, as he well
might, to a familiar acquaintance with all faculties and to the
ability to fill any chair with honor.   His signature in my son's
album runs thus: " Godofredus Christophorus Beireis, Pri-
marius Professor, Medicinæ, Chemicæ, Chirurgiæ, Pharmaceu-
tices, Physices, Botanices, et reliquæ Historiæ naturalis: Helm-
stadii d. XVII. Augusti a. MDCCCV."

From the above it will appear that his natural-historical collections might have been judiciously made, but that those which
he most prized were mere curiosities fitted to excite attention
and admiration only on account of the high price at which they
had been procured, it being particularly impressed on the visitor
that at their sale emperors and kings had been outbidden.

In any case he must have had considerable sums of money
at his command.   Then, as one could easily see, he had been as
careful to await a favorable time for such purchases as to show
himself, perhaps more than others, in the light of a solvent man.
The subjects above specified he displayed minutely, no doubt
with interest and complacency, but his joy in them seemed, to
a certain extent, only historical.   In showing his pictures, however, his most recent fancy—a field on which he had entered
without the slightest preparation—he bored you incessantly
with his passionate eloquence.   It was incomprehensible how
completely he had been gulled, or how he attempted to gull us.
We were treated in particular to certain pet curiosities.   Here
was a " Christ," at the sight of which a Göttingen professor had
burst into a flood of tears.   There, again, on the table of the
disciples at Emmaus was a loaf, in truth naturally enough
painted, but at which an English dog had been seen to bark.
There, too, was the image of a saint wondrously saved from a
fire—and such like.

His way of showing the pictures was strange enough, and

seemed, to a certain extent, calculated. Instead of having them hung in enjoyable order beside each other on the clear, broad walls of his upper rooms, they lay piled above one another along the walls round his great canopy-bedstead, in his sleeping-chamber, whence, refusing all assistance, he fetched them and whither he replaced them himself. Some were left in the room ranged round the spectators, and being always pressed closer on their attention, the patience of our fellow-traveller at length suddenly gave way, causing his retirement.

This was a real relief, for such torments are more easily endured alone than in the company of a friend of insight, from whom, if not from the other side as well, you are every moment in dread of an explosion.

And Beireis went fairly beyond all bounds in his impositions on his guests. He had three pieces in the first, second, and last style by the most renowned artists. As he presented and described them, the utmost power of face at the command of man scarcely sufficed to enable one to maintain his gravity. The scene was ridiculous and aggravating, insulting and lunatic.

The first apprentice-trials of a Raphael, Titian, Carracci, Corregio, Domenichino, Guido, and who not? were nothing more nor less than feeble pictures and even copies of pictures by second-rate artists. Beireis now begged of you to exercise indulgence toward such beginnings, then he proceeded to laud and admire the extraordinary progress shown in the later works. Among those said to be of the second epoch you found a good deal that was meritorious, but in point of talent and time a whole world removed from the names assigned to them. The same was the case with the last series, in respect of which, too, Beireis expatiated complacently in empty phrases such as pretentious ignoramuses make use of.

In proof of the genuineness of such and other pictures he produced the auction catalogues, and prided himself on the printed laudation of each number bought by him. No doubt among them were some veritable though strongly restored originals. In short, anything like criticism on the part of this ctherwise valuable and worthy man was quite out of the question.

It must be said, too, that if most of the time you had to exercise all possible patience and forbearance you were yet occasionally consoled and rewarded by the sight of excellent pictures.

Invaluable seemed to me Albrecht Dürer's portrait, painted by himself, with the year 1493 attached to it, consequently in his twenty-second year; half life size; a bust; two hands; the elbows cut off; a purple-red cap with short, pointed embroidery; the neck bare down to beneath the collar-bone; shirt having embroidered front; the plaits of the sleeves bound beneath with purple-red ribbons; a blue-gray loose coat edged with yellow lace—dressed, altogether, quite daintily in the style of a fine youth; in his hand, significantly, a blue-blossoming *eringium*, in German, *Mannstreue* (man's fidelity); an earnest youthful face; sprouting beard about the mouth and chin—the whole splendidly drawn, rich and innocent, harmonious in its parts, although painted with a very thin color which in some places had shrunk together.

This praiseworthy, altogether invaluable picture painted on a thin board, which a true lover of art would have set in a golden frame and protected in the most handsome case, he left without any frame, without any care for its preservation. Every moment in danger of splitting, it was fetched forth with less precaution than was taken with every other picture, set up for inspection and then put aside, while the guest's entreaties that such a jewel should be carefully guarded were treated with indifference. Like Hofrath Büttner he seemed to take a wilful pleasure in regular disorder.

I must further note a happy free picture by Rubens, somewhat long, not too large, in the manner in which he liked to execute such sketches. A huckstress sitting in the fulness of a well-supplied vegetable store; cabbages and salad of all kinds, roots, onions of all colors and shapes. She is just engaged in a bargain with a stately burgess's wife whose comfortable dignity forms a very pretty contrast with the quietly proffering character of the woman selling her wares, behind whom a boy about to stead some fruit is threatened by an unexpected slap from her maid. On the other side is seen the respectable burgess's wife's maid standing behind her mistress, carrying a shapely basket already in part supplied with market provisions. She, too, is not idle. Her eye is directed toward a stripling whose finger signs she seems to reply to by a friendly look. Scarcely anything was ever better in conception or more masterly in execution, and had we not determined on closing our annual exhibitions we should have given out this subject as already described for our prize-theme, in order to find out who were the artists who, yet uninfected by the prevailing false taste for gold grounds, sympathized heartily with fresh, robust life.

At the dissolution of the cloisters, Beireis had succeeded in getting more than one considerable picture illustrative of the history of art. I regarded them with interest, and noted down many things in my pocket-book, where I find that beside the first above described all the others might belong to the fifteenth or perhaps the sixteenth century. For a more precise appreciation my knowledge was not thorough enough, and in the case of some, if I might have been able to hit nearer the mark, our whimsical collector constantly dunning into me his fantastic dates and names served always to confuse me.

For in his possessions as in his person he was once for all eccentricity incarnate. The first Byzantine piece, he let you know, belonged to the fourth century. Then he showed you an uninterrupted series dating from the fifth, extending through the sixth, and so on down to the fifteenth century. All this he told you with such an assurance and conviction as was fit to turn your head. When palpable nonsense is confidentially communicated to you as self-evident truths, you find yourself in a dilemma in which you can neither believe in your own self-deception on the one hand, nor in the possibility of such brazen-faced effrontery on the other.

Such inspections and contemplations were very agreeably interrupted by festivities. Here the odd man continued to play his youthful part with all comfort to himself. He joked with the mothers as though they were old flames of his, with the daughters as though he were about to offer them his hand. Nor did anyone take the least offence at these displays of his gallantry. Even the talented men of the company treated his follies with some degree of indulgence, and it was evident that his house, his treasures in nature and art, his money and funds, his wealth real or boastingly exaggerated imposed on many, and that the respect for his merits was strained to extend to respect also for his whimsicalities.

In truth nobody was more shrewd and expert than he in creating the instinct of legacy-hunting. Nay, it seemed to be his aim to procure himself in this way a fictitious family and the *un*-pious piety of a number of people toward himself.

In his bed-room there hung the picture of a young man, a picture like hundreds of others, nothing distinguished either in the way of attraction or repulsion. This picture he usually let his guests see, lamenting at the same time how this young man, on whom he had expended much, to whom he had intended leaving his whole fortune, had proved unfaithful and ungrateful to him, that he had been obliged to turn him off, and was now in vain looking about for a second person with whom he might enter into a like but more fortunate relationship.

There was no doubt some roguish feeling at the bottom of this representation. For as in looking over a lottery programme each one thinks of himself as the winner of the big prize, so to each hearer of Beireis's mournful tale a star of hope seemed, at least for the moment, to rise in the firmament.

Even prudent men I have seen for some time allured by this *ignis fatuus*.

The greatest part of the day we spent with him, and in the evening he treated us on Chinese porcelain and silver to rich sheep's milk, which he praised and pressed on us as highly healthy nourishment. Once you had accustomed yourself to the taste of this uncommon dish, it cannot be denied but you began to like it well enough, and could admit its claim to be considered wholesome.

We next had a view of his older collections, to the happy accumulation of which historical knowledge sufficed without the addition of taste. He had made a most complete collection of the gold coins of Roman emperors and their families, the authenticity of which he made haste to prove by the catalogues of the Paris and Gotha cabinets, demonstrating at the same time his superiority over them in this respect by their failing to possess certain specimens which he had acquired. What however you had most to admire in his collection was the perfection of the impressions, which appeared as distinct as if fresh from the mint. An observation to this effect he was well pleased to hear, and assured you he had one after the other exchanged the single pieces, till with heavy sacrifices he had obtained the best specimens, in the acquisition of which, however, in spite of the sacrifices, he deemed himself a lucky man.

The busy possessor bringing forth new drawers for our contemplation from a neighboring press, we were at once transported into another time and place. Very beautiful silver coins of Greek cities were spread before us, which having been kept sufficiently long in a damp, close air, their well-preserved impressions showed a bluish tinge. There was just as little want of rose-nobles, older papal coins, bracteated medals, enticing satyric seals, and what of extraordinary was to be expected in such a large antique collection.

It was not to be denied that in this department he was well-informed and in a certain sense a connoisseur. In earlier years he had published a little treatise on the method of distinguishing genuine from false coins. Nevertheless in this, as in other things, he seems to have indulged himself in a little arbitrariness. He obstinately maintained in triumph over all medal-experts that the golden Lysimachs were entirely false, and therefore treated with the utmost contempt a few fine specimens lying before us. We let this as so much else pass, and turned for delight and instruction to the really extraordinary treasures open to our view.

Amid all these curiosities, the ample time Beireis devoted to our amusement was ever now and again interrupted by his medical labors. Now he would return early in the morning from the country, where he had gone to attend some peasant's wife in being delivered of a child, now he was engaged and prevented from keeping us company by some grave consultation.

In explanation of the fact that he was always ready day and night for business of this kind, and always in a position to appear with like outward dignity, he called our attention to the mode in which he kept his hair. He wore hanging locks, rather long, fastened with pins, fast glued over both ears; the front of the head was adorned with a *toupet;* all firm, smooth and strongly powdered. In this way, he said, he had his hair trimmed every evening, going to bed with his hair firmly done up, and whatever hour he might be called to a patient, he could ever appear in the same becoming state as when going to company. And in truth on all occasions he was ever pranked in his light blue-gray complete dress, in black stockings, and shoes with large buckles.

In the whole course of these lively conversations and uninterrupted diversions, he had yet put forward little that was incredible. Later on, however, he could not quite omit gradually communicating to us the litany of his legends. One day, while he was treating us to a really well-furnished table, the sight of a plentiful dish of particularly large crabs much excited our curiosity, the country round about being so very poor in streams and waters. In answer to our inquiries, he assured us that his fish-press was at no time permitted to be without a supply of these creatures; he owed so much to them; he deemed them not only a fine treat for guests, but so beneficial to health that he had them always about him as a most efficacious medicine in extreme cases. He now passed to some mysterious communications. He spoke of total exhaustion induced by highly important but also highly dangerous work performed in the endeavor to master the most difficult process of the highest science. In such a state he lay all unconscious, in the last throes past all hope, when a young scholar and attendant heartily attached to him, impelled by an instinct like inspiration, brought a dish of large boiled crabs to his lord and master, urging him to eat sufficiently of them. He was thereby marvellously restored to life and has ever since cherished great reverence for such a dish.

Waggish friends asserted that Beireis had on occasion given some people to understand that by means of the "universal"! he knew how to transform may-bugs into young crabs, which then, by means of a particularly spagyrian food, he contrived to fatten to a remarkable size. We of course deemed this a legend invented in the spirit and taste of the old wonder-worker,

like so many more imputed to him, and which (as jugglers and
other thaumaturgists also find advisable) he was by no means
disposed to explode.

Hofrath Beireis had a well-established reputation as physician
in the whole district, having also, as their family doctor, a welcome reception in the house of Count Veltheim at Haubke, to
which, therefore, he at once declared himself ready to introduce us.   Having sent in our names we entered.   Stately farm
buildings formed a spacious court in front of the high and somewhat antique castle.   The count bade us welcome, and was
glad to make in me the acquaintance of his father's old friend;
for with his father we had through the medium of others been
in correspondence for several years in the study of mining,
though it was mainly with a view to the explanation of problematic passages in old authors that the father cultivated a
knowledge of nature.   If in this study he might be accused of
temerity, no one could yet deny him the possession of remarkable acumen.

Facing the garden, the somewhat old, ornate, respectable
castle had a particularly fine situation.   Stepping from it you
at once entered on smooth, fair levels girdled in by hills of soft
ascent shadowy with bushes and trees.   Convenient roads next
conducted you to cheerful views of neighboring heights, and
your eye gradually took in the wide sweep of the domain, resting in particular on the well-stocked woods.   Fifty years before the grandfather had given himself earnestly to the cultivation of forests, endeavoring also to naturalize North American
growths in the German soil.   We were now guided to a well-
stocked wood of Weymouth pines, grown respectably strong
and tall, within whose confines, as so often before in the Thüringian woods, stretched on the moss we enjoyed a good breakfast, delighting our eyes, too, on the regular arrangement of
the plantation.   For this ancestral forest yet showed the style
of the first planting, the trees disposed in rows all grouping
themelves into squares.   In the same way in each division of
the forest, in each species of tree, the intention of the provident grandsire could be quite distinctly read.

The young countess, just near her confinement, remained,
unfortunately, invisible, denying us the personal testimony we
should have been so glad to have had, of her celebrated beauty.
With her mother, however, a widowed Frau von Lauterbach
from Frankfort-on-the-Main, we enjoyed agreeable conversation on the family relations of the old free town.

The best entertainment, the most graceful intercourse, instructive conversation, in which gradually, point after point,
the advantages of so large an estate came more distinctly to

view, especially in the present case, where so much was done
for the tenantry and dependents; all this evoked the silent wish
to continue our stay there for some time longer, a wish which,
unexpectedly, was met by a kind pressing invitation to that
effect. Our dear fellow-traveller, however, the excellent Wolf,
who found here no incitement in his pursuit, and was therefore
soon violently overtaken by his customary impatience, demanded a return to Helmstädt with such urgency that we were
obliged to determine on parting from so agreeable a circle. It
was destined, however, that at our parting a mutual relation
should be formed. The friendly host, out of his fossil treasures, was pleased to honor my son with the gift of a costly en-
crinite, and we were afraid we should be unable to do any
equal politeness by way of return, when a problem connected
with forests turned up for discussion. In Ettersburg, near
Weimar, namely, according to the information of a popular
journal, a beech-tree had been found, which in size and other
qualities evidently approached the oak. The count, with his
hereditary bias toward arboriculture, wished some twigs of it,
and whatever else might contribute to a more precise knowledge of the tree to be sent to him; particularly, however, if possible, some living plants. In the sequel we were so happy as
to procure him the gratification of his wishes and ourselves the
fulfilment of our promise, having the pleasure of sending him
living offshoots from the tree, and years later of hearing the
glad news of their thriving.

On the way back, as on the way thither, we had a great deal
to hear respecting the great achievements of the old enchanter
who conducted us. We now learnt from his own mouth what
had already been narrated to us concerning his earlier days.
Critically regarded, however, there was a perceptible monotony
in the legend of this saint. As a boy, bold determination; as a
scholar, headlong self-defence; academic quarrels, expertness
in the use of the rapier, artistic skill in riding, and other bodily
accomplishments. Courage and skill, strength and endurance;
constancy, and love of enterprise—all that lay behind him in
the obscure past. Three years' travels also lay veiled in mystery, and many other things hovered indefinitely in his communications, and still more cloudy did they appear when you
began to sift them.

Seeing, however, that the striking sensible result of his course
of life was an apparently immeasurable accumulation of preciosities and incalculable wealth, he had no want of believers or
adorers. Such preciosities and wealth are a species of house-
gods, toward which the crowd devoutly and eagerly bend their
eyes. When, now, such acquisitions are not hereditary and

of obvious derivation, people in their obscurity regarding them are ready to admit any kind of wonder in association with them, and to leave the possessor to picture his fabulous existence in any colors he pleases. For a mass of coined gold and silver is a reality which imparts respectability and importance even to a lie; people let the lie pass and fall to envy the hoards of money.

The possible or probable means by which Beireis attained to such possessions are unanimously and simply accounted for. He is said to have invented a color to take the place of cochineal, and to have communicated to the heads of factories more advantageous processes of fermentation than were till then known. The man conversant with the history of chemistry will judge whether in the latter half of the last century receipts of that kind could be smuggled about, and will know how far they have in modern times become matter of public and universal knowledge. May not Beireis, for example, have perhaps come to an early knowledge of the improvement of madder?

But over and above all this, the moral element in which and on which he worked must be borne in mind, I mean the time, its peculiar sense, its peculiar wants. The communication between citizens of the world was not then so swift as at present. Anyone living in a remote place like Swedenborg, or in a small university like Beireis, had always the best opportunity of wrapping himself up in a mysterious obscurity, invoking spirits and laboring at the philosopher's stone. Have we not in modern times seen how Cagliostro, sweeping swiftly across large spaces, could now in the south, now in the north, now in the west, carry on his juggleries and everywhere find adherents? Is it, then, too much to say that a certain superstitious belief in demoniac men never dies out, so that at all times a place is to be found where the problematic true, for which in theory alone we have respect, may most conveniently in practice associate with a lie?

The agreeable company in Helmstädt detained us longer than we had intended. In every sense Hofrath Beireis showed himself kindly disposed and communicative, yet his chief treasure, the diamond, he had not yet spoken of, much less shown us. None of the Helmstädt academic people had seen it, and an oft-repeated fable that this invaluable treasure was not in the place served, as we heard, to excuse him from showing it even to strangers. In seeming confidence, he was accustomed to relate that he had made up twelve sealed packets completely alike, in one of which was the precious stone. These twelve packets, now, he distributed among friends at a distance, each of whom fancies he has the treasure. He himself alone, however, knows where it is. We were therefore afraid that to our inquiry also he would likewise deny possession of the wonder of nature. Happily, however, shortly before we departed the following happened:

One morning he showed us, in a volume of "Tournefort's Journey," the picture of certain natural diamonds, which, in the form of an egg, with partial deviation into the shape of a kidney and nipple, had been found among the treasures of the Indians. Having now well impressed on us this shape, he produced from the right pocket of his trousers the important production of nature. About the size of a modern goose-egg, it was perfectly clear and transparent, yet without any trace of its having been polished. On its side was seen a faint knob, a kidney-like outgrowth, giving the stone a complete resemblance to the diagrams above referred to.

With his usual composure he made some ambiguous experiments by way of testing its genuineness as a diamond. On its being moderately rubbed the stone attracted paper-clippings, and the English file seemed in no way to affect it. Still he went cursorily over these proofs and related the oft-repeated story how he had tried the stone under a muffle, and how, in his admiration at the splendid spectacle of the developing flame, he had forgotten to subdue and extinguish the fire, thus in a short time depreciating the value of his stone by over 1,000,000 thalers. He nevertheless accounted himself happy in having seen an illumination denied to the sight of emperors and kings.

While he was thus expatiating over this theme, mindful of chromatic tests, I held up the wonderful egg right before my eyes, in order to take note of the horizontal window-bars, but found the color boundaries not broader than in the case of a mountain-crystal. I was therefore for the future justified in entertaining some doubts as to the genuineness of the celebrated treasure. Our stay was accordingly quite appropriately crowned by an exhibition of the most extravagant rodomontade on the part of our whimsical friend.

In the course of joyous confidential intercourse at Helmstädt, in which the peculiarities of Beireis formed the principal topic of conversation, another whimsical character, a nobleman, was several times mentioned. His seat lying not far off the road we should take, on our return journey by way of Halberstadt, it was suggested that we might also pay him a visit, and so extend our knowledge of eccentric men. We were all the more readily disposed for such an expedition that the gay-tempered, ingenious Provost Henke volunteered to accompany us thither, an addition which seemed to guarantee that in any case we should be safely tided over any rudeness or incivilities that might be offered us by the notorious man.

We, therefore, all four got into our carriage, Provost Henke
with a long, white clap pipe, with which alone he could enjoy
a smoke, and which, as he assured us, he could carry uninjured
in a carriage through long journeys.

In lively and instructive conversation we sped over the way
and at length reached the estate of the man known far and wide
by the name of the Mad Hagen, settled like a species of dangerous cyclops on a fair property. The reception we met was itself
characteristic enough. He drew our attention to the sign-
board of his new-built inn, hanging to solid smith-work, a sign-
board to serve for attracting guests. To our surprise, however, we here saw executed by no unskilful artist, the
counterpart of the one on that sign-board in reference to which
the " Traveller to the South of France " expatiates so circumstantially. Here, too, was seen an inn bearing a representation
of the doubtful sign and spectators standing around it.

Such a reception inspired in us no doubt the worst forebodings, and I was all the more on my heed that it just occurred
to me how our new worthy friends at Helmstädt might have
contrived this adventure for us in order that after the noble
drama in which we had there played part they might entrap
us as actors in a sorry satyrical farce and enjoy the fun of seeing
us hoaxed.

I scared away the suspicion, however, as soon as we trod the
perfectly respectable-looking courtyard. The farm buildings
were in the best condition and the courts in proper order,
though without a trace of any æsthetic tendency. The master's
occasional treatment of his dependents could not be styled
otherwise than harsh and rough, though a seasoning of good-
humor perceptible in it made it the more endurable. The good
people, too, seemed accustomed to his manner and followed
their duties in all quietness, as though he had addressed them
in the blandest terms.

In the large, clean, bright dining-room we found the mistress
of the house, a slim, well-formed lady, who, however, the picture of mute suffering, seemed to take interest in nothing, thus
at once betraying to us the heavy troubles she had to bear.
There were, furthermore, two children; a Prussian ensign on
furlough and a daughter from the Brunswick boarding-school
on a visit, neither of them yet twenty, mute like the mother,
and gazing with an air of stupefaction when her looks betokened
manifold sorrow.

The conversation at once assumed a certain brusque soldierly
tone, the burgundy got from Brunswick was really excellent;
the mistress, by her well-served and well-appointed table, did
the honors of the house. So far, then, all was quite tolerable,

only you could not look much about you without becoming
aware of the faun-ear which made itself conspicuous all through
the household management of a well-to-do country gentleman.
In the corners of the room stood clean-kept casts of Apollo and
other statues. Strange, however, it was to see how he dressed
them. He stuck on them cuffs he had taken off, and which he
thought helped, like fig-leaves, to adapt them to good society.
Such a sight wakened no little apprehension in me, it being
certain that one bad taste implies another, as in point of fact
was also verified here. The conversation was still conducted,
on our side at least, with some degree of propriety, yet in the
presence of adolescent children it was not altogether becoming.
When, however, in the course of the dessert the children had
been sent away, our eccentric host stood solemnly up and removed the cuffs from the statues, by way of signifying that
now it was time to allow one's self a little more latitude and
freedom in his behavior. We contrived, by a pleasantry, to
procure our hostess, truly worthy of commiseration, furlough
as well, for we suspected what our host might be driving at,
when he set before us a yet better burgundy, to which we
did not show ourselves averse. This, however, did not hinder
us, when the dinner was finished, from proposing a walk. The
night setting in, he compelled his distressed wife to sing some
songs of her own choice, in accompaniment to the harpsichord,
which, being well executed, gave us some real pleasure. At
last, however, he could not refrain from expressing his disgust
at such insipid songs and demanding something with more
life in it, whereupon the lady was compelled to accompany with
the harpsichord a highly inappropriate and absurd strophe.
Indignant at this repulsive scene, and inspired by the burgundy,
I now felt the time was come for me to show my paces and give
a specimen or two of the mad escapades with which in the wan-
tonness of youthful spirits I was wont to indulge myself.

After he had at my request several times repeated the detestable strophe, I assured him the poem was excellent, only he must
endeavor, by skilful execution, to do justice to its precious contents, nay, even to enhance their value by due expression. Now
the talk revolved first about forte and piano, then about the finer
shadings and accents, till in the end the antithesis of lisping
and shouting came to be discussed. Under all this folly, however, was hidden some germ of instruction, while I imposed
on him a multitude of requisitions, which he seemed to dispose
of as an ingeniously quaint man. Yet he sometimes tried to
interrupt this pile of demands heaped on him by filling up our
glasses with burgundy and offering us cake. Our Wolf, bored
to death, had already retired. Abbot Henke walked up and

down with his long clay pipe, and, watching his opportunity, emptied the glasses of burgundy forced on him out of the window, awaiting with the greatest composure the close of all this nonsense.   Nor did it come soon, for there was no end in my demands for arch expression on the part of my humorously learned pupil.   At last, toward midnight, I rejected as naught all that he had yet achieved.   He had only learned his lesson by rote, I said, and that was worth nothing.   He must now, out of his own head, discover the true, which had remained hitherto concealed, and thereby, as an original, compete with poet and musician.

He was clever enough to catch some inkling of the fact that under all these follies a certain sense was hidden; nay, he seemed to find pleasure in such wanton abuse of really respectable doctrines.   He had meanwhile, however, grown tired, and, so to say, mellow, and when I at last concluded that he must now seek repose and await what light a dream might perhaps bring him, he readily yielded and let us go to bed.

The next morning we were all early astir and ready for our departure.   At breakfast things passed in quite a human manner.   It appeared as though he were not willing we should go away with wholly unfavorable notions of him.   As land-councillor, he could give very pertinent, though in his own way quaint, account of the condition and the affairs of the province.   We parted in a friendly spirit, and could not enough thank our companion, who returned to Helmstädt with unbroken pipe, for his kindness in conducting us on this doubtful adventure.

Entirely peaceful and rational, on the other hand, was a lengthy stay we made at Halberstadt.   Gleim had now some years ago gone over to the company of his earliest friends.   A visit I had long ago paid him had left but a faint impression behind, the tumultuous, diversified life following on that visit having nearly blotted out of my memory the peculiarities of his person and circumstances.   Nor could I then, as later on, ever succeed in knitting a relationship to him.   His labors, however, had never been foreign to me.   I heard much of him through Wieland and Herder, with whom he always remained in correspondence and vital connection.

On this occasion we were very kindly received into his dwelling by Herr Körte.   The house indicated clean well-to-doness, peaceful life, quiet, social comfort.   His past achievements we celebrated in the works he had left behind him; much was related of him, a great deal shown to us, and Herr Körte promised, by a complete biography and an edition of his correspondence, to furnish every man with material sufficient to recall to his consciousness in his own way such a remarkable individual.

By his poems Gleim appealed most immediately to the general German character, discovering himself as an eminently loving and lovable man. Technically his poetry is rhythmic, not melodious. He, therefore, for the most part, makes use of the freer metres. His productions, now in the form of verse and rhyme, now of letter and treatise, convey the impression of a kindly disposed common-sense working within conscientious limits.

More than by anything else, however, we were attracted by his temple of friendship, a collection of portraits of persons with whom he was associated in older and more recent times. It afforded a beautiful testimony to his appreciation of his contemporaries and gave us an agreeable recapitulation of so many distinguished figures, a recollection of the noteworthy spirits they represented, of their relations to each other and to the valued man who gathered most of them for a time around himself, and was careful to retain, at least by picture, about him the departing and the absent. In such contemplation, however, many a grave consideration was forced on you. Among all these poets and men of letters, numbering over 100, was not one single musician or composer. What, should the venerable old man, who, as far as his word was concerned, lived and breathed apparently only in song, have no feeling of song in the peculiar sense? of the art of music, the true element, at once the origin and fruition of all poetry?

If now you tried to gather up into one conception all your sentiments in reference to the noble man, you might say the basis of his character was a passionate benevolence, which, both by word and deed, he endeavored to make good and effective. Inspiring encouragement by speech and writing, diffusing abroad the general pure feeling of humanity, he approved himself a friend of every man, helpful to the needy, full of furtherance in particular to necessitous youth. In him, as a good householder, beneficence appears to be the one fond fancy on which he spends his superfluity. The most he gives is out of his own resources, seldom, and only in later years, did he make use of his name and reputation to acquire some influence for the furtherance of his projects with kings and ministers, and this without any great success. He is treated with honor, his active exertions tolerated and praised, a helping hand, too, reached out to him, but usually some scruples are entertained about joining heartily in his purposes.

On the whole, he must be allowed to have in every respect the most emphatic burgess-like mind. As man, he stands on his own feet, performing the duties of a considerable public office, and for the rest shows himself a patriot toward town, province, and kingdom, a genuine liberal toward the German Fatherland and the world. Everything revolutionary, on the other hand, that discloses itself in his later years is highly hateful to him, as was everything which at an earlier period set itself in hostility to Prussia's great King and his realm.

Further, while every religion should promote the pure, peaceful intercourse of men among each other (but the Christian evangelical religion is specially qualified to effect this end), Gleim innately, by a necessity of his nature, practising the natural religion of the upright man, could acknowledge himself as the most orthodox of men, and in the hereditary confession, as in the simple established *cultus* of the Protestant Church, find ample satisfaction for his wants.

After calling up these lively representations of the departed man, we were destined to see an image of him in the person of his dying niece, whom he greeted on her sick-bed. Under the name of Gleminde she had for many years been the ornament of a poetic circle. Her graceful though sickly frame harmonized finely with the great purity of her surroundings, and we conversed with her on the good, by-gone days ever associated in her mind with the life and labors of her excellent uncle.

At length, to close our pilgrimage in an earnest and worthy manner, we entered the garden and went round the grave of the noble old man, to whom, after many years' sufferings and sorrows, activity and endurance, it was granted to rest in the spot dear to his affections, surrounded by monuments of friends.

We repeatedly visited the desolate, damp aisles of the cathedral. Though deprived of its former religious life, it yet stood unshaken in its original dignity. Such buildings have in them something peculiarly attractive. They bring home to us solid though sombre states of existence, and it being sometimes grateful to our spirits to wrap ourselves in the semi-obscurity of the past, we welcome the shudder and foreboding that close in on us bodily, materially, spiritually, affecting our feelings, imagination, and disposition, and so moulding us into a moral, poetic, and religious mood.

The Spiegelberge (heights overgrown with green bushes, outspurs of the neighboring Harz) now through the strangest formations become an arena for hateful creatures, as though an accursed company returning from Blocksberg had, by God's unfathomable decree, here become petrified. At the foot of the ascent a huge vat serves as bridal salon for an abominable race of dwarfs, thence through all walks of the grounds lurk monsters of every kind, so that the malformation-loving Prætorius might here see completely realized his Mundus Anthropodemicus.

The thought was here forced on you how necessary it is in education not to neglect imagination, but to regulate it, to awaken in it by the early presentation of noble pictures the love of the beautiful, the need of the excellent. Of what use is it to bridle sensuousness, to cultivate the understanding, to secure reason her sovereignty? Imagination lurks in the man as his deadliest enemy; by nature she has an irresistible impulse toward the absurd, an impulse which operates powerfully even in cultivated men, and, to the contempt of all culture, displays in the midst of the most becoming circles the inherited savagery which takes pleasure in caricatures.

Of the rest of my return journey I need speak only in hasty touches. We visited the Bodethal and the long-known Hammer. Thence, for the third time in my life, I now passed along by the rushing waters shut in by granite rocks, and here it again occurred to me that in our thoughts we are never so much thrown back upon ourselves as when revisiting, after a long interval, highly significant objects, in particular decidedly characteristic scenes of nature. In such a case we shall, on the whole, remark that on each successive visit the object ever assumes more prominence; that if in the earlier visits our feelings were in the ascendant, and the scene was associated with joy and sorrow, cheerfulness and tumult, our self now gradually retires into the background, and we do justice to the external situation, recognizing its peculiarities and ever more highly appreciating its properties, so far as our minds can penetrate them. The first kind of contemplation is conditioned by the artistic sense, the second by the sense of the natural philosopher; and though at first it gave me pain to perceive how the former mode of viewing nature was gradually waning in me, I was soon comforted by the discovery that the latter mode was all the more vigorously developing itself in my eye and spirit.

1806

The interim hopes with which like Philistines we had for many years been beguiling ourselves, we still cherished in the present. No doubt all ends of the earth were in flames; Europe had become transfused into another shape; by sea and land fleets and towns were shattered to pieces. Middle and North Germany, however, still enjoyed a certain feverish peace, in the possession of which we resigned ourselves to a problematic security. The great realm in the West had established itself, and shot out roots and branches on all sides. Meanwhile Prussia had apparently conceded to it the privilege of fortifying itself in the North. It first garrisoned Erfurt, a very important

9

halting-point, nor did we oppose the quartering of Prussian
troops from the beginning of the year within our borders.   The
Ostin regiment was followed in the beginning of February by
fusiliers ; next entered the regiments of Bork, Arnim, Pirsch ;
people had already become accustomed to this disturbance.

The birthday of our revered duchess, January 30th, was
this time celebrated pompously enough, it is true, yet still
with sad forebodings.   The Ostin regiment boasted an un-
equalled band of trumpeters; by way of welcome they entered
the theatre in the form of a half-circle, giving proofs of their
extraordinary skill, and at last accompanying a song, whose
universally known melody devoted to an island king, and by
no means yet surpassed by any performance of the kind on the
part of the patriotic Continent, exercised its full heart-elevating
power.

A translation, or recast, of Corneille's " Cid " was next performed ; then " Stella," for the first time with tragic catastrophe.
" Götz von Berlichingen " followed, also " Egmont."   Schiller's
" Bell," with all apparatus for casting and for finished representation, a feature we had now as matter of instruction long attempted, was given; the whole company taking part in it, the
special dramatic, artistic, and artisan parts falling to the master
and the journeymen, the remaining lyric parts to the male and
female members, an appropriate piece being allotted to each.

" Dr. Luther," brought by Iffland for representation, excited
attention on the whole, though we hesitated to adopt it.

During our lengthened stay in Carlsbad, the next theatre season engaged much of our thought, and it was attempted to accommodate Oehlenschläger's meritorious tragedy " Hakon
Jarl " to our stage, clothes and decorations to this purpose having already been looked out and found.   Later on, however, it
appeared dubious, at a time when crowns were played with in
earnest, to turn such a sacred ornament into jest.   The past
spring all that could be done was to maintain the extant repertory, and to a certain extent enlarge it.   Toward the end of
the year, when the pressure of war threatened the rupture of
all ties, we deemed it our duty to keep up the theatre as a public
benefit, an important part of the common weal of the town.
Only two months were our representations interrupted, our
scientific pursuits but a few days, and Iffland's " Calendar " for
the theatre served to reanimate the German stage with fresh
bounding hopes.

The projected new edition of my works compelled me to a
revision of them all.   I devoted to each single production the
attention I deemed due, but held fast by my maxim to make no
essential recast of anything nor even alterations to any great
extent.

The two divisions of the " Elegies," as they are now to hand, were disposed of, and " Faust," in its present form, fragmentarily treated. In this way I reached the fourth part inclusively, but a more important task was engaging me. The epic " Tell " again stirred in me in the form in which in 1797 I had conceived him in Switzerland and afterward set aside in favor of Schiller's dramatic " Tell." Both Schiller's and my " Tell " could very well exist together. Schiller was well acquainted with my plan, and I was satisfied with his having used my main conception of a self-dependent " Tell " (independent of the other conspirators). In the execution, however, in obedience to the tendency of his talent and the necessities of the German theatre, he had necessarily to pursue another road than mine. The epic-peaceful-grandiose treatment still remained wholly at my disposal, while the two bodies of motives, even where they touched on each other, assumed in the two works entirely different figures.

I longed once more to try my hand at hexameters, and my good relationship to the Vosses, both father and son, inspired in me the hope that in this splendid form of verse, also, I should progress with ever greater assurance. The days and weeks, however, were so full of foreboding, the last months so stormy, revealing so little hope of a free breathing-time, that a plan conceived in unrestrained nature on the Vierwaldstädter lake, and on the way to Altorf, did not well admit of execution in an anguished Germany.

If publicly we had now renounced our relationship to plastic art, it yet inwardly remained dear and precious to us. Sculptor Weisser, an art-associate of Friedrich Tieck, worked with Glück at the bust of the Duke of Brunswick, who died here, a bust which, standing in the public library, gives a beautiful testimony to his much-promising talent.

Copperplates are, in general, the handiest form of art for the entertainment of connoisseurs and amateurs. I accordingly received from Rome, at the hands of Gmelin, the excellent print inscribed " The Temple of Venus according to Claude." It was all the more valuable to me that the original did not become known till after my departure from Rome, so that I was first able to convince myself of the excellencies of the work from this artistic copy.

In quite a different province, yet cheerful and talented enough, appeared Riepenhaus's prints to " Genoveva," with the original drawings of which we had before been acquainted. These young men, who had formerly practised themselves on Polygnotus, now turned toward the romantic, a direction which literary talent had rendered popular, and thus proving that to a greater degree than is supposed the plastic artist is dependent on the poet and author.

In Carlsbad I found instructive entertainment in a collection of copperplates in the possession of Count Lepel. The large water-color pen-drawings of Ramberg no less testified to the talent of that artist, a talent cheerful, happy in its conceptions, disposed occasionally for extempore efforts. These, as also some works of his own, beside very beautiful landscapes in opaque colors, belonged to Count Corneillan.

The collections here were increased by an addition of drawings of a high class. Carstens's artistic legacy was inherited by his friend Fernow, and, a fair arrangement having been come to with the latter, our museum was enriched by several drawings of the most various size: larger cartoons, smaller pictures, studies in black chalk, in ruddle, water-colored pen-drawings, and other things to which an artist is induced from various motives.

Wilhelm Tischbein, who on his removal from Naples had, under the favor of the Duke of Oldenburg, nestled into a peaceful happy situation, let us hear occasionally from him, and this spring sent us no little of a pleasing nature.

He was the first to communicate the remark that pictures the swiftest in execution are often the happiest in thought, an observation suggested to him by the sight of many hundred paintings by excellent masters, splendid in thought, but not the most careful in execution. And truth it is that the most finished pictures of the Netherland school, with all their wealth and luxury of detail, sometimes disappoint you on the side of genius, of intellectual invention. It would appear as though the artist's careful conscientiousness and determination to satisfy completely every demand on the part of the connoisseur and dilettante impeded the free flight of his spirit. On the other hand, the artist knowing nothing of these considerations, but yielding himself freely and wholly to the conception which dominates him, is apt to deliver himself all the more happily and immediately. Tischbein sent us some water-color copies, two of which remain. " Diggers for Treasure in a deep Town-moat and Casemates "—night-time, inadequate exorcisms, evil spirits molesting them, loss of the treasures which had been discovered and half-seized. Grace of effect is not entirely studied in this picture. The matter represented and the execution both suggest dread and secrecy. Still more, perhaps, is this the case with the second picture. " A Horrible Scene of War "—killed and plundered men, disconsolate wives and children, in the background a cloister in flames, in the foreground ill-used monks; a picture likewise to be preserved in a case.

Tischbein further sent the duchess Amalia a moderate folio volume of water-color pen-drawings. Here Tischbein is particularly happy, his practised talent giving visuality to thoughts, chance ideas, whimsies, without any great expenditure of labor, and without danger of losing his time.

The representation of animals was always a passion with Tischbein, and here may be mentioned an ass of his, eating with all comfort pine-apples instead of thistles.

In another picture your eye is carried over the roofs of a large town toward the rising sun. Quite close to the spectator, in the fore-front, sits by the chimney-stack a sweep-boy. Everything on him capable of receiving color is glorified by the sun, and it is in truth a charming thought that the son of the most miserable trade should yet be the only person among many thousands favored with such a heart-rejoicing view of nature.

These communications of Tischbein were imparted under the condition that a poetic or prosaic interpretation should be given to his moral-artistic dreams. The little poems we sent him in return are to be found in my collection. Duchess Amalia and her circle took their due share in these things, and responded by their own hand to the friendliness of the donor.

I, too, was induced in Carlsbad to impress the various important subjects coming under my observation on my memory by means of imitations. The more perfect sketches had some value for me, and I began to collect them.

A cabinet of medals, giving a sufficient view of the course of sculpture from the second half of the fifteenth century onward, was considerably increased, offering ever more complete representations on the subject.

A collection of autographic leaves of distinguished men was in like manner considerably enlarged. An album of the family of Walchi, dating from about the beginning of the eighteenth century, and in which Maffei has a prominent place, was highly valuable, and I expressed my great obligations to the friendly givers. An alphabetic list of the autographic collection was printed, and I inserted one such in every letter I wrote to my friends, and in this way the album was ever more and more extended.

As to artists, Rabe from Berlin again visited us, and commended himself as well by his talent as by his politeness.

A letter from Hackert, however, could not but sadden me. This excellent man, having been struck down by an apoplectic fit, had only so far recovered as to be able to dictate and sign a letter. I was distressed to see the hand which was wont to pen so many firm strokes able only tremblingly and incompletely to indicate a name formerly flourished off so joyously and happily.

The Jena museums were swelled by the influx of so many new subjects that an extension had to be taken in hand and a different arrangement adopted.

Batsch's reliques entailed on us new trouble and inconvenience. He had founded the Natural Research Society, and conducted it through a series of years, collecting also for its instruction a museum of all kinds of subjects, a museum increased both in bulk and importance by his own private collection methodically distributed through it. After his death the directors and members of the society demanded a part of the property, in particular the museum specially belonging to it. The heirs demanded the rest, a demand which, as the hitherto director was only supposed to have made a present of his collection, could not be refused. On the side of the ducal commission it was determined to interfere, but an arrangement with the heirs having failed there was no help for it but to divide and distribute the lot. What arrears had to be paid were made up, and the Natural Research Society had a room assigned it in the castle, whither the specimens belonging to it were conveyed. People engaged to do something toward their preservation and increase, and so this business was set to rest in rather a hopeful state.

When I returned in September from Carlsbad I found the mineral cabinet in the fairest arrangement, also the geological orderly disposed.

Dr. Seebeck spent the whole year in Jena, and forwarded in no small degree our insight into physics generally, and in particular into the theory of colors. While in reference to those subjects he labored at galvanism, his other experiments on oxidation and deoxidation, on warming and cooling, on kindling and extinguishing, were for me of the greatest importance in a chromatic sense.

An experiment by our worthy Göttling to turbify glass-panes did not succeed, but in fact only for the reason that his efforts were too laborious, this chemical effect, like all effects of nature, proceeding from a breath, from the most delicate of conditions.

With Professor Schelver one was able to exchange truly beautiful observations. The tender and solid qualities of his nature came very amiably to light in conversation, the converser in this respect having the advantage over the lecturer, who, as in the case of all too recondite monologues, always felt himself so far estranged from his audience.

Sömmering's " Diagrams of the Human Organs of Hearing " carried us back to anatomy. Alexander von Humboldt's kind missives called us into the wide open world. Steffen's " Principles of the Philosophical Natural Sciences " offered sufficient matter for thought, people living generally in dissentient unity with him.

To instruct myself in mathematics to the limits of my capacity, I read Montuclas's " Histoire des Mathématiques," and having again cleared up to myself, as far as possible, the higher views from which each particular is derived and attempted to plant myself midway between the kingdoms of nature and freedom, I drew up the scheme of the " General Science of Nature " in order to find a sure standpoint for my special chromatics.

In the domain of antiquity, whither I am so disposed to retreat, I read Agricola's " De Ortu et Causis Subterraneorum " for the sake of again impressing on my mind the model of a common-sense contemplation, and in doing so remarked that, while in this way wandering backward into the past, I found the most credible intelligence of a meteor stone in the " Thüringian Chronicle."

Nor must I omit mentioning two beautiful incitements I experienced in the province of botany. The large " Charte botanique d'après Ventenat " rendered the family relations of plants more striking and impressive to me. It hung in a large room of the Jena Castle, in the first floor of which I lived, and remained there on the wall when I suddenly made way for Prince Hohenlohe. It served for the occasional entertainment of his educated staff of generals, as also, later on, for Napoleon's, and when after so much storm and commotion I again took possession of my peaceful lodging, I found the chart hanging in the old place still uninjured.

Cotta's " Observations on the Sap in Vegetables," with specimens of cut woods appended, was for me a very pleasing gift. They again resuscitated in me those tendencies of mind I had followed for so many years, and were the principal cause that, turning anew to " Morphology," I determined on reprinting the " Metamorphosis of Plants " and other things attaching themselves thereto.

My preparations with the " Theory of Colors," labors which had employed me without interruption for twelve years, had now made so much progress that the various parts began more and more to round themselves into each other and to figure forth the near-approaching whole. The physiological colors were now completed to the full scope of my intentions and capabilities, the beginnings of the historical part also lay in finished form before me, and the printing of the first and second parts of the work might, therefore, at once be taken in hand.

I now turned to the pathological colors, and in the historical section investigated Plinius's " Observations on Colors."

While thus the single parts were in progress, a scheme of the whole was in constant execution.

The physical colors now in their turn claimed my whole attention. The consideration of the means and conditions of their appearance absorbed all my faculties. Here now I had to pronounce my long-confirmed conviction that colors appearing only through and in *media*, the doctrine of turbidity, as the most delicate and the purest material to be treated, is the initial rudiment whence is developed the whole science of chromatics.

Convinced that in the earlier part, within the circle of the physiological colors, this truth must inevitably demonstrate itself even without any assistance on my part, I advanced to the redaction of all I had thought and established with myself and others on the subject of refraction. For here, in fact, was the citadel of that bewitching princess who in an array of seven colors had befooled the whole world; here lay the grim sophistic dragon threatening everyone who presumed to try his fortunes with these illusions. The importance of this part and the chapters devoted to it was great. I endeavored in the execution to do the work full justice, and was under no apprehensions of neglecting anything. It was firmly established that if on refraction colors came to light, an image, a boundary must be shifted. How in the case of subjective experiments black and white images of every kind appear at their boundaries when looked at through the prism, how the same happens with gray images of all shades, with bright images of every color and degree, in the case of stronger and lighter refraction—all this was strictly demonstrated, and I am persuaded that the competent man examining all these appearances in experiments will miss nothing either in the phenomenon itself or in the presentation.

Next followed the catoptrian and paroptian colors, and in respect of the former it was to be remarked that in the case of the mirage, colors only then appeared when the reflected body was brilliantly taken in a scratched or thread-like form. In the case of the paroptian the bow was denied and the colored stripes were derived from double lights. That each of the edges of the sun throws a shade of its own was strongly evidenced in the case of an annular eclipse.

The sensuously-moral effect of color was then taken in hand, and in the historical part Gautier's " Chroagénésie " considered.

With the printing we had reached the thirteenth sheet of the first part and the fourth of the second, when the most dreadful havoc broke in upon us, threatening the entire destruction of the papers which had been prematurely hurried away for safety.

Happily enough we were able, when shortly afterward we had rallied our spirits, to take up this task anew, along with other business, and in composed activity again to prosecute our daily work.

The necessary tables were now, before everything else, carefully elaborated. A correspondence carried on with the good and worthy Runge enabled us to append his letter to the conclusion of the " Theory of Colors," as Seebeck's increased experiments also proved of advantage to the whole.

With lightened heart we thanked the Muses for the aid they had so manifestly deigned us. Hardly, however, had we to some extent fetched a free breath when we found it necessary, if we were not to stand still, to take up the repugnant polemical part, and to compress within practical compass and conclude all our arguments in respect of " Newton's Optics," as also the examination of his experiments and the inferences drawn from them. The introduction of the polemical part was accomplished by the close of the year.

With the poetical merits of strangers, sympathy was at least inwardly felt if not in large measure publicly expressed. " The Wunderhorn," antique and fantastic, was appreciated according to its merits, and a review written out in a kindly spirit. Hiller's poems of nature, of quite an opposite character, belonging wholly to the present and the real, were with fair criticism received according to their style. Oehlenschläger's " Aladdin " met no less with a good reception, though everything belonging to it, especially in the course of the fable, could not be commended. And if among the studies of an earlier time I find the " Persians " of Æschylus mentioned, it appears to me as if a presentiment of what was in preparation for us had impelled me thither.

To quite a national interest, however, had the " Nibelungen " grown. The appropriation of them was the passion of several meritorious men sharing equal predilection for them with us.

Schiller's remains continued a principal concern, though remembering with pain that former attempt of mine, I at once emphatically renounced all participation in an edition of his works and a biographical sketch of my excellent friend.

Adam Müller's lectures came to my hands. I read and studied them, but with divided feeling, for if an excellent mind is really patent in them, you also became aware of many uncertain steps which must gradually by logical sequence lead the best *naturel* on false ways.

Hamann's writings were from time to time brought forth from the mystic vault in which they rested. The strong spirit here operating through the strange garment of language in

which the thoughts are clothed always anew attracted the lovers
of pictures till, tired and confused by so many riddles, one laid
them aside and yet could not suppress the wish for a complete
edition of the works.

Wieland's translation of Horace's "Epistle to the Piso's"
really seduced me for some time from other employments.
This problematic work will appear differently to one from what
it will to another and differently to the same person again every
ten years. I ventured on bold and whimsical interpretations
of the whole as of single parts, and could wish I had them
written down if only for the sake of the humor of the views.
These thoughts and fancies, however, like so many thousand
others expressed in conversation, passed away like so much
vapor.

The great advantage of living with a man devoting himself
to the thorough cultivation of a subject was richly imparted to
us by Fernow's abiding presence.   By his treatise of the Italian
dialects he this year transplanted us into the midst of the life
of that remarkable country.

The history of modern German literature had also much
light shed on it; first by Johannes Müller's "Autobiography,"
which we greeted with a review, then by the publication of
Gleim's letters, for which we had the well-informed Körte to
thank; next by Huber's "Life," due to his faithful and in so
many respects highly valuable wife.

Of older historical studies I find nothing remarked except
that I read Lampridius's "History of the Emperors," and I
still vividly recall to mind the horror which seized me in the
contemplation of the anarchy there disclosed.

To keep alive my interest in the higher, moral-religious life,
Daub and Kreuzer's studies came to hand, as also the seventy-
second part of the "Halle Missionary Reports," gifts which I
owe to the kindness of Dr. Knapp, who, convinced of my sincere sympathy in the spread of moral feeling by religious means,
had now for years forwarded me news of the blessed progress
of an ever vital institution.

On another side I was instructed in the present political situation by Gentz's "Fragments from the History of the Political
Equilibrium of Europe," while I still remember the light that
was thrown on particular events of the time by an Englishman
of mark living among us, Mr. Osborn, who circumstantially
and graphically set forth the strategy of the battle of Trafalgar,
its great plan and bold execution.

Since 1801, when, after serious illness, I went to Pyrmont,
I had visited no watering-place for the sake of my health; in
Lauchstädt I had spent much time attending to the theatre, in

Weimar attending to the exhibition. Meanwhile, however, many ailments had announced themselves in my body, but of which with patient indolence I took little heed till, now at last urged by friends and physicians, I determined on a visit to Carlsbad, all the more that an active and dexterous friend, Major von Hendrick, offered to take upon himself the whole care of the journey. At the end of May, accordingly, I drove off with him and Riemer. On our way we had the adventure of seeing the " Hussites before Naumburg." Another embarrassment was occasioned us in Eger, where we found that we were not provided with passes, these having been forgotten in the hurry and bustle of starting, and through a strange complication of circumstances not been demanded at the frontiers. The police officials, however, at Eger, with the politeness and expertness which such junctures are apt to call forth, managed to help us over our difficulty. They gave us a paper of safe conduct to Carlsbad against our promise to forward them the passes.

In this watering-place, where, in order to recovery, one should leave all cares behind him, we arrived just in the midst of anxiety and apprehension.

Prince Reuss XIII, always graciously disposed toward me, was there himself and was pleased to open up to me with diplomatic skill the havoc threatening our situation. The same confidence was shown me by General Richter, who enabled me to throw many a glance into the past. He had experienced in his own person the hard fate of Ulm, and I was favored with a diary of the events dating from the third of October, 1805, to the seventeenth of October, the day of the surrender of the fortification. In such circumstances July came round; one important item of news followed the other.

Toward the advancement of geological studies Joseph Müller had been faithfully working throughout the years I did not visit Carlsbad. This worthy man, born at Turnau, and trained as a lithographer, had tried many things in the world, and at last settled in Carlsbad. There he was practising his art of lithography, when the thought struck him to cut and polish the stones of the Carlsbad fountain in tables, whereby a knowledge of these celebrated stalactites was gradually spread among the lovers of nature in the world. From these productions of the warm fountains he turned to other striking products of the mountains, collecting the twin-crystals of the felspar to be found detachedly in the surrounding country.

Years ago he had accompanied us in our walks, when, with Baron von Racknitz and other lovers of nature, I investigated important species of stone, and later on he had spared neither time nor trouble to set up a manifold characteristic collection, number them, and in his own way describe them. As he had followed the structure of the mountain, it was found that the things he had collected fitted pretty well into each other, and it did not require much labor to arrange them in an order more available for scientific purposes, a rearrangement which with some little reluctance he complied with.

Of all his investigations, that which promised to yield me the greatest profit was the attention he had devoted to the transition-stone which precedes the granite of the Hirschensprung, presents a granite veined with hornstone and containing pyrites, as also, finally, calcareous spar. The hot springs gush immediately out of this stone, and people were not disinclined to explain the heating of the waters and the solution in them by the mingling of water with this remarkable geologic formation, and so solving the mysterious problem.

He carefully showed me the traces of the above stone, a thing not easily done, seeing that the buildings of the Schlossberg rest on it. We then proceeded together through the district, visited the basalts reposing on the granite above the Hammer, and close by a field where the twin-crystals are to be found opened up by the plough. We drove to Engelhaus, observing in that place the lithographic granite and other stone deviating only in a little degree from granite. The clinkstone rock was mounted and duly hammered, and the character of the wide though not cheerful prospect fairly noticed.

To add to our good-fortune, Councillor of the Embassy Herr von Struve, as erudite in this province as he is communicative and polite, showed us, to our edification, his beautiful grades he had brought with him, taking an important part also in our geological observations, and himself producing an ideal cutting of the Lessau and Hodorf chain of mountains. This cutting clearly demonstrated the connection between the subterranean fire and the under and laterally lying mountain-chain. The specimens before us, both of the fundamental rock and its alteration by fire, conclusively established to our eyes the fact of that connection.

Walks arranged with reference to this matter were at once instructive and cheerful, while they also served to divert our minds from the events of the day.

Later on, Counsellor of Mines Werner and August von Herder joined us, the former for a prolonged, the latter for a shorter time. Though now, as is generally the case in scientific discussions, diverging, nay, opposing views came to light, still, as the conversation was directed to experience, a great deal was always to be learned. Werner's derivation of the fountain from coal-strata in constant combustion was too well known to me that I should have ventured on communicating to him my latest views. To the transition species of rock of Schlossberg, too, which for me was of so much importance, he gave only a subordinate value. August von Herder communicated to me some beautiful observations on the contents of the mountain-veins, which are different according to the different directions in which they run. It is always a beautiful experience to see the incomprehensible embodied before one's eyes.

In reference to a pedagogic-military institution in the French army, we received exact intelligence from an excellent clergyman from Bavaria. A kind of catechization, it was explained to us, was held on Sunday by officers and under-officers, in which the soldier was instructed, not only in his duties, but also in knowledge which might be serviceable to him within his sphere. The object here aimed at was plainly the training of thoroughly acute and expert men accustomed to rely on themselves. This, no doubt, presupposed a great mind in the leader, which, in spite of all instruction on the part of his subordinates, towered conspicuously above each and all, fearing nothing from *raisonneurs*.

Anxiety and danger, however, were increased by the brave, stubborn spirit of German patriots, who zealously and undisguisedly bent on organizing and effecting a popular rising, passionately concerted the means to this end. While threatened by heavy thunder-clouds in the distance, we thus saw our immediate firmament overcast with cloud and vapor.

Meanwhile, the German Confederation of the Rhine was concluded, and its consequences were easily to be overseen. On our return journey by Hof we also read in the newspapers how the German Empire was dissolved.

In the midst of these disturbing subjects of conversation we were, nevertheless, in many ways diverted. Landgrave Karl von Hessen, all along devoted to deeper studies, liked to converse on the primitive history of mankind, and was not averse from acknowledging higher views, although, by strict logical steps, one could not arrive at unanimity with him.

Carlsbad at that time gave one the feeling of living in the land of Goshen. Austria was compelled to make ostensible peace with France, and in Bohemia at least you were not, as in Thuringia, every moment alarmed by marches and counter-marches. But scarcely had you reached home when you heard the threatening thunder actually rolling in your ears, the most decided declaration of war by the marching hither of immeasurable masses of troops.

A passionate commotion revealed itself in the minds of men,

according to their different circumstances, and fables being a
never-failing product of such a temper, a report spread of the
death of Count Haugwitz, an old friend of my youth, formerly
recognized as an active and polite minister, but now hateful
to the whole world, he having drawn on himself the indignation
of the Germans by the declaration wrung from him of adher-
ence to the French supremacy.

The Prussians continue to fortify Erfurt, and our prince, as
a Prussian general, prepares for departure. It would be difficult to express the anxious negotiations I carried on with my
faithful and forever unforgettable business friend, the State
Minister von Voigt, as also the pregnant conversation with my
prince in the head-quarters at Niederrossla.

The dowager duchess occupied Tiefurt. Leader of the
Orchestra Himmel was there, and music was performed with a
heavy heart. Even in moments of so much seriousness, pleasure and work are wont to follow each other with the same sad
regularity as eating, drinking, and sleeping.

The Carlsbad specimens of the mountain-stone series had
arrived in Jena. I repaired thither on the twenty-sixth of September to unpack them, and, with the assistance of Director
Lenz, to catalogue them for the present. A list, too, was written out for the " Jena Literatur-Intelligenzblatt " and sent to
the printer.

Meanwhile I had withdrawn to the side wing of the castle
to make room for Prince Hohenlohe, who was reluctantly moving hither with his division of troops, though he would rather
have been marching on the way toward Hof to meet the enemy.
In spite of all these sad views, many a philosophic chapter was,
in the old academic way, gone through with Hegel. Schelling
published a declaration, answered by Ths. I dined with Prince
Hohenlohe, met again many important men and extended my
acquaintance; not one of us felt assured, but, on the contrary,
all were in despair, a feeling betrayed, if not by words, at least
by demeanor.

I had a wonderful scene with the hot-headed Colonel von
Massenbach. With him, too, the inclination for writing came
in the way of political prudence and military activity. He had
composed a strange work, nothing less than a moral manifesto
against Napoleon. Everybody apprehended and dreaded the
ascendancy of the French. The printer, therefore, accompanied by some advisers, came to me, and all pressingly entreated me that I would divert the printing of the manuscript,
which, if published, would on the entrance of the French army
inevitably bring destruction on the town. I had the work given
over to me, and found a series of periods, the first of which

began with the words, " Napoleon, I loved you ; " the last, however, ending with " I hate you." The interval between these periods was taken up with the expression of the hopes and expectations men at first cherished regarding the greatness of Napoleon's character, it being supposed that such an extraordinary man must be actuated by morally human purposes. At last, in strong language, he was reproached with all the wrongs which in recent times people had to suffer at his hands. With a few alterations, the paper might have been interpreted as the expression of the vexation felt by a jilted lover at the infidelity of his lady love, the composition thus appearing as ridiculous as it was dangerous.

Urged by the importunities of the worthy Jena citizens with whom I had for so many years stood on a good footing, I broke through the rule I had prescribed for my conduct not to mix myself up in any public quarrel. I took up the sheets and found the author in the large, antique rooms of the Wilhelm Dispensary. After renewing acquaintance with him, I advanced to the delivery of my protestation, and found, as was to be expected, that I had an obstinate author to deal with. I, on my side, however, showed myself as obstinate a citizen, and with vehement eloquence assailed him with all the arguments at my command, which, to be sure, were sufficiently weighty, till at last he yielded. I remember a tall, straight Prussian, apparently an adjutant, was present on this occasion, standing in unmoved posture and with unchanged features, but who might, inwardly, well be surprised at this boldness on the part of a citizen. In short, I parted from the colonel on the best terms, weaving into my thanks all the persuasive reasons which properly should have been sufficiently influential by themselves, but which now produced a mild reconciliation.

On Friday, the third of October, I waited on excellent men. I found Prince Louis Ferdinand able and friendly according to his nature ; Lieutenant-General von Grawert, Colonel von Massow, Captain Blumenstein, the last, half a Frenchman, friendly and confiding. At noon to dinner with them all at Prince Hohenlohe's.

Amid the great confidence expressed in the Prussian strength and skill in war, my ear was every now and again strangely assailed by admonitions to the effect that people should endeavor to hide their valuables, their most important papers, etc. In these circumstances, divested of all illusions of hope, I called out just as we commenced eating larks, " Now, should the heavens fall, there will be no dearth of these creatures."

On the sixth I found Weimar all in commotion and consternation. The strong characters were composed and decided, it was now time to consider and make resolutions.   Who should remain?   Who should flee?   That was the question.

1807

At the end of last year the theatre was again opened; balconies and boxes, pit and gallery, were soon refilled, as a sign and symbol that in town and State everything had resumed its old course.   It was fortunate for us to be sure that the Emperor remained true to his main maxim, to live in peace and good-will with all bearing the Saxon name, without allowing any subordinate circumstance to interfere.   General Dentzel, who so many years before had studied theology in Jena, and on account of his local knowledge was summoned to that great expedition, showed himself as commandant quite disposed to treat us with friendliness.   The younger Mounier, educated among us and attached to many a house by the ties of friendship, was appointed *Commissaire Ordonnateur,* and his mild procedure gradually appeased the excited minds of the people. Everyone had something to relate of the evil days, and felt some complacency in the remembrance of the havocs he had survived.   People, too, submitted willingly to many a burden, being no longer under apprehensions of a sudden visitation of fresh horrors.

I and those immediately associated with me, therefore, endeavored to revive the old vitality of the theatre, and in an accidental way, though not without preparation, it attained to a new splendor by means of a representation which served to reestablish the truest harmony among ourselves.   "Tasso" was performed, having been learned, certainly not amid the storms we had just passed through, but long ago in private; for as it was a custom with young actors entering our boards to practise many parts they were by no means ripe to exhibit in public, so our old actors often conned pieces not at all suitable for immediate representation.   In this way "Tasso" had for a long time been concerted among the actors, its parts distributed among them and studied, while I would frequently surprise them in the act of perusing it, without, however, feeling my obstinate scepticism on the subject of its suitability for public performance in any way shaken by that circumstance.   Now, however, when much seemed on the point of coming to a standstill, when both occasion and spirit failed for undertaking anything new, and when festival days imperatively demanding celebration at our hands pressed close upon us, my dear pupils began anew to importune me, so that at last, half angrily, I yielded to a request I should have eagerly and thankfully hastened to meet.   The applause the piece enjoyed corresponded completely with the maturity which through cordial and long-continued study it had attained in the minds and persons of the actors, and I willingly confessed my error when the project I had stubbornly refused to entertain as being impossible was by our company presented as a sensible and complete success before my eyes.

With persistent, faithful oversight the theatre was directed throughout the next months, young actors being guided and instructed in everything pertaining to their professional culture, trained in particular to observe a certain natural moderation and to free themselves from all mannerisms. Of higher importance in the future for us was the " Resolute Prince," which, having once engaged our attention, continued in private constantly to occupy our minds. Another problematic theatrical piece of quite a different character, the " Broken Jar," also attracted us; and notwithstanding the many misgivings it excited in us, we brought it to our boards, where, however, it met with a most unfavorable reception. Not, however, till after its transference to Halle and Lauchstädt and a lengthy stay there, where, subjected to the criticism of a cultivated public, it was stimulated to its utmost capacity, did our Weimar theatre recover its former vigor. The repertory of its representations this summer is, perhaps, the most important that our staff can boast of within such a short period; a repertory to which, perhaps, no other theatre could produce a match within the same limits of time.

Very soon after the performance of " Tasso "—so pure a representation of court and world scenes, tender, intellectual, and loving—Duchess Amalia, to the grief of us all, and to my special sadness, left her native soil, which for her had been so deeply disfigured, nay, even defaced beyond recognition. A hasty composition I threw off, more in the way of business than in any higher sense, was intended only as an acknowledgment of my far greater obligations to her. The sketch, however, will shortly be communicated.

To rid myself, however, of all these distresses and enable my mind to recover its wonted freedom I returned to the study of organic nature. More than once responses had reached me testifying how the mode of thought which had rendered me happy was developing itself in kindred spirits. I therefore felt myself induced to reprint the " Metamorphosis of Plants," and to rummage many old bundles of papers to see whether I could not light on something pleasant and profitable for the lovers of nature. I thought I had so far succeeded as to be justified in announcing in the catalogue of the Easter fair " Goethe's Ideas on Organic Structure," as a work that might shortly appear.

10

The observations and studies connected with this subject were now, therefore, pursued more earnestly than ever. I set myself especially to master Kaspar Friedrich Wolf's " Theoria Generationis." The old osteological views, especially the discovery made by me in Venice in 1790, that the skull is formed from the vetebræ, were more minutely set forth and discussed with two sympathetic friends, Voigt junior and Reimer. These two in astonishment brought me the news that this high significance of the skull bones had, in an academic programme, just been sprung upon the public; a fact, as to which, seeing they still live, they can testify. I besought them to compose themselves, seeing that it was all too palpable to the scholar that in the programme referred to the matter was not ably handled nor drawn from its source. Many attempts were made to induce me to a public utterance, but I was too knowing to break silence.

All adherents to the doctrine of organic metamorphosis were, next, favored by a happy accident. The *Monoculus apus* is sometimes, though seldom, to be found in stagnant water in the neighborhood of Jena. Some specimens were brought to me, and nowhere is the transformation of one member always remaining the same into another form more strikingly illustrated than in this creature.

While for so many years ascending mountain after mountain and hammering rock after rock, I had not neglected either to inspect pits and excavations. The natural appearances in the latter direction I had, in part, myself taken a drawing of, for the sake of impressing their character and manner on my senses, in part caused to be drawn, in order to gain and preserve more accurate diagrams. In the course of these observations there always hovered before my mind a model which would serve to render into more distinct visuality the impression I had received from nature. On the surface a landscape should be represented rising from a plain to the highest chain of mountains. A section of this whole ascent having been made and its various parts discriminated from each other, the inner profile should show the depressions, the strata, and other desirable characteristics. This first plan I kept for a long time with me, endeavoring, from time to time, to give it greater completeness. While so engaged I encountered problems not so easily solved. I was therefore much pleased with an offer on the part of the worthy natural-historian Haberle, whom Counsellor of the Embassy Bertuch had introduced to me. I laid my work before him, requesting him to prosecute it further. After talking the matter over with him, however, I all too soon became aware that we could not agree on the mode of treatment. I nevertheless committed the plan to him, hoping for his further labors with it, but he having left Weimar from irritation at some false views in meteorology, I never saw it again.

In the first half of this year I felt myself highly favored by Herr Alexander von Humboldt's dedicating to me in a distinguished manner a work of great importance illustrated with diagrams, " Ideas towards a Geography of Plants, with a Diagram of the Vegetation of the Tropics."

Out of friendship for the noble author, a friendship dating from the earliest days and strengthening with the advance of time, and in response to this latest and so flattering challenge addressed me, I hastened to study the work, but the profile map belonging to it was still wanting and only announced as shortly to follow. Impatient that my full appreciation of such a work should be kept in suspense, I at once undertook, in accordance with his data, to transform a certain area of paper into the picture of a landscape with mountain-masses at the side. Following his directions, I first elaborated the tropics on the right side, as the side of light and sun, and then constructed the European heights on the left, as the side of shade. In this way arose a symbolic landscape not unpleasing to the eye. This product of accident, so to say, I dedicated with an inscription to the friend to whom I had owed its conception and execution. The " Industrie Comptoir " published a copy of it with a portion of text, a copy which was received with so much favor abroad that an engraving appeared at Paris.

With no little trouble and endeavor after accuracy a clean copy of the long-prepared tables of the " Theory of Colors " was gradually finished and engraved, while the printing of the design was steadily prosecuted and at the end of January completed. The field was therefore so far cleared for the polemical part. Newton, by joining together several instruments and preparations, having perpetrated an experimental incoherence, the phenomena produced by prisms and lenses operating on each other were explained, and in general Newton's experiments minutely examined, one after the other. The polemical parts could thus be sent to the printer, while the historical part was by no means lost sight of. Nuguet " On Colors," in the " Journal de Trevoux," was highly welcome. A retrogression was also made into the Middle Ages; Roger Bacon came up for discussion, and by way of preparation the scheme of the fifteenth century was written.

Friend Meyer studied the coloring of the ancients and began to write an essay on the subject. The merits of those old classic men, never to be enough appreciated, were honestly set forth in their perfect naturalness. An introduction to the " Theory of Colors " and then a preface to the introduction were penned. A sympathizing friend attempted a translation into French, and the sheets of this translation, still in my hands, ever remind me of the pleasantest hours. The polemics had, meanwhile, to be continued, and the printed sheets of both parts corrected. At the end of the year thirty proof-sheets of the first and five of the second part were in my hands.

Subjects long meditated and appropriated become almost like familiar friends, till at last they accompany us into all provinces, and may be introduced into all manner of topics either in the way of jest or earnest. I shall thus have occasion in my literary communications to mention a couple of happy thoughts which occurred to some lively friends.

The manuscript of my writings is despatched piece by piece. The first printed copy arrived.

I hear of Hackert's death. Biographical essays and sketches are sent me according to his direction. I write his life in epitome, at first for the " Morgenblatt."

My stay in Carlsbad last year had so far improved my health that unquestionably I may ascribe the fact of my not having succumbed to the great havoc of war which burst upon us, to the careful use I then made of that watering-place. I, therefore, determined on another journey thither, and that soon, arriving there in the latter half of May. This season was rich for me in smaller stories planned, commenced, continued, and completed. Slung together on a romantic thread, under the title of " Wilhelm Meister's Travels," they were to compose a strangely attractive whole. To this purpose are marked " Conclusion of the New Melusine," " The Man of Fifty," " The Witless Wanderer."

I was no less happy with Joseph Müller's Carlsbad collection. The preparations of the past year were careful and adequate; I had acquired a sufficient supply of specimens of the rocks to be found in that district, and, resolutely following out my purposes, I had them deposited in the Jena Museum, conferring with Counsellor of Mines Lenz on their nature and their arrangement in accordance with the order in which they had been found.

This time, therefore, I arrived in a well-furnished state at Carlsbad, where Müller had amassed an abundance of stones. With little deviation from last year's order, in which I found a specimen-collection still to hand, but with good-will and conviction on the part of the old stone-lover, the decisive, new order was adopted, an essay being at once composed and repeatedly and carefully revised.

Before, however, the little essay could be printed it had to receive the approval of the upper authorities at Prague, and on one of my manuscripts, therefore, I have the pleasure of seeing the " Vidi " of the Prague censor. These few sheets were intended to serve myself and others in the future in the way of a guide and to induce a more special examination. Another purpose aimed at by this publication was that of smuggling certain geological convictions into the acknowledged science of the day.

For the good Joseph Müller it had also the happy effect of drawing attention to his collection, so that, shortly after, he received several orders. Yet so deep was his secrecy on the source of their supply (a secrecy rendered no doubt necessary by the competition for them), that he would never discover even to me the place where certain numbers were to be found, but rather contrived the strangest evasions to mislead his friends and patrons.

In riper years, when one is no longer so impetuously hurried far and wide by the distractions of his nature, when one is no longer so desperately nailed by his passions to one spot, a season at a watering-place offers an excellent field for the study of human life in the manifold assemblage there from all quarters of so many important persons. This year in Carlsbad proved in this respect highly favorable to me, not only affording me the richest and most congenial entertainment, but enabling me to form a connection very fruitful in the future. Here I met Von Reinhard, who with his spouse and children had chosen this as a place of residence where to rest and recruit themselves from the hard blows of fate. In earlier years entangled in the French Revolution he had successively accommodated himself to a series of generations, and by ministerial and diplomatic services had risen to a high position. Napoleon, who did not love him, yet knew his value, sent him to an ungrateful and dangerous post at Jassy, where he stayed for some time, abiding faithfully by his duties, till, seized by the Russians, he was conducted with his family over many tracts of country, and at last on suitable representations again set free. Of all these things his highly·cultivated wife, a Hamburg lady, the daughter of Reimarus, had composed an excellent narrative, imparting a more precise insight into the complicate and anxious situation, and exciting true sympathy.

The moment which brought before me a new, worthy countryman of Schiller's and Cuvier's was itself important enough to induce at once a nearer relation. Both husband and wife, truly upright and German in their dispositions, cultivated on all sides, the son and daughter, too, graceful and amiable, they soon drew me into their circle. The excellent man attached himself all the more closely to me that, being the representa-

tive of a nation which at the moment was working woe on so
many men, he could not be regarded with kindly feelings by
the rest of the social world.

A man of business accustomed to attend to the most foreign
affairs, in order to attain with the utmost swiftness a clear
comprehension of them, lends everyone his ear, and so this
new friend indulged me with continuous attention, while I
could not deny myself the gratification of expounding to him
my "Theory of Colors." He very soon became conversant
with it, and undertook the translation of some passages. Nay,
we made the strange experiment of a mutual communication;
I, one morning, extemporaneously delivering to him the history and fortunes of the "Theory of Colors," from the oldest
to the most recent times, and all the pains I had subjected myself to on this matter, and he the next day relating, likewise
in a summary way, the history of his life. We thus at the
same time became acquainted, I with what befell him, he with
what most vitally concerned me, and in this way a more heartfelt participation in our mutual interests was facilitated.

I have next to take note of the princess Solms, a princess of
Mecklenburg by birth, who always, wherever I met her, showed
me gracious attention. On each occasion she pressed me to
read something to her, and I always chose the product which
had most recently issued from my head and heart. The poetry
I read to her being, therefore, each time the expression of a
true feeling carried with it the evidence of truth, and proceeding from the heart also penetrated to the heart. A friendly
minded court lady, Fräulein l'Estocq, was present with her
good understanding at these confidential communications.

The name of Reinhard was now, again, to sound gratefully
in my ears. The chief court preacher of the Kingdom of Saxony was visiting the warm springs with the object of recruiting
his very infirm health. Painful though it was to see this worthy
man laboring under such serious bodily illness, it was yet enjoyable to have conversation with him. His beautiful moral
nature, his well-cultivated mind, his upright will, his practical
insight into everything worthy of being desired and sought
after, shone forth everywhere with a dignified amiability. Although he could not entirely sympathize with my way of expressing myself on forthcoming matters, I had yet the happiness of completely according with him on certain main points
in opposition to ruling views; and he might well perceive that
my apparent liberal indifferentism, practically at one with him
in all that was most deeply earnest in his nature, might be but
a mask behind which I endeavored to protect myself from
pedantry and self-conceit. I gained his confidence in a high

degree, and thereby shared in much that was excellent. Our moral communings with each other touching the imperishable served to turn away or blunt the sting of the war news which day after day reached our ears.

Renewed intercourse with the meritorious prefect of the district, Von Schiller, likewise afforded me many an agreeable hour, notwithstanding the manifold labors falling to the lot of this overburdened man of business. I was also surprised by the presence of Captain Blumenstein, whom a year before, on the dreadful eve of our unhappy days, I had found sympathetic and sincere. Full of insight, good humor, and happy ideas, he was the best of company, and we bandied many a jest with each other, though as a passionate Prussian he could not forgive my too confidential acquaintance with a French diplomatist. Yet with the help of some merry fancies the dispute between us was soon happily composed.

Another circle, however, was opened for me. Princess Bagration, beautiful, charming, attractive, gathered about her a considerable company. Here I was introduced to Prince Ligne, whose name had been familiar to me for so many years, and whose personality, from his relation to friends of mine, had become highly interesting to me. His presence made good his reputation; he appeared ever in good spirits, ingenious, equal to all occasions, everywhere welcome, and at home as a man of the world and of action. The Duke of Coburg distinguished himself by his handsome figure and his gracefully dignified manner. The Duke of Weimar, whom in relation to myself I should have first mentioned, seeing it was to him I owed my honored reception into this circle, inspired it with his animation. Count Corneillan, by his earnest, quiet demeanor and his pleasant conversation on works of art, was also ever welcome. In front of the princess's residence, in the middle of the meadow, were at all times to be found some members of this company, among them, too, Hofrath von Gentz, who, with great insight into and comprehension of the recent events of the war, very frequently communicated his thoughts to me, describing the positions of the armies and the consequences of the battles, and finally giving me the first intelligence of the Peace of Tilsit.

Carlsbad was at this time blessed likewise with doctors. I first mention Dr. Kapp, from Leipsic, who made my time at the bath uninterruptedly happy for me, his conversation being altogether instructive and his care of those intrusted to him most conscientious. Hofrath Sulzer, from Ronneburg, a faithful, scientific investigator and diligent mineralogist, attached himself to us. Dr. Mitterbacher, as far as his business would allow him, was also ready with his counsel. Dr. Florian, a

Bohemian from Manetin, was likewise of our company. We thus had the opportunity of becoming initiated into more than one method of medical thought and treatment.

The town and government, too, seemed disposed to do more than they had hitherto done toward honoring the warm springs and rendering the locality agreeable to the strangers who had been enticed hither. A hospital set up at the side of the Bern-hard rock suggested hopes for the poorer classes, while the higher classes rejoiced in the anticipation of a more convenient and becoming walk to the new fountain. I was shown the plans, which could not but be approved, and with many thousand others I was gladdened by the near prospect of exchanging a place of resort crowded to a degree extremely unpleasant for a stately hall.

My taste for mineralogy was promoted in many ways. The porcelain factory in Dalwitz again confirmed me in my conviction that geognostic knowledge in general and in particular is of the greatest moment in every undertaking in this direction. What used to be thought peculiar to this and that country alone is now to be found at a hundred places; for example, the porcelain Saxon clay once prized as a jewel, but now everywhere to be met with.

Toward a better knowledge of precious stones, Zöldner, from Prague, staying at the baths, told me much of great interest, though I bought but little of him; his communications, while a pleasure to me at the time, proved profitable to me in the future.

I will not omit mentioning the notice I find in my diary of the honor and confidence with which our company received the narrative of Dr. Hausmann's journey to Norway.

The presence of Werner, counsellor of mines, at Carlsbad was, too, during the last days of my stay there, as always, animating in the highest degree. We were acquaintances of many years' standing, and harmonized with each other, perhaps more, however, from mutual forbearance than from agreement in our principles. I avoided touching his derivation of the wells from coal layers, though in other things I was open and communicative, while with a politeness really exemplary he would out of his rich experience readily help me with my dynamical theses, though he regarded them as fanciful.

I was then more than ever intent on bringing forward the porphyritic formation in opposition to the conglomerate, and though this view of mine found no response in him, yet in answer to my question, he made me acquainted with a highly important stone, which, with an excellent definition of his own, he called granulous date-quartz, a stone to be found at Prieborn

in Silesia. He gave me a drawing of the style and character
of the phenomenon, and thereby induced many years' investigations.

It is a curious experience we make in our travels when meeting with strangers or persons we had long before lost sight of,
that we find them altogether different from the idea we have
been accustomed to associate with their names. We think of
this or that public man as peculiarly and passionately attached
to this or that branch of knowledge, we meet him and desire
instruction in his particular department, and, lo! his mind has
taken quite a different direction, and the inquiries we address
him are completely out of his horizon. This was now my experience with Werner, counsellor of mines, who rather avoided
oryctognostic and geognostic conversations, and directed our
attention to quite other subjects.

Philology was now his peculiar field, the origin, derivation,
and relationship of languages giving full scope for his sharp-
sighted industry, and he did not need much time to interest us
in his pursuit. He carried about with him a set of bandboxes,
in which, methodically arranged (as becomes such a man), he
kept a whole library of books pertaining to this subject of inquiry, thereby facilitating for himself a free intellectual communication.

That this, however, may not appear too paradoxical, let one
think of the necessity which impelled this man into such a department. Every branch of knowledge requires a second, a
third, and so on; we may follow the tree in its roots or in its
branches and twigs; the one always issues out of the other, and
the more vital any branch of knowledge grows in us the more
are we driven to pursue it in its connection forward and backward. In his department, Werner, as he advanced, employed
for the naming of particular objects such terms as had been in
favor with his predecessor; but new subjects pressing daily on
his attention, he felt the necessity, for the sake of distinction,
of inventing names himself.

Naming is not so easy a business as is commonly supposed,
and a right solid philologist would be incited to many strange
reflections were he to write a criticism on the usual oryctognostic nomenclature. Werner was very sensible of all this, and
no doubt made a wide circuit when, in order to name the subjects of a certain department, he resolved to study languages
in general in their origin, development, and structure, and so
learn from them what he required for his purpose.

No one has the right to prescribe to an intellectual man the
field of his study. The mind shoots its rays from the centre
to the periphery; if it encounter a terminus at this point, it re-

tires into itself and shoots forth again out of the centre new lines of endeavor, so that if it cannot transcend its orbit it may yet become acquainted with it and fill it out to the utmost possible degree. And even if Werner, in his elaboration of the means, had forgotten the purpose he originally intended by them, a thing we can by no means assert, we were yet witnesses of the joy with which he pursued the business, and learned from and by him how one should set limits to himself in any undertaking, and find for a time within those limits happiness and satisfaction.

Otherwise I had neither leisure nor opportunity to enter into more ancient treatises of the history of nature. I studied "Albertus Magnus," but with little success. It was necessary to realize the character and features of his century in order to comprehend in any measure what was here intended and accomplished.

Toward the end of my stay in the watering-place, my son came to Carlsbad, as I wished to indulge him with the sight of a place so often the subject of conversation at home. This gave occasion for some adventures disclosing the inner disquietude of society. At that time it was fashionable to wear a kind of short shooting-coat, green, and largely set with lace of like color, very convenient for riding and hunting, so that its use soon became widely extended. This attire several Prussian officers, dispersed by the war, had adopted as an interim uniform, with which they might roam about unrecognized among farmers, landlords, hunters, horse-dealers, and students. My son had put on a coat of this kind. Meanwhile, in Carlsbad some of these masked officers had been scented out, and in a very short time this dress came to be taken as the indication of a Prussian.

No one knew of the arrival of my son. I stood with Fräulein l'Estocq at the Tepel-wall before the Saxon salon; he passes by and greets us; she draws aside and says vehemently, "That is a Prussian officer, and what frightens me is that he looks very like my brother." "I will call him hither," I answered; "will examine him." I was gone when she shouted after me, "For God's sake, no pranks." I brought him back, presented him, and said, "This lady, sir, desires some information. Would you discover to us whence you come and who you are?" The two young persons were both embarrassed, the one as much as the other. My son was silent, puzzled as to the meaning of it all, while the lady likewise silent appeared to be meditating some plausible escape. I therefore took up the word, and with a jocular turn declared it was my son, and we must esteem it a fortune of the family, if in any measure he resembled her brother. She did not believe this representation, till in the end the fable assumed the air of probability, and at last of certainty.

The second adventure was not of so happy a nature. We had now reached the month of September, the season when the Poles are wont to assemble more numerously in Carlsbad. Their hatred of the Prussians had for a long time been intense, and after the last misfortunes had passed into contempt. Under the green jacket, properly Polish, being of Polish origin, they might on this occasion have scented out a Prussian. My son goes about on the space fronting the houses on the meadow; four Poles walking in the middle of the sandy way meet him, one of them parts from his companions, passes by my son, looks him in the face, and then rejoins the others. My son makes a manœuvre so as to meet them again, walks up to them in the middle of the sandy way, and passes through the four, at the same time explaining quite curtly what his name was, where he lived, and that as he intended leaving next morning, whoever had any business with him should despatch it with him that evening. We passed the evening without any disturbance, and set off the next morning. It looked as though this comedy of many acts might, like an English comedy, not end without an affair of honor.

On my return from Carlsbad the singers gave me a serenade, in which I could read affection, good-will, progress in their art, and much else of a gladdening nature. I was now pleased, for the sake of enlivening society, to wed known melodies to new songs, the contents of which were drawn from present events. Mademoiselle Engels rendered them with appreciation and life, and so we gradually appropriated the most popular melodies, as though they had been originated for our circle. We diligently rehearsed musical pieces for several voices, and the first Sunday thereafter, the thirtieth of December, was celebrated before a large company.

The Weimar theatre gained at Michaelmas an agreeable and promising tenor voice, Morhard. His culture was promoted by an older musical friend, who was distinguished by a particular skill of his own in leading concerts, and who with the violin would assist the song, infusing a sense of security, courage, and pleasure into the singer. This gave occasion to musical instruction, by way of preparatory practice, as in the case of dramatic pieces, the singer being in this way introduced to parts which only later on might perhaps be assigned to him in public. It was also intended by this means to render persons whose voice was not first-class, available for light simple operas, which are always welcome as a break. Out of this proceeded practice in songs of several voices, which was bound sooner or later to redound to the advantage of the theatre.

Nor as poet would I remain idle for the stage. I wrote a prologue for Leipsic, where our actors were to figure for a time; further, a prologue for the thirtieth of September, to celebrate the reunion of the princely family after that repugnant separation.

As the most important undertaking, however, I remark that I began to work at " Pandora's Return." I did it for the sake of two young men, friends of many years' standing, Leo von Seckendorf and Dr. Stoll. Both being of literary aspirations, they thought of bringing out a " Musenalmanach" in Vienna, and the mythological crisis at which Prometheus appears being ever present with me and, indeed, grown to a living fixed idea, I set to work on this subject not without the most earnest intentions, as anyone will be convinced who attentively considers the piece as far as it goes.

To the volume of my epic poems " Achilleïs " was to be added. I again took the whole in hand, but had enough to do to mature the first book to such a point that I was able to commence it formally.

I must now mention another work which was called forth by a feeling of friendship. Johannes von Müller had at the beginning of the year written an academic oration to the memory of King Frederick II, and was violently attacked for doing so. Now, since the first years of our acquaintance, he had shown me much love and faithfulness, having rendered me essential service. I therefore thought of doing him some politeness by way of return, and believed it would be agreeable to him if approval of his undertaking were testified from any side. A friendly response in the shape of a harmless translation appeared to me most suitable; the translation appeared in the " Morgenblatt," and he thanked me, though the matter was not thereby improved.

" Pandora's Return " was planned, and the execution went on bit by bit. Only the first part was finished, but that alone will show the intention with which this work was undertaken and carried out.

The little stories already repeatedly referred to occupied me in happy hours, and the " Elective Affinities " were also in this way to be briefly treated. They, however, soon extended themselves. The material was altogether too important, and had struck too deep root for me to be able to dismiss it in so light a fashion.

" Pandora " and the " Elective Affinities " both express the painful feeling of resignation, and could therefore very well advance side by side. The first part of " Pandora " arrived at the right time toward the end of the year in Vienna. The plan of the " Elective Affinities " had advanced far, and many preliminary labors were in part completed. Another interest appeared in the last quarter of the year; I turned to the " Nibelungen," of which, indeed, much was to be said.

Through Bodmer's labors I had long known of the existence of this poem. Christoph Heinrich Müller sent me his edition, unfortunately in an unstitched state; the precious work remained in my hands in this unsatisfactory form, and, involved in other business, tendencies, and cares, I continued as insensible to its merits as the rest of the German world. Only by accident I read an outside page at the place where the mermaids prophesy to the bold hero. The passage struck me, without, however, stimulating me to dip deeper into the whole: I rested satisfied rather with humming to myself an independent ballad suggested by the contents, a ballad which would again and again sing itself in my imagination, though I never brought it so far as to conclude and complete it.

But as everything tends toward maturity, the interest in this important product of antiquity became, through patriotic exertions, more general and the access to it more convenient. The ladies to whom I had still the happiness of giving readings on the Wednesdays made inquiry about this work, and I did not neglect acquiring for them the desired knowledge. I immediately got hold of the original and worked my way into it with so much success that with the text before me I could read off line for line an intelligible translation. The tone, the course of the poem was duly rendered, nor did the contents suffer anything at my hands. Such an exercise comes off most happily when purely extempore. You must have all your senses about you, your mind must be in full swing; it is a kind of improvisation. While in this manner I went the whole round of the poetical work, I did not neglect a critical study of it to such a degree that when questions were put to me I could give satisfactory account of its details. I drew up a list of the persons and characters, made hasty sketches of locality and history, morals and passions, harmony and incongruities, planning at the same time a hypothetic map for the first part. By this means I gained much for the immediate purpose, more for the future, rendering myself better able to judge, enjoy, and profit by the earnest continuous labors later on of German students of language and antiquity.

Influence from Munich in the person of Dr. Niethammer urged me to two works of wide research: a historic religious book for the people and a general collection of songs for the edification and enjoyment of the Germans. Both of them were meditated for a time and planned; but, on account of many misgivings, the enterprise was dropped. Still the papers in connection with those two works were collected and laid past, so as to be serviceable for me in the event of my undertaking a similar task in the future.

I made earnest preparations for a biography of Hackert. The task was a difficult one, for the papers delivered to me were to be regarded neither as entirely raw nor as entirely worked-up material. The data committed to me were neither wholly to be taken to pieces, nor in their present form were they completely available. The work, therefore, gave me more trouble and pains than if it had been an entirely original production, and it cost no little perseverance, as it also required all the love and respect I had for my departed friend, to keep me from abandoning the undertaking. The noble man's heirs, who set a very high value on the manuscript, often met me, not in the most friendly way.

The polemical as also the historical part of the " Theory of Colors " advances slowly, to be sure, but yet steadily. Of the historical studies there remain as the chief authors Roger Bacon, Aguillonius, and Boyle. At the end of the year the first part is mostly finished, the second corrected down to the ninth sheet.

The Jena institutions, after the storms of war from which happily they were miraculously saved, had completely recovered themselves. All persons interested had set themselves zealously to work, and when in September they were all inspected, their founder, our gracious master, on his happy return, received a satisfactory account of them.

1808

The social personalities in Carlsbad had this summer assumed quite a different character for me. The Duchess of Courland, graceful herself and with a graceful surrounding, Frau von der Recke, accompanied by Tiedge, and others attaching themselves to these, formed a highly joyous centre of life there. You met each other so often in the same place, in the same relations, finding your friends ever in the old style and fashion, that you seemed to have lived years with them; you confided without properly knowing each other.

The family of Ziegesar composed another more decided, more indissoluble circle. Parents and offspring I knew through all their ramifications; the father I had always highly respected—I may well say reverenced. The joyous activity of the mother,

an activity knowing no decline, permitted nobody to be in her
company without being satisfied. Children, on my first entrance into Drackendorf not yet born, here met me in the figure
of grown-up, stately, amiable persons. To these were attached
acquaintances and relations. A more united, a more harmonious circle could nowhere be found. Frau von Seckendorf, by
birth Von Uechtritz, and Pauline Gotter were no small ornaments of this company. Everyone endeavored to please the
other and was pleased with the other, the company naturally
resolving itself into pairs, and excluding everything like envy
or misunderstanding. These unsought relationships produced
a mode of living which with more important interests would
have adorned a novel.

Away from home as we were, and living in rented rooms,
such relations appear quite natural, and in the case of social
wanderings quite inevitable. The intercourse between Carlsbad and Franzensbrunn, regulated as a whole by calculation,
but in particular always induced casually, at first arranged by
the prudence of the parents, but in the end confirmed by the
passion of the younger members, caused even the mischief produced by such communication to be ever delightful, as also in
remembrance highly agreeable, everything in the end being
made up and happily composed.

From the first, and still more within the last few years, convinced that the peculiar function of newspapers is only to amuse
the public and beguile them in regard to the aspects of the day—
whether the reason be that the editor is prevented by an external
power from telling the truth or that his inward partisan feeling
forbids his doing so—I ceased reading them. Of the main
events of the day I was informed by friends, who took pleasure
in learning and communicating news, and otherwise in the
course of this period I had nothing to make inquiry after. The
" General Gazette " (" Allgemeine Zeitung "), however, regularly sent me by favor of Herr Cotta, accumulated on my hands.
The impressions of 1806 and 1807 having been nicely bound
by the good offices of an order-loving chancery colleague, I
found them in this state just as I was about to set off for Carlsbad. Though now I had been taught by experience to take
few books with me on such occasions, as being not at all likely
to be read, yet as one is disposed to read those casually given
him by friends, I found it convenient and pleasurable to take
this political library with me; and not only did I find unexpected instruction and entertainment in it, but friends, who
became aware of the volumes, begged them of me in turns, so
that at the end I could not gather them together again. The
particular merit of this paper consisted, perhaps, in the fact

that though with prudent delay it occasionally kept back news, it did not fail conscientiously to communicate, piece by piece, as much as enabled the thoughtful observer to understand the situation of affairs.

Meanwhile, the present outlook was still sufficiently full of anxiety, so that the different peoples meeting at such a health resort were not without certain apprehensions the one of the other, and therefore avoided all political conversation. All the more must the reading of these newspapers in the way of substitute for political conversation be felt as the satisfaction of a want.

I must not forget the ruling duke, August von Gotha, who was pleased to present himself in a problematic light, and under a certain soft exterior to show himself sometimes agreeable and sometimes repugnant. I have no reason to complain of him, but it was always a matter of anxiety to accept an invitation to his table, it being impossible to foresee which of the guests he might by chance be disposed to treat in an unsparing manner.

I will next mention the Prince Bishop of Breslau, and a mysterious Swede, in the list of visitors called Von Reiterholm. The former was in bad health, but with a truly personal dignity, friendly and obliging. With the latter the conversation was always important, but, people desiring to respect his secret, and yet afraid of touching on it by accident, we came little in contact with him—we not seeking his company and he avoiding us.

Prefect of the District von Schiller always showed himself disposed to avoid rather than attach himself to the spa visitors, a line of conduct very necessary in his place, as in the event of any police cases occurring he was at liberty to regard people only in so far as they were in the right or in the wrong, and no personal relationship inclining one to be favorable or unfavorable could be permitted to come into play.

With Von Herder, counsellor of mines, I continued the customary conversations as though we had but a little before parted from each other; as also with Wilhelm von Schütz, who soon let it be seen that he was likewise advancing steadily on his course.

Counsellor of Mines Werner joined us as usual later on. His presence was always instructive, whether you considered him and his mode of thought or made acquaintance through him with the subjects to which he devoted himself.

A lengthy residence in Franzensbrunn enables me to pay frequent visits to the problematic Kammerberg (chamber-mountain) at Eger. I collect its products, make accurate observations of it, describe and draw it. I find myself impelled to deviate from Reuss's view, which regards the mountain as pseudo-volcanic, and to hold it for volcanic. In this sense I write an essay which can speak for itself. The question, however, may not be quite solved by this treatise and a return to Reuss's interpretation seem very well advisable.

In Carlsbad it was gladdening to see how Joseph Müller's collections were gaining in favor, though the constantly convulsed war-like times were prejudicial to all scientific pursuits. Müller, in no way discouraged, gathered his heaps of stones, and, accustomed to the new order, he cut them so neatly that in his collections of greater or smaller size the pieces of each heap were of like proportions, lying clean and instructive before one's eyes. Among the stones broken under the hammer the fit or important one was always to be found, and those of no value having been cast away, he could always provide the amateur to his entire satisfaction. But there was no inducing him to put his raw store in order, his fear of losing his monopoly and his habituation to the disorder made him deaf to all good counsel. With every fresh collection he began to pick the stones out of the chaotic heap, and, according to the new order, distribute them in numerical sequence on boards divided by bars into squares, and so gradually fill up the cases. I daily visited him on the way to the New Well, enjoying ever an instructive conversation, for there is no district of nature, however limited, but will always offer something new, or at least present some striking aspect of the old.

After such subjects, appearing perhaps all too dry and material, renewed relations with worthy artists were to stimulate and animate me in a peculiar manner.

The presence of Kaaz, the excellent Dresden landscape painter, gave me much joy and instruction, especially as he knew how to transform in a masterly way my dilettante sketches into a fair-looking picture. Making use of a style which easily conjoined water and opaque colors, he roused even me out of my fantastic scrawling to a freer handling. And as a proof how the presence of a master raises and supports one, I still keep in my possession some leaves from that period, which, like illuminated points, indicate that in such circumstances one can accomplish what would appear impossible before and after.

I next had the agreeable surprise of an impetuous visit in the old style from a friend who had attached himself to me for many years. It was the good, talented Bury, who, in the suite of the hereditary Princess of Hesse-Cassel, had put up for some time in and around Dresden, and now on furlough, came hither for some days.

I wrote a poem to the honor and pleasure of this worthy lady,

11

who was also friendly to me, a poem which, written in fair hand
in the middle of a large sheet of paper, was to be enclosed in
the most pictorial frame, representing the districts through
which she travelled, the subjects to which she devoted the most
attention, and which afforded her the most enjoyment. A
complete sketch was devised and drawn, and everything so zealously taken in hand that there could be no doubt of a happy
result. The poem is to be found printed among my others.
On this occasion Bury again drew my portrait in small size and
contour, a portrait which my family in the future prized as a
joyous monument of that time. This summer residence was
thus enriched for me on the side of plastic art, and though it
assumed quite a different character from that of the former
summer, it was also valuable and fruitful in results to me.

On my return I was summoned to still higher art contemplation. Mionet's invaluable plaster-of-Paris casts of Greek coins
had arrived. You here looked into an abyss of the past, and
were astonished at the most splendid pictures. You endeavored
in the midst of this wealth to attain to a true appreciation, and
felt beforehand that here you had matter of instruction and
edification for many years. Cut stones of importance added to
my collection of rings. Albrecht Dürer's pen-drawings, in
lithograph, came repeated and increased to us.

Runge, whose tender, pious, amiable efforts had found good
reception with us, sent me the original drawings of his days'
rich thoughts and images, which, though so faithfully and carefully executed in copper-plate, yet in natural, immediate expression showed to great advantage in the original. To these were
added other sketches, mostly half complete, of no less value.
All were thankfully returned, though there was much which,
had it been possible to do so without indiscretion, we would
willingly have retained among our collections, in memory of an
excellent talent.

In autumn, too, the most agreeable contemplation and entertainment were afforded by a number of landscape drawings
by Friedrich. His beautiful talent was known and appreciated
by us, the thoughts of his work were tender, nay, pious, but
from the stricter artistic point of view not altogether to be approved. However that may be, many beautiful testimonies of
his merit have become incorporated with us. At the close of
the year we were visited by the everywhere welcome Kügelgen.
He painted my portrait. His personality must necessarily exercise the tenderest influence on our cultivated social circle.

A serenade given me by the singers before my departure for
Carlsbad assured me at the time of their affection and persevering diligence even in my absence, and on my return accord-

ngly I found everything in the same good course. The private musical practice was continued, and social life by that means acquired a highly joyous harmony.

Toward the end of the year manifold differences came to light in the theatre, which, though not interrupting the course of the representations, yet embittered December for us. After many discussions a new arrangement was agreed to, in the hope that this would hold good for some time.

Much of a personally joyous nature was apportioned to me this year. To our young master and mistress Princess Marie was born, to the joy of all, and me especially, who here saw a new twig sprout forth from the princely tree to which I had devoted my whole life.

My son August went to the Academy of Heidelberg full of vigor and good spirits, my blessing, my cares, and hopes, following him thither. With introductions to important friends formerly of Jena, Voss and Thibaut, he might be considered here as under his parents' roof.

On his way through Frankfort he greeted his good grandmother, just in time, as later on in September she was snatched away from us, to our grief. Toward the end of the year also occurred the death of a man, comparatively young, whom we regretfully blessed. Fernow died after much severe suffering. The distension of the artery of the neck tormented him through long, distressed days and nights, till one morning sitting upright he was found, as is usually the case in such troubles, to have suddenly breathed his last.

His was a great loss for us, as the source of the Italian language, which, since Jagemann's decease, had sunk into comparative neglect, now dried up for us the second time. People will not appreciate and appropriate a foreign literature till it is pressed upon them, till it is made cheaply and easily accessible to them. Thus on account of neighborhood or other influence we find in eastern Germany the Italian, in western, the French, and in northern, the English language particularly cultivated.

The Congress of Erfurt, which first assembled in September in the neighborhood and then advanced to our quarters, is of such great importance and the influence of this period on my situation so weighty, that a particular description of these few days may well be given.

September

In the first half of the month the news is confirmed of the
meeting of the monarchs at Erfurt.

23. March of the French troops thither.

24. Arrival of the grand-duke Constantine in Weimar.

25. The Emperor Alexander.

27. The princes to Erfurt. Napoleon comes as far as
Münchenholzen.

29. The duke called me to Erfurt. In the evening " Andromache " in Théâtre Français.

30. Grand dinner at the duke's. Evening, " Britannicus."
Then great tea at Frau Präsidentin von der Reck's. Minister
Maret.

October

1

Levée at the Emperor Napoleon's.

Government. Stair, ante-room, and room.

Great bustle.

The familiar old place and the people all different.

Medley.

Old and new acquaintances.

Poet as prophet.

The Prince of Dessau remained to audience.

Many assembled in the convoy-office at the Duke of Weimar's.

The prince returns and relates a scene between the Emperor
and Talma, which might occasion misconstruction and tittle-
tattle.

I dined at Minister Champagny's.

My neighbor at table was Bourgoing, French ambassador at
Dresden.

2

Marshal Lannes and Minister Maret had probably spoken in
favorable terms of me.

The former knew me since 1806.

I was ordered to the presence of the Emperor at 11 A.M.

A stout chamberlain, a Pole, intimated to me to stay.

The crowd removed.

Presented to Savary and Talleyrand.

I am called to the Cabinet of the Emperor.

At the same moment Daru sends in his name and is at once admitted.

I therefore hesitate.

Am again called.

Step in.

The Emperor sits at a large, round table, taking breakfast; at his right stands Talleyrand at some distance from the table, at his left, rather near, Daru, with whom he converses on the contribution affairs.

The Emperor nods to me to come forward.

I stand at becoming distance from him.

Having looked at me attentively, he said, "*Vous êtes un homme.*" I bow.

He asks, "How old are you?"

"Sixty years."

"You carry your age well. You have written tragedies?"

I answered what was necessary.

Here Daru took up the word. In some measure to flatter the Germans on whom he had to work so much woe, he spoke of German literature; being also well conversant with Latin and himself editor of Horace.

He spoke of me in much the same way as my patrons in Berlin might have spoken; at least I recognized in his words their mode of thought and sentiment.

He then added that I had translated from the French, and that Voltaire's "Mahomet."

The Emperor replied, "It is not a good piece," and set forth with great detail how unsuitable it was for the conqueror of the world to make such an unfavorable description of himself.

He then turned the conversation on "Werther," which he seemed to have studied thoroughly. After various very pertinent remarks he pointed out a certain passage and said, "Why have you written so? It is not according to nature;" opening up his meaning at large and setting forth the matter with perfect accuracy.

I listened to him with an expression of pleasure, and, with a smile of gladness, answered that I, indeed, was not aware that any person had made me the same reproach; but I found his censure quite correct, and confessed that in this passage there was something demonstrable as untrue. Only, I added, it might, perhaps, be pardoned the poet if he made use of an artifice not easily to be discovered in order to produce certain effects he could not have accomplished in a simple, natural way.

The Emperor seemed satisfied with this, returned to the

drama, and made very important remarks, in the manner of a criminal judge who contemplates the tragic stage with the greatest attention, having deeply felt the deviation of the French theatre from nature and truth.

He then referred to the fate-plays with disapproval—they had belonged to a darker time. " What," said he, " have people now to do with fate? It is politics that is fate."

He next turned again to Daru and spoke with him of the great contribution affairs. I retired a little, and came to stand just at the corner, where, more than thirty years ago, along with many a glad hour, I had also experienced many a sad one, and had time to remark that to the right of me, toward the entry door, Berthier, Savary, and yet another person stood. Talley- rand had removed.

Marshal Soult was announced.

This tall figure with a profusion of hair on his head entered The Emperor inquired jocularly about some unpleasant events in Poland, and I had time to look round me in the room, and to think of the past.

Here, too, was yet the old tapestry.

But the portraits on the walls were vanished.

Here had hung the likeness of the duchess Amalia, in mas- querade dress, a black half-mask in the hand, the other like- nesses of governors and members of the family, likewise all gone.

The Emperor rose, went up to me, and, by a kind of manœu- vre, separated me from the other members of the row in which I stood.

Turning his back to those, and speaking to me in a lower voice, he asked whether I was married, have children, and other personal matters of usual interest. In the same manner, like- wise, he inquired after my relations to the princely house, after the duchess Amalia, the prince, the princess, etc. I answered him in a natural way. He seemed satisfied, and translated it into his own language, only in a somewhat more decisive style than I had been able to express myself.

I must remark, generally, that in the whole conversation I had to admire the multiplicity of his expressions of approval, for he seldom listened without some response, either nodding reflectively with the head or saying, " Oui," or " C'est bien," or such like. Nor must I forget to mention that when he had finished speaking, he usually added, " Qu'en dit Mr. Göt? "

And so I took the opportunity of asking the chamberlain by a sign whether I might take leave, which he answered in the affirmative, and I then, without further ado, took my departure.

3

Much conferring as to a representation to be given in Weimar. In the evening " Œdipus."

4

To Weimar for arrangement of the theatre.

6

Great hunt.—The French actors arrive with their director.—Evening, " Death of Cæsar."—Minister Maret and those connected with him lodged with me.

7

Marshal Lannes and Minister Maret.—Particular conversation on account of the imminent Spanish expedition.—From the Jena-Apolda hunt all back and farther.—Hofrath Sartorius, from Göttingen, and Frau call on me.

14

I receive the order of the Legion of Honor.—Talma and Frau and Minister Maret's secretary, de Lorgne d'Idonville, meet in my house.

1809

This year, in consideration of the beautiful results it yielded me, must ever remain dear and precious in my memory. I spent it without any stay abroad, partly in Weimar, partly in Jena. It thus gained more in unity and compactness than other years, which mostly split in the middle by journeys to watering-places suffered in manifold distractions.

My work in Jena would, I hoped, be favored by a quite unbroken residence there; but this, however, was not indulged me. Unexpected events of the war penetrated to our quarter and compelled me to change my place of abode several times.

Tumults of war far and near in Spain and Austria could not but excite fear and apprehension in every man. The march of our *chasseurs* on the fourteenth of April for the Tyrol was sad and serious. Immediately on the back of that came the quartering of soldiers. The Prince of Ponte-Corvo as leader of the Saxon Army Corps moved toward the borders of Bohemia, and on the twenty-fifth of April marched from Weimar to Kranichfeld. Long accustomed, especially during the last years, to shut myself completely off from the outer world, attend to my own affairs, and cultivate the productions of my mind, I now repaired, on the twenty-ninth of April, to Jena. There I worked at the " History of the Theory of Colors," fetched up my review of the fifteenth and sixteenth centuries, and wrote the history of my own chromatic conversion and progressive studies, a work which, concluded for the time being on the twenty-fourth of May, I laid aside, and did not resume till toward the end of the year, when Runge's " Globe of Colors " set our chromatic contemplations again in motion.

In this epoch I brought the " Theory of Colors " down to the end of the eighteenth century. At the same time the printing of the second part continued without interruption, and attention was next directed to the controversy with Newton. In all these labors Dr. Seebeck was sympathetic and helpful.

To come, now, to poetical labors, the " Elective Affinities," the first conception of which engaged my mind a long time ago, had not again been out of my thoughts since the end of May. No one fails to see in this novel a wound of deep passion which nurses itself and shuns healing, a heart which dreads recovery to soundness. Some years ago the main thought was seized, but the execution evermore extended and developed in many directions, threatening to transgress the limit of art. At last, after so many preparations, the resolution was taken, the printing should now begin, many a doubt would be put an end to, the one point held fast, the other at last determined.

In the swift progress which now ensued I was, however, all at once disturbed. The news of the powerful advance of the French into Austria having been heard with dread, the King of Westphalia began a march toward Bohemia, so that on the thirteenth of June I returned to Weimar. The intelligence as to this strange expedition was very uncertain when two diplomatic friends following the head-quarters, Von Reinhard and Wangenheim, unexpectedly visited me, puzzling me with the announcement of an inexplicable retreat. On the fifteenth of July the King comes to Weimar. The retreat appears to degenerate into flight, and on the twentieth the roving Oels corps inspire us and the neighborhood with anxiety. This thundercloud, too, however, soon draws off in a northwest direction, and on the twenty-third of July I go back to Jena.

Immediately thereafter the " Elective Affinities " gradually gets printed. This impelling me to diligence, the manuscript soon definitely shapes and rounds itself, and the third of October relieves me from the work, though I did not yet feel completely freed from the personal interest of its contents.

In social conversation the interest turned almost exclusively on the early times of the North and of romance in general. The extempore translation of the " Nibelungen," evermore succeeding, entirely chained the attention of a noble company who constantly gathered every Wednesday in my house. " Fierabras " and other heroic sagas and poems, " King Rother," " Tristan and Isolde," followed each other to their mutual enhancement. Attention was, however, specially directed to the " Wilkina Saga " and other Northern relations and productions, when the strange pedestrian Rune-antiquarian Arndt called on us, and, by his personal communications and discourses, endeavored to make himself tolerable to our company if he did not gain us over to his side. Dr. Majer's " Northern Sagas " contributed their part to make us feel well at ease under the dull sky. At the same time nothing was more natural than that the antiquities of the German language should come into prominence and be evermore prized, a tendency promoted by Grimm's stay among us, while a thorough study of grammar was revived in a charming manner by " The Boy's Horn of Wonder."

Cotta's publication of my works likewise demanded much of my time. It appeared and gave me the opportunity, by the sending of copies, of calling my patrons and friends to memory. Of this mention will be made at another place.

That part of my labors this year, however, which pointed most decidedly to the future were my preparations to the considerable undertaking of an autobiography. In view of the misgivings attending the endeavor to recall long-elapsed seasons of youth, the work had to be proceeded with carefully and circumspectly. Yet the resolution was at length taken, with the determination to deal sincerely with myself and others, and to strive after the truth to the utmost degree, as far as memory would help me to it.

The new arrangement, too, which in view of the main business devolving on me was lately chosen, required my longer stay in Jena this year. Our gracious master had, namely, appointed that all institutions having for their immediate object the cultivation of science and art should be put under one head direction, be paid out of one treasury, and be relatively conducted in one spirit. His Highness had confided to Privy Councillor von Voigt and me the faithful and judicious fulfilment of these intentions. The institutions above referred to (in no way connected with similar institutions or involved in older relationships, but wholly dependent on the will of the prince, who, out of his own means, defrayed their expenses) comprise in Weimar the library and cabinet of coins, as also the free drawing-school; in Jena, the different museums and other scientific establishments founded since the beginning of the duke's government, and set up without the co-operation of the other high gentlemen supporting the academy. With the union now of all these institutions formerly under separate jurisdictions, it devolved on the officials appointed to superintend them, to determine each time where, according to circumstances, money was to be expended and assistance given to this or that branch, an arrangement which, under immediate supervision and the influence of unprejudiced sentiments, was all the more feasible that the prince did not so much want to hear proposals in respect of what should be done, as to receive reports and obtain personal knowledge of what was being done.

The Jena institutions above specified, and which had been founded and regulated within the last thirty years, having suffered little by the French invasion, we were animated with all the greater zeal to restore them completely to their former vigor and even to erect others in connection with them. The extension, however, of too confined places and the judicious revision of existing arrangements demanded thorough individual inspection and rendered necessary the personal presence of him who was authorized to decide these questions, all the more that no final comprehensive plan could for the present be entertained, and what was needed was tact in dealing with the momentary situation.

In Weimar, again, it became necessary to add to the building of the ducal library, in order to supply new rooms for the ever-increasing stock of books, copperplates, and other articles of art. The Prussian architects Gentz and Rabe, at present in Weimar superintending the completion of the castle, assisted us with their advice, and so arose a building useful as it was both pleasant in outward aspect and well adorned inside.

Yet the extension of rooms and the increase of collections did not absorb all our care. Our treasury, thanks to economy, was now in such a good state that we were enabled to send a young natural-historian, Professor Voigt, at the proper time to France, who, being well instructed and making the best use of his stay in Paris and other places, returned well furnished in every respect.

The theatre, after weathering the light storms which had assailed it, pursued its quiet course. In commotions of this kind, the question never is, Who is to effect some settlement? but, Who is to influence and command? If differences are only composed, everything is just where it was; at most no better, if not worse. The repertory was well provided and pieces were repeated, so that the public became accustomed to, without getting tired of, them. The latest productions, " Antigone " by Rochlitz, Knebel's translation of Alfieri's " Saul," the " Daughter of Jephtha " by Robert, were in turn well received. To favor Werner's considerable talent, a representation of the " Twenty-fourth February " was carefully prepared, while the pleasing, cheerful pieces of Steigentesch insinuated themselves into the favor of the public.

Mademoiselle Häsler, a singer of much promise, and Moltke, a highly agreeable tenor, joined our stage, taking part in the instructions which were faithfully and zealously carried on. Werner attempted tragedies great and small, though there was little hope of seeing them become available for the theatre.

The household musical entertainments through more earnest arrangements grew ever more in value. The chorus of singers under the leadership of Eberwein more and more improved. Thursday evening was rehearsal, after which came mostly a merry repast: Sunday, performance before a large, good company, with breakfast. These private exercises suspended for some time during the summer were at once resumed toward the end of harvest, while, in the meantime, the theatre and the public musical performances were animated and regulated through the accession to us of Orchestra Leader Müller. Nor must it be forgotten what gratification was afforded us in the course of this year by the varied talents of Fräulein aus dem Winkel.

Plastic art, too, to which we were always most heartily devoted, brought us this year the most beautiful fruits.

In Munich were published the hand-drawings of Albrecht Dürer, and now for the first time, it may be said, did we recognize the talent of the highly revered man. Liberated from the painful conscientiousness which cramps both his pictures and his woodcuts, he here moved freely in a field where work was but a subordinate element, where he had but so much space given him to adorn. Here appeared his splendid *naturel* in all its cheerfulness and humor; we had here, indeed, the most beautiful present of vernal lithography.

Painting, too, came to our homes in quite a friendly manner. Kügelgen, the good artist, whose company is so prized by all, stayed with us for several weeks. He painted Wieland's and my portrait from life, Herder's and Schiller's from tradition. Man and painter were united in him, and those pictures, therefore, ever present a double value.

As by his presentation of the human figure Kügelgen directed attention both to his own work and to the subjects of it, so Kaaz exhibited several landscape pictures, in part his own idea from nature, in part in imitation of the best predecessors. The exhibition gave the happiest occasion both here and in Jena for intellectual social unions, and brought people together who otherwise were not wont to meet.

Hirt's work, " Architecture according to the Principles of the Ancients," stimulated us to new attention and interest in this direction, his restoration of the Temple of Diana, at Ephesus, as also of Solomon's Temple, carrying our thoughts back to those past ages. The imagination was compelled to take her flight into ancient history and survey erections now in ruins. We took a lively part in these studies and were incited to similar attempts.

A present of the greatest importance in respect of ancient art was given us by Herr Dr. Stieglitz. He honored us with sulphur casts of his considerable collection of coins, and in this way, as also by the appended list, he did no small service toward research in the field of ancient art.

Our medal departments were at the same time enlarged by medallions of the fifteenth and sixteenth centuries. Studies of them were taken in hand by way of programmes for the " General Jena Literature-Gazette." The able artist Schwerdgeburth with conscientious precision engraved some outline-tables for this purpose.

To all these things was added a collection of metal utensils of unknown shapes dug out at Köstritz, and to which I devoted much attention. I made a great deal of research in reference to them in the older history, particularly in that epoch when Heathendom and Christendom reeled against each other in Franconia and Thüringia. Among the books I then consulted, the " Antiquitates Nordgavienses " were especially remarkable to me, and induced a minute consideration of the heathenish customs which were banned by the first Frankish councils. I convinced myself anew that our heathen forefathers had superstitious customs based on dismal presentiments of nature, but no grimacing idols. A written essay on these subjects was received in a friendly manner by the princely Reuss proprietor, and I was honored in return with a copy of the puzzling antiquities which had been found.

My collection of autographs of important persons was also, this year, considerably increased through the favor of friends. They tended to confirm the belief that the handwriting has a decided relation to the character of the writer and his situation at the time, though one could account to himself and others for the fact more through presentiment than by a clear conception, just as in the case of all physiognomy, which, though it has a genuine basis in nature, fell into discredit through the attempt to make a science of it.

Of events in nature I mention the violent storm of the night of the thirtieth and thirty-first of January, which raged far and wide, and wrought me also a very sensible damage, throwing down an old venerable juniper-tree in my garden on the Stern, and thus tearing from my side a faithful witness of happy days. This tree, the only one in the whole district—in which the juniper is found almost solely in the form of a bush—had probably come down from those times when horticulture was not yet practised. All sorts of fables were abroad respecting it. A former possessor, a schoolman, was said to have been buried under it. Between it and the old house near which it stood, ghosts of maids, it was pretended, had been seen sweeping the place clean. In short, it formed part of the wonderful complexity of that residence in which so many years of my life had passed, and which, through affection and habit, through poetry and illusion, had become so dear to the heart of myself and others.

I had the overthrown tree drawn by a young artist, a drawing still to be seen at the duke's library. Below it is the following inscription:

" The tree above drawn stood in the garden of Herr Privy Councillor von Goethe, on the Stern. Its height from the ground to the point where it parted into two branches was 12 feet, its whole height 43 feet. At the base on the ground it was 17 inches in diameter; at the place where it divided into two branches 15 inches. Each branch 11 inches, and then it narrowed upward, till it ended in tender twigs at the top.

" Of its extreme old age no one ventures to say anything definite. The trunk was dry inside, its wood cut through by horizontal fissures, as is wont to be seen in coals, its color yellowish, worm-eaten.

" The great storm which raged during the night of January 30th-31st, 1809, tore it up. But for this extraordinary event it might have stood for a long time yet. The tops of the branches and the ends of the twigs were entirely green and vital."

1810

An important year with alternations of activity, pleasure, and profit, so that with a superabundant whole I feel embarrassed how to present the parts in due order.

Above everything else the scientific part deserves particular relation. In this direction the beginning of the year was toilsome enough. So great progress had been made with the printing of the " Theory of Colors," that it was deemed not impossible to accomplish the conclusion of it before the festival. I closed the polemical part, as also the history of the eighteenth century. The tables engraved according to my careful drawings were colored, the recapitulation of the whole was finished, and with pleasure the last leaf was seen going to press.

This happened eighteen years after first wakening to a sense of an error of very old date, and in consequence of increasing efforts and the discovery at last of a point round which the whole must cohere. So great was the burden I had hitherto borne that I regarded the sixteenth of May, when I stepped into the carriage to drive to Bohemia, as the happy day of my deliverance. About the results I was little concerned, and did well in being so. Such a complete want of sympathy, such an offering of the cold shoulder, I was still, however, unprepared for. I pass it over in silence, and rather mention how much, in the case of this and of my other scientific and literary works, I owed to an inmate of my house for several years, a fellow-traveller, a fellow-worker, as learned as skilful and friendly, Dr. Friedrich Wilhelm Riemer.

Seeing, however, that once accustomed to toil and travail, one lightly and readily imposes new tasks on himself, there arose in my mind while again surveying the plan of the " Theory of Colors," the kindred thought whether the theory of sound could not also be comprehended under a similar view. And in this way there originated a table in which were represented in three columns, subject, object, and copula.

And seeing that none of our faculties is to be easily enticed out of the way it has once struck in, whether conducting to a true or a false goal, the same mode of representing things was applied to physics universally; the subject in exact consideration of its organs of apprehension and knowledge; the object, over against it, as a something in any case knowable; the appearance, through repeated and manifold experiments, in the middle. In this way a quite peculiar kind of inquiry was prepared.

The experiment, as proof of any subjective judgment, was rejected; there arose what has long been called " Inquiry addressed to Nature." And inasmuch, then, as all invention may be construed to be a wise answer to a rational question, one could convince himself at each step that he was on the right road, seeing, as he did, in particular and in general, only gains on either hand.

How very much, however, my happy surroundings favored my steady assiduity in this study will be seen from the fact that Dr. Seebeck, both at home and abroad, was almost ever by my side. Professor Voigt returned from France and communicated many a beautiful experience and insight. From his lips in our own mode of speaking and thinking we heard of the scientific situation in Paris, and with pleasure we acknowledged that he had made a good use of his time both for himself and us.

As to cultivation of music for the good of the theatre, both in the first and last months of the year, I have shortly to report that the volunteer band continued their practice regularly. On Thursday evening we had rehearsal before some friends; on Sunday morning, performance before a large company. Theatre singers, younger and older, choristers, and amateurs took part. Eberwein conducted these performances in a masterly manner. Pieces for several voices by Zelter and other great Italian composers were introduced and anew impressed on our memories. Pleasure and profit, practice and progress, went hand in hand.

The fact that the rehearsal was kept completely separate from the performance entirely excluded all slovenly dilettanteism which will content itself with trying its parts in the very moment of the performance, nay, will leave unsettled to the last moment the question what it can and is to perform.

Thursdays were critical and didactic; Sundays, days of fruition and enjoyment for everyone.

Toward the end of the year public entertainments could be given in the theatre by this company. Such musical pieces were performed as the public have otherwise no opportunity of hearing, and from which every cultivated man should draw, at least once in his life, refreshment and enjoyment. As an example I mention " Johanna Sebus," composed by Zelter, a piece which leaves an ineffaceable impression on all hearts.

The instructions were commensurately carried on with the reciting players; with the most instructed only in the case of new pieces, with the juniors on each fresh practice of an old part. This latter point is, properly, the most important part of the instruction; only by such repetition and revision will a harmonious ensemble be maintained.

" Zaïre," translated by Peucer, again proved the ripeness of our *personnel* in pure recitation and declamation. The first rehearsal was so perfect that a cultivated public might have been present at it all through.

The " Twenty-fourth February," by Werner, performed on this day, was a complete triumph of perfect representation. The dreadful aspect of the material vanished before the purity and precision of the performance. The attentive connoisseur found nothing wanting that was desirable.

Shifting tableaux were represented to us by the distinguished talent of Frau Hendel-Schütz. Earnest representation in public, and cheerful, jocular, nay, comic entertainment in private, afforded new views of art and a great deal of enjoyment.

The presentation toward the end of the year of the opera " Achill," by Brizzi, in the Italian language, opened up to us a new field, and, at the same time, under the most earnest and faithful exertions of the actor Wolff and his highly improved talent, the " Resolute Prince " was brought near the longed-for performance.

In respect of plastic art, there likewise occurred a remarkable epoch. The brothers Boisserée sent me from Heidelberg, by the hands of the bookseller Zimmer, who was travelling to the Leipsic fair, their precious drawings of the cathedral. With pleasure I recalled the feelings of those years when the Strasburg minister forced admiration from me and impelled me to strange, enthusiastic, yet deeply felt utterances. The study of that more antique, peculiar architecture was now again seriously and integrally revived in me, while this important subject excited the interest also of the Weimar lovers of art.

A fit which came over me to draw sketches of landscapes I did not try to throw off. During walks in spring, especially near Jena, I seized hold of some subject or other suited to a picture and then endeavored at home to reduce it to paper. In equal measure my imagination became easily excited by narratives, so that I was at once seized with a longing to design places described in conversation. This experience continued vital in me throughout the whole of my journey and up till my return, when it left me, never to visit me more.

Nor in the course of this year was there any want of opportunity of dedicating many a poem and many a representation to festal days. The " Romantic Poesy," a great masquerade act, was dedicated to the thirtieth of January, and repeated on the sixteenth of February, on which occasion there figured a characteristic row of Russian tribes, while the piece was likewise accompanied by poetry and song. The presence of the Empress of Austria in Carlsbad called forth agreeable services at my hands, and many more smaller poems unfolded themselves in private.

Hackert's biography was, meanwhile, earnestly taken in hand, a work which cost much time and trouble, in which, however, the remembrance of our departed friend sustained me. For although the papers intrusted to me were important and furnished sufficient material, the dissimilarity in its form was difficult to master, resisting re-fusion into a coherent whole.

Dissipations of the journey, the passing sympathy of friends I met in smaller compositions, put me in mind of the many details still detached and awaiting conjunction with each other, in order to present themselves partly anew, partly for the second time, to the public. The thought of the " Travels," so naturally following the " Apprenticeship," matured more and more, occupying me in odd hours which could not otherwise have been utilized.

With respect to the copyright of authors, it could not but
be deemed remarkable that Minister Portalis should ask me
whether I could give my consent to a Cologne bookseller's reprinting the " Elective Affinities." I answered, " With all my
heart, as far as myself is concerned," but referred the matter
to the lawful publisher. So much higher even then stood the
French in their views of intellectual possession, and the equal
rights of the higher and lower classes, a height to which the
good Germans will not so soon elevate themselves.

In Carlsbad I contemplated the waste caused by the spring
with great interest. From the back windows of the White Stag
I carefully drew this strange situation from reality, and committed myself to the remembrance of many years' considerations
and inferences, of which I must here make but brief mention.

<h1 style="text-align:center">1811</h1>

This year distinguishes itself by persistent outward activity.
The " Life of Philipp Hackert " was getting printed; the papers
put into my hands carefully edited according to each particular
requirement. By this work I was again attracted to the South;
the events I had passed through in Hackert's presence or in his
neighborhood became active in my imagination; I had reason
to ask why I should not undertake for myself what I was doing
for another. Before the completion of that volume I therefore
turned to my own earliest history. Here, to be sure, I found I
had delayed the task too long. It should have been taken in
hand during my mother's life-time, when I should myself have
been so much nearer the scenes of my childhood, and, with the
help of her powerful memory, completely transplanted thither.
Now, however, I had to conjure up by my own unaided exertions those vanished ghosts, and with toil and contrivance collect many a help to memory, thus furnishing myself, as it were,
with a necessary magic apparatus. I had to represent the development of a child grown to be considerable, how, in given
circumstances, the bent of my genius had asserted itself, presenting the history in such a way, moreover, as to satisfy the
penetrating student of human nature.

In this sense, modestly enough, I called such a work executed
with careful fidelity " Poetry and Truth," most inwardly convinced that man in presence, much more in remembrance, fash-
ions and moulds the outward world according to his peculiarities.

This business plunging me for a long time in historical
studies, in recalling places and persons, so absorbed me when
at rest and when in motion, at home and abroad, that my actual

12

situation assumed a subordinate character, although wherever
and whenever summoned out by the demands of life I at once
reasserted myself there and then with my full force and with
all my senses.

For the theatre much was done, the ever-rising talent of the
excellent Wolff appearing in the best light. The " Resolute
Prince " was acted with general applause, and quite a new province was thus conquered for the stage. Wolff appeared also as
" Pygmalion," and his representation made one forget how in-
admissible and unsatisfactory this piece is.

Alfieri's " Saul," translated by Von Knebel, the " Daughter
of Jephtha," and " Tasso " were repeated. " Romeo and Juliet " was prepared for the theatre, a task in which both Riemer
and Wolff zealously co-operated. For the immediate future,
also, Calderon's " Life a Dream " was prepared.

Mademoiselle Franck, from Mannheim, earned as Emme-
line and Fanchon great applause. Brizzi repeated his visit.
The representation of " Achilli " again went its brilliant
course. The second great " Opera Ginevra " could not come
up with the former. Here, too, was verified the old lesson that
a worthless text will secretly work the ruin of the music and
representation. A villain and traitor everywhere, at last a sorry
figure, worst of all on the theatre where the course of his vil-
lanies is unravelled and displayed before our eyes.

The newly built theatre at Halle afforded all the advantages
of the Lauchstädt one. Its dedication gave occasion for a prologue which met with a good reception.

I was not so happy in respect of music. I became sensible
that my house-chorus, as I had ventured a year ago to call it,
was inwardly in danger of breaking up. No one else perceived
any change, but certain elective affinities had begun to operate
in it which at once gave me apprehension, though it was out of
my power to provide a remedy. At the beginning of the year
things still went their usual course, yet no more with the same
regular weekly sequence. We still produced genuine old pieces,
while several new canons by Ferrari sustained the pleasure of
the singers and provoked the applause of the hearers. I had,
however, already resigned myself to the loss, and when, at the
end of April, as I was about to enter on my summer tour, a break
had to occur, I resolved not to resume the course. This was
a very great loss for me, and I had to look earnestly about after
compensation elsewhere.

While this edifying entertainment was still active I wrote the
cantata " Rinaldo " for his Serene Highness Prince Friedrich
of Gotha. It was composed by the meritorious leader of the
orchestra, Winter. Executed by the graceful tenor voice of

he prince and accompanied by choruses it afforded a beautiful
enjoyment.

Particular attention was paid to older plastic arts. Meyer
labored without intermission at the history of arts, and all investigations prompted by this study furnished material for
nstructive conversation. Mionet's plaster-of-Paris casts of old
Greek coins as the worthiest documents of that time opened the
most assured prospects.

The pleasure of realizing the past continued operative, and
with the help of a good calculator we endeavored to re-erect the
funeral-pile of Hephæstion, especially, however, the huge am-
phitheatre in the midst of which it was set up, and to which the
walls of Babylon had to contribute earth and rubbish, as also
bricks for the *rogus*. The whole of the Grecian army looked
without inconvenience on the solemnity.

We had next many centuries to shoot across when Dr. Sulpiz
Boisserée visited us with an important series of drawings and
copperplates calling our art contemplations into the Middle
Ages. We lingered there very willingly, while a well-considered series of accordant monuments lying before us transported
us into a time gloomy, no doubt, yet worthy of honor and sympathy. The lively interest of the exhibitor and his thorough
knowledge of the conditions and intentions of that period were
communicated to us. As by a change of the theatrical decorations you were here carried away pleasurably into times and
places in the irrevocable past. In this way we entered into an
alliance of mind and heart with our noble guest—an alliance
which promised to be fruitful of consequences for the rest of
our lifetime.

Dr. Sulpiz Boisserée had also brought with him drawings
by Cornelius, illustrative of the " Nibelungen " poems. Their
antique brave sense, expressed with a technical skill quite incredible, excited our high admiration.

As an echo of our former Weimar Art Exhibition, and in consequence of good relations with living artists originating in that
undertaking, a great deal in this department was sent us. The
meritorious Nauwerck at Ratzeburg sent drawings and paintings. Drawings left by Kaaz, the too-early departed landscape
painter, were forwarded to us. Princess Caroline, of Mecklenburg, herself possessing a fine sense for landscape drawing, and
a graceful hand in execution, procured a selection from both the
above sets.

We also became acquainted for the first time with the hopeful
talent of a man who died in his youth, of the name of Wehle,
whose artistic remains had been bought by Baron Schönberg-
Rothschönberg. Both in sketches and in completed designs

after nature there was here revealed a happy artistic glance into
the world, and the interest in these leaves was enhanced by the
strange foreign localities represented. He had penetrated as
far as Tiflis, and objects distant as well as near he had committed to paper with characteristic ease.

In reference to scientific studies we were disposed in some
measure to discretion. Still, at intervals, I studied the history
of physics, in order to bring home to myself to the utmost degree possible the course of this highest science, for only through
comprehension of the past is the present intelligible. Like
every human institution and arrangement, a science is a monstrous juxtaposition of truth and falsehood, of freedom and
necessity, of sanity and disease. All that we perceive from day
to day we can yet in the end regard but as symptoms which, in
order to genuine instruction, must be reduced to their physiological and pathological principles.

I withdrew myself personally from experiments of every
kind, but an Indian white fire, kindled on the Landgrafenberg
by Professor Döbereiner, lighting up the valley, and especially
the mountains on the other side, formed a highly surprising
phenomenon.

After this splendid effulgence, the shining comet which next
riveted our attention could be seen for a long time, serving to
delight our eyes and summon out our inward faculty into the
all-wide world.

My stay in Carlsbad this year assumed quite a different character from that of former years. The love of dogging nature
of drawing and copying, had wholly forsaken me; nothing in
this direction would any longer succeed with me; and as for
rummaging among and hammering all too well known masses
of rocks, I was completely tired of it. Müller, far advanced in
years, no longer stimulated me, and with indifference I looked
at the efforts made to wrest the fountain into its old channel
consoled by the remark that though people were fond of flattering old-established prejudices they yet longingly desired to prevent a like evil.

In the company of jovial friends of both sexes, I gave myself
up to a day of dissipation. The usual promenades and carriage
drives offered sufficient scope for excursions on all sides.
Places of pleasure, near as well as distant, were visited, while
a new resort was added to the number through an almost ridiculous accident. In Weheditz, a village over the Eger, and
lying toward Dalwitz, a peasant, having carted goods to Hungary and returned laden with new, savory wines, had set up a
tavern. The low value of the paper money, standing in the
proportion of almost ten to one, enabled you to get a bottle of

good Hungarian wine for a few pence. The novelty, the rarity, the very inconvenience of the house, joined to the cheapness of the wine, gave a certain charm to the affair. We got out, laughed, made merry with ourselves and others, enjoying ever more of the insinuating wine than was altogether good for us. In reference to such a pilgrimage, the following anecdote went abroad. Three aged men went to Weheditz to drink wine:

Colonel Otto, aged . . .	87 years
Lithographer Müller, aged . .	84 "
An Erfurt man, aged . . .	82 "
	253 years

They caroused lustily, and only the last on his way home betrayed some traces of tipsiness. The two others seized their younger boon companion by the arms and brought him safe back to his house.

Such a general frolic was favored by the great depreciation of paper money. A patent was issued which confused everybody. The existing notes had lost all value; new, so-called anticipation notes were expected. Sellers and receivers could not keep pace with the declining value of the paper. Buyers and spenders also lost by it; they squandered away their groschen, and so gradually got rid of their dollars. The situation was of a kind to put the best head at fault.

The day, however, is too long to be passed without some useful employment, and therefore, with Riemer's assistance and by dint of constant conversation on the subject, I continued my task of the "Autobiography," writing out the immediate matter on hand in full and drawing up plans of the more distant parts. In the way of reading and study, too, I had the shorter writings of Plutarch always by me, while the great confluence of important persons in this place, enjoying unlimited leisure, and delighting to converse on the subjects they had most at heart, could not fail to supply me with a great deal of experience and instruction.

As to persons who this year called on me in Weimar, I find the following mentioned: Engelhard, architect from Cassel, on his way to Italy. It was asserted that he had been the prototype of my artist in the "Elective Affinities." Raabe, as skilful as he is polite, stayed some time with us, and painted my portrait in oil on a copperplate. Ritter O'Hara, the best of company, a good host, and a man of honor, chose Weimar for some time as his place of residence. The stories of his many years' wanderings, which he knew how to season with jests on himself, diffused a pleasant confidential tone round his table.

It was no small merit on his side that his cook prepared capital beefsteaks, and that his banquets were crowned with the most genuine mocha coffee. Lefevre, French secretary to the embassy, coming from Cassel, and introduced by Baron Reinhard, resuscitated to our most agreeable entertainment French speech, poetry, and history. Professor Thiersch paid us a passing visit, leaving behind him, and also taking with him, it is to be hoped, good impressions. The married couple Von Arnim took up quarters for some time with us. Our old confidential relations with each other were at once renewed; but through this very freedom and unreservedness of communication there came to light a difference which had developed since our former unanimity. We parted in hopes of closer union at a future time.

Of important books whose influence was lasting, I read St. Croix's " Examen des Historiens d'Alexandre," Heeren's " Ideas on the Politics, Intercourse, and Trade of the most distinguished Peoples of the Ancient World," and Dr. Gerando's " Histoire de la Philosophie." They all forced the reader to extend and widen his views in the domain of past times.

Jacobi, on " Divine Things," made on me an impression the very opposite of beneficial. How could the book of a friend so dear to my heart be grateful to me, a book endeavoring to prove that nature hides God? With the sincere, deep, structural, and habitual sentiment and thought of my whole nature, a sentiment, a thought impossible to call in question, the very basis of my existence, namely, that God is in nature and nature in God—with this as a primary and ultimate fact—how was it possible that such a detached, unsupported, lifeless judgment should not alienate me forever from the noblest man whose heart I reveringly loved? Yet I did not give way to the feeling of pain and vexation, but turned for relief to my old asylum, to Spinoza, in whose ethics I found daily entertainment for several weeks, and, as since the date of my last acquaintance with him, my culture had been deepened and purified, I now found, to my admiration, a great deal in him new and unexpected, exercising on me an influence fresh and all its own.

Umaroff's project for an Asiatic academy attracted me to those regions whither, without that attraction, I was for a considerable time disposed to wander. Hebel's new " Alemannian Poems " gave me the agreeable impression we always feel on being introduced to family relations. This was not the case with Von Hagen's "Book of Heroes"; here an all-transforming period had intervened between me and the book. Busching's " Poor Henry," a poem considered by itself highly valuable, also pained me both physically and æsthetically. It is scarcely possible to get rid of the loathing we feel toward a leprous man,

for whom the bravest girl sacrifices herself; in fact, a century
in which the most repulsive disease had continually to furnish
motives for passionate deeds of love and daring fills us with
aversion. The horrible disease which in the above poem is
made the basis of heroic acts, works, on me at least, so repul-
sively that I feel myself infected by the very touch of the book.

By a peculiar accident there next came to my hands a work
from which an immoral infection might have been dreaded.
Seeing, however, that from a certain presumptuous self-conceit
a man feels more confident in guarding against spiritual than
bodily influences, I read the volumes with pleasure as also with
haste, seeing they had to be returned in a short time. They
were the "Novelle galanti," by Verrocchio. In poetical and
historical value they are about equal to those of the Abbate
Casti, though artistically Casti is more compressed and more
master of his material. On the suggestion of a friend, I immediately thereafter took up the "Novelle del Bandello." "The
Adventures of the Knights Grieux and Manon l'Escot," as of
a kindred nature, were next tackled. Still, to do myself justice,
I must testify that after all this course of wicked reading, I
returned at last with innocent enjoyment to the "Vicar of
Wakefield."

1812

The family of Kobler opened the year with highly graceful
ballets. "Romeo and Juliet," next "Turandot" are repeated,
the representation of "Life a Dream" prepared. The exertions required for the worthy representation of such pieces gave
new occasion for deeper and more searching study and raised
our acting altogether to a higher level. A young actor of the
name of Durand joined us, furnished with all the accomplishments heart could wish in a young amateur, except that one
missed a certain inward fire, the enthusiasm which should have
carried him out of himself and forced him on the public com-
pelling their sympathy and recognition. It was, however, hoped
he would soon himself become sensible of this defect.

Theodor Körner had come forward as a dramatic author.
His "Toni," "Zriny," and "Rosamunde," as echoes of a period
shortly past, were easily taken up and rendered by the actors,
and being in style and sentiment in sympathy with the public
were also favorably received by them. For higher purposes
Calderon's "Great Zenobia" was studied, and through Griesen's
translation "The Wonder-Working Magus" was brought
home to us.

Wolff and Riemer drew up a plan for the representation of
"Faust," causing the poet to occupy himself anew with this

subject, to bethink himself of many an intermediary scene, even to design decorations and other requirements. The above-mentioned friends, with their unceasing activity, likewise planned a recast of " Egmont," restoring the Duchess of Parma, whom they would on no account dispense with. The presence of Madame Schönberger gave rise to the happiest representations. Iffland closed the year in the most successful manner, appearing in several parts. From the twentieth of December to the end of the year the following pieces were acted : " Clementine," " Self-Control," " The Jew," " The Artist's Earthly Pilgrimage," " Don Ranudo," " The Poor Poet," " The Merchant of Venice," " The good-hearted Roisterer."

The following actors from our well-appointed company took parts along with him, and their performance, as a whole, having done no dishonor to his high art, we mention their names. Gentlemen : Durand, Deny, Graff, Genest, Haide, Lorzing, Malkolmi, Oels, Unzelmann, Wolff. Ladies : Beck, Eberwein, Engels, Lorzing, Wolff.

The second volume of the " Biography " was prosecuted and concluded, the third volume commenced, planned as a whole, and some pieces of it completed. In consequence of the Mosaic history having been introduced into the first volume, I took up from old papers my account of the " Wanderings of the Children of Israel through the Wilderness." The work was, however, set aside to be used for other purposes.

Three poems for their imperial Majesties, written in the name of the Carlsbad citizens, furnished me with an honorable and pleasant occasion of once more trying my hand at verse.

On the field of plastic art much that was favorable occurred. The news of the discovery at Ægina opened out new prospects for the history of art, on which, with our friend Meyer, who was constantly advancing in his pursuits, we instructed and delighted ourselves.

The thought of supplying from the stock of old medals we had in hand the remembrance of lost works of art had so great a charm for us, and had, moreover, such a solid basis in fact, that, following the lines marked out in the essay on " Myron's Cow," we zealously endeavored to restore the Olympian Jupiter, the Polycletian Juno, and many another worthy image.

A little silver centaur, about a span long and admirably executed, called forth a lively dispute whether it was antique or modern. The Weimar lovers of art, convinced that in such things there was no possibility of unanimity and decision, admired it, edified themselves by it, and then took sides with that party which contended that it was old and dating from the time of the emperors.

I acquired an old Florentine copy of Michael Angelo's " Sitting Moses," not quite an ell high, cast in bronze, and by burins and other sculpturing instruments most diligently elaborated to the utmost completeness; a beautiful monument of careful, almost contemporaneous copying of a highly valuable work of art of that period, and an example of how a little image which, though it cannot, of course, represent the greatness of the original, may yet, by elaborate execution in details, attain quite a peculiar value.

Natural science had many a conquest to boast of. Ramdohr, on the " Digestive Organs of Insects," confirmed us in our views as to the gradual development of organic life. Otherwise, however, attention was more directed to the general field of natural science.

Dr. Seebeck, ever studious of chromatic matters, tackled the second Newtonian experiment, which in my polemics I had touched only so far as necessary. He elaborated the subject in my presence, and many important results were achieved, showing, among other things, how that doctrine of Newton's, when once you pass from primary prisms to lenses, becomes entangled in an almost inextricable labyrinth.

We were called to wide contemplation and to the elevation of our minds by the writings of Jordanus Brunus, of Nola, though, to be sure, the task of separating the solid gold and silver from the mass of metal layers so unequally furnished with the precious material, was almost more than human powers were equal to; and whoever feels innately impelled in that direction, would do better to turn himself immediately to nature than exhaust his strength in grappling with the strata, perhaps the dross-heaps, of past centuries.

In Carlsbad you found yourself again swept away by the current of geological studies. The extension of the space round the New Well, a bold undertaking, perhaps inconceivable in former times, confirmed us in the views we had hitherto entertained. A remarkable stone was also there obtained, the strong water of the Tepl and the violent ebullition of the hot wells appeared simultaneously, circumstances which seemed to point to the hypothesis that this great operation of nature was to be regarded as a vast galvanic experiment.

From Teplitz we visited Dr. Stolz, in Aussig, and drew instruction from his excellent fund of knowledge and his collections. Fossil bones in Bohemia were also the subject of conversation.

Home again, we stayed first in Jena, to give our glad attention to the museums there on their first entrance on a favorable epoch. Her imperial Highness the hereditary princess destined a considerable sum to this purpose, and the mechanician Körner was preparing an air-pump for the physical cabinet. Other instruments and provisions were likewise being fitted in, and to gain the more space the upper rooms of the Jena castle were arranged for the reception of a part of the museum collection. Von Trebra honored us with plates of remarkable transition stones, as documents of his former geognostic wanderings on the Harz. His work, "Observations in the Interior of the Mountains," is again taken in hand, giving rise to conversations on older and more recent views.

The so-called sulphur springs in Berka, on the Ilm, above Weimar, the drying of the pond in which they sometimes appeared, and their utilization for a watering-place occasion the resuscitation of geognostic and chemical studies. On this occasion Professor Döbereiner took a most lively, cordial, and influential part.

1813

The presence of Brizzi had again infused new life into the opera and made operatic representation in Italian possible. No singer is an entire stranger to this language, for he must frequently exercise his talent in it, and in general any person whom nature has favored with a fine ear will not find Italian difficult to learn. For greater convenience and more rapid progress, a teacher of the language was engaged. Iffland's presence, too, roused the powers of our actors to the utmost, and they were all full of emulation to stand worthily by his side. To anyone who saw far enough into the matter it was plain that the harmony and unity of our company made it completely easy and convenient for this great actor to carry out all his own ideas here to their utmost scope, without stumbling on any impediment. After his departure everything was continued in the same earnest and faithful spirit. Every artistic tendency, however, was so far lamed by the dread of war tumults pressing ever closer on us that we had to content ourselves with keeping within the bounds of the repertory we already had.

My poetic gains this year were not rich. Three romances, "The Dance of the Dead," the "Faithful Eckart," and "The Walking Bell," deserve some mention. "The Lion's Seat," an opera founded on old tradition, which I afterward embodied in the ballad "Die Kinder, sie hören es gerne," came to a standstill and stuck there. The epilogue to "Essex" may also be mentioned.

The third volume of my "Biography" was finished and printed, and, in spite of some untoward external circumstances, enjoyed a good effect. The Italian journal was more minutely gone into, and preparations made for its elaboration. A composition to the " Memory of Wieland " was read in the masonic mourning lodge, and for friendly communication sent to press.

In the field of literature, a great deal old, modern, and of near interest was taken up and prosecuted more or less to some definite goal. Here is specially to be mentioned the study devoted to Shakespeare in relation to his predecessors.

Geographical maps with a view to the sensuous representations of the distribution of languages over the world were, with the participation of Wilhelm von Humboldt, elaborated, defined, and colored. In the same way I was induced by Alexander von Humboldt to draw a comparative landscape picture of the mountain masses of the old and new world.

It will now be opportune briefly to express how I endeavored to earn the happiness of living in intimate communication with the most distinguished men of my time.

From the standpoint where God and nature had been pleased to place me, and where, next, I did not neglect to exert my faculties according to circumstances, I looked all about me to mark where great tendencies were in operation and lastingly prevailed. I, for my part, by study, by performances of my own, by collections and experiments, endeavored to reach forth toward those tendencies, and faithfully toiling upward to the level of the achievements I could not myself have accomplished, in all simplicity, innocent of all feeling of rivalry or envy, with perfectly fresh and vital sense, I presumed to appropriate to myself what was offered to the century by its best minds. My way, therefore, ran parallel with very many beautiful undertakings till it would next turn toward others. The new accordingly was never foreign to me, nor was I ever in danger either of adopting it in a state of unpreparedness, or, by reason of old-fashioned prejudice, rejecting it.

As indication of my attention to the most curious things, I may mention that I brought copy-tracings of pictures out of an old manuscript of the " Sachsenspiegel " (a German law-book of the Middle Ages) to the hands of connoisseurs and amateurs, who then made the most praiseworthy use of them, and quite cleverly and convincingly interpreted the symbolism of an age completely childish in respect to plastic art.

To mention here the most recent of all occurrences, Abbate Monti, remembering former relations, sent me his translation of the " Iliad."

As art treasures there arrived at my house gypsum casts of Jupiter's colossal bust, small hermæ of an Indian Bacchus of red, antique marble, gypsum casts of Peter Vischer's statues of the apostles on the monument of St. Sebaldus, at Nürnberg.

Papal coins in particular enriched one of my most precious collections, doubly gratifying, partly because they filled up gaps, partly because they in general gave excellent insight into the history of plastic art and sculpture.   Friend Meyer continued his " History of Art "; Philostrat's pictures shone with their original splendor; Heine's works on that subject were studied; the colossal statue of Domitian, described by Statius, it was likewise endeavored to realize, restore, and set in its place.   The philologists Riemer and Hand were politely ready with their counsel.   Visconti's " Iconographie Grecque " was again taken in hand, while a highly welcome present carried me immediately into those old times.   Herr Bröndsted presented to me, in name of those who had travelled to Greece on so important a mission, with a palm branch from the Acropolis, fashioned into a walking-stick, a valuable large silver coin taking the place of the knob.

To hold one to correct views of these objects, opportunity was found of leisurely contemplating the Dresden collection of the originals, as also of the casts.

The mastery which modern times have acquired in many branches of art was next feelingly regarded.   On observing the Ruysdael works a small essay was penned, " The Landscape Painter as Poet."

Of contemporaries, opportunity occurred of making acquaintance with the works of Kersting, and one had cause to value them highly.

Natural sciences, especially geology, did not fall into neglect. From Teplitz I visited the tin works of Graussen, Zinnwalde, and Altenberg.   In Bilin I had the pleasure of being conducted by the experienced, clear-thinking Dr. Reuss; under his guidance I reached the foot of the Bilin rock, which, based in a mass of clinkstone, immediately towers up in the form of columns. A slight change in the conditions may easily have effected this change in its structure.

The garnets which are to be found in the neighborhood of Bilin, their assortment and preparation, were likewise made fully known to me.

A visit of Dr. Stolz, in Aussig, was just as interesting on another side.   You here become sensible of the great merit of a man who first makes himself thoroughly conversant with all the features of his district, and then, in a trice, communicates to the stranger visiting it more knowledge than a lengthy residence would have enabled him to acquire.

As to my manifold study of books, Trebra's " Observations of the Interior of Mountains," and Charpentier's works fall here to be mentioned.   It was my way to attend especially to the views and convictions of contemporaries, and all the more when they did not chime with the penny whistle of the day.

The sulphur bath intended to be established at Berka gave rise to many discussions. We attempted what was seen beforehand to be practicable, and what was not to be achieved we let alone.

The entoptic colors excited attention. Independently of this I had written a paper on "Iceland Crystal."

By way of conclusion I remark that the instruments for the Jena observatory were ordered and Kluge's work on "Animal Magnetism" considered.

Important persons were met by me. In Tharand, Ranger of the Forest Cotta; in Teplitz, Dr. Kapp, Count Brühl, General Theilmann; Captain of the Horse Von Schwanenfeld, Professor Dittrich of the gymnasium at Komotau, the grand duchesses Catharine and Maria.

After the battle of Leipsic, I met in Weimar: Wilhelm von Humboldt, Count Metternich, State-Chancellor Von Hardenberg, Prince Paul of Würtemberg, Prince August of Prussia, the Electoral-Princess of Hesse, Professor of Chemistry John Hofrath Rochlitz.

I must here call to mind a peculiarity in my mode of procedure. When any momentous threatening event loomed forth in the political world I obstinately turned my mind to a subject as remote as possible from such a consideration. This will account for the fact that from the time of my return from Carlsbad, and onward, I set myself earnestly to the study of the Chinese world. Having regard to the unhappy performance of "Essex," which had been extorted from me, and to please the actress Wolff, as also to make her fatal part in some measure brilliant, I wrote, intermediately, the "Epilogue" to that play on the very day of the battle of Leipsic.

On behalf of my own "Biography" I extracted from the Frankfort "Gelehrten Anzeigen" of the years 1772 and 1773 the reviews which, in whole or in part, belonged to me. To transport myself the more into those times, I studied Möser's "Fantasias," then Klinger's works, which called very characteristically to mind the indefatigable activity of a quite peculiar nature. For more general instruction in æsthetic matters I continued the assiduous reading of Ernesti's "Technology of Greek and Roman Oratory," and contemplated myself there with a view to my own edification and entertainment, in no little degree composed by the fact here presenting itself as a striking proof of man's narrow limits—the inevitable recurrence, namely, after a couple of thousand years of the same virtues and faults in my own writings.

Of events I remark for the present: the French ambassador is seized unawares in Gotha and escapes. A small body of Prussians occupies Weimar and will have us believe we are safe under its protection. The volunteers behave badly, and do not ingratiate themselves into people's favor. I depart; events on the way. In Dresden, Russians are quartered; at night torch-illumination. Likewise the King of Prussia. In Teplitz, confidential communications. Provisional indications of a general union against Napoleon. Battle of Lützen. The French in Dresden. Armistice. Stay in Bohemia. Sham manœuvres between Bilin, Osseck, and Duchs. Manifold events in Dresden. Return to Weimar. The latest French guard retires. General Travers, whom I had known as the attendant of the King of Holland, is, to his extreme wonder, quartered in my house. The French all march forward. Battle of Leipsic. The Cossacks slink hither; the French ambassador here gets taken; the French pushing hither from Apolda and Umpferstedt. The town is fallen upon from Ettersburg. The Austrians march in.

1814

In the theatre was represented Müllner's "Guilt." Such a piece, whatever else may be thought of it, is so far of great advantage to the stage that it compels every member to exert himself to the utmost if he is to do any justice whatever to the part he plays.

The happy solution of the problem imposed on us by the above piece encouraged us to several excellent representations of "Romeo and Juliet," "Egmont," Wallenstein's "Camp," and "Death." The change of parts which occurred in these pieces was turned to careful account in the way of instruction, in order to bring players of different degrees of cultivation into harmony with each other.

In looking about for fresh, foreign, and at the same time important pieces, something good, it was thought, could be made out of the plays of Fouqué, Arnim, and other humorists, their frequently very happy subjects, to a certain degree also dramatically favorable, being deemed capable of adaptation to the stage. The enterprise, however, did not succeed, any more than in the case of the earlier works of Tieck and Brentano.

The visit of Prince Radziwill likewise stirred up a longing difficult to appease. His composition to Faust, full of soul and enthusiasm though it was, did not inspire us with more than a distant hope of seeing the strange piece on the stage.

Our theatrical company had the pleasure this time, as hitherto, of giving representations throughout the summer in Halle.

The worthy Reil, to whom the stage there owed its origin, had
died; a prelude was desired by way of paying the last honors
to the excellent man. During my stay in spring at Berka on
the Ilm, I thought out a plan for such a prelude. When, however, unexpectedly, on the challenge of Iffland, I undertook the
" Awaking of the Epimenides," the piece in honor of Reil was
handed over for elaboration to Riemer. Leader of the Orchestra Weber visited me on the subject of the composition of the
" Epimenides," on which we came to an agreement.

The monodrama " Proserpina " was, according to Eberwein's
composition, studied with Madame Wolff, and a short but highly
significant performance prepared, in which recitation, declamation, mimicry, and plastic representation of noble figures
vied with each other; at the end a great tableau representing
Pluto's kingdom and crowning the whole—all this left behind
a very favorable impression.

The " Sages' Banquet," a dramatic-lyric pleasantry, in which
the different philosophers facetiously answer or rather evade
those importunate metaphysical questions the common people
often dun them with—not suited for the theatre, but very well
adapted for social music—had, for fear of giving offence, to be
disposed of among the " Paralipomena."

Musical enlivenment through Zelter's presence and Inspector
Schützen's rendering of Bach's sonatas.

Celebrations in honor of the arrival of the duke from the
happy campaign induced preparations for the architectural ornament of the streets. Editing of a collection of poems and
their publication afterward under the title of " Welcome."

Meanwhile the new edition of my works was prepared. The
third volume of the " Biography " was published by the time
of the festival. The " Italian Journey " proceeded apace; the
" West-Eastern Divan " was laid. The journey to the Rhine,
Main, and Necker lands yielded a rich booty in knowledge of
personages, localities, art works, and art remains.

In Heidelberg, at Boisserée's, study of the Netherland School,
pictures of that class being collected there. Study of the Cologne Cathedral, and other old edifices after sketches and plans.
The latter study continued in Darmstadt, at Moller's. The
old high-German School in Frankfort, at Schütz's. Of this
rich material in respect of men, districts, works of art, and art
remains, communication is made in the periodical " Art and
Antiquity on the Rhine and Main."

Natural science was greatly promoted by the polite communications of Cramer, chief councillor of mines at Wiesbaden, on
minerals and by his notes on mining in the Westerwalde. The
Darmstadt Museum. Stay with Privy-Councillor von Leonhard, in Hanau. On my return fears about Jena.

Of public events I remark the capture of Paris, and that I was present at the first celebration of the eighteenth of October in Frankfort.

1815

As early as last year the complete poems of " Hafiz " in Von Hammer's translation came into my hands, and if formerly I could make nothing of occasional translations in periodicals of detached pieces of this splendid poet, the · whole now produced all the greater impression on me, and I found myself urgently impelled to productive efforts in order to assert my own genius in conflict with this new mighty force. The German translation unsluiced the full tide of its influence on me, and everything of kindred sense latent in me started up in emphatic response, and with all the greater impetuosity that it had now become a poignant necessity for me to fly the actual world and escape into an ideal world more conformable with my taste, capacity, and will.

Not wholly a stranger to the peculiarities of the East, I turned to the language to naturalize myself, as far as indispensable, to the air of that clime; I turned to the written characters themselves, with their idiosyncrasies and ornaments. I betook myself to the " Moallakats," some of which I had translated immediately after their appearance. I familiarized myself with the state of the Bedouins. " Mohamed," by Oelsner, with whom I had long stood on terms of friendship, again came to my assistance. My relation to Von Diez was tightened. The book " Cabus " opened to me the theatre of foreign modes of life in a highly important time—a time having some resemblance to our own—when a prince had ample cause to instruct his son in a lengthy treatise how, under the worst of fates, one may get through the world with a business or trade. " Medschnun " and " Leila," as examples of a boundless love, were again brought home to my heart and imagination; the pure religion of the Parsees was raised out of its decline and restored to its beautiful simplicity; the travellers Pietro della Valle, Tavernier, Chardian, long before studied, were again carefully perused. The material thus accumulated, and my knowledge increased to such an extent that at last I was able without misgiving to seize hold of and appropriate out of the Eastern stores what at any moment I might need. Diez was politeness itself in answering my curious questions; Lorsbach highly sympathetic and helpful, bringing me into contact also with Silvestre de Sacy; and although these men could not distantly conjecture, far less comprehend, my proper drift, they all contributed toward speedily making me at home in a province into which

I had occasionally sallied, but in which I had never stayed long enough to look seriously about me. Von Hammer's translation being daily in my hands, and becoming, indeed, for me the book of books, I did not fail to pick many a jewel out of its treasures.

The political heaven seemed, meanwhile, gradually to clear up. The wish to roam about in the open world, especially in my free native district, to which my mind now fondly turned, impelled me to a journey. The blithe air and the nimble motion stimulated several growths in me of the new Eastern genus. A healthful stay at a watering-place, rural residence in a district I had roamed all over in youthful days, meetings with dear friends of cultivated mind—all this quickened and enriched me, raising me to the happy state which every man of feeling will find reflected in the " Divan."

Toward the end of this pilgrimage my papers were so enlarged that I was able to distribute the matter according to a certain order, divide it into books, measure the proportions of the different branches, and bring the whole, if not to completion, yet nearer to a conclusion. And so, in the midst of lively distractions, I had gained more than the quietest days in an equal space of time could have yielded me.

Before my departure four volumes of the new edition of my works were sent me. I began, too, to edit the " Sicilian Journey," but my interest in the East soon absorbed all my powers. Fortunately enough!—for had this instinct now been thwarted or diverted I should scarcely again have recovered the way to such a paradise.

With the exception of Persia, little that was foreign affected me. Still, I took great interest in modern Greek songs, which were communicated both in the original and in translations, and which I wished soon to see printed. Herren von Ratzmer and Haxthausen had undertaken this choice work.

In literary matters the " Göttinger Anzeigen " furthered me in no small measure, many volumes of which I found in the Wiesbaden library, and which I perused in order, with genial attention. Here you became aware of what you had experienced and lived through, and how important such a work is which, being the circumspect product of the time, continues to act on the times. It is highly agreeable from this point of view to contemplate what is long past. You see what is being and what has been wrought in their connection; everything of subordinate value is winnowed away, the false interest of the moment has vanished, the voice of the crowd has subsided, and the pure weighty matter which remains cannot be sufficiently appreciated.

13

The older German architecture should next fall to be mentioned. My conception of it became more and more developed and purified.

A journey to Cologne in the flattering company of the State Minister von Stein crowned this matter. With astonishment, for which, however, I was prepared, I saw the sad monument of incompleteness,* and was yet able to grasp with my vision the measure of the entirety it should have attained, though it still ever remained incomprehensible to one's mental capacities even at their utmost stretch. Of ancient painting much was to be seen and a great deal to be appreciated in the collection of Professor Walraff and other private persons. The stay, short though it was, left imperishable impressions behind. These were confirmed and raised by the pleasant company of Sulpiz Boisserée, with whom, on my travels from Wiesbaden by way of Mainz, Frankfort, and Darmstadt, I carried on conversations almost exclusively on this subject. Arrived at Heidelberg, I found the most hospitable reception at his hands, and had the fairest opportunity of contemplating for several days his invaluable collection, of convincing myself of its characteristic excellence in detail, and gaining instruction as much historical as artistic. A great deal was written down to help my memory and to be turned to best account in the future.

In respect to architecture during my Cologne journey, there was so much important conversation, in presence of the objects, on ground-plans and designs of older German, Netherland, and French buildings, that we managed to thread our way through a vast, often whimsical and confusing mass toward the pure and beautiful whither the human mind under each particular form had been striving. The first two books of Moller appearing at the moment furnished us with the desired aid. As to technics, an old printed copy, "The Stone-Cutters' Fraternity," gave us remarkable testimony of the high importance of this guild. You here saw how workmanship and art co-operated.

On this journey, too, I became sensible to how small a part of my native country, owing to the unhappy prevalence of war and tyranny, I had been confined, and how much, to my misfortune, I had missed and lost in the way of progressive culture. In Frankfort I was again able to admire Städel's treasures, and to rejoice in the patriotic sense of the collector. Yet I was seized with impatience at the sight of so many resources unused, for, in my opinion, with far less means the establishment might have been founded and erected and artists set in activity. Thereby, too, would art have been bearing beautiful fruit for years past—a rich compensation for all that might perhaps have been lost to the capital in the way of interest.

* The Cathedral, at that time, still unfinished.

Brentano's collection of paintings, copperplates, and other works of art afforded double enjoyment on account of the living sympathy of the professors, and their friendly desire to share their treasures with others.

Dr. Crambs, who was disposed to add his art treasures to those of Städel, let us several times see in part his excellent possessions, paving the way to a more thorough knowledge.

Hofrath Becker in Offenbach showed us important paintings, medals, and gems, being generous enough, moreover, to give this and that valuable article to the amateur.

In reference to natural history we saw Hofrath Meyer's collection of birds, not without fresh instruction on this splendid branch of the kingdom of nature.

The Senckenberg foundation in Frankfort was found to be in the best hands. The activity of the present suggested the near prospect of a new epoch for this beautiful institution.

In Carlsruhe, through the complaisance of Herr Gmelin, a cursory but sufficient survey of the highly considerable cabinet was afforded us there. The short time there indulged us was, indeed, altogether usefully as it was agreeably employed.

With all these journeys hither and thither, geognosy could but reap some profit. Von Hövel's "Mountains of the Mark Country" were, especially with the assistance of the officials of the place, instructive even in the distance. In Holzapfel, the highly remarkable vein there occasioned a discussion of Werner's "Theory of the Origin of Veins" (of 1791), as also of the "Dislocation of Veins" (of 1810), by Schmidt, who had been placed there. This important phenomenon, so often contemplated by me and ever remaining mysterious, again appeared before my mind, and I had the happiness in the valley of the Lahn, nearly opposite a suppressed abbey, to find on a neglected declivity plates of clay-slate with quartz veins running crosswise, and shifting their direction more or less, where the ground-phenomenon was at least seen with one's eyes, if one could not account for it to one's self or explain it to others.

I had a peculiar happiness at Biberich in that the hereditary Duke Karl, R.H., after an interesting conversation, graciously honored me with a description of his campaigns, and with highly accurate and neatly drawn maps. On these altogether valuable papers was traced the district of the Lahn from Wetzlar to Neuwied, and I remarked that a good military map is of the very greatest service for geognostic purposes. For neither soldier nor geognost inquires to whom river, land, and mountain belong; the former being interested only in so far as those features will serve his operations, the latter, so far as they may supplement or corroborate his observations. A journey into

different districts on both sides of the Lahn, begun, and for th
most part completed, with Cramer, the head councillor of mines
furnished much happy knowledge and insight, and would wel
deserve to be ranked among the little geognostic excursions.

I shall ever look back with pleasure on my return journe
as well.   The way from Heidelberg to Würzburg was traverse
in company with Sulpiz Boisserée.   Our parting being painfu
for us both, it was better it should happen on foreign than o
native soil.   I next travelled by way of Meiningen and the Thü
ringian Forest to Gotha, arriving on the eleventh of Octobe
in Weimar, having been away on those foreign travels for man
weeks.

Arrived at home, I mention first the visit of Dr. Stolz, th
worthy physician of Teplitz, when we ardently renewed th
mineralogical and geognostic conversations which had formerl
given us so much instruction and delight in Bohemia.   On m
next stay in Jena, Professor Döbereiner guided me into th
secrets of stoicheiometry.   He also made repeated experiment
with the white fire which, lighting up the country all down th
Jena Valley, afforded a magically surprising sight.

In the " Theory of Colors " some progress was also mad
The entoptic colors remained a principal study.   My meetin
with Dr. Seebeck was of great profit for me.   Beside conver
sation embracing general principles, he brought clearly befor
us the theory of the Iceland spar, and the relations of the axe
of such doubly refracting bodies.   A further comparison wa
made of the theory of sound with the " Theory of Colors.
Professor Voigt pursued his observations, principally on th
colors of organic bodies, and over my whole natural-historica
endeavors hovered Howard's theory of clouds.

After so much said on the subject of nature it is proper t
return to art.   In the Weimar Theatre we were constantly en
gaged with Calderon.   The " Great Zenobia " was represente
The first three acts succeeded excellently.   The two last havin
but a national-conventional and temporary interest, nobod
could either enjoy or criticise them, and after this last experi
ment the applause which had been so richly bestowed on th
first pieces partly died away.

The monodrama " Proserpina " with Eberwein's compositio
was happily performed ; " Epimenides " was prepared for Be
lin ; and to the memory of Schiller and Iffland a small piec
was written in co-operation with Peucer.   In this epoch
might well be said that the Weimar Theatre, in respect of pur
recitation, powerful declamation, natural and at the same tim
artistic representation, had attained a considerable height of ex
cellence.   In outward respects, too, it gradually improved ; th

wardrobe, for example—through emulation, first of the ladies, then of the gentlemen. Exactly at the right time we gained in the decorator Beuther an excellent artist trained in the school of Fuentes, who, by means of perspective, was able to enlarge our small spaces endlessly, by characteristic architecture to multiply them, and by taste and ornament to render them highly agreeable. Every kind of style he subjected to his perspective skill. In the Weimar Library he studied the Egyptian as also the old German architecture, and thereby gave to the pieces requiring such illustration new attraction and peculiar splendor.

And it may, accordingly, be said, the Weimar Theatre had at this epoch reached the acme of its development—a height promising, however, a desirable continuance for the immediate and subsequent future.

It would therefore here be opportune to add some well-weighed words on a business which for so many years had earnestly engaged my faculties.

The theatre, like everything about us, has two sides, an ideal and an empiric—an ideal, in so far as it continues to work in a regulated manner according to its inward nature; an empiric, which by reason of the most diverse changes to which it is subjected appears unregulated. We must therefore consider the theatre from both sides, if we are to form right conceptions regarding it.

From the ideal side, the theatre stands very high, so that almost nothing man produces by dint of genius, intellect, talent, technics, and practice can be co-ordinated with it. If poetry, with all its laws, giving rule and direction to imagination, is worthy of reverence; if rhetoric, with all its historic and dialectic requirements, remains highly estimable and indispensable; while no less praiseworthy is personal oral discourse, which cannot be conceived of except in conjunction with a certain moderate degree of mimicry—we see how the theatre absolutely comprises within its grasp these highest qualifications of man. Add to this the plastic arts—all that architecture, sculpture, and painting contribute to the complete development of the stage; take account, moreover, of the high ingredient of music—and it will be acknowledged what a host of human splendors are massed into this one institution.

All these great, nay, prodigious qualifications pervade all representations, from the highest to the lowest, without visible effort, as if spontaneously; and the all-important question is whether the direction, with set purpose and clear knowledge or from zeal and experience, determine on elevating their stage, in the whole or in parts, or, on the contrary, by their incapacity let it sink into contempt.

It is owing to the fact that I had all along, thanks especially
to Schiller's influence, endeavored to raise our stage in the
whole and in parts, according to our powers, means, and possibilities—it is owing to this fact that for several years our theatre
was looked up to as one of the most excellent in Germany.

And therein properly consists all true theatrical criticisms—
the observing, namely, whether the stage is rising or sinking
and to do this implies a comprehensive view of all requirements
—a comprehensive view seldom to be found, and in consideration of the multiplicity of influences and changes to which the
empiric theatre is subjected, almost impossible—for the present
which is ever under the influence of prejudice, and also for the
past, the impression of which becomes indistinct.

It may now be allowed us to pass from the narrow playhouse
stage to the stage of the great world.   Napoleon's return terrified the world; we had to live through a hundred days pregnant
with fate; the troops hardly gone away were summoned back
I found the Prussian guard in Wiesbaden; volunteers were
called up, and the peacefully busied citizens, who had scarcely
recovered breath, had to reaccommodate themselves to a situation for which physically they were not equal and about which
morally they were not unanimous.   The battle of Waterloo, re
ported in Wiesbaden as lost, to the great horror of everyone
was next announced as won—to overwhelming, nay, stupefying
joy.   In fear of the quick dispersion, as formerly, of French
troops over provinces and lands, visitors at watering-places had
made preparations for packing off, and, recovering from their
alarm, could by no means regret their needless foresight.

As to persons, I have yet reverently and thankfully to name
The hereditary duke Karl, in Biberich, the grand duchess Cath
arine, in Wiesbaden; the Duke and Duchess of Cumberland, a
Frankfort, the hereditary Grand Duke of Mecklenburg, at the
same place; in Carlsruhe, the counts Von Hochberg, Herren
Weinbrenner and Hebel; after reaching home, the whole suite
of the reigning Empress of Russia; Count Barclay de Tolly.

1816

The many important things I had a year before seen, experienced, and pondered in my own mother-country could not possibly fail to transfigure themselves somehow or other into a new
body.   A paper, "Art and Antiquity on the Rhine and Main,"
was undertaken, and at the end of last year more than one pre
liminary essay made in this business; the older Netherlanders
Van Eyck and his productions, thoroughly studied; the former
problematic picture " Veronika " reduced in size and engraved

for future use. Büsching's "Wöchentliche Nachrichten" co-operated toward this purpose, and, sharing in the spirit which animated me, the Weimar lovers of art turned piously to the old pictures of the saints which we got fetched from Heilsberg in the Thüringian Forest and had repaired before our eyes. As, however, in modern complicated times one thing always works into another, and one extreme calls forth the opposite, we were transported into admiration of the great deeds of Blücher, and the propriety of a heroic picture, as a likeness of his personality, suggested itself to our minds.

If the hero with danger of his life and reputation measures himself with the fates of the world, and happily comes off victorious, the astonished patriot, in order to find some expression for his admiration and worship, craves the aid of the artist.

After an interchange of writing with Herr Director Schadow, it was at last resolved to have a heroic figure moulded in accordance with the conception of the olden time, yet clad in costume approaching to that of the modern. The first model having been injured, the artist brought us a second, in regard to which, after many conferences, we heartily united on certain changes such as a fully executed work almost always suggests. This image stands, accordingly, as if on the line of demarcation between the ancient and the modern time: on the border on one hand of a certain conventional idealism satisfying the memory and the imagination of the spectator; and on the other hand, of an absolute truth to nature, which binds art, in spite of itself, to an oppressive realism.

From Berlin I was glad to receive transparent pictures illustrative of my "Hans Sachs." For, as imitation of the faithful, earnest, characteristic poetry of the olden time had in a former period long delighted me, it was a pleasure to me to find it now reappear in the way of reaction on modern artists. Drawings to "Faust," by Cornelius and Retzsch, had in their way a like effect; for though one neither can nor should recall a past mode of representing things, it is yet praiseworthy to exercise one's self historico-practically on it, and by modern to revive the memory of an antique art, in order after recognizing its merits to rise with the greater relief into freer regions.

In social circles the love of tableaux vivants had always increased, and if not immediately furthered, they were yet occasionally accompanied by me with a few verses.

As an echo of the Rhine impressions the picture of St. Roch, when, stripped of all, he enters on his pilgrimage from his palace, was designed and sketched by the Weimar lovers of art, then carefully cartooned, and at last painted by a delicate lady-hand, it was favorably received into the friendly Chapel of St. Roch.

An engraved reduced sketch duly stands as frontispiece to the
second " Rhine and Main " volume.

From Offenbach I received some beautiful bronze medals,
which again transplanted me back into the beginning of the sixteenth century.   Count Cicognara's " Storia della Scultura "
came at the right time to help me in these attractive studies.   To
higher regions, however, were we transported by Quatremère
de Quincy's " Olympian Jupiter " ; here was much to be learned
and pondered.   The arrival of the Elgin marbles excited great
longing among all lovers of art ; meanwhile, too, Burtin's
" Connaissance des Tableaux," which afforded us insight into
another important field, was not unheeded.

The restoration of the Dresden pictures came under discussion.   To show in some measure what a vast undertaking this
was, I drew attention to the restoration academy in Venice,
consisting of one director and twelve professors, which had
occupied in its labors the large rooms of a cloister.   Such a
restoration and preservation of old works of art is more momentous than is supposed, and is not to be undertaken on the
spur of the moment.

The Weimar drawing-school had to undergo a great change.
The old building having been devoted to other purposes, and
no place of like magnitude having been found, the classes were
divided into two.   For the first class, a building on the Espla-
nade was bought, the two others being relegated to the so-called
Hunter's House in front of the Frauenthor.   This change well
deserved, like the preceding ones, a special notice, not remaining without good consequences for the institution itself.

At the same time a distinguished sculptor of the name of
Kaufmann was called from Rome, who infused fresh life into
this art.

If I am to call to mind my own works, I have, first of all, to
mention the " Divan."   It was always attaining more fulness
and definiteness of form, some of it being intended for the
" Ladies' Calendar."   For the historical and explanatory part
I was ever collecting more preparatory material.   Von Diez's
" Memorabilia," his dispute with Hammer, and the latter's
" Oriental Mines," I studied attentively, everywhere inhaling
fresh Eastern air.   Knox's " Ceylon " came at the right time to
hand ; Hyde's " Persian Religion " appeared to me, however,
particularly valuable, and, in accordance with my nature, which
involuntarily demanded a reconstruction of any important subject which engaged my mind, I designed an Eastern opera, and
began to work at it.   It would, too, have attained completion,
the conception being really vital in me for a length of time, had
there been a musician at my side and a large public before me,

so that I should have been spurred to meet the capacities and accomplishments of the former and the taste and demands of the latter.

Fantastic folk, such as are to be found in this world, misled by Schiller's edition in chronological order, demanded the like of me, and had almost brought the impression already entered on into derangement. My reasons for declining compliance with their solicitations were, however, approved, and the business went its course without further molestation. The ninth and tenth volumes were revised; the Italian tour, especially to Naples and Sicily, assumed ever more definite shape, and as one work always calls forth another, I could not omit adding some main events in the fourth volume, so long delayed and awaited, of " Truth and Poetry." The " Rhine and Main " paper, second part, was pushed on, " Reineke Fuchs " looked through, and the " St. Roch Festival " written.

The second set of my works arrive. The " Paralipomena " are, of course, attended to, and a song for the Berlin artists' festival written. On the other hand, owing to want of time and incitement, a large cantata intended for the Luther festival was dropped soon after the conception, the drawing up of the plan, and a little execution, never to be resumed.

My interest in foreign works was specially directed to the poems of Byron, who grew ever more significant and more attractive for me, though formerly his hypochondriac passion and violent self-hatred had repelled me, and while I was disposed to approach his great personality, I felt estranged from his muse. I read the " Corsair " and " Lara," not without admiration and sympathy. At the same time appeared Nelson's letters, with his life, giving much matter for melancholy reflections. Gries, by the publication of the second part of his " Calderon," brought us into more intimate acquaintance with Spain of the seventeenth century. Anatole transferred us to a new Paris, and awakened our admiration for a beautiful romance. The " Prisoners of Peace," by Lawrence, one of the rarest productions, compelled us to pay all attention to a quite accursed situation. English travellers arrested in Verdun, according to modern maxims of international law, on the outbreak of a war with Albion; republican Frenchmen, especially a commandant and commandant's lady promoted from a humble station during the Revolution; secret emigrants taken for Englishmen, disguised people of distinction, and such-like figures—these compose a quaint picture which deserves to go down to posterity, since, under this condition alone could it have been conceived by a fellow-sufferer of ingenious observation, and completed more with hatred than love.

Rückstuhl wrote on the German language, and the inexhaustible work of Ernesti, " Technologia Rhetorica Græcorum et Romanorum," was always in my hands; for this latter work enabled me again and again to discover how far in my literary course I had done rightly and wrongly. I must not, however, omit a highly remarkable piece of description, perhaps without a rival; it is the diurnal and horal book of the battle of Leipsic, by Rochlitz, of which I have spoken elsewhere.

The immediate institutions in Jena devoted to natural science in general and natural history in particular, had to rejoice in the most attentive care bestowed on them. In almost all divisions the inward activity had so increased that though with good management they could all be compassed within the limits of present arrangements, our thoughts were necessarily directed to a new and extended set of museums on a new scale. Döbereiner's dwelling-house was finished, a piece of garden ground at the observatory bought, and added to this possession. The veterinary institution in Jena took firm footing. Professor Renner began his course, and I handed over my old horse-skulls sawn in pieces and otherwise prepared for an elementary course of lessons, for which they had formerly served me.

The long-interrupted diggings of the very old grave-hill at Romstedt were continued, and yielded us several skulls. Through special care, too, a whole skeleton was brought to Jena, and carefully deposited in good order. A skull which from the swelling of the bones had expanded to quite a monstrous size was brought in gypsum casts from Darmstadt through the kindness of Herr Schleiermacher.

I again called to remembrance Kaspar Friedrich Wolf, and studied completely Jäger " On the Misgrowths of Plants," as also Philibert's " Diseases of Plants." Von Humboldt's work on the " Division of Plants on the Globe " was highly welcome, and Nees von Esenbeck's most complete work on fungi and sponges made me regret an excellent telescope, which a strange fate had destroyed in the most pleasant moments of life.

Out of the animal kingdom, a wonderful creature, the *Proteus anguinus*, was shown us by Herr Professor Configliacchi, who, having carefully kept it in a glass of water in his bosom on the journey, had brought it alive to us.

In the mineral kingdom we were much favored. The important collection of Privy Councillor Heim, at Meiningen, was kindly sent by him to Jena for our institution, where it was set up in accordance with his wishes. Of remarkable things the ball-syenite of Vallinco from Corsica deserves special mention. In consequence of my journey last year there were added to my collection minerals from Westerwald and the Rhine, also a hyalite from Frankfort exhibiting the largest surface with which perhaps it has ever been met, seven inches in diameter. Privy Councillor Von Leonhård's " Significance and Place of Minerals" enriched us on the theoretic side.

Howard's cloud terminology was diligently applied to atmospheric appearances, and we arrived at particular expertness in parallelizing them with the state of the barometer.

In other physical departments, an attempt was made to light Jena with gas; as through Döbereiner we also learnt the way of extracting different substances by pressure.

In chromatics, the entoptic phenomena were the order of the day. I put together the observations I had hitherto made, and transferred them into a short essay, the inadequacy of which being, however, soon felt, compelled me to further investigations which brought me ever nearer the truth.

Professor Pfaff sent me his work on the theory of colors, with an impolite importunity native to the Germans. I set it aside for a future day when I should have come to a final conclusion on the subject with myself. It is always most profitable to follow one's own way, for it has the happy advantage that it leads us from errors back on ourselves again.

Dr. Schopenhauer came as a kind friend to my side. We discussed a great deal in agreement with each other. At last, however, we could not avoid deviating from each other to a certain extent, like two friends who have kept company with each other up to a certain point, when they shake hands, the one to go north, the other south, soon to lose sight of each other.

Color experiments with vegetable extracts repeatedly served to demonstrate the very high congruity of the theory of colors.

I must now, however, bring forward in its connection an interlude in which a great deal occurs I would not like to have split up under different heads. On the approach of good weather I thought of again enjoying to my own heart's content such beautiful days as I had enjoyed last year in my native country. Friend Meyer was minded to accompany me; nature and art were to pour on us a superabundance of their treasures. Preparations were made, plans designed as to how everything was to be enjoyed and utilized. And so we sat snugly seated in a nice carriage. The half of our way to Erfurt was, however, not passed when we were capsized, the axle having broken. My friend had received an injury on his brow, and we were obliged to turn back. From vexation and superstition we gave up our intended journey, perhaps prematurely, and without long consideration we betook ourselves to Tennstädt, where a

Thüringian mineral water (of sulphur) promised good effect. There, according to my usual humor, I became interested in the locality and history of the place; for the Thüringian fore-world had a great deal to do with the Unstrut. I therefore read the "Thüringian Chronicle," which on the spot gave us many clear views of that quarter. The immediate and surrounding situation of the town was contemplated, and it was easily seen why, in the earliest time, tenements should have been planted there. We visited Herbsleben on the Unstrut, Kleinwallhausen, and other near-lying places, and found in the plain dried-up beds of lakes, tufa stone quarries and fresh-water conchylians. On almost all excursions we had the back of the Etterberg before our eyes and could easily think ourselves at home. A crowd assembled on the occasion of a shooting at the popinjay, as also of a well-festival, which a procession of children made a right hearty affair.

"Agamemnon," translated by Humboldt, had just come into my hands, and afforded me the comfortable enjoyment of a piece I had ever idolized. Marcus Cornelius Fronto, from Niebuhr, paid me a visit. Privy Councillor Wolf appeared unexpectedly. The conversation was important and edifying, and Meyer took a penetrating and artistic part in it. Both friends happened to leave me on the twenty-seventh of August, and I had therefore time enough again to celebrate my birth-day in still composure, and to consider the value of the garlands with which I saw my room decorated by my kind hostess. For the rest, I was indebted to the composure and quiet I found at this place for the full description of the St. Roch Festival.

I have further to celebrate the high enjoyment a Hermstedt concert and private exhibition gave me, for, having been now a long time absent from musical friends, I had become almost a stranger to this splendid element of art and nature.

Public events which nearly affected me this year I mention with joyous and sad memories. On the thirtieth of January the Order of the Falcon was founded, and the grand cross was at once apportioned me. Duke Bernhard's marriage inspired the fairest hopes. On the other hand, the death of the Empress of Austria put me in such a state that the feeling of it has never left me. The State minister, Von Voight, a dear aged colleague and promoter of my well-intended undertakings, celebrated his jubilee of service—an occasion which I greeted with a poem and the most heartfelt good wishes.

Of visits I remark the following, all awaking remembrances of earlier and earliest times: Mellish, Dr. Hufeland, Max Jacobi, Von Laffert, Dr. Chladni, Zelter and Wilken, Count and Countess O'Donell, Hofräthin Kestner from Hanover.

Inward peace was favored by the outward peace of the world, when, after freedom of the press had been decreed, the " Isis " was announced, and every right-thinking, sensible man anticipated with alarm and regret the immediate consequences easily to be calculated and the further consequences not to be calculated.

1817

I foresaw that for more than one reason I would this year have to stay a long time in Jena, and therefore had a great deal of my own manuscripts, drawings, apparatus, and collections carried thither.   First of all, the institutions were all inspected, and finding a great deal remarkable in reference to the formation and transformation of plants, I set up a botanical museum of my own, placing and disposing in order in it considerable collections of dried plants, the beginnings of a collection of all kinds of seed, also samples of the different kinds of wood, monstrosities of special importance being arranged in a long series.

The transference of the court mechanician, Körner, from Weimar to Jena, placed in our neighborhood an able, expert, active man.   A transit instrument made by him in Weimar was, on account of some buildings which required to be provided at the observatory, first set up in the castle.

Further, the manifold gifts brought by his Serene Highness from the Milan journey were distributed among the different departments.

The expenses had increased, the state of affairs had again to be investigated, chapter by chapter ; I, therefore, wrote a circumstantial report, and a clear summary was then presented at highest quarters.

In the last three months of the year, however, there again came into agitation a matter which had been a subject of our solicitude for years, but, on account of the great difficulties connected with it, we had always postponed taking effective measures toward its settlement.   Among all the institutions which had been improved or even newly founded, partly on the sole initiative and at the sole expense of his Serene Highness, partly with aid from the Gotha Court, one could not, unfortunately, reckon the University Library.   It lay hopelessly embarrassed, without its being possible to lay the blame of this bad plight on anyone in particular.   To its beginnings, which had been laid 300 years ago, there had gradually in manifold ways—by legacies, purchases, and other contracts—been added a considerable number of separate book collections, as also single books, till now the whole stood heaped in

layers, the one cargo above and beside the other in the most
heterogeneous fashion, mostly as accident had directed.   How
and where a book was to be found was almost the exclusive
secret of the library-attendant rather than of the higher officials.
The rooms no longer sufficed; the Buder Library was closed,
scarcely accessible; according to the will of the founder, it was
to remain forever untouched.

But not these strange complications alone were to be unravelled and this chaos brought to order.   The Büttner library,
formerly in the castle, it was likewise sought to incorporate into
the main mass.   If you surveyed the whole, if you inspected
particular parts, you would have to confess that on an entire
rearrangement of the library very few volumes, perhaps, would
be left beside each other in the old order.   In these circumstances nobody could well be censured if he hesitated about
putting a precipitate hand to such a business.   At last, however, on the fourteenth of October I received by a gracious
rescript the commission to undertake the affair without further
delay.   There was nothing, therefore, left for it but to think
the matter through anew, and to defy all obstacles in the way,
an attitude necessary in the case of every important undertaking, especially when one must set boldly to work under the
clause, *non obstantibus quibuscunque*.   And so I set to impetuously and proceeded without pause.

The dampness of the lower hall had for years long been a
subject of lamentation; but still no remedy had been devised,
far less carried out.   This, then, was the first thing to be taken
in hand.   The confining wall, toward the moat, was, in spite
of a lively, nay, underhand protestation, removed, and the accumulated rubbish carted away.   Above everything else, however, the office-rooms were so arranged that one could work
in them without discomfort.   While other buildings were being prepared and bargained for, the year passed away.

The Veterinary School had now principally to be looked
after.   Step by step it was brought into order.   On the scientific side, I fetched my portfolio of comparative anatomy to
Jena, and framed the drawings I found most important.

Professor Renner demonstrated different things to me, especially in respect to the lymphatic system.   A dead phoca is
bought from the keeper of a strolling menagerie and dissected,
important preparations being made.

Spix's " Cephalogenesis " appears; on repeated use of it unpleasant obstacles are encountered.   The method of general
representation, and the nomenclature of the different parts,
have neither of them been brought to maturity.   You also
notice in the text that more second-hand matter is presented
than matter of original thought.

Herold, of Marburg, in his " Anatomy of Caterpillars and Butterflies," makes us an agreeable present. How much progress have we not made in the thoughtful observation of organic nature, since the time of the diligent and over-exact Lyonnet?

I work heartily on the second sheet of the " Morphology," and observe historically the influence of the Kantian doctrine on my studies.

Geognosy, geology, mineralogy, and kindred subjects were the order of the day. I thought over the doctrine of the veins generally, and made myself at home with Werner's and Charpentier's views. The remarkable clay-slate plates from the valley of the Lahn I put together in the order most adapted for instruction. Specimens of the coagulating of the rock masses I sought out everywhere, and thought I found much which testified to the porphyry-like origin of so many conglomerates. A complete set procured by his Serene Highness from Chamouny was arranged in order in the museum; no less were many Swiss rock species, models, and panoramas, each in its way preserved, utilized, and examined.

The neighborhood of Baden, through Cimbernat's examination and treatment, excited a growing interest, and his geological map of that district communicated to us from a high quarter, was altogether welcome for the immediate requirements of our studies. Brocchi's " Valley of Fassa " challenged us to the study of the Wacke formation, in accordance with his views and those of others.

Herr Chamberlain von Preen, on a journey thither, had procured for me the most beautiful specimens.

Mawe's paper on Brazil, and the precious stones there, brought us on that side into nearer acquaintance with those lands. I entered into immediate relationship with him, and received through his provision a fine collection of pieces of English tin-ore now, as always, obtained immediately from primitive rock, and, in this instance, in chlorite stone.

Privy Councillor Von Leonhard's large tabular works, published in co-operation with other natural-historians, facilitated the arrangement of my private cabinet.

No little enlightenment in geology and geography I owed, however, to Sorriot's map of the European mountains. The ground and soil of Spain, for example, so treacherous to a commander-in-chief, and so favorable for guerilla warfare, became all at once clear to me. I drew his principal water-sheds on my map of Spain; and every route of travel, as also every campaign, every regular and irregular beginning of the kind, became plain and comprehensible to me; and whoever makes this colossal chart the intelligent basis of his geognostic, geo-

logic, geographic, and topographic studies, will find himself
furthered in the highest degree.

Chromatics busied me uninterruptedly in private. I endeavored to realize the views held regarding it in England,
France, and Germany. I studied four English writers distinguished in this department: Bancroft, Sowerby, Dr. Reade,
and Brewster. On one side I observed with pleasure how
through pure observation of the phenomena they had approached the way of nature, nay, in some points touched it;
but, to my regret, I soon became aware that they were not able
to free themselves entirely from the old delusion that color is
contained in light, that they made use of the traditional terminology, and therefore fell into the greatest entanglements.
Brewster, especially, seemed to think that by an endless series
of experiments the subject is substantially advanced, whereas
manifold and exact experiments are rather, in the case of true
lovers of nature, only preparations in order to be able to express a pure result freed from all non-essential adherents.

The most repugnant thing, however, which ever met my
eyes was Biot's chapter on the entoptic colors, there called
polarization of light. Thus, according to the false analogy of
a magnet, light was distorted into two poles, and colors, as
formerly, explained by the differentiation of that which is most
unchangeable and most integral.

Now, however, in order to brazen out a fallacy with demonstrations, the whole armory of mathematics was put in motion
to oust nature, bag and baggage, out of both the outward and
inward sense. I was compelled to look on the whole affair as
a pathologic case, just as if an organic body had got a splinter
thrust into it, and a skilful surgeon, instead of extracting it in
order to effect a speedy cure, took the utmost pains with the
swelling to appease and divide it, while in the meantime the
sore aggravated inwardly till it became incurable.

It was, accordingly, quite horrible to me when a university
professor, after introducing a programme of Hofrath Meyer
in Göttingen, with incredible composure and assurance flourished the most impudent juggleries before high and intelligent
persons. After gazing and gazing, after blinking and blinking
(with aching eyes), you were quite at a loss to know either
what you had seen or what you were intended to see. At the
first preparations I got up and went off, and on my return
heard without surprise the course of this demonstration, as I
had foreseen it. I was also taught on this occasion, by the
illustration of billiard-balls, how the round molecules of light,
if they strike the glass with the poles, penetrate quite through,
whereas if they meet it with the equator they are sent back with
protest.

Meanwhile I endlessly diversified the entoptic colors, so that at last I could not but discover the simple atmospheric origin. To one's entire conviction the main conception was confirmed on the seventeenth of June under a clear sky. I now set to work to winnow away the many details as chaff and hulls, and by word spoken and written to communicate the kernel to friends of nature and art. I hereby, too, discovered that a light favorable or unfavorable to the painter is due to the reflection being direct or indirect. Professor Roux had the politeness to deliver me exact copies of the entoptic color-pictures. Both sides, the bright as well as the dark, you now saw in heightened succession beside each other; every spectator exclaimed that he saw the Chladnian figures colored before his eyes.

Leonardo da Vinci's essay on the cause of the blue color phenomenon on distant mountains and objects repeatedly gave me great satisfaction. Simply as a man apprehending nature by immediate observation, as an artist meditating on the appearance itself and piercing through it, he had hit the mark. No less came sympathy from several attentive and thoughtful men. State Councillor Schulz, in Berlin, sent me the second essay on physiological colors, in which I saw my main conceptions carried into life. Just as edifying for me was Professor Hegel's agreement. Since Schiller's decease, I had quietly withdrawn from all philosophy and sought only to mature to ever greater certainty and precision the method innate in me, applying it to nature, art, and life. It could not, therefore, but be of great value for me to see and consider how in his way a philosopher would understand that which I on my side had produced in my way. And in the present case I was allowed the most complete right to contemplate the mysterious clear light as the highest energy, everlasting, single, and indivisible.

In the way of plastic art a great deal of instruction came this year. Of Elgin's marbles we heard ever more and more, and the desire to see with our eyes anything belonging to Phidias was so passionate, that one fine, sunny morning, stepping out of doors without any special purpose, overtaken by my passion I turned on the spur of the moment, without any preparation, toward Rudolstadt, and there gazed for a long time on the truly astounding heads of Monte Cavallo. Nearer acquaintance with the Ægina marbles was likewise apportioned me through drawings of the artist in Rome commissioned with the restoration, and under a like incitement I turned to one of the most splendid productions of modern art.

I was enabled to study more minutely Vossi's works on Leonardo da Vinci's " Supper," by means of the copy tracings

14

which our prince had brought with him from Milan. Comparative study of them busied me a long time, and otherwise a great deal was brought home to our contemplation. The architectural remains of Eleusis, contemplated in the company of our chief building director Coudray, afforded views into an incomparable time. Schinkels's great and admirable pen-drawings, the most recent Munich lithograph sketches to Castil's fables of animals by Menken, a copperplate collection from a Leipsic auction, an estimable little oil-painting, with which we were honored by Rochlitz, all these chained my attention on many sides. At last I found opportunity to procure an important collection of majolicas which, in consideration of their merit, might certainly be classed among modern works of art.

Of my own works I report the following. For the sake of the " Divan " I always continued my studies of Oriental peculiarities, and spent much time on the subject. Handwriting, however, being in the East of so great importance, it will hardly be thought strange that, without a special study of the language, I yet devoted myself zealously to caligraphy, and both in the way of jest and earnest, endeavored to copy as neatly as possible, nay with many traditional ornaments, Oriental manuscripts lying before me. The influence of these intellectual technic exertions will, on close inspection of the poems, not escape the attentive reader.

The third set of my works, from Volume 9 to Volume 12, appears at Easter. The second " Rhine and Main Sheet " is concluded, the third commenced and finished. The " Journey to Naples and Sicily " is printed, the biography generally again taken in hand. I draw the " Meteors of the Literary Heaven," and busy myself with extracting the " Critical Words of French Critics " from Grimm's correspondence. A paper on the hollow coins, called " Regenbogenschüsselchen " (Rainbow Dishes), I communicate to the lovers of such curiosities. The celebrated Heilsberg inscription I get printed with an explanation by Von Hammer, which however does not come off happily.

Of poetical works I have nothing to show but the " Orphic Primitive Words," in five stanzas, and an Irish death song translated from " Glenarvon."

In the way of knowledge of nature I here mention an important *aurora borealis* in February.

Agreement between the substance and the form of plants was the subject of an animated conversation between me and Hofrath Voigt, whose " Natural History," contributing so much to that study, was to be thankfully accepted. I directed a great deal of observation to the dispersion of the seed of the barberry flower, and of the yellow outgrowths of older twig-leaves there indicated. Through the politeness of Hofrath Döbereiner I was able to make further progress in the stoicheiometric science in general. I casually set myself the task of purging an old edition of Thomas Campanella, " De sensu rerum," from errors of the press—in consequence of the extremely attentive reading I devoted anew to this important monument of his time. Count Bouquoy rejoiced his absent friends, as well as those immediately about him, by further printed communications, in which his intellectual activity called forth the remark from us that it again brought home to us his personal intercourse.

Closer study of Howard's forms of clouds seeming to suggest the conclusion that their different forms corresponded with their different atmospheric altitudes, by way of experiment they were carefully inserted into that former table of altitudes, and the mutual relations in general thus visualized, and thereby so far prepared for examination.

In speaking of books, the translation of the Indian " Megha-Duta " comes naturally and agreeably to mind. After brooding so long on clouds and the forms of clouds we were able to follow in spirit with all the more certain observation this messenger of clouds in his thousandfold variety of forms.

English poetry and literature took, this year, the precedence of the productions of all other countries. Lord Byron's poems excited the more interest the more one studied the peculiarities of this extraordinary mind. Men and women, spinsters and bachelors, seemed to forget everything German and national. The procuring of his works having been facilitated, I also busied myself with him. He was for me a dear contemporary, and I willingly followed him in thought along the dubious courses of his life.

The novel of " Glenarvon " would, it was thought, yield us much light on many a love adventure of the poet; but the interest of the voluminous work was not commensurate with its bulk; it repeated itself in situations, especially in intolerable situations. You could not deny it a certain value which, however, you would have acknowledged more heartily had it been compressed within two moderate volumes.

Having so long heard of the name of Peter Pindar, I wished to associate with it some distinct conception. I obtained satisfaction on that point, but only now remember that he appeared to me as a man of parts, inclining to the side of caricature. John Hunter's Life seemed to me highly important, as a monument of a splendid mind which, with but little school education, developed itself in the sphere of nature nobly and powerfully. Franklin's Life had, in general, the same character, though, in details, heaven-wide from the former. On remote, hitherto inaccessible regions, Elphinstone's "Cabul" gave us information, while the better known parts of the world had no ordinary light thrown on them through Raffle's "History of Java." At the same time the splendid work on "Indian Hunting" by Howett reached us, and its excellent pictures came to the help of the imagination, which, without such a basis of reality to confine it, would have lost itself in the indefinite. On North America manifold information was imparted to us.

Of books and other publications and their influence I remark the following: Hermann, "De Mythologia Græcorum antiquissima," interested the Weimar philologists in a high degree. In a kindred sense Raynouard's "Grammar of the Roman Language." "Manuscrit venu de St. Helène" engaged all the world. Its authenticity or spuriousness, its half or whole originality, was the subject of conversation and argument. That a great deal from the hero had been overheard was plain and indubitable. "The Primitive History of Germany" by Barth struck into our studies of the time; on the other hand, "Whit Monday" by Professor Arnold, in Strasburg, was a highly amiable publication. It is a decidedly pleasing feeling we experience—a feeling it is well not to insist on rendering too distinct to the understanding—when we perceive a nation reflected in the peculiarities of its members. It is, indeed, only in specialties we recognize our relatives. In generalities we feel our relation to others only in the common derivation from Adam. I busied myself much with this work and expressed my satisfaction with it sincerely and circumstantially.

Of events I remark but little, though that little of importance for myself and others. Notwithstanding that I had wandered for forty years up and down in all directions through Thüringia, in carriage, on horseback, and on foot, I had never yet come to the Paulina cloister, though often not many miles from that place. It was not then the habit to regard these church ruins as in any high degree important and venerable. At last, however, I heard so much about them, younger people, both native to the quarter and who had travelled into it, praised so much the grandeur of the view, that on my birthday this year—a day I always liked to celebrate quietly—I resolved on a solitary excursion thither. A very bright day favored the enterprise, but friendship too prepared me an unexpected festival. The chief forest-ranger, Von Fritsch, from Ilmenau, had arranged with my son a pleasant repast, where at our ease and to our glad content we could contemplate the old structure which had been put in order by the Schwarzburg-Rudolstadt authorities. Its origin dates in the beginning of the twelfth century, when the half-circular arch still prevailed. The Reformation banished such a building into the wilderness where it had arisen. The clerical object for which it was intended had fallen into neglect; but it remained a centre of worldly privilege and income down to the present day. It was never destroyed, but in part carried away, in part disfigured, for economical purposes. In the brewery, for example, you can still find some of the old colossal bricks hard burnt and varnished; nay, I do not doubt but in the official and other buildings you might discover some of the primitive rafters of the flat roof and other original timbering.

From abroad came news of destruction and re-establishment. The Berlin Theatre was burnt to the ground; a new one was erected in Leipsic. A symbol of sovereignty was given to the people of Weimar by a striking ceremony. The Grand Duke from the throne invested the Prince of Thurn and Taxis, in the person of his deputy, with the postal revenues, on which occasion the whole body of us servants appeared in becoming attire according to our respective ranks, and on our side recognized the supreme authority of the Prince. Meanwhile, in the course of the same year, a general festival of German students on the eighteenth of June, at Jena, and still more important, on the eighteenth of October on the Wartburg, announced a counter-effect full of foreboding.

The jubilee of the Reformation disappeared before these fresh younger endeavors. Three hundred years ago, able men had undertaken great things. Now their great deeds appeared superannuated; and something altogether different might be expected from the latest open-secret aspirations.

Personal renewal of former favors and affection was destined to gladden me frequently this year also. The hereditary Princess of Hesse never knew me to be in her neighborhood without letting me be personally assured of her continued graciousness toward me. State Minister Von Humboldt called on me, carrying on, on this occasion also, an instructive and stimulating conversation with me. Quite a peculiar influence, however, I received for a long time from a considerable number of young Greeks studying in Jena and Leipsic. They ardently wished to acquire German culture in particular, in order that their country might reap the benefit of this acquisition on their part. Their diligence was commensurate with their high aims; only it was noticeable that in regard to the chief idea of life they were ruled more by words than by clear conceptions and purposes.

Papadopulos, who frequently visited me in Jena, once in
youthful enthusiasm praised to me the lectures of his philosophical professor.   It sounds, he exclaimed, so splendid when
the excellent man speaks of virtue, freedom, and country.
When, however, I inquired what this excellent professor meant
by all that, I received for answer that he could not exactly tell
me, but word and tone constantly resounded in the hearing of
the soul: Virtue, Freedom, and Country.

He is the same person who translated my " Iphigenia " into
modern Greek.   And wonderfully enough, if you consider this
piece in this language and under this relation you will find it
expressing quite peculiarly the longings of a Greek in travel or
in exile.   The general longing for one's native country is here
specifically expressed under the feeling of longing for Greece
as the sole land of human culture.

A new and agreeable acquaintance I made in a Fellenberg
assistant, of the name of Lippe, whose calm clearness, decision
of purpose, and confidence in the good result of his labors
attracted my highest esteem, and at once confirmed me in the
good opinion I had entertained of him and the institution to
which he had devoted himself.

Of very manifold effect was the much-desired visit of an old
friend.   Wilhelm von Schütz, from Ziebingen, renewed his
former earnest and deep intercourse with me.   We had quite
a curious experience of each other.   At the beginning of every
conversation we entirely concurred in all premises.   With the
progress, however, of our exchange of views, we diverged even
more and more from each other, till at last no common understanding was any longer to be thought of.   Generally the same
thing happened in our correspondence and occasioned me
much pain, till in the end I had the happiness to terminate this
strange contradiction.   That I might become acquainted with
all kinds of occurrences, the very reverse experience now
fell to my lot.   Hofrath Hirt, with whom I could never agree
on principles, gladdened me by a visit lasting for several days,
during the whole course of which never once did the least
variance come to light between us.   When I reflected on the
two incidents just mentioned, I found that the explanation of
them was the following: Von Schütz proceeded from general
principles, on which I stood in conformity with him, to more
general principles, whither I was unable to follow him.   Hofrath Hirt, on the other hand, let the mutually incompatible
general principles of us both entirely alone, and entered into
details which he had thoroughly mastered ; you listened to his
thoughts with pleasure and heartily accorded with him in his
convictions.

The visit of Berlin friends, State Councillor Hufeland, Langermann, and Varnhagen von Ense, redounded in blessings on my head (to talk the language of the pious); for what is richer in blessings than the encounter of congenial, like-minded contemporaries unintermittently progressing on a course of culture of themselves and others.

A younger Batsch, reminding you of his father both by his friendly, active demeanor, and by his correspondingly pleasing, intellectual personality, returned from Cairo, whither he had gone in connection with the business of some European merchants. He had brought home with him drawings of places there, accurate, indeed, but by no means artistic; also small antiquities of Egyptian and Greek origin. He looked like a man striving with all his active faculties to accomplish in practical business what his father had theoretically achieved in the domain of natural science.

1818

Throughout the winter the " Divan " had continued to be cherished and nursed with so much affection, love, and passion that by the month of March I no longer hesitated about sending it to press. Not that I then broke off my studies on this subject, for I continued writing notes and detached papers in the hope that they would contribute to a better understanding of the matter. I was, of course, quite prepared to see the German stop short in perplexity when a phenomenon out of an entirely different world was precipitated on his notice. The trial, too, in the " Ladies' Calendar," had embarrassed rather than assisted the public. The uncertainty as to whether the foreign arrival was a translation, an imitation, or an appropriation, did the enterprise no good. I did not, however, think it proper to enlighten them on this point. I was accustomed to seeing the German public eying a strange dish suspiciously before they would fall to and partake.

Above everything else, it appeared to me necessary to enlighten myself and others on the seven chief Persian poets and their achievements. For this purpose I set myself to the faithful and earnest study of Von Hammer's important works. To ferry me into those distant times and places, I made requisition of all available crafts, Anquetil's " Religious Customs of the Ancient Persians," Bidpai's " Fables," Freytag's " Arabian Poems," Michaelis's " Arabic Grammar."

Meanwhile the rarities brought by our Prince from Milan, the greater number of which referred to Leonardo's " Supper," had in the highest degree excited my attention. After zealous study of Vossi's work on this subject, after comparison of the copy-tracings lying before me, after consideration of many other works of art and events of that time, I at last wrote the treatise as it still exists in print and had it at once translated into French, to render it accessible to the Milan friends.   At the same time a dispute as to antique and modern, such as was being agitated in Germany, was reported to us from that quarter; whence, too, we heard news of polemical discussions regarding classical and romantic.

Intermediately, at every pause occurring during all this affair, mightily attracted to Greece, I pursued an old pet thought, that Myron's " Cow " in its main conception was preserved on the medals of Dyrrachium; for what is more desirable than a distinct remembrance of the highest achievements dating from a time which will never return?   This sentiment it was which prompted me to take up again Philostrat's pictures, with a view to renovating the ruinous past by resuscitating in me the dormant soul of that period.   What other things I endeavored to explicate to myself is testified in " Art and Antiquity," fourth part.

A wonderful situation under bright moonshine brought me the song, " At Midnight," which is all the more dear and precious to me that its origin and drift both alike transcended my private consciousness.   Summoned to produce a poem, I produced it at the end of a year—a poem, clearer, therefore, than " At Midnight " in its origin, but just as incalculable as the latter in its execution—demanded, conceived, introduced, and finished all in a short time.   In homage to her Majesty, the dowager empress, a masked procession was thought of to represent in separate groups the many years' poetical achievements of the Weimar muses' circle.   These groups flowing by in succession, lingered each for a moment in the presence of her Highness to recount its special characteristic in a becoming poem.   The affair came off on the eighteenth of December, and rejoiced in a favorable acceptance and a lasting remembrance.

Shortly before, the seventeenth and eighteenth volumes of my works had reached my hands.

My stay in Jena was this time fruitful to me in more ways than one.   I had quartered myself in the bow-windowed room of the Tanne at Camsdorf, and enjoyed at my convenience the free fair views extending before and around me, especially the characteristic cloud-appearances.   In accordance with Howard, I observed them in relation to the barometer and acquired insight in many ways.

At the same time the entoptic chapter of colors was the

order of the day. Brewster's experiments to impart to the
glass, by pressure, as is otherwise produced by heat, the same
quality of the regular display of colors which is seen in a mirage, succeeded perfectly well; and I, for my part, convinced
of the agreement of the technical-mechanical with the dynamic-
ideal, had the Seebeck crosses stitched on damask stuff, and
could now, by changing the light at pleasure, see them on the
same plane either bright or dark. Dr. Seebeck visited me on
the sixteenth of June, and his presence was on this occasion, as
always, helpful to me at the right time.

In Carlsbad, I saw, to my great regret, a well-wrought
brazen tube with sextant, intended to prove the polarization of
light. It was made in Paris. Here in confined space you saw
only partially what we had long known how to represent fully
and completely in the open air. All the more agreeable to me,
therefore, was an apparatus for the same purpose with which
I was honored on my birthday by Professor Schweigger, an
apparatus performing everything that can be desired in this
respect.

The most handsome contributions to geognosy, with important specimens, had come to us from Italy. Brocchi's
works on Italian fossils, Sömmering's fossil lizards and bats.
Thence we raised ourselves again into older regions and
studied Werner's theory of veins and Friesleben's Saxon tin
formation. A collection of minerals announced to us from
the North arrives, also petrifactions sent us from the island of
Rügen by Kosegarten, and minerals from Sicily and the island
of Elba by Odeleben. The position of the celestin at Dornburg is investigated. By a special occasion we are brought
into better acquaintance with the geognosy of the United
States. The advantage thus accruing to us is returned in a
friendly and creditable way.

In Bohemia, geognosy in general was all the more earnestly
promoted through the short visit of a young far-reaching geologist of the name of Reupel, who had the politeness to illustrate
for me a map of the kingdom, he having the intention, in a
work of his own, to prosecute this branch of inquiry further
and make it publicly known. We visited Haidinger's porcelain factory in Elbogen, where, beside the material of the
pure, disintegrated felspar, we also made the acquaintance of
peat widely used for fuel, and were at the same time instructed
regarding the mine of the hemitrope crystals. We visited
Surveyor of Mines Beschorner in Schlackenwalde, received
much pleasant instruction from his collection of minerals, and
on the same day obtained, also, a kind of survey of the locality
of the thrackscat. Portions embedded in granite, or rather

contained in it, and which through exposure to the weather
have resolved themselves into distinct appearances—for example mica-balls—were observed and picked up. I had also
very instructive crystallographic conversations with Professor
Weiss. He had some crystallized diamonds with him, with the
course of whose development he made me acquainted in accordance with his higher views. A small collection of Müller's,
specially instructive, was put in order. Rosequartz from
Königswart reached me, while I also procured some Bohemian
chrysoliths. On my return I found at home minerals from
Coblenz and other instructive materials of this kind.

The University of Jena was peculiarly favored by the zealous attention of the high personages supporting it; it was now
furnished with new apparatus and staff. The older statutes it
was sought to bring into conformity with recent times; and I,
too, in so far as the immediate institutions affected the university, had contributed my part by serviceable proposals. The
affairs of the library, however, since the beginning of the year,
demanded incessant and enlarged activity. The place of the
library was carefully considered, the question being especially
discussed both from an artistic and business-like point of view,
how much room might be secured without incurring too great
expense, and how far, in accordance with our plans, the necessary work might be begun and prosecuted. All our proposals
in this business received the approval and sanction of the supreme authorities, and contracts with the tradesmen were at
once concluded. The main requirement still continued to be
the drying of the lower large hall. As externally, toward the
moat and the garden, the ground had been cleared and opened
to free ventilation, we now set to work to accomplish a similar
result internally by deepening the court. Everything else
likely to promote the security and dryness of the building was
the subject of careful deliberation, and our decisions were immediately put in operation. Plastering the outside, for example, was at once taken in hand. After certain difficulties
connected with the inside also had been energetically overcome, the castle library was transferred to the new quarter, a
business conducted with the utmost care and precaution, the
books being again set up in the old order not to disturb the
use of them till the new arrangement was concluded. It re-
dounds generally to the honor of the superintendents of this
business, that with all the revolutions made in the whole and
in single parts, the use of the library throughout the whole
course of this change was not only not suspended, but, on the
contrary, very considerably facilitated.

It is now my part to discharge a debt by mentioning the gentlemen who in this highly complicated and confused business approved themselves faithful and competent fellow-laborers. Professor Güldenapfel, hitherto Jena librarian, had suffered so much from the old imbroglio in this department, that he joyfully offered his aid toward its improvement, and devoted to this object an almost hypochondriac degree of care. Councillor Vulpius, librarian in Weimar, had hitherto superintended the Büttner Library, which was kept in the castle, and did not refuse his services toward its transportation, furnishing us also, with great expertness, many new lists which had become necessary. Dr. Weller, a young, energetic man, undertook the management of the buildings, a task which was no sinecure, seeing that the employment of the different places to new purposes, and the reutilization of book-shelves and other wooden erections demanded incessant and skilled oversight and direction. The clerk of the chancery, Compter, and the keeper hitherto of the castle library, Färber, performed each in his place and in his way all that was possible; so that in this whole business I cannot sufficiently praise the devotion of all to the common task, as also their personal attachment to me.

During this toilsome period, the sale of the highly important Gruner Library was announced, and the commission was at once given to purchase the whole, and then afterward get rid of the duplicate copies. Strongly averse from such a procedure, in which the gain at best would be problematic, I had the Gruner catalogue compared with the catalogues of the whole of our libraries, and had signified by letters on said Gruner catalogue what works were already in our possession, and where they were to be found. By this laborious and tedious job, often censured at the time, we learned what a large quantity of excellent works was already in our hands. As to what had still to be acquired, inquiry was made of the faculty of medicine, and at moderate expense we found ourselves in possession of the contents of the whole of the Gruner collection. Now, however, that our library had acquired solidity and an academic reputation, it began to attract attention from abroad. The Duke of Egerton sent us, accompanied with a friendly notice, the whole of the works published by him. In November the directors gave in their chief report, which enjoyed all the greater approval at the hands of our patrons, that the circumspect Prince had at every step personally informed himself of the course of the business.

The head direction over all the immediate institutions had another special duty to discharge in connection with internal matters. The activity in particular scientific departments had increased to such an extent, the claims they asserted had risen to such a degree, that the present administration no longer sufficed to overtake all the business. By good economy, no doubt, that could in some measure be compassed as a whole. Still it behooved all element of uncertainty to be excluded; nay, for the sake of greater clearness, new heads in the department of accounts and a new arrangement of the administration were become indispensable. At this crisis the officer of the exchequer acting hitherto as our accountant, was transferred from the ducal chamber to another post, and the troublesome task of closing the old accounts, finally winding up all past concerns, and establishing a new administration with a fresh system of accounts, devolved almost exclusively on me, who had been intrusted with the management of the whole, and who, on account of the peculiarity of affairs, was scarcely in a position to avail myself of the services of a competent man of business.

In this year, too, falls an undertaking which perhaps should not have been entered on—the removal of the Löber Gate. The new library building, of a cheerful aspect outside as well as inside, having provoked a desire to see the grounds immediately surrounding it tastefully laid out so as to gratify the eye of the spectator, it was proposed to take away both the outer and inner Löber Gate, to fill up the moats, to prepare a market-place for wood and fruit wagons, and over and above to open communication between the town and the ponds, so as to be serviceable in case of fire. The latter task was soon accomplished. When, however, we came to the inner buildings, by the removal of which we hoped to obtain a stately entrance from the town, we were arrested in our labors by opposition—opposition which obstinately based itself on the modern maxim that the claims of the individual are to be held sacred in the face of whatever advantage might accrue to the community from overriding them. An aggravating eye-sore had thus to be left standing—an eye-sore which, in the near future, it is to be hoped, there will be an opportunity of removing, so that our posterity may not suffer from the same affliction.

In the way of insight into higher plastic art, this year opened a new epoch. Reports and drawings of the Ægina marbles had already reached us, the sculptures of Phigalia we saw before us in drawings, sketches, and more complete copies. The highest, however, still remained remote from us; and we made diligent inquiry after the Parthenon and its pediment statues as they had still been seen by travellers of the seventeenth century. In reply to our inquiries we received from Paris a copy of that drawing, which, though but lightly executed, yet afforded us a more distinct conception of the plan of the whole than, after so much destruction, was possible in more recent times. From the school of the London painter, Haydon, there were sent us copies in black chalk, of equal magnitude with the marbles; and the sight of Hercules and the figure resting in the bosom of another, together with the third figure in a sitting posture and belonging to the group, on a reduced scale, threw us into the astonishment they were calculated to produce. Some Weimar lovers of art had repeatedly seen the gypsum casts likewise, and maintained that here was to be witnessed the acme of aspiring art in antiquity. At the same time a valuable consignment of copperplates belonging to the sixteenth century enabled us to gaze into another epoch of art, likewise animated by thoughts of the highest earnestness. The two volumes of " Bartsch," xiv and xv, were studied in reference to these pictures. The things belonging to that period which we already possessed were looked through, and with our modest dilettanteism we bought only a few, the prices asked being very high.

Likewise highly instructive, though in another sphere, was a large packet of copperplates from a Leipsic auction. For the first time I saw Jackson's woodcuts almost entire. After duly arranging them I contemplated this acquisition, finding it important in more senses than one. Every technical art becomes remarkable when it is directed on excellent subjects, nay, even when it ventures on such as go beyond its powers.

From the French school I received many drawings at the cheapest price. All neighborly feeling toward France was at that time changed into such intense hate that nobody would allow her any merit, nor purchase anything derived from her. I therefore succeeded, at some late auctions, in procuring for a trifle important, large, well-engraved drawings, famous in the world of art and art-history, and enhanced in value through anecdotes and peculiarities of the artists; as also original etchings by several celebrated and popular artists at two groschens apiece. Among others I secured Sebastian Bourdon's etchings, and thereby learned to appreciate in detail an artist I had always esteemed in general.

A medal the Milan people had stamped in honor of our Prince, as a remembrance of his stay there, gives me the opportunity of returning to plastic art. I acquired at the same time an eminently beautiful coin of Alexander's. Several small bronze coins of importance also came into my possession at Carlsbad, partly through purchase and partly in the way of presents from friends. Count Tolstoi's bas-reliefs, of which I knew but a few, were sent me by the benevolent artist

through the hands of a passing courier, and, to grasp together
some scattered events, the copperplate work of Campo Santo,
in Pisa, renewed the study of that older epoch, while, in
strangest antithesis, the "Omaggio della Provincia Veneta
alla S. M. l'Imperatrice d'Austria" brought before my eyes
the wonderful sentiment and thought of contemporaneous
artists.   Of two horseheads ordered in Paris, the one Venetian
and the other Athenian, the former arrived first, enabling us
to appreciate its merits before they were thrown into the shade
by the arrival of the latter with its superabounding greatness.

1819

Of personal events there are the following to report: the
Queen of Würtemberg dies at the beginning, the hereditary
Grand Duke of Mecklenburg at the end, of the year.   State
Minister Von Voight leaves us on the twenty-second of March,
creating a great gap for me, the loss of a principal fellow-
laborer in the circle of my activity.   Of late he felt his strength
severely impaired by the revolutionary forces constantly at
work, and I accounted him happy that he was safe out of the
hearing of Kotzebue's murder, which occurred on the twenty-
third of March, and that the violent tumults which next agitated Germany could no longer distress him.

In the otherwise quiet course and procession of the world
the Empress of Russia called at Weimar; at this time, too, I
saw Count Stourdza and State Councillor Von Köhler.

As a happy event in connection with the princely house, a
son was born to Duke Bernhard, an event which diffused universal joy.   The stay in Dornburg and Jena called forth many
rejoicings.   The princesses had taken possession of their
garden in Jena, causing much movement hither and thither;
and the society of the high personages was increased by the
Duke of Meiningen and Prince Paul of Mecklenburg staying
some time in Jena for the sake of their studies.

In Carlsbad I saw Prince Metternich and his diplomatic
circle, and found in him, as usual, a gracious master.   I made
the personal acquaintance of Count Bernstorff, having for
many years previously heard him spoken of to his advantage,
and having also learned to esteem him for the intimate faithful relations in which he stood to dear friends of mine.   I also
met Count Kaunitz and others who had been in Rome with
the Emperor Francis, but among them all found none who
had a good word to say of the exhibition of German piety in
the Caffarelli palace.   To my great pleasure I also found
Karl Harrach, whom I had known intimately so many years

ago in Carlsbad when he determined on devoting himself to medicine; finding him the same good friend as ever, and now passionately attached to his profession. His lively description, given in all simplicity, of mobile Vienna life fairly confused my senses and understanding the first evening I spent with him. In time, however, I became accustomed to the representation of such a giddy whirl of events, all the more when he confined himself more particularly to a picture of his professional work, his relations to people as physician, and the remarkable scenes which fall under the observation of a man like him, a man of position, of the world, and of medicine. I thus learnt much that was new and foreign to me.

Privy Councillor Berends, from Berlin, a medical man who at once awakened your confidence, was a neighbor much prized by me, as also by my companion, Dr. Rehbein, a young doctor whose insight was as excellent as his character was conscientious. The widow of the intendant of mines Von Trebra reminded me of the great loss I had sustained in the death of her husband a short time ago, an aged friend as indulgent as he was helpful to me. In conversation with Professor Dittrich, of Komotau, I was called back to former Teplitz experiences, thus renewing old joys and sorrows.

At home and in Jena I had the pleasure of meeting many persons staying and passing. I mention Counts Canicoff and Bombelles; next, friends of older and later date, sympathetic and instructive, Nees von Esenbeck, on his way to and from Berlin, Von Stein from Breslau. Of joyous influence were my manifold conversations with this latter friend, an active, robust man, and a former pupil. A like relation was renewed with Counsellor of Mines Von Herder. General Superintendent Krause looked very ill, and many a silly expression of his was perhaps to be imputed to his inward incurable trouble. He recommended " Tiedge's Urania " as a classical work to the upper classes of the gymnasium, not thinking how the scepticism which had been so happily overcome by the excellent poet was now quite out of date; how nobody any longer entertained skepticism about himself, and how, as to skepticism about God, people were too busy to concern themselves with the like of that. His presence did not attract me; I have seen him but once, and regretted he could not give a share of his celebrated intelligence and activity to our Weimar churches and schools. I found myself more at home in the midst of the numerous family of Seebeck, who were removing from Nürnberg to Berlin, regretting with inward affection their happy residence in the former place, calling to mind in a lively manner our former relations to each other in Jena, and looking forward to Berlin with joyful hope. A visit of Dr. Schopenhauer, a meritorious young man, mostly misunderstood, and difficult to understand, stimulated me, and was profitable in the way of our mutal instruction. A young man from Berlin, holding an official post, who by talent, temperance, and diligence had worked himself up from circumstances full of solicitude to a considerable position, economic ease, and a pretty young wife. Major von Lück, the Mainz humorist, who, entirely like himself, dropped in on me unexpectedly, cut short his visit without any occasion, and in his precipitate haste missed the coach. Franz Nicolovius, a dear relative, stayed longer, and gave me the opportunity of knowing and valuing a youth full of promise. Privy Councillor Von Willemer, who was magnanimously endeavoring to divert the consequences of an affair of extreme sadness to himself, travelling to Berlin to entreat pardon of his Majesty the King for the opponent of his son. The Greek, Ghika, visited me frequently. I had always received in a friendly way his countrymen who had come to Germany for the sake of higher culture. President Von Welden, from Bayreuth, like every man in authority, much disturbed by academic turbulence, visited me, and unfortunately nothing of a gladdening nature could be reported respecting public events then of so pressing a character. The Weimar and Gotha plenipotentiaries Von Conta and Von Hoff likewise spoke with me on the academic troubles. A son of Baggesen gave me pleasure by his presence and his unembarrassed conversation. Ernst von Schiller, who could not get on here, was going to a post in the Prussian service. I next made the acquaintance of a young man studying chemistry, of the name of Runge, who appeared to me on the right road.

I have now to mention the sympathy people were pleased to show me in many places and from many sides on the occasion of my seventieth birthday. From a strange fancy rooted in self-willed embarrassment I was always disposed to shun the celebration of my birthday. This time I spent the day on a journey between Hof and Carlsbad; I arrived at the latter place in the evening, and in my narrow-mindedness I thought I had got happily through. On the twenty-ninth of August, however, I was invited to a supper in the Posthof, an invitation I had to decline on the solid ground of the state of my health. Much kindness also surprised me from a distance. In Frankfort-on-the-Main, on the twenty-eighth of August, a beautiful and important festival was celebrated. The Society for Older German Historical Intelligence had named me an honorary member; the paper formally conferring this honor on me I received officially. The Mecklenburg States honored me on this day with a gold medal as memorial of the artistic share I had taken in the erection of Blücher's statue.

1820

After observing on the twentieth of March an eclipse of the moon, we directed our attention toward an annular eclipse of the sun announced for the seventh of September. At the observatory of Jena provisional drawings of it were got ready. The day came on, but, alas! with a sky quite overcast. In the princesses' garden, arrangements were made for the admission of several persons. His Serene Highness visited his dear grandchildren in good time; the cloud about the sun became lighter, beginning and middle could be perfectly observed, and to see the exit, the end, we betook ourselves to the observatory where Professor Posselt with other experts was busy. Here, too, the view was successful, and we had reason to be entirely satisfied, while in Weimar a clouded sky balked all observation.

On a journey to Carlsbad I studied without interruption the forms of clouds, and there systematized my observations. I continued such a nubarium to the end of July and later, whereby I became even more initiated into the development of the visible atmospheric conditions out of each other, and was able at last to undertake a tabular assortment of the forms of clouds in different fields. Returned home, I talked over the matter with Professor Posselt, who took a very intelligent part in the subject. Meteorological observations were also sent me from Eisenach. Of books, Brande's "Meteorological Intelligence" and other essays in this department were most helpful to me. Dittmar's labors were utilized, though, of course, not in the sense the good man might wish.

Botany was not lost sight of. The Belvedere catalogue was drawn up; and I found myself induced to write the history of the Weimar botany. Hereupon I had a French publication translated, which, in a gallant discourse, recommended and directed the increase of the Ericæ. Jäger on the "Misgrowths of Plants," De Candolle's "Medicinal Virtues of Plants," Henschel on "Sexuality," Nees von Esenbeck's "Manual," Robert Brown on the "Syngenesists" were all perused, a stay in the botanical garden giving me the most desirable leisure for such work.

Important honey-dew was observed and described on the spot. Herr Dr. Carus communicated a delicate web of lime-roots from a churchyard in Saxony, roots which, having

15

reached down to the coffins, had enveloped both them and the corpses inside as with filigree. I continued nursing the *bryophyllum calycinum*, plants which celebrate in the light of day the triumph of metamorphosis. Meanwhile the liveliest hopes were excited by the journey of Austrian and Bavarian students of natural science to Brazil.

On my journey to Carlsbad I went by way of Wunsiedel to Alexandersbad, where, for the first time after many years—since 1785—I again observed the strange ruins of a granite mountain. My horror of explaining things by extraordinary forces, such as were here abundantly imputed—earthquakes, volcanoes, deluges, and other titanic events—was increased when, on the spot, after calm contemplation, I observed that, through partial dissolution and partial persistence of the original rock—consequently through the standing, sinking, and tumbling of huge masses, this astonishing phenomenon was accounted for in a perfectly natural way. This subject was both literally and figuratively developed in my scientific papers; I doubt, however, whether such a calm view will content such a turbulent age.

In Carlsbad I again arranged the old geognostic series in instructive specimens, among which beautiful pieces of the granite of Schlossberg and the Bernhard rock, interlined with veins of horn-stone, agreeably caught the eye. To this was appended a new more special series referring to porcelain and earthenware manufacture, containing at the same time the natural unchanged pieces. This complete collection I showed to the Prince of Turn and Taxis and his circle, on a visit they kindly paid me, and they seemed satisfied with the exhibition.

I likewise paid renewed attention to the pseudo-volcanic mountains, the openings made in the mountains in the neighborhood of Dalwitz and Lessau, on account of the construction there of a new road, offering me a favorable opportunity in this way. Here you were struck by the fact that the original layers of the mountain formerly disposed in horizontal strata—at one time most closely mixed up with masses of coal, then set in a glow of combustion—continued firmly in their old situation in the character of bright porcelain-jasper. A whole layer also of rod-like iron-stone, for example, distinctly displayed itself intermediately. We were thus enabled to enrich Müller's and our own collection and the cabinets of friends with large and instructive pieces.

Next climbing the mountain of Kammerberg, near Eger, which, on account of the construction of the road, was always getting more and more opened up, I carefully and minutely inspected its regular layers, and felt myself obliged to revert to the views of Councillor of Mines Reuss, and to regard this problematic phenomenon as pseudo-volcanic. Here was a mica slate intercalated with coals; there lay beds of clay-layers of later date, made red hot, melted, and in this way more or less changed. This view, the result of my fresh observation, it cost me no pains to adopt in spite of a printed paper of my own advocating an opposite theory. It is no wonder if an honest investigator, endeavoring to account for an important phenomenon of nature, should sometimes change his opinion.

The small basalts of Horn, a high mountain in the neighborhood of Elbogen—basalts about the size of a child's fist to which one could often attribute a definite form—the ground-type out of which, apparently, all the other forms were developed, was imitated in clay, and specimens were sent to Herr Von Schreibers, in Vienna.

In the Jena museums I make a fresh survey of the Carlsbad set, and as the geologist is always disposed to institute experiments of combustion of a higher and lower temperature in order to achieve appearances parallel to those resulting from natural combustions, I caused experiments of this kind to be made in a bottle factory at Zwetzen, and am sorry not to have preserved the chemical results in the order introduced in the catalogue, especially as some rocks, after the most intense combustion, shaped themselves with extreme regularity. At the same time there were sent us from Coblenz, natural clay, and tiles burned to an extraordinary degree from that clay—tiles which also showed themselves in the form of slag and of regular structure.

Younger friends provided me with specimens of the primitive bowlders at Danzig, as also at Berlin, out of which could be arranged a completely systematized collection of stone species, and that in their hardest rock- and vein-parts.

The stone-cutter Facius showed us an example of a formation of the latest possible date. In a tufa-stone conglomerate containing various rounded bowlders he had also found a cut chalcedon, on which was an obelisk with all sorts of non-Egyptian signs, a man kneeling in prayer on one side, a man standing sacrificing on the other, of tolerable workmanship. It was sought to explain this plainly accidental appearance by the circumstances in which the stone was situated, which, however, this is not the place to develop. The Mecklenburg Chamberlain, Herr Von Preen, honored me with important minerals he had brought with him from a journey in Tyrol; Count Bedemar, the royal Danish chamberlain, with beautiful opals from the Faroe Isles.

The following books afforded me much pleasure: Rose

" On the Genesis of Basalts," an old contemporary, clinging also to old notions; also his " Symbol." An extract from the first of these two books I communicated in print; an extract from the second is still among my papers. Herr Von Schreibers's " Aerolites " was helpful to us in this field. From England came, with much welcome to us, " The First Principles of Geology, by G. H. Greenough, London, 1819." To recognize in a foreign language the Werner views, to which we had now for so many years become accustomed, was stimulating and delightful. A large geologic map of England was, by reason of its particular completeness and distinctness, highly instructive. I for my part contributed to " Morphology and Natural Science " the third sheet of the first volume.

Fresh enthusiasm for the theory of colors produced the " Entoptic Colors." With great care I concluded my composition in August this year, and transmitted it to press. The deduction which I had followed in my " Theory of Colors " was here, too, made good; the entoptic apparatus was always being more simplified. Mica and gypsum leaflets were applied in experiments, and their effects carefully compared. I had the pleasure of once more going through this matter with Herr State Councillor Schultz; I then betook myself to various paralipomena of the theory of colors. Purkinje's " Contributions to the Knowledge of Seeing in a Subjective Respect " were extracted, and the opponents of my endeavors produced in the order of years.

In the way of sympathy from friends, my attention was directed to " Nouvelle Chroagénésie, par Le Prince," a work which might be regarded as the effect and confirmation of my theory of colors. On nearer inspection, however, an important difference came to light. The author had come by the same road as myself to the discovery of Newton's error, but for all that he did not mend matters either for himself or others, setting up, as he does, like Dr. Reade, something just as untenable in room of the old fallacy he seeks to displace. This caused me to consider anew how man, arrested in his errors and enlightened, will yet relapse so quickly again into the darkness of his individuality, where he pitifully struggles to help himself forward a bit with the light of a faint glimmering lantern.

I make various observations on the path pursued by the sciences—on progress and retardation, nay, retrogression. The inter-relation of all physical phenomena, ever more and more advancing into notice, yet ever more mysterious, was modestly considered, and in this way the Chladni and Leebeck figures were parallelized, when all at once, through Professor

Oersted's discovery of the relation of galvanism to the magnet needle, an almost dazzling light burst on us. On the other hand I contemplated with horror an example of the most dreadful obscurantism, studying more minutely Biot's labors on the polarization of light. One gets fairly sick at the sight of such craziness; theories, demonstrations, and deductions of such a kind are veritable *necroses* against which the most vital organization cannot maintain its sanity.

The large lower hall of the Jena Library was now in all substantial respects restored; the book-shelves which, formerly disposed lengthwise, had darkened the room, were now arranged diagonally, so as to admit due light into the place. A colored old German window, the gift of his Serene Highness, was fitted in, and beside it the gypsum busts of the two foster-fathers. In the upper hall a large desk was set up, and in this way the requirements of the institutions were being successively satisfied. To lend some air of attraction to rooms all too plain, unadorned, and offering little to delight the eye, we thought of symbolic pictures representing the different intellectual faculties, which, accompanied with apophthegms, should draw the attention of the visitor to the scientific institutions. This was to some extent carried out, a part being prepared through the kindness of Herr Schinkel; the most, however, was left only in the form of a sketch, nay, even of a mere thought. Buder's "Deductions" were catalogued by Vulpius, a Bohemian manuscript referring to Huss's times was translated by Dr. Wlokka, a general report of the library given in, a comprehensive continuation of the whole business being rendered possible by complete diaries and Dr. Weller's personal reports.

In connection with the botanical institution we were busied with the plan of a new glass-house under the orders and special co-operation of his Serene Highness. The design was examined, contracts for the work concluded, and the business completed in due time. The purchase of Stark's collections of preparations for the anatomical cabinet was also approved and concluded, though, as it required a new place for its reception, its transportation was postponed. The lower large hall in the castle which, since the removal of Büttner's Library, had still remained in confusion, was again completely put in order for the preservation of different curiosities. An important model of the Amsterdam Council-house which, through being frequently shifted about, had got much damaged, was repaired and set up again.

Things in Weimar went on in due course. The cabinet of medals was given over to Vulpius for definite arrangement, and the archives were also duly disposed of.

Last year in honor of my birthday the respected Society for Older German Historical Intelligence in Frankfort-on-the-Main had paid me the compliment of naming me an honorary member of their body. Now when I more carefully considered the claims of the society and what part they might desire me to take in furtherance of their purposes, it occurred to me that it would be to my advantage to get initiated into a new field of inquiry. In the Jena Library lay a prized manuscript of the Chronicle of Otto von Freysingen, as also other papers, a description of which would be welcome to the society. Compter, the secretary of the library, had a special talent for things of this sort, was remarkably successful in imitating the old written characters, and would therefore find such a work quite to his mind. I drew up a careful plan according to which the codices should be compared point for point. This done, Compter began to compare the said manuscript of Von Freysingen with the first Strasburg printed copy—a work, however, which was not continued. Still, on the whole, the business was carried on for a considerable time, and my connection with Herr Büchler in Frankfort kept up.

At the same time the hereditary grand duchess purchased, at the auction of Canon Pick, at Cologne, a well-preserved silver vase, on which an engraved representation and an inscription seemed to refer to the baptism of Friedrich I, and to a godfather called Otto. It was lithographed for Frankfort, where, and at other places, it was subjected to comments. It now came to light how impossible it is for antiquarians to agree in their opinions. A document drawn up on the subject gives a remarkable example of the diversity of antiquarian criticism; and I do not deny that this experience fairly robbed me of all further pleasure and confidence in the matter. I, too, had written out an explanation of the vase for my gracious Princess, but one contradiction trod so closely on the heels of another that at last you were fairly puzzled to know whether the silver vase you held in your hands really existed, or whether there was any image or inscription on it at all.

"The Triumphal Procession of Mantegna," cut in wood by Andrea Andreani had, among the art-works of the sixteenth century, from the beginning attracted my greatest attention. I had some plates of it in my own possession, and I never saw in any collection this production complete without going through the whole with lively interest. At last I received it myself, and was able to view them beside and following each other; I also studied Vasari, who, however, was not to my taste. The present resting-place of the originals, however, which having been painted on tables, had been carried away

from Mantua, remained to me a secret. One morning I had
my prints spread out in full in the garden-house of Jena, in
order to contemplate them more particularly, when young
Mellish, a son of my old friend, entered, and at once declared
this was to him the renewal of acquaintance he had lately made,
having, shortly before his departure from England, seen such
a collection, in good preservation, at Hampton Court, in the
royal rooms. Research became easier; I renewed my relations with Herr Dr. Noehden, who in the friendliest way endeavored to meet all my wishes. Number, measure, condition,
nay, the history of their possession from Karl I downward, all
was rendered clear, as I have circumstantially set forth in
" Kunst und Alterthum," vol. iv, 2d part. The original
copperplates of this series, by Mantegna himself, likewise
came, by favor of friends, to my hands, and I could now completely recognize them as a whole, comparing them with
Bartsch's references, and make myself entirely conversant with
such an important point in the history of art.

From youth up I had peculiar pleasure in the company of
plastic artists. With free, light exertion a picture would arise
in conversation before our eyes: our mutual intelligence was
perfect. This pleasure was now allotted to me in a high degree. Herr State Councillor Schultz brought with him three
worthy artists from Berlin to Jena, where towards the end of
summer I was staying in my usual garden residence. Herr
Privy Councillor Schinkel admitted me into the plan of his
new theatrical building, and showed me invaluable landscape
pen-drawings, the acquisition of his Tyrol travels. Herren
Tieck and Rauch moulded a bust of me, the former also a
profile of Friend Knebel. On this occasion sprang up a lively,
nay, passionate conversation on art, and I may well reckon
these days as among the fairest of the year. A model having
been finished in clay, Kaufmann, the Court-sculptor, prepared
a gypsum cast. These friends left for Weimar, whither I followed them, renewing the most pleasant hours. So much in
the way of production had been compressed into these few
days—design and completion, plans and preparations, matter
of instruction and delight—that the remembrance of them will
ever be stimulating for me.

As to the state of art in Berlin I was now most completely
instructed, Hofrath Meyer communicating to me the diary of
his stay there. His essays also on art schools and art collections chained my vital attention to art and art works in general
till the end of the year. In modern plastic art, I received the
most complete collection of medals cut in brass by Count
Tolstoi in honor of the great war of deliverance. How highly

praiseworthy was this work is more particularly set forth by
the Weimar lovers of art in " Kunst und Alterthum."

Leipsic auctions and other occasions contributed to the increase of my copperplate collection. Brown prints copied
from " Rafaelino da Reggio," of an entombment, the original
of which had already been in my possession for some time,
shed the clearest light on the procedure of artists and imitators.
The " Sacraments of Poussin " gave us deep insight into the
naturel of so important an artist. Everything here was justified at the court of the understanding, was based on an irre-
fragable conception of art, but you felt the almost entire
absence of a certain naïveté which delights in communicating
itself, and also captivates the hearts of others. From this point
of view a series of such important and revered subjects was of
the greatest furtherance to us.

Good prints of Von Haldenwang's aquatinta, after Nahl's
careful drawings of the four Cassel Claude Lorraines, also
came into my hands. These excite our continual astonishment, and are all the more prized that the originals snatched
away from our neighborhood are accessible to but a few
people in the far North.

The worthy, diligent Friedrich Gmelin, who never failed in
affectionate remembrance of the Weimar lovers of art, sent us
most of the proofs of his copperplates to the Virgil of the
Duchess of Devonshire. However much his skill in this work
was admired, it could not but be regretted that he should lend
his hand to such originals. These prints, intended to accompany a magnificent edition of the " Æneid " by Annibale Caro,
give a mournful instance of the modern realistic tendency
which prevails mostly in England. For what can well be
sadder than to seek to illustrate a poet by the representation
of desolate tracts which the liveliest imagination refuses to
cultivate, refuses to people? Can one be so stupid as not to
perceive, or, perceiving, not to act in conformity with the perception, that it was opportune enough for Virgil in his time
to endeavor to recall the original state of the Latin world, and
to dress in some measure in poetical attire before the eyes of
his contemporary Romans, the long-deserted, vanished, entirely changed castles and towns of the primitive time, but
that to outrage the eyes of the modern reader of Virgil with
the literal copy of places waste, level with the earth, weltering
in swamps, is to impose paralysis on the reader's imagination,
to clip the wings of his fancy which would otherwise soar up
to the height of the poet's musings?

The Munich lithographs enabled us, from time to time,
to contemplate the unresting progress of such a highly

important branch of technics. A very distinct and exact copy of the engravings to " Faust," drawn by Retsch, appeared in London. A historical engraving representing the assembled ministers at the Vienna Congress, a present of the Duchess of Courland, took its place in the portfolios of the largest size.

The oldest principle of chromatics that the bodily color is a dark shade which can be observed only when light shines through, was confirmed by the transparent Swiss landscapes which König, from Berne, exhibited to us. One which was powerfully shone through, took the place of the one which was brightly shone upon, and so overpowered the eye, that at last, instead of a decided pleasure, one felt painfully affected.

In conclusion, I have yet thankfully to remember a lithograph which in celebration of my birthday this year was kindly sent with a poem from Mainz. The sketch also indicated a monument which my dear countrymen had intended for me. As a graceful ornament to an idyllic garden-scene—as was signified in the first friendly thought—it would have been proper thankfully to recognize it, but as a great, architectural, independent, magnificent erection, it was more becoming modestly to beg its being put a stop to.

To higher, however, nay, to the highest considerations of art we were summoned when the architecture and sculpture of Greece pressed more closely on our attention. We were drawn anew to the Parthenon, while more particular intelligence reached us of the Elgin marbles, and no less of the Phigalian. We were here sensible of the utmost limits of human achievement in art of the highest kind, conjoined with the truest imitation of nature, and accounted ourselves happy to have lived to see such excellence.

A contemporary friend chained our bias and imagination to antiquity. The latest number of Tischbein's sculptures to Homer gave rise to many comparisons. The Milan codex of the " Iliad," although dating from a late period, was of great consequence for art views; splendid works of art of older date being manifestly imitated therein, and in this way their remembrance preserved for us.

The residence of Herr Raabe, in Rome and Naples, had not remained fruitless for us. On an initiative from higher quarters we had assigned to him some tasks from which very beautiful results were transmitted us. A copy of the Aldobrandinian nuptials, in the state in which the artist found this work, made a very agreeable comparison with an older copy, executed also very carefully thirty years ago. To recall to mind the coloring of the Pompeian pictures we had desired several copies of them, and the worthy artist highly delighted us with the imitation of the well-known centaurs and female dancers. The tender feeling of the ancients in chromatics here displayed itself as entirely commensurate with their other merits. And, indeed, how was it possible for such a harmonious humanity to fail in this main particular? How was it possible that with the want of such a capital artistic qualification their nature should have betrayed a most serious effect.

As, however, our worthy artist on his return to Rome exhibited this work of his, the Nazarenes there hooted it as useless and ill-advised. He did not, however, allow himself to be led astray, but on our advice drew and colored in Florence some works after Peter of Cortona, again strengthening our conviction that this artist was endowed by nature with a fine sense of beauty, especially in the field of color. Had, since the beginning of the century, our influence on German artists not been quite frustrated, had cant with its deadening influence not resumed its sway over the minds of men, we should have given occasion for a collection of such a kind as would have presented in examples to an eye instructed purely in nature and art, a history of more ancient and more modern coloring such as has been already composed in words. Seeing, however, things were once for all destined otherwise, we sought to strengthen only ourselves and the few immediately allied to us in rational views, while that crazy sectarian spirit was not ashamed to proclaim its old exploded cant to be the fundamental maxim of all artistic procedure.

In Weimar we were not lucky in our own artistic productions. Heinrich Müller, who had practised lithography in Munich, was encouraged to transfer to stone different drawings which were in our hands, among them Carstens'. He succeeded not amiss, it is true; but the first number published under the name of the "Weimar Pinakothek" found no purchasers, the market being glutted with wares, some of them of excellent quality. He tried some more plates, but we found it advisable to suspend the business, in the hope of resuming it in the future with improved techniques.

As in some measure allied to plastic art, I remark here that this year my attention again revived in the direction of autographic handwritings of distinguished persons, in consequence of the publication of a description of the castle of Friedland with fac-similes of Wallenstein and other important personages of the Thirty Years' War, a work which I at once attached by way of supplement to my original documents. At the same time there also appeared a portrait of that remarkable man in full figure from the facile practised hand of Director Bergler in Prague, the spirit of those times being thus conjured back to us in a twofold manner.

Of my equal interest in works of various kinds, a great deal might be said. Hermann's programme on the nature and treatment of mythology I read with the high respect I had always given to the works of this excellent man, for what can more profit us than to be admitted into the views of men of deep and penetrating mind who have consecrated all their faculties toward one object? One remark of his could not escape me, and that is that the primitive people who fashioned languages were, in the naming of natural phenomena, and in their reverence of them as ruling deities, influenced more by fear than by love, recognizing more the tumultuously destructive than the silently creative deities. And as this human race of ours never fairly outgrows its original fundamental characters, it struck me how our latest theorists in geology remained true to the instincts of their ancestors, and could conceive of no way of creating a world than by vomiting fire out of mountains, convulsing the earth, rending it into chasms, torturing it internally by pressure and contusions ($\pi\iota\acute{\epsilon}\sigma\mu\alpha\tau\alpha$), sweeping it with storms, deluging it with floods and such-like universal hurly-burly.

Wolf's " Prolegomena " I again took in hand. The works of this man, with whom I stood in intimate personal relations, had long since served to lighten up my way before me. In the study of the above work, I watched myself and the operations of my mind. In this way I became aware how systole and diastole were constantly alternating in me. I was accustomed to regard the two Homeric poems as wholes, and here were they each with great knowledge, penetration, and ability sundered and taken to pieces, and, while my understanding readily concurred in this procedure, a traditional feeling at once recomposed into a whole all those detachments, and a certain tolerance which overcomes us in the appreciation of all true poetical productions, caused me tenderly to overlook the gaps, variations, and defects I had been made sensible of.

Reisig's observations on " Aristophanes " appeared shortly after Wolf's work. Although grammar proper was outside of my sphere, I appropriated out of this book all that belonged to me. Lively conversation with this young man, and mutual intellectual communications afforded me, during my lengthy stay on this occasion in Jena, the most agreeable hours.

The French literature, old and modern, excited this time also my special interest. The novel " Anatole," the reading of which was almost forced on me, I had to approve as satisfactory. The works of Madame Roland excited wondering admiration. The fact that persons of such character and talents are produced will no doubt be the chief advantage handed down by unhappy times to posterity. They it is who impart such a high value in our eyes to days of world-history otherwise so repulsive. The history of Joan of Orleans, in its whole detail, produces the same effect, only that at the distance of several centuries it acquires a certain *chiaroscuro*. In the same way the poems of Marie of France appear dearer and more graceful on account of the vapor of years which intervenes between us and her personality.

Of German productions " Olfried und Lisena " was highly welcome to me, an appreciation also heartily expressed at the time. The one misgiving, which to a certain extent was also confirmed in the sequel, was that the young man had probably spent his time too early in such a circle. Werner's " Mother of the Maccabees," and Houwald's picture affected me, each in its own way, disagreeably. They seemed to me like knights who, to surpass their predecessors, seek reward outside the lists. Henceforth I refrained from everything modern, committing the enjoyment and the judgment of such to younger hearts and minds ; berries of that sort, though no longer tempting to me, might yet be toothsome to them.

Transplanted, however, into an earlier period by Blumauer's " Æneid," I shuddered in the endeavor to realize to myself how such boundless insipidity and platitude could ever have been popular or conform with the sense of any time. " Touti Nameh," by Iken, drew me away again unexpectedly into the East. My admiration of these fables, especially those according to the older edition, of which Kosegarten in the appendix gives examples, was raised, or rather revived ; the living presence of the unsearchable and incredible it is which here attracts us with such powerful delight. How easy it were to destroy to the feelings and imagination such invaluable naïve things by the application of mystic symbolism ! By way of complete antithesis, I mention a literary collection of Letti's songs which, just as limited as the above are limitless, moved in the most natural simple circle.

My interest was next withdrawn to foreign countries, and transported into the most dreadful African situations by Dumont's " In Morocco Slavery "; into states of rising and sinking culture, older and more modern, by Laborde's " Journey to Spain." A written diary of Zelter's travels led me to the German Ocean, a diary which anew confirmed my view that the affection we cherish for the traveller is a most infallible means toward realizing distant places and manners.

Important persons far and near, called forth my interest. The biography of " Hess " written by Landolt, prefect of

Switzerland, especially with its autographic additions, renewed my idea and conception of that wonderful child of man—a figure such as perhaps could be born and become great only in Switzerland. In 1779 I had come to know the man personally, and, as a lover of oddities and eccentricities, viewed with wonder this astonishing, sound piece of humanity, and delighted myself also with the fables told of him. Those earlier days were now recalled to me, and I was all the better able to comprehend such a physical phenomenon, that I summoned to the help of imagination and reflection his personal presence and the surroundings in which I had found him.

Of nearer interest for me was the misunderstanding which broke out between Voss and Stolberg and which gave occasion for various considerations.

We often see how, after twenty years' married life, a couple who have been living secretly at variance with each other, seek divorce, and everyone exclaims, "After having so long endured each other, why can't you do so to the end?" This reproach is, however, highly unjustifiable. He who adequately considers the high dignity environing the married state in regulated and cultivated society will be sensible of the dangerous consequences of divesting himself of such a sacred connection, and will often put the question to himself, whether it is not better to endure the bitterness of the present, so long as it is not altogether intolerable, and even to drag on a wretched life, rather than precipitate a result which, unfortunately, when the ills of married life at last grow unendurable, of itself springs violently into the light of day.

Similar is the case with a friendship formed in youth. In the first days of radiant dawning hope, one enters absolutely, heart and soul, into such a connection; a rupture is inconceivable for the present, inconceivable through all eternity. Such committal of the soul in friendship stands much higher than the alliance two passionate lovers vow at the altar; it is wholly pure, unstimulated by desire, the gratification of which might be apt to induce a retrocession. It, therefore, seems impossible to untie a bond of friendship which has been contracted in youth, even though more than once differences should crop up threatening to dissolve it.

If one looks minutely into Voss's grievances against Stolberg, he will find in the very first conditions of their acquaintance, a pronounced divergence which there was no hope of ever seeing composed. Two brothers of the rank of count, distinguished from others at the students' café by their better plate and confectionery, whose ancestral line in the background ever overshadows their existence in many ways—how can an able, blunt, downright, isolated *Autochton* enter into true, lasting alliance with such men? The reciprocal relation is, moreover, loose to the utmost degree; a certain youthful liberal good-nature under the action of æsthetic influences draws them together, without uniting them; for what avails a bit opining and rhyming against innate qualities, modes, and conditions of living?

On leaving the university, had they separated, the one for the North, the other for the South, a certain relationship by letters and writings might, at all events, have been continued. But, instead, they approach each other topographically, bind each other to reciprocal services and gratitude; live as neighbors to each other; come in contact in their businesses with each other; inwardly disunited they tug and strain fretfully together, held to each other by elastic bands.

The possibility, however, how such torture could be so long endured, such a desperate relation be perennially maintained, is a problem not to be solved by everyone. I, however, am convinced that this wonder was due to the amiable, intermediating influence of the Countess Agnes. I myself once rejoiced in the radiance of her fairest years, once delighted myself in her most graceful presence, recognizing in her a nature before which all disaffection, all discord could not help at once dissolving and vanishing. Her ascendancy was not that of the moral nature, of the understanding, of intellect, but of a free, gay, harmonious personality. Never did I see her again, but in all relations as peacemaker between husband and friend I recognize her perfectly. All through, she plays the part of the "Angel Grazioso," plays a part equally lovely, unerring, and effective so that I have asked myself whether it would not have moved the admiration of a Calderon, the master of such a province. Not without a consciousness of her power, not without a feeling of her serene superiority, she moves between the two alienated friends and fascinates them into concord by the charm she suggests of the possible paradise lying in relations where yet, inwardly, they already detect the premonitions of hell.

The god-like lady hastens back to the source of her being; Stolberg gropes after a lost prop, and the tendril clings round the cross. Voss, on the other hand, lets himself be overcome by the indignation he had so long nursed in his heart, and presents to us as an injustice on the other side what was only a reciprocal incompatibility. Stolberg with a little more strength, Voss with a little less tenacity would never have allowed the affair to go the length it did. Had they found union on a sober footing impossible, a separation would yet have been rendered more tolerable and mutually pardonable.

In any case both were to be pitied. They would not let the former impression of friendship die away, not considering how friends who shake hands with each other at the parting of the roads are already as good as lost to each other. If their dispositions run in mutually opposite directions, how is the one to communicate his inmost secrets to the other? It is very odd, therefore, to see Voss blame Stolberg for keeping secret what had no right to be imparted to him, and which, when it at last came to the light of day, affected the most sober and sensible men with despair.

How did Jacobi and many others demean themselves on that event? And will the matter be found as important in the future as it then appeared at the moment? I know not; but a like scandal will unquestionably arise should Catholicism and Protestantism, however long in the shade they may have crept beside each other in outward truce, suddenly on some particular occasion come into glaring conflict with each other.

But not alone religion will produce such phenomena; political, literary differences unexpectedly coming to light will have the same effect. Let one but call to mind the unhappy discovery by Friedrich Jacobi of Lessing's secret leanings in favor of Spinoza's way of thinking, a discovery which was literally the death of Mendelssohn. How hard was it for the Berlin friends, who thought they had grown into such close intimacy with Lessing, to have all at once sprung on them the fact that all his life he had kept secret from them a view of things in deep antagonism to theirs!

I had a visit from Ernst Schubarth, whose personal acquaintance was highly agreeable to me. The affection with which he had comprehended my works could not but make him dear and precious to me, and his thoughtful presence raised my appreciation of him still higher. Though, true the peculiarity of his character gave me some apprehension as to how he would like and fit himself into civil life, there now presented itself an opening where he might hope to make his way under favorable auspices.

Some labors and preparations busied me greatly. I again took in hand the " Second Residence in Rome," in order to attach it by a necessary continuation to the " Italian Journey "; I next found myself disposed to work at the " Campaign of 1792 " and the " Siege of Mainz," etc. I therefore made an extract from my diaries, read several works relative to these epochs, and endeavored to recall many things to remembrance. I further wrote a summary chronicle of the years 1797 and 1798, supplied two numbers of " Art and Antiquity," as a conclusion to the second volume, and prepared the first number of the third volume, in connection with which work I have to remember another careful development of the motives of the " Iliad." I wrote the " Self-betrayer," also the continuation of the " Nut-brown Maid " and furthered the ideal connection of the " Travels." The free unembarrassed feeling of travel allowed me to come again in contact with the " Divan "; I extended the " Book of Paradise," and found a great deal to intercalate in the preceding parts. By a symbolic poem I endeavored thankfully to reply to the friendly celebration from so many sides of my birthday. Stimulated by the sympathetic inquiries addressed to me, I wrote a commentary to the abstruse poem, the " Harz Journey in Winter."

In foreign literature, " Count Carmagnola " engaged my attention. The truly amiable author, Alessandro Manzoni, a born poet, was, on account of a theatrical local offence he had given, accused by his countrymen of romanticism, of whose improprieties, however, not the slightest trace attached to him. He held by a historical course, his poetry had the character of a complete humanity, and though he luxuriated little in tropes, his lyric utterances were yet highly praiseworthy, as even envious critics had to acknowledge. Our good German youths might see in him an example of how a man in simple greatness exerts power naturally—an example which might, perhaps, lead them back from the altogether false *Transcendiren.*

Music was sparely, yet sweetly, apportioned me. A children's song, composed for the Nepomueks festival in Carlsbad, was rendered back to me by Friend Zelter in fit style and high sense. Music Director Eberwein turned his talent happily to the " Divan," and the charming execution of his wife gave me many delightful social hours.

Some things in reference to persons I will write down without further connection as I find them marked. The Duke de Berri is murdered, to the horror of all France. Hofrath Jagemann dies, to the regret of Weimar. I make the long longed-for acquaintance of Herr von Gagern, who pays me a friendly visit, in which the peculiar individuality of this excellent man is displayed to me. His Majesty the King of Würtemberg honors me with his presence in the company of our young masters. I have, next, the pleasure of making the acquaintance of worthy men, his Majesty's cavaliers, in attendance on him. In Carlsbad I meet both patrons and friends. Countess von der Recke and the Duchess of Courland I find as formerly gracefully and sympathetically disposed toward me. Literary conversations are continued with Dr. Schütze. Councillor of the Embassy Conta takes part with much insight in the geognostic excursions.   The specimens we collect in these wanderings and otherwise are viewed with interest by the Prince of Thurn and Taxis and his circle.   Prince Karl of Schwarzburg-Sondershausen shows me kindness.   Good-fortune brings me into the company of Professor Hermann, of Leipsic, and we come mutually to increased instruction.

And so, at last, in the way both of jest and earnest, I may also mention a marriage in civil life which was celebrated at the shooter's house, the so-called little Versailles.   A pleasant valley at the side of the Schlackenwald way was profusely sprinkled with citizens in their finery, who, in part guests of the young pair, lustily moved about, smoking their tobacco pipes in hearing of dance-music drowning all other sounds, or sat by the ever refilled glasses and beer-cans, enjoying themselves to their hearts' content.   I joined them and in a few hours gained a clearer conception of the state of the town proper of Carlsbad than in many years before I could have attained, when I looked upon the place as only a large hotel and hospital.

My subsequent stay in Jena was greatly enlivened by the fact of my patrons spending a part of the summer in Dornburg, which afforded me a more lively sociality than usual and a great deal of unexpected entertainment.   For example, Krtom Balahja, the celebrated Indian juggler and sword-swallower, astonished us on this occasion by his extraordinary feats.

Quite a number of visits blessed and gladdened me in the old garden-house and the scientifically planned botanic garden conveniently adjacent to it: Madame Rodde, by birth Schlözer, whom I had seen many years before at her father's house, where as the most beautiful, most promising child, she grew up in happy development to the joy of the strict, almost surly-tempered man.   There I saw also her bust fashioned shortly before, by our countryman Trippel in Rome, when the father and daughter were there.   I would like much to know whether a cast of it still remains, and where it is to be found; it should be multiplied; father and daughter deserve to have their memory preserved.   Von Both and his lady from Rostock, a worthy couple with whom I became more intimate through Herr Von Preen, brought me the productions of a poet of nature and the nation, D. G. Babst, which compare very favorably with the works of his coevals.   Highly valuable are his occasional poems, which recall to us an old bygone state, revived in festal moments.   Count Paar, adjutant of the Prince of Schwarzenberg, to whom I had attached myself in a friendly

16

way in Carlsbad, assured me by his unexpected appearance
and by his continued confidential conversations, of his inviolable affection. Anton Prokesch, likewise adjutant to the
Prince, was introduced to me by him. Both thoroughly conversant with the Hahnemann doctrine described it to me minutely, and from their communications it appeared to me that
whoever was careful about himself and subjected himself solely
to a diet conformable with his state and constitution, would so
far unconsciously act in accordance with that method.

I had to thank Herr Von der Walsburg for much joyous
light shed on the Spanish literature and the deeper insight
into it thereby afforded me. A son of Fallenberg brought
me the philanthropic plastic efforts of his father more distinctly to sense and soul. Frau Von Helvig, by birth Von
Imhoff, awakened by her presence agreeable remembrances
of former relations, as her drawings also showed how she had
been always building on the foundations she had laid years
before in the company of lovers of art in Weimar. Count
and Countess Hopfgarten, as also Förster and his wife, brought
me personally the assurance of faithful interest in my life and
labors on the part of friends known and unknown. Privy
Councillor Rudolphi, of Berlin, as also Professor Weiss, gave
us but a flying visit, yet their fleeting presence served to enliven and instruct me.

Our circle at this time looked forward to the visit of Herr
General Superintendent Röhr. What great profit was here in
store for us was immediately on his entry to be foreseen, if
not to be precisely calculated. He came at a good time for
me; his first clerical act was the baptism of my second grand-
child, whose undeveloped being seemed already to forecast
much good. Privy Councillor Blumenbach and family delighted us for some days with their presence; he was ever
the same cheerful, circumspect, erudite man with an all-retentive memory, standing on his own feet, a true representative
of the great learned institution in which he had for so many
years labored as a highly important member. My dear relatives, Councillor Schlosser and wife, from Frankfort-on-the-
Main, stayed some days with us, raising by their personal
presence to a higher degree of confidence our many years'
active friendly relationship with each other. Privy Councillor
Wolf animated our deep literary studies by his instructive
spirit of controversy, and it happened that on his departure
Dr. Reisig, who had been called to Halle, could accompany
him thither—Dr. Reisig, a young man whom I was very sorry
to part with, not alone on my own account. Dr. Küchel-
becker, from St. Petersburg, Von Quandt and his lady, Von

Arnim and Painter Ruhl by their interesting conversations greatly variegated our social days.

On the side of our princely family, we were gladdened by the visit of Duke Bernhard with his spouse and children. Almost at the same time, however, by an unhappy slip the grand duchess broke her arm, causing sorrow and apprehension to the whole of her friends.

By way of supplement I have yet to remark that at the end of September the revolution broke out in Portugal; that personally I escaped a business the undertaking of which, with the great responsibility attaching to it, threatened me with no end of worry.

1821

I found much inducement to self-activity. The many years' affection and friendship of Count Brühl demanded a prologue from me for the opening of the new Berlin Theatre, a prologue which, as time pressed, had to be conceived and executed almost extemporaneously. The good effect it produced was highly delightful to me; for I had longed for an opportunity of testifying to dear Berlin my sympathy with it in important epochs of its history.

I again put hand to the " Paralipomena." Into this compartment I stowed away different accumulations, whatever in the way of poems I had yet unprinted and unassorted. From time to time—such a work being apt to become irksome if too long protracted—I would arrange them, and, a good number among them being occasional poems, annotate them as well. " Zahme Xenien " I also pieced together; for although one should avoid marring the catholicity of his poetical works by peevish and ill-natured personalities, one cannot help now and again giving vent to his nature on this side. Of small productions originating in this way, I set apart the most admissible, sticking them into pasteboard covers.

For some years now, Howard's " Formation of Clouds " had busied me, and proved highly advantageous in the contemplation of nature.

In honor of his memory, I wrote four strophes containing the principal words of his terminology, and then at the request of London friends an exordium of three strophes serving to clear up and complete the sense.

Lord Byron's invectives against the Edinburgh reviewers interested me in many a sense, and I began to translate them, though my want of information about many particulars soon compelled me to leave off. I had, therefore, all the more freedom to write poems in return for a transmission of Tischbein's drawings, as also poems referring to landscapes he had etched after my sketches.

I next had the unexpected happiness of paying homage in my own house and garden to their Imperial Highnesses the Grand Duke Nicolas and his consort Alexandra, in the suite of our most gracious sovereign. Her Imperial Highness the Grand Duchess was graciously pleased to allow me to write some poetical lines in her homage in her magnificent album.

On the incitement of a kind friend I endeavored to collect my scattered scientific poems, printed and written, and arranged them in the order of subjects.

At last an Indian legend which had long hovered in my mind, and which I had occasionally compressed into shape, resuscitated itself in me, and I endeavored to make a complete appropriation of it.

To pass now from poetry to prose, I have to report that the " Travels " awoke to new life in me. I took the manuscript in hand, consisting of detached little stories, in part already printed, concatenated by the wanderings of a well-known figure—stories which, though not all of one web, should yet appear dominated by one idea. There was little more remaining to be done, and even the refractory contents stimulated new thoughts and goaded me to the completion of the work. The printing was begun in January, and ended in the middle of May.

" Art and Antiquity," third volume, second number, was at the same time on the loom, a great deal being worked into it which should be agreeable to cultivated friends.

Curiously enough I was transiently seized by the desire to work at the fourth volume of " Poetry and Prose "; a third of it was written, which, of course, invited one to fetch up the rest. A pleasant episode in connection with Lili's birthday was produced particularly *con amore;* other things indicated and written down. From such occupation, however, in which success is possible only in tender confidential hours, I soon found myself wrenched away by other employment which caused those biographical memories again to subside into the shade.

Some novels were projected; dangerous negligence, ruinous reliance on habit, and other such-like quiet simple features of life, were fetched forth from the usual indifference with which they are regarded, and raised to the high importance really attaching to them.

In the middle of November I began the " Campaign of 1792." The assortment and concatenation of the materials in my hands required all my attention. I wanted to be true all through, and yet at the same time not to disparage the due euphemism. "Art and Antiquity," volume three, third number, likewise went its course. Lighter efforts, such as the preface to the "German Gil-Blas," and smaller biographies for the "Trauerloge," succeeded pleasantly in quiet intervals.

Outwardly, with reference to me and my works, there appeared a great deal that was agreeable. A translation of Howard's "In Memoriam" showed that I had hit the sense of the English, and had given them pleasure by my high appreciation of their countryman. Dr. Noehden, who had a post in the London Museum, translated, with annotations, my treatise on "Da Vinci's Supper," which, in an excellent edition and most tastefully bound, he transmitted me. "Rameau's Nephew" is translated in Paris, and passes for some time as the original, and in the same way my theatrical pieces are also gradually translated. The interest I took in foreign and in German literature I can certify to the following extent:

It will be remembered what a painful sensation was diffused among those who loved and enjoyed the art of poetry when the personality of Homer, the unity of the author of those world-renowned poems, was so boldly and ably disputed. The world of culture was agitated to its deepest depth, and if unable to refute the arguments advanced by the powerful antagonist, it could not yet quite extinguish the old feeling and prejudice that there could be but one source whence so much that was precious was derived. This conflict now lasted over twenty years, and it required a revolution in the whole sentiment of the literary world to reassert in some measure the old mode of representing things.

The majority of the classically cultivated world were growing impatient of a state of destruction and dismemberment. Tired of unbelief they longed to attain again to belief, to rally out of detachment into union, out of criticism into enjoyment. A fresh crop of youths had grown up as instructed as they were full of life; with courage and freedom they undertook to recover the advantage we in our youth had also enjoyed, namely, without peddling scrutiny to let the appearance of an effective whole pass for a whole. Altogether youth has no liking for dismemberment, the time in many a sense had powerfully struggled toward synthesis, and the former spirit of reconciliation was again felt ruling in the minds of men.

Schubarth's "Ideas on Homer" found more and more response; his ingenious treatment, in particular the pronounced favor shown to the Trojans, excited a new interest, and people felt themselves disposed to his view. An English essay on Homer, in which, in a kindly way, it was also sought to main-

tain the unity and indivisibility of these poems reached us at
the right time, and, convinced that, in accordance with the
usual procedure to which such works are subjected, down
even to the present day, the last editor and thoughtful tran-
scriber strove to the best of his ability to weld the poems into
one, and hand them down as a whole, I again fetched forth
the abstract of the " Iliad," which in order to a swifter survey
of the work I had composed many years before.

The fragments of " Phaëthon " communicated by Chevalier
Hermann stimulated my productiveness. I hastily studied
many pieces of Euripides to make myself at home again with
the mind of this extraordinary man. Professor Göttling translated the fragments, and I busied myself for a long time with
a possible supplement.

" Aristophanes," by Voss, gave us new views and a fresh
interest in the most singular of all theatrical poets. Plutarch
and Appian are studied, this time for the sake of the triumphal
processions, in order to be the better able to appreciate Mantegna's drawings, the representations of which he evidently
drew from the ancients. In doing so, we were at the same
time admitted, here and there, to a view of highly important
events and states in Roman history. Von Knebel's translation of " Lucretius," which after manifold studies and labors
at last appeared, compelled us to wider views and studies in
the same field ; we had to make ourselves conversant with the
high state of Roman culture half a century before the birth
of Christ, and with the relation of the poetical and oratorical
art to the system of war and the State. Dionysius of Halicar-
nassus could not be neglected ; and so charming was the subject that several friends found entertainment with and in him.

The interest in English literature was now kept constantly
alive by a multitude of books and writings, especialy also by
Hüffner's highly interesting reports in writing sent from London. Lord Byron's former controversy with his weak and
unworthy reviewers brought before my mind the names of
many writers in poetry and prose who had grown remarkable
since the beginning of the century, and I therefore read with
attention Jacobson's biographical anthology, in order to obtain a more particular knowledge of their circumstances and
talents. Lord Byron's " Marino Faliero," as also his " Man-
fred," in Döring's translation, kept that prized and extraordinary man ever before our eyes. " Kenilworth," by Walter
Scott, read attentively in lieu of many others of his novels,
enabled me to appreciate his excellent talent for transforming
historical matter into a living picture, and generally to recognize his very high proficiency in this species of poetry and
literature.

Through the medium of English, and under the guidance of the worthy Professor Kosegarten, I turned again for some time to India. By his exact translation of the beginning of " Megha-Duta," this invaluable poem again appeared alive before my soul, and gained immensely from such a faithful reflector. " Nala " also was studied with admiration, and I only regretted that with us sentiments, morals, and intellectual habitudes have developed in a way so different from that of this Eastern nation, that such an important work can gain among us only a few readers, perhaps only readers by profession.

Of Spanish productions I name first an important work, " Spain and the Revolution." A travelled man, very well acquainted with the customs of the Peninsula, with its state, court, and financial relations, portrays to us here, in a methodic and trustworthy manner, the interior aspect of the country in these respects during the years in which he personally witnessed all he describes, and communicates to us a conception of what is being accomplished in such a land by revolutions. His way of looking at things and of thinking does not correspond with the spirit of the times, which therefore dooms the book to inviolable silence, a kind of inquisitionary censure which the Germans have largely applied.

Two pieces by Calderon gave me the highest pleasure; the most absurd subject in " Aurora of Copacabana," the most rational and natural in the " Daughter of the Air," both handled with equal mind and superabounding talent, so that the power of genius to control the most refractory elements is here most indubitably manifested, raising our appreciation of such productions double and threefold.

A Spanish anthology I received through the politeness of Herr Perthes was highly pleasing to me. I appropriated from it all I could, though with my little knowledge of the language I encountered many obstacles.

From Italy only a few things reached our circle. " Ildegonda," by Grossi, excited my whole attention, though I did not find time publicly to express my opinion on it. Here is displayed the most manifold activity of a pre-eminent talent which, though in a strange way, can boast of great ancestors. The stanzas are excellent, the subject disagreeably modern, the execution highly accomplished after the style of great predecessors. Tasso's grace, Ariosto's skill, Dante's repugnant, often horrible greatness—you have the patterns of them all here, one after the other. I should not care to read the work again for the sake of a more exact appreciation; I had quite enough to do to get the horrible ghosts the first reading had conjured up in my imagination gradually exorcised.

With the greater welcome, therefore, I saluted "Count Carmagnola," a tragedy by Manzoni, a true congenial poet of clear comprehension, deep penetration, and human sympathy.

Of modern German literature I could not acquire much knowledge; for the most part only so much as had immediate reference to myself and which I could take up into my other labors. Zauper's principles for a German theoretical-practical poetry, brought me face to face with myself, and as if I were viewing myself in a mirror gave occasion for many considerations. I said to myself: "Seeing, that for the instruction of youth and their initiation into a language, chrestomathies are employed, it is not at all amiss to take one's self up with a poet who, more from impulse and fate than from choice and intention, attains to being himself a chrestomathy; for such do sense and taste cultivated by study of many predecessors in fact become. To addict one's self to such a poet has by no means a narrowing effect on the young man who adopts such a course, but rather compels him after he has wilfully wandered about long enough in a certain circle, to make his flight into the wide world and into distant ages. An example of this we have in Schubarth, who, having confined himself for a long period to my circuit, felt himself by this means only strengthened for the task of grappling with the most difficult problems of antiquity and effecting an ingenious solution of them." I said a great deal to the good Zauper which might be helpful to him, and replied to his "Aphorisms" he had sent me in manuscript, by short observations not without use for him and others.

The affection with which Dr. Kannegiesser endeavored to decipher my "Harz Journey" induced me to return to that very early period in my life, and furnish some explanations in regard to it.

A manuscript of the fifteenth century, painting at large in the most fabulous manner the legend of the three saintly kings, happening to fall into my hands, interested me in many a sense. I busied myself with it, and an ingenious young man, Dr. Schwab, was disposed to translate it. This study gave rise to the observation of the way in which fables and histories in the different epochs interlace and conflict with each other so that they are hardly to be disentangled, and by disentangling them you only so far destroy them.

On each occasion of my stay in Bohemia I engaged myself in some measure with history and language, if only in the most general way. This time I again read Zacharias Theobaldus's "Hussites' War," and to both my pleasure and profit made a better acquaintance with Stransky's "Respublica Bohemiæ," with the history of the author, and with the value of the work.

Through the arrangement of the university library at Jena, a collection of pampnlets of the sixteenth century became accessible to us; pamphlets which, in default of newspapers, served at that time to communicate intelligence to the public, and in which you obtain a more precise and immediate idea of the original *factum* than now, when on each particular occasion each party communicates only what suits its own views and intentions, so that only after the event is all over can you read the papers with profit and true insight.

Boisserée's invaluable collection, which gave us a new idea of former Low-German painting, and so pretty well filled up a gap in the history of art, was now to be made known by excellent lithographs to those who could no longer contemplate the originals, while at the same time people who had not yet seen the originals should by means of these lithographs be enticed to draw near personally to those treasures. Strixner, already long celebrated for his Munich works, showed himself here too to great advantage, and although the striking value of the original pictures consists in their splendid color, we, nevertheless, here make acquaintance with the thought, expression, drawing, and composition; and as by copperplates and wood-cuts we come to an appreciation of the works of the High-German artists, so here also, by a newly invented mode of imitation, we become conversant with the masters of the fifteenth and sixteenth centuries who had hitherto scarcely been named among us. Every copperplate collector will willingly procure himself these sheets, as in consideration of their intrinsic value their price is to be accounted moderate.

There next appeared the Hamburg lithographs, mostly portraits, excellently designed and executed by artists staying and working together. We wish every amateur the happiness of possessing these prints.

Much else that the time produced, and which may well be deemed boundless, is mentioned and appraised in another place.

We will now call to mind a labor of our own, a Weimar-lithographic number with explanatory text, which we published under the title of "Pinakothek." The intention was to bring to the notice of the public a great deal on our hands worthy of communication. However that might be, this small attempt acquired many patrons, it is true, but few purchasers, and was continued only slowly and in private to keep the

brave artist from falling out of practice and to maintain alive
a technical art, to promote which every community, great or
small, should account it an advantage to itself.

Now, however, after long waiting the engraver's art brought
us a print of the greatest significance. In the most beautiful
clearness and distinctness, a picture of Raphael's dating from
his fairest youthful years is here delivered to us; here is already as much accomplished as there is much to be hoped.
The long time the engraver had expended on this work must
be regarded as happily spent, so that we could not at all grudge
him the recompense he thereby laboriously achieved.

Almost at the same time pattern prints for manufacturers
and hand-workers reached us from Berlin, which, too, could
not but be highly welcome to every artist. The purpose is
noble and beautiful, to communicate through inanimate forms
to the whole of a great nation the feeling of the beautiful and
pure. In these patterns, therefore, everything is exemplary;
choice of subjects, composition, sequence, and completeness—
virtues which together will evermore display themselves in
these desirable sheets.

After such excellent works extending almost over the whole
field of art, I may now speak of a single drawing which refers
immediately to me, but as a work of art is not without merit.
It is due to the efforts which Dawe, an English painter, during his lengthy stay here, made in regard to my portrait. In
its way it is to be pronounced a success, and well deserved
being carefully engraved in England.

We were called forth into the free world by the landscape
drawings of David Hess, of Zürich. A very beautifully colored water-color series conducted as to the road over the
Simplon, a colossal structure which caused a great deal of
talk in its time.

The drawings to the Prince of Neuwied's " Brazilian Journey " transplanted us into distant regions. The wonderful
nature of the subject seemed to be in rivalry with the artistic
representation.

Another performance in the way of art I have to record,
which as a puzzle engaged and agitated every good ingenious
head; it was the invention how to take a larger or smaller
impression from a copperplate. I saw such proof-sheets in
the hands of a traveller who had just brought them as a great
rarity from Paris, and, in spite of the improbability, we had on
close inspection to admit that the greater and smaller impressions were really to be recognized as of one origin.

To report now something weighty in reference to painting
as well, we do not fail to set forth that when on initiation from

higher quarters means were granted to the talented Captain
Raabe to go to Italy, we were able to give him the commission to copy various things which might be worthy of remark
in the history of coloring and be of furtherance for this important branch of art itself. What in the course of his travels
he achieved and sent home, and what after their completion
he brought back with him, was exactly the praiseworthy contribution we wanted. The Aldobrandinian wedding in its
latest state, the invaluable female dancers and Bacchic centaurs, whose figure and composition were already known to
us in the North through copperplates, were now presented
to us in colors, so that we were able to admire with joy the
great antique taste in this respect as well. German art
scholars, bewildered in modern error, would, of course, not
see into the value of such labors; but we did not let this circumstance discompose either ourselves or the understanding
artist.

Brought near as we thus were to the antique mind, Mantegna's " Triumphal Procession " again appeared in the highest degree pleasing to our eyes. Following the great artist's
own copperplate, we had the picture intended to take the
tenth place in sequence behind the triumphal chariot drawn in
commensurate style and size, and thereby brought to view a
concluded series most highly instructive.

Copies of old glass-paintings of St. Gereon's Church in
Cologne, imitated with the greatest care in respect to drawing
and color, excited everyone's admiration, and gave a remarkable demonstration as to how an art, advancing from its
primary elements, was able to achieve its ends.

Through the kindness of the Boisserée circle, other works
of this Low-German school, more advanced and more complete, were shown us, while at a later date from Cassel a more
modern effort of art, aspiring to the antique, was presented to
our eyes—" Three Singing Angels," which on account of completeness and precision we had reason to view with special
attention.

In contrast, however, to this strict, self-retarding art there
came to us from Antwerp a joyous picture, " Rubens as a
youth, presented by a fair, stately lady to the aged Lipsius,"
and that in the very room which has come down to us from
that time unchanged, the room in which this man, excellent
in his way, had worked as a corrector of the press for Plantin's
printing-house.

In immediate accord with this was a copy from a painting
of the sons of Rubens in Dresden, which shortly before Countess Julie von Egloffstein had finished in a lively and happy

manner.   We at the same time admired her highly practised
and accomplished talent in a drawing-book, in which with no
less skill than truth to nature she had delineated the portraits
of friends, as also country family seats.

At last my own lame talent also came to be considered,
distinguished and valued collectors demanding something
from my hand, to whose wishes, then, I yielded, though with
some backwardness.   At the same time I united into one volume a considerable number of leaves of more than usual distinctness; they were those of the year 1810, when for the last
time the impulse to express nature in my way animated me
for some months.   For the sake of the singular circumstances
in which they originated, these leaves might have some value
for me.

My relation to architecture was, properly, only historical,
theoretical, and critical.   Surveyor-in-Chief Coudray, solid,
skilful, as active as he was talented in this domain, instructed
me with reference to the buildings to be undertaken by us,
and the conversation on these subjects was of the greatest
furtherance to me.   Together we perused many important
copperplate works, the new work by Durand, "Partie Gra-
phique des Cours d'Architecture," reminding us of a time
shortly passed, Richardson's "The New Vitruvius Britannicus," and in detail the always exemplary ornaments of Alber-
tolli and Moreau.

Highly welcome to me in this province was a drawing, sent
me from Berlin, through the kindness of the theatre-manager,
the scene, within which at the opening of the theatre, the
prologue composed by me was recited.

Boisserée's treatise on Cologne Cathedral called me back
into former centuries.   The manuscript, however, was needed
sooner than I liked, and the thread of reflection, which with
momentary interest began to spin itself, was snapped, and its
zealous reattachment was destined to be subjected to many
accidents.

If in that work we had seen the old German architecture
at its highest regulated summit, other representations, the old
architectural monuments in the Austrian Empire, for example,
enabled us to see only an art diverging from the traditional
into a capricious style.

We were, however, reminded of one good time in the history of this Austrian style of architecture by a very old Jewish synagogue in Eger, once transformed into a Christian
chapel, now destitute of religious service either of the Old or
of the New Testament.   The number of the year of an old
Hebrew inscription standing high on a pillar was undecipher-

able, even to a Jewish student travelling by the place. The same dubiety which renders highly uncertain both the number of the year and of the people of the Hebrews, prevails here also, and caused us to desist from further investigation.

In plastic art some activity was shown, if not in many, yet in important subjects. Some busts in gypsum and marble by the court-sculptor, Kaufmann, receive applause, and a smaller medal with his Serene Highness's image to be executed in Paris was the subject of conversation and deliberation.

Theory and criticism, as also other things of influence on art, pursued their course and were profitable, now in a more contracted, now in a more extended circle. A paper of the Weimar *Kunstfreund* for Berlin respecting art-schools and academies, another in reference to museums, written with full conviction, if not everywhere received with approval; a treatise on lithography praising the masters of such an art, and certainly grateful to them; all this testifies to the earnestness with which on our side it was sought, in manifold ways, to promote the welfare of art.

A very pleasant conversation with foreign friends called forth, with the help of copperplates, many observations on conception, technical and higher composition, invention, and the effectual representation of motives. The high value of copperplate art in this historical sense was at the same time set forth, we extolling it as a great boon.

Music likewise promised to revive in my household circle. Alexander Boucher and his wife, with violin and harp, first moved a small circle of assembled friends to admiration and astonishment, and then produced a like effect on the Weimar public, next on the great public of Berlin, accustomed to everything that is excellent. The talents for musical production and execution of Director Eberwein and his wife gave us repeated enjoyment, and by the middle of May a large concert was able to be arranged. To listen to and direct recitation and rhythmic delivery was an old, not quite extinguished passion with me. Two persons of decided talent in this department, Countess Julie von Egloffstein and Fräulein Adele Schopenhauer, took great delight in reciting the Berlin prologue, each in her way penetrating into the inmost spirit of the poetry, and representing it with a pleasing variety in accordance with the difference of their idiosyncrasies. Through the care and skill of a long approved friend, Hofrath Rochlitz, a Streicher harpsichord, which he had thoroughly tested, came to us from Leipsic—a very happy event, for soon after Zelter brought us a pupil of his, Felix Mendelssohn, who excited our highest admiration, but whose incredible talent would, without the medium of such a mechanism, never have been brought home to us. In this way, too, a great and important concert was next achieved, in which Hummel, the leader of the orchestra, whose talent one can never sufficiently praise, likewise took part. Subsequently, Hummel, from time to time, entertained us with some remarkable performances, which caused us to regard the possession of this excellent instrument as an invaluable treasure.

From music I turn to natural science, and before everything else I have to mention Purkinje's work on subjective seeing, which especially interested me. I made an abstract of it, appending notes, and with a view to the use I intended making of it, had the annexed table copied—a laborious and difficult work, which, however, the careful artist readily undertook, because at an earlier period he had himself been distressed by appearances similar to these there delineated, and was glad to learn that they were natural, and no symptom of a morbid state.

Seeing that on the pure conception of turbidity the whole theory of color depends—as by it we attain to the observation of the original phenomenon, and its circumspect development will explain to us the whole world of vision—it was well worth while to take a comprehensive view of the modes in which the different nations have expressed themselves on this subject, from what point they have proceeded, and how, as they were more rude or more refined, they have made use of analogies nearer or more remote in that respect. We endeavored to obtain certain Vienna drinking-glasses on which a turbid varnish represented the phenomenon more beautifully than it could otherwise be seen.

Different chromatic observations were looked out from former papers for the fourth number, Bernardinus Telesius being studied, both from a general point of view as also specially for the sake of color. Seebeck's lecture on the unequal excitement of warmth in the prismatic sun-image was highly welcome, and my former ideas on those remarkable appearances again revived.

Körner, the court mechanician, busied himself with the preparation of flint-glass, and, according to French prescriptions, set up in his workshop an instrument for the so-called polarization experiments. The result, as we had long been instructed to expect, was pitiful, and it was remarkable enough that just at this time a feud between Biot and Arago began to transpire, which to experts showed still more conspicuously than ever the nullity of the whole of this doctrine.

Herr Von Henning visited me from Berlin. In consequence

of my conversations with him, he became completely initiated into the theory of colors, and showed the courage to adopt it publicly. I communicated to him the table which should show to him what kind of phenomena in a chromatic exposition are to be observed and considered, and in what order.

In the knowledge of the surface of our globe we were much furthered by Count Sternberg's " Flora der Vorwelt " in the first and second number. To this was added the " Knowledge of Plants," by Rhode, in Breslau. The primeval ox, brought from the Hassleber peat-pits to Jena, well deserves mention here, as one of the latest evidences of the earlier animal forms. The " Archives of the Primitive World " had already come on a thought of this kind, and I had the particular pleasure on this occasion of renewing in Halberstadt my former friendly relation to Herr Körte.

Keferstein's intention of publishing a geological atlas for Germany met my most earnest wishes; I took a zealous part in the matter, and as far as the coloring was concerned, was ready with my advice and my views. Unhappily, on account of the indifference of the technical artists appointed to execute the work, this principal feature was not quite successful. If color is to serve the map at all in the way of exhibiting essential distinctions, it is necessary that the greatest attention should be given to it.

The Marienbad rocks were collected with care. Arranged in Jena, they were then communicated to the public by way of experiment, to meet a repeated request for them, as also to furnish successors in this field of labor with such a valuable provision. Sartorius deposited in the Jena museum a series of rocks coming from the Rhone, in confirmation of the views of his treatise on the volcano.

In this year, too, not despairing of ultimate success, I diverted the attention of my Silesian friends to the Prieborn organized sandstone, or by whatever name this wonderful species of rock may be called, as also to the vitreous tubes at Massel, in former times abundant but unknown.

In the most general way I received furtherance from D'Aubuisson de Voisin's " Geognosy " and from Sorriot's map of the heights of Europe.

Meteorology was diligently prosecuted. Professor Posselt did his part; Conductor Schrön cultivated his talent ever more completely; Court Mechanician Körner was ready with his most careful aid in all technical preparations, and everything contributed to advance to the utmost possible degree the intentions and arrangements of the Prince. A manual of instruction was prepared for the whole body of observers in the grand duchy, new tables being drawn and engraved. The atmospheric observations in the middle of April were remarkable, as also the height of smoke on the twenty-seventh of June. The young Preller made a neat copy of my cloud drawings, and, that we might miss no kind of observations, the tower warden in Jena was instructed to take notes of certain meteors. Meanwhile Dittmar's prophecies gave people much to talk about, but neither profit nor applause was reaped by them.

To give a tolerably complete account of the activity at Belvedere in the culture of plants would require a whole paper to itself. We shall only mention the erection of a palm-house, at once satisfactory to the man of science and gratifying to the taste of every visitor. The opposite end to that of the tropical vegetation was furnished with dried specimens of plants from the island of Melville—specimens, however, which by their particularly sickly and wasting appearance only showed us the last traces of an otherwise well-known species of plants. The log of the trunk of a tree which had been injured, but had again coalesced, gave rise to many investigations into the recuperative powers of nature.

In Jena the botanical garden began to flourish with fresh life. Hofrath Voigt, head superintendent of the garden, and Baumann, the art gardener, made a journey to Berlin, bringing home with them much that was profitable both for themselves and the establishment.

I held it expedient to close the two volumes of " Natural Science and Morphology " with the fourth number, reserving so much material as would suffice for the preparation of a subsequent volume.

1822

Two important works conducted me to the old German architecture, to examination of its character through appreciation of its sentiment, and to a comprehension of the time in which it originated. Möller's " German Architectural Monuments," the first number of which was now completed, lay displayed to our view. After several proof-prints appeared the first number of Boisserée's work on the cathedral. A great part of the text which I had formerly studied in manuscript was appended, and now on my perusal of the whole it became clear as sunlight, as indubitable as the most palpable fact, that the religion, the morals, the peculiar phase of art, the peculiar spiritual needs, the physical and mental structure of the centuries in which this peculiar style of architecture bloomed forth so exuberantly—that these are never detached features, but only compose one great living unity. From this point of view it was to be explained how chivalry allied itself with ecclesiasticism, pursuing a different aim, yet animated with a kindred spirit.

Plastic art produced not many, but yet important fruits. The smaller medal with his Serene Highness's image and the inscription *Doctarum frontium proemia*, was cut in Paris by Barre. A little Bacchus in bronze, a genuine antique and of the greatest elegance, became mine through the kindness of Herr Major Von Staff. On the Italian campaign he had made his way through Italy to Calabria, and had the opportunity of procuring many a pretty work of art. Knowing my predilection in this direction, he honored me with the little image, which never fails to enliven me as often as I look at it.

Tischbein, out of old friendly affection, surprised me by a gem with stork and fox; the execution rough, thought and composition, however, quite excellent.

I receive " The Climate of England," by Howard, two volumes. Posselt writes a review. Inland observations under all the different headings continue, and are regularly transferred into tables. Inspector Bischoff, of Dürrenberg, urges the value of comparative barometrical observations, a proposal which is favorably received. Drawings of cloud-forms were collected and attentively prosecuted. Observation and reflection go hand in hand, thereby by means of tabular representation the uniform course of so many, not to say all, barometers whose readings naturally stood parallel, suggests the finding of a telluric cause and the ascription of the rising and falling of the quicksilver, within certain limits, to the earth's constantly changing power of attraction.

During my stay in Bohemia this time, the geological collection of the Marienbad district was again taken in hand, and completed in relation to the documents and the list in press. The specimens, carefully arranged in a case, were at my departure given over to Dr. Heidler as basis for future investigation in natural science. The Tepler Museum honors me with beautiful lime-slate with fishes and plants from the Walsch estate. Agreeable and instructive conversation with Herr Von Buch in passing. In Eger I met Herr Councillor Grüner, a diligent student of nature, engaged in raising a primitive colossal oak which had been lying deep sunk across the bed of the river. The rind was completely of the nature of peat. We next visited the quondam chalk pit of Dölitz, whence was derived the mammoth's tooth which had been long preserved as a remarkable heirloom by the family owning it, and was

17

now intended for the Prague Museum. I had a cast of it taken
to show it for closer examination to Herr d'Alton.

With strangers, also, passing through the place the collection was contemplated and the problematic Kammerberg
again visited. In the course of all this, Dlask's " Natural
History of Bohemia " was of furtherance and assistance.

Herr Von Eschwege, who had come from Brazil, shows us
jewels, metals, and stones. His Serene Highness makes a
considerable purchase. On this occasion is made over to me
the collection of precious stones formerly purchased from
Brückmann's legacy. It was highly interesting to me to re-
vise a series which had been gathered and arranged by a passionate amateur and connoisseur trustworthy and circumspect
for his time, to intercalate later acquisitions and give to the
whole as good an appearance as possible. Fifty unpolished
diamond crystals, remarkable when looked at separately, still
more so when viewed in a series, which were now described
and arranged according to their structure by Herr Soret, gave
me a perfectly new insight into this striking and highest product of nature. Herr Von Eschwege further showed us the
Brazilian species of rocks which again demonstrated that the
rocks of the New World in their first original appearance
completely accord with those of the Old ; a fact on which both
his printed and manuscript observations throw laudable light.

As a contribution to the knowledge of plants, I wrote the
" Plan to the Culture of Plants in the Grand Duchy of Weimar." I obtained a clump of beechwood, admirably drawn,
as a pathological phenomenon. It was a split log from a beech
trunk, in which, several years before, the rind had been regularly marked with a cross cut into it, which, however, healing
to a scar and overgrown, became incorporated into the trunk,
the form and impression of the cutting being still distinctly
traceable in the log.

My relation to Ernst Meyer imparted to me new life and
stimulus. The species *Juncus* which he has more particularly
defined and elaborated, I brought, with the help of Host's
" Gramina Austriaca," under my observation. In conclusion,
I must thankfully mention a gigantic *Cactus melocactus* sent by
Herr Andreä at Frankfort.

Of general interest appeared several important works: The
large map of natural history by Wilbrand and Ritgen, in relation to the element of water and to mountain height, showing how organization everywhere is modified by the situation.
Its value being at once recognized, the beautiful and striking
design was hung on the wall, produced for daily use, made
the subject of conversation in social meetings, and constantly
studied and utilized.

Keferstein's "Geognostic Germany" was in its continuation likewise of great furtherance, and with more precise coloring would have been still more so. In maps of this kind one has frequent occasion to remark that if distinctions are to be made by means of colors, the colors must themselves be distinguishable from each other.

The fourth number of my essays in morphology and natural science was carefully thought out and elaborated, concluding, as it did for the present, the two volumes on that work.

"The History of the Changes of the Earth's Surface proved by Tradition," by Herr Von Hoff, gave us a new pleasure. Here lies a treasure to which one would like to add something, while enriching himself by it.

To the revival of my mountain and stone studies I received important impressions of plants in coal slates, through the careful hands of Mahr, an officer of the exchequer, a man devoted to these studies. Minerals of the Fichtel mountains I receive from Redwitz, along with much else from Tyrol; on the other hand I send my friends different things. Herr Soret increases my collection by many important gifts, from Savoy as also from the island of Elba and more remote regions. His crystallographic knowledge was of the greatest assistance in the determination of diamonds and other minerals requiring to be more particularly discriminated. His printed papers he readily communicated and talked over.

In chromatics it was for me a great gain when at last the hope appeared that a younger man would take on himself the task of championing this weighty business and fighting its way through to general recognition. Herr Von Henning visited me, bringing with him entoptic glasses of felicitous device, as also black glass mirrors, which, united, presented fully before the eyes, without much further trouble, all desirable phenomena. Communication with him was easy; he had familiarized himself with the main part of the business, and I could very soon satisfy him on many points on which he still desired instruction. He told me of his lectures and how things stood in that respect, communicating also to me his introduction to them. We exchanged views and experiments; I handed over to him an older essay on prisms in connection with lenses, an aspect of the question which had hitherto been wrongly interpreted. He on the other hand urged me to arrange my chromatic documents and papers in a more complete and business-like form. All this happened in autumn and gave no little measure of composure.

An entoptic apparatus was prepared for Berlin, while the simple entoptic glasses with black glass mirrors opened up a new road, added to the number of discoveries, expanded the view, and then gave rise to the entoptic quality of melting ice.

The table of colors was revised and printed; an instrument prepared with the greatest care to show the phenomena of the polarization of light according to French principles was set up in my house, and I had the opportunity of making myself completely acquainted with its mechanism and performance.

In zoology I was furthered by " Carus on the original parts of the Skull and Bone Structure," and no less by a table in which the filiation of all vertebrate transformations was sensibly set forth. Here, for the first time, I received the reward of my past labors respecting general principles, what I had only divined being now palpably produced in detail before my eyes. A similar experience was granted me when I reperused an earlier work of D'Alton's on horses, and next delighted and instructed myself with his book on " Sloths and Thick-skinned Animals."

The antediluvian ox found in the turf-pit behind the Ettersburg engaged my attention a long time. It was set up in Jena, restored as far as possible, and united into a whole. This study brought me into contact again with an old well-wisher, Herr Dr. Körte, who showed me on this occasion a great deal to my entertainment.

Heinroth's " Anthropology " shed light on my procedure in observing nature, at the very moment that I was busied with my number on natural science.

Herr Purkinje visited us, conveying the indubitable impression of a remarkable personality and of extraordinary exertions and self-sacrifice.

While for my own enlightenment I endeavored to acquire more accurate knowledge and a more sensible idea of Kunkel's art of glass-making, concerning which I was still enveloped in the dimness of prejudice and without true appreciation, I had much communication with Herr Professor Döbereiner, who opened up to me the latest phases and discoveries in this branch of human endeavor. Toward the end of the year he came to Weimar to show his Serene Highness and an intellectually cultivated company important experiments illustrating the reciprocal influence of galvanism and magnetism, giving also oral explanations on the subject, an entertainment which the much-enjoyed visit a short time previous of Herr Professor Oersted had excited all the greater appetite for.

In the way of social intercourse, this year was very favorable to our circle. Two days in the week were set apart for submitting important things to our most gracious superiors in my house, the necessary explanations being also given. Each meeting suggested something new, and a great variety of subjects came under our review; things old and new, art and science, all finding friendly and intelligent hearers.

Every evening a more select circle, consisting of well-instructed persons of both sexes, gathered around me. That the interest might not slacken, but on the contrary intensify, Tuesday night was singled out as a night when there should be no doubt of a good company round our tea-table. Music, too, of a high order was from time to time introduced, raising our hearts and minds. Englishmen of culture took part in these entertainments, and as, beside, about noon, I was wont gladly to receive short visits from strangers, I was thus, while confined to my own house, ever in contact with the outside world, perhaps more intimately and integrally than if I had been stirring about abroad hither and thither.

A young man conversant with libraries and archives makes a repertory of all my works and unprinted writings, after having sorted and arranged everything.

On this occasion there was a provisional attempt made to draw up a chronicle of my life, which had hitherto been missed; a work which came to the help of my affairs in a very special manner. Immediately thereafter I took the work again in hand with fresh zest, elaborating particular parts of it at greater length.

Van Bree, from Antwerp, sent me his papers on the theory of the art of drawing. Tischbein's " Homer," part VII, arrived. The great mass of lithographic drawings by Strixner and Piloty I arranged in the order of schools and masters, whereby, for the first time, the collection acquired true value. Lithographs on all hands continued to be made, bringing many a picture under our observation. For the sake of a friend I explained a couple of problematic copperplates, Polidor's " Manna," and a sheet of Titian's, a landscape, " St. George with the Dragon and the Beauty in Peril." Mantegna's " Triumphal Procession " was further edited.

Painter Kolbe, from Düsseldorf, exhibited some works here and completed various portraits. It was a pleasure to make the personal acquaintance and enjoy the talent of this strenuous man whom we had known since the days of the Weimar art exhibitions. Countess Julie von Egloffstein made considerable progress in art. I had the etchings after my sketches tinted and painted in order to present them to friends.

A fair copy of Meyer's " History of Art " was at last written out and handed to the printer. Dr. Carus wrote a paper on landscape painting, in the beautiful style of his own productions, a paper of excellent thought and feeling.